The NFL's
60-Minute Men

The NFL's 60-Minute Men

*All-Time Greats
of the Two-Way Player Era,
1920–1945*

Chris Willis

McFarland & Company, Inc., Publishers
Jefferson, North Carolina

This book has undergone peer review.

LIBRARY OF CONGRESS CATALOGUING-IN-PUBLICATION DATA

Names: Willis, Chris, 1970– author.
Title: The NFL's 60-minute men : all-time greats of the two-way player era, 1920–1945 / Chris Willis.
Other titles: NFL's sixty minute men
Description: Jefferson, North Carolina : McFarland & Company, Inc., Publishers, 2024. | Includes bibliographical references and index.
Identifiers: LCCN 2024006254 | ISBN 9781476691329 (paperback : acid free paper) ♾
ISBN 9781476650647 (ebook)
Subjects: LCSH: Football players—United States—Biography. | Football—United States—History—20th century. | National Football League—History—20th century. | BISAC: SPORTS & RECREATION / Football
Classification: LCC GV939.A1 W574 2024 | DDC 796.332092/2 [B]—dc23/eng/20240215
LC record available at https://lccn.loc.gov/2024006254

BRITISH LIBRARY CATALOGUING DATA ARE AVAILABLE

ISBN (print) 978-1-4766-9132-9
ISBN (ebook) 978-1-4766-5064-7

© 2024 Chris Willis. All rights reserved

No part of this book may be reproduced or transmitted in any form or by any means, electronic or mechanical, including photocopying or recording, or by any information storage and retrieval system, without permission in writing from the publisher.

Front cover: Detroit Lions running back/defensive back Dutch Clark (7) stiff-arms Carl Brunbaugh of the Chicago Bears on his way to a 51-yard touchdown run on Thanksgiving Day, November 26, 1936, at the University of Detroit Stadium (courtesy of the Detroit Lions)

Printed in the United States of America

*McFarland & Company, Inc., Publishers
Box 611, Jefferson, North Carolina 28640
www.mcfarlandpub.com*

Table of Contents

Preface   1

Introduction   17

No. 1. Dutch Clark	34		**No. 24.** Albert "Turk" Edwards	175
No. 2. Don Hutson	44		**No. 25.** Ox Emerson	179
No. 3. Sammy Baugh	52		**No. 26.** Arnie Herber	184
No. 4. Mel Hein	60		**No. 27.** George Trafton	188
No. 5. Guy Chamberlin	68		**No. 28.** Ray Flaherty	192
No. 6. Bronko Nagurski	73		**No. 29.** Clyde "Bulldog" Turner	198
No. 7. Verne Lewellen	79		**No. 30.** Tuffy Leemans	204
No. 8. Sid Luckman	85		**No. 31.** Duke Slater	208
No. 9. Cal Hubbard	92		**No. 32.** Ward Cuff	213
No. 10. Paddy Driscoll	98		**No. 33.** George Musso	218
No. 11. Pete "Fats" Henry	103		**No. 34.** Joe Stydahar	223
No. 12. Dan Fortmann	110		**No. 35.** George Christensen	226
No. 13. Clarke Hinkle	115		**No. 36.** LaVern "Lavvie" Dilweg	230
No. 14. Roy "Link" Lyman	120		**No. 37.** Joe Kopcha	233
No. 15. Bill Hewitt	125		**No. 38.** Cecil Isbell	238
No. 16. Mike Michalske	131		**No. 39.** Jack McBride	243
No. 17. Benny Friedman	135		**No. 40.** Red Dunn	247
No. 18. Ernie Nevers	139		**No. 41.** Ed Danowski	251
No. 19. Cliff Battles	147		**No. 42.** Ace Parker	256
No. 20. Ken Strong	152		**No. 43.** Charley Brock	261
No. 21. Johnny "Blood" McNally	158		**No. 44.** Glenn Presnell	266
No. 22. Red Grange	163		**No. 45.** Roy "Father" Lumpkin	272
No. 23. Fritz Pollard	168			

The Best of the Rest 278
Final Analysis 281
Appendix I: The Author's All-Time Two-Way Teams 283
Appendix II: Historical Sources of NFL All-Pro and All-Time Teams, 1920–1945 285
Chapter Notes 291
Bibliography 301
Index 303

Preface

The idea for this book came about in 2019 when I was asked by football historian John Turney, who runs the pro football history blog *Pro Football Journal*, to write a series of posts on the greatest players of the pre–World War II era. That year the NFL celebrated its 100th season, so it was perfect timing to make the list of players. During the summer I researched and wrote the list of players. I made a list of the best two-way players from each of the seven different positions: end; tackle; guard; center; quarterback; halfback/wing back; and fullback.

The list of players was posted on *Pro Football Journal*. Each entry had just a sample bio of the player—maybe a paragraph or two—but there always seemed to be more to say about this era of players, who played both ways and competed for 60 minutes of action. That same year the NFL itself choose a 100th Anniversary All-Time Team that consisted of 100 former star players. On that squad were just *seven* men who played in the era of two-way players—gridiron men who played 60 minutes on both offense and defense. Those men were Sammy Baugh (quarterback); Dutch Clark (running back); Dan Fortmann (guard); Mel Hein (center); Cal Hubbard (tackle); Don Hutson (wide receiver); and Bill Hewitt (defensive end).

That's a small number of players from that era which covered the NFL's first 25 years (1920–1945) before the end of World War II. So, who were some of the greatest players from the two-way era? There must be more than just seven great players.

Very little has been documented about the early days of pro football and the pioneers who had a major influence on the history of the NFL. Ranking some of the greatest two-way players would help us understand more about what that era of professional football was like in an age of leather helmets, no television, dirt fields, small salaries, and playing for the love of the game.

I did more research to come up with the greatest NFL two-way players of all-time. I set out to find as many All-Time teams, selected by men who played, coached, and/or officiated in that era, as possible. I also tried to find every All-Pro team selected from that era, usually selected by newspapers or coaches who had an expert opinion on who they thought was the best of that year. I plowed through all of the game recaps of NFL games from the newspapers that covered the games (1920–1945) to get better insight into who was playing well during this two-way era. One of the more enjoyable aspects of the research was going through all the game footage I could find; watching film of these players was pure joy and I hope to find more footage in the future.

I also listed my choices of the NFL's retroactive MVPs from 1920 to 1945, giving more credence to who was the elite of the elite during the NFL's first 25 years. Lastly, and probably most importantly, I tried to find as many interviews, quotes, and testimonials as I could to help with my research. Throughout this book you'll hear from the players and coaches themselves telling you why someone was great, as well as how they played the game in the two-way era. These are important because they show us what the players thought about who was great and why they were great.

Certainly, this list will bring up discussions and debates among football writers, historians, and fans of pro football.

Explanation of Rankings

The National Football League (NFL) was founded on September 17, 1920, in a Canton, Ohio, Hupmobile showroom. For the next 25 years (1920–1945), the NFL saw 3,760 players play at least one game in the league. Among the 3,760 players, only 788 of them played at least 25 games. The average playing career of an NFL player during this time period was roughly two years. These players played a different game than we see today. The biggest difference is that the pioneers of the NFL played both ways—offense and defense. They played a "60-minute" game.

Among the more than 3,000 players from the league's first 25 years we arrived at some of the greatest during the two-way era. With the task of narrowing down the field, I came up with certain criteria to be able to rank the players fairly.

First, I chose to cut off the time period at the end of World War II—the NFL's first 25 years of action. This two-way era stopped right before the establishment of a rival league, the All-America Football Conference (AAFC), in 1946, and where the NFL/AAFC had more specialized play on both offense and defense, which would occur right before the end of the decade and the beginning of single-platoon football and unlimited substitutions, which came into the pro game starting in 1950.

Second, the player must have played at least three years during the time period from 1920 to 1945. That meant players such as ends Paul Robeson and Charlie Berry weren't eligible, since both only played two years in the NFL. Examples of Hall of Fame players playing only one or two years are Bill Dudley (1942, 1945); Bob Waterfield (1945); and Steve Van Buren (1944–1945), as well as players whose careers started post–1945, such as George Connor (1948); Chuck Bednarik (1949); and Charley Trippi (1947), none of whom make this list. The player must have played at least three seasons between 1920 and 1945.

Finally, below is the list of criteria used to rank the players. There are 12 separate standards that were used. They are in no particular order, and none was weighted over the others, as each one was considered in the ranking of the players.

Preface

1. Interviews/Testimonials: Maybe the most interesting of the rankings were the quotes and testimonials from the players and coaches from this time period. These quotes are significant because they represent the opinions of those who played or coached against the subjects on the field. I used as many quotes as possible to supplement the rankings and show how and why the players were great.

2. Game Film: As they always say, the eye in the sky don't lie. Watching footage of this era can be arduous, because not every game was filmed, especially in the 1920s, and the camera work is spotty at best. But finding and going through the footage was another key step in ranking the players. I looked at more than 200 NFL games from this era, mostly full games, as well as newsreel highlights.

3. NFL All-Pro Teams: The next several items on the criteria list are the honors of the players—starting with All-Pro teams selected by players, coaches, and mainly the newspapers/sportswriters of the era. I was able to find 42 different sources for All-Pro teams. These All-Pro teams selected first, second, and sometimes honorable mention selections.

4. NFL All-Decade Teams: In 1969 the Pro Football Hall of Fame selectors selected All-Decade teams to celebrate the NFL's 50th year. These All-Decade teams—of the 1920s, 1930s, 1940s—are just a gauge of who were the best of their decade. But in 1969 some of the choices were chosen because of their name: for example, Jim Thorpe selected as a halfback for the 1920s instead of Green Bay Packers halfback Verne Lewellen. Thorpe was past his prime when the NFL was established, not having any good seasons in the 1920s, while Lewellen was First Team All-Pro four straight seasons (1926–1929) and guided Green Bay to the 1929 NFL championship.

5. NFL All-Time Teams (selected by players, coaches, executives, officials): Another key element in deciding the rankings was the selection of All-Time teams. During my research I've tried to find as many players, coaches, executives, and game officials selecting their All-Time teams. Just like with the testimonials, Hall of Famers selecting their greatest teams proved very valuable. I've also included the NFL's official All-Time teams for their 50th, 75th, and 100th anniversaries.

6. Championships Won and Postseason Performances: Another easy one is the number of championships won or lost. I also took into consideration their performances in playoff and championship games, as well as in big games that occurred before the NFL championship game era began in 1933.

7. Retro-MVPs: In 1938 the NFL named its first official MVP with the selection of Giants center-linebacker Mel Hein. The MVP trophy was named in honor of its late president, the Joe F. Carr Trophy, but before that no award existed. I decided to re-create the voting and name Retro-MVPs for the years before the Carr MVP Trophy was awarded, the years 1920–1937. I've also done research on the years the Carr MVP Trophy was awarded to see if the

sportswriters got the vote right. These Retro-MVPs are included in the player profile chapters, explaining why they won, as well as in the front matter with the Top 5 voting.

8. Statistics (two eras: 1920–1931 unofficial/1932–1945 NFL official): Of course, statistics heavily influenced the rankings. NFL stats are broken into two eras: from 1920 to 1931 are unofficial stats, while from 1932 to 1945 are official NFL stats, since the league didn't start keeping statistics until the 1932 season. The NFL stats used during the time period 1920–1931 come from the play-by-plays and newspaper sources of the time. The stats were used to compile the book *Pro Football: The Early Years* written by Richard Cohen and David Neft. They are incomplete, as of now; I hope in the future they will become "official," so the following rankings take that in consideration.

9. Newspaper Recaps of NFL Games (1920–1945): The rankings were supplemented by going through game recaps from newspapers of all NFL games from 1920 to 1945.

10. Signature Game/Moment/Season: Taken into consideration are the players' signature plays, greatest seasons, and greatest moments.

11. Pioneer/Changed the Game: Also, if the player did something to change the game or was a pioneer in a certain skill or aspect of the game, that was considered.

12. Team Honors: Lastly, if the player has been honored by their team/franchise, for example, if they have had their jersey number retired or been inducted in the team's Hall of Fame or Ring of Honor.

All 12 standards were considered in ranking the players.

In the following pages, the reader will find a list of the Top 5 voting for the Retro-MVPs from 1920 to 1945. In addition, the sources used for the NFL All-Pro teams and NFL All-Time teams have been included in appendices.

NFL Retro-MVPs, 1920–1945

If you check the *2023 NFL Record & Fact Book*, on page 524, you'll see listed the NFL's Most Valuable Players selected by the Associated Press. The only problem is that the first year the AP selected a league MVP was 1961, although there was a Most Outstanding Player Award from 1957 to 1960. But nothing before 1961. How can that be?

Major League Baseball first had an MVP Award back in 1911 called the Chalmers Award (1911–1914). It also awarded an MVP throughout the 1920s, and the current MVP awards for the American and National League have been given out annually since 1931. But the NFL didn't honor the best player in the league until 1961. America's best sport was behind the times when it was growing up during its formative years. Newspaper men didn't have the time to choose the game's best player for a specific season.

Preface

In 1938 the NFL did establish the Joe F. Carr Trophy to select the league's Most Valuable Player (MVP). It was given out until 1946 when it suddenly stopped being awarded. Just nine awards were given out. I've gone back to look at those selections from 1938 to 1945 to see if the sportswriters voting at that time got the selection right.

As an historian I went back and researched each NFL season, going through every game recap I could find. I also tried to find every All-Pro team to see which players stood out above the rest for each season. Below are the Top 5 rankings of the NFL's MVPs from 1920 to 1945—selected by the author. More detailed seasonal recaps appear in the player chapters.

1920 American Professional Football Association (APFA)

1. Fritz Pollard, Akron Pros, back
2. Al Nesser, Akron Pros, guard
3. Jimmy Conzelman, Decatur Staleys, back
4. Al Mahrt, Dayton Triangles, back
5. Swede Youngstrom, Buffalo All-Americans, guard

Shifty Akron halfback Fritz Pollard beats out his guard teammate Al Nesser for the league's first-ever MVP. Pollard provided the offensive spark, while Nesser the brute force up front for the Akron Pros, who won the league's first title in 1920. Pollard was named First Team All-Pro by the *Rock Island Argus* while scoring 42 points. Nesser helped anchor a line that was productive on offense and nearly perfect on defense as the Pros gave up only one touchdown all season.

1921 APFA

1. Dutch Sternaman, Chicago Staleys, back
2. Elmer Oliphant, Buffalo All-Americans, back
3. Swede Youngstrom, Buffalo All-Americans, guard
4. Fritz Pollard, Akron Pros, back
5. Guy Chamberlin, Chicago Staleys, end

Staleys back Dutch Sternaman helped guide the Staleys to a title (9–1–1 record) by scoring a team high 41 points. Back Elmer Oliphant, who led the NFL in scoring with 47 points, and guard Swede Youngstrom put the pressure on Sternaman's Staleys with their fine performances guiding the Buffalo All-Americans to a second-place spot—one game behind the Staleys.

1922 NFL

1. Guy Chamberlin, Canton Bulldogs, end
2. Paddy Driscoll, Chicago Cardinals, back

3. Link Lyman, Canton Bulldogs, tackle
4. Dutch Sternaman, Chicago Bears, back
5. Pete Henry, Canton Bulldogs, tackle

The Canton Bulldogs player-coach, Guy Chamberlin, was the best player on the best team. He finished third in the NFL in scoring with 42 points and guided the Bulldogs to an unbeaten record of 10–0–2. What stood out most about Chamberlin was that he scored seven touchdowns in four different ways—rushing, receiving, interception return and fumble return.

1923 NFL

1. Pete Henry, Canton Bulldogs, tackle
2. Link Lyman, Canton Bulldogs, tackle
3. Dutch Sternaman, Chicago Bears, back
4. Paddy Driscoll, Chicago Cardinals, back
5. Curly Lambeau, Green Bay Packers, back

Winning back-to-back NFL championships, the Bulldogs were led by their dynamic tackle combination of Pete Henry and Link Lyman. The Bulldogs scored a league high 246 points and the stout defensive line gave up just 19 points. Henry gets the edge by playing stout line play and a dominating kicking performance as he finished second in the NFL in scoring with 52 points (behind Driscoll, 78 points) and by leading the NFL with 25 extra points and finishing second in the league with nine field goals.

1924 NFL

1. Link Lyman, Cleveland Bulldogs, tackle
2. Joey Sternaman, Chicago Bears, back
3. Tex Hamer, Frankford Yellow Jackets, back
4. Benny Boynton, Buffalo Bisons, back
5. Guy Chamberlin, Cleveland Bulldogs, end

The Bulldogs continued their dominance over the NFL, this time in Cleveland. Tackle Link Lyman proved again that he was one of the best players in the league—scoring four touchdowns—becoming a stalwart from his tackle position, both on offense and defense.

1925 NFL

1. Paddy Driscoll, Chicago Cardinals, back
2. Joey Sternaman, Chicago Bears, back
3. Jimmy Conzelman, Detroit Panthers, back
4. Jack McBride, New York Giants, back
5. Red Dunn, Chicago Cardinals, back

Paddy Driscoll, quarterback, Chicago Cardinals, ca. 1923 (courtesy Arizona Cardinals).

The Pottsville Maroons were declared ineligible for the NFL title on December 29, 1925, so their players are also ineligible for NFL MVP, which eliminates Charlie Berry (end) and Tony Latone (fullback). Cardinals back Paddy Driscoll continues his fine play in 1925, scoring 67 points for a Cardinals team that was awarded the NFL title with an 11–2–1 record.

1926 NFL

1. Paddy Driscoll, Chicago Bears, back
2. Ben Jones, Frankford Yellow Jackets, back
3. Henry "Two-Bits" Homan, Frankford Yellow Jackets, back
4. Ernie Nevers, Duluth Eskimos, back
5. Jack McBride, New York Giants, back

After getting sold from the Cardinals to the crosstown Bears, nobody played better in 1926 than back Paddy Driscoll. He led the NFL in scoring with 86 points (second was Nevers with 71) and field goals made with nine. Despite his great individual play, his Bears (12–1–3) came up one game behind the Frankford Yellow Jackets (14–1–2) who were led by the dynamic backfield of Ben Jones and Henry "Two-Bits" Homan. Driscoll became the first player to win back-to-back MVP awards.

1926 American Football League (AFL)

1. Al Kreuz, Philadelphia Quakers, back
2. Eddie Tryon, New York Yankees, back
3. Bull Behman, Philadelphia Quakers, tackle
4. Red Grange, New York Yankees, back
5. Bob Dinsmore, Philadelphia Quakers, back

The American Football League, rival league to the NFL in 1926, had a close MVP race. The biggest star, Red Grange, played well but wasn't the best in the league. The Philadelphia Quakers won the '26 title behind the play of back Al Kreuz (34 points scored), tackle Bull Behman and back Bob Dinsmore, each making the top five. Yankees halfback Eddie Tryon (72 points scored) actually out-played Grange to finish in the runner-up position.

1927 NFL

1. Jack McBride, New York Giants, back
2. Benny Friedman, Cleveland Bulldogs, back
3. (tie) Cal Hubbard, New York Giants, end; Al Nesser, New York Giants, guard
4. Paddy Driscoll, Chicago Bears, back
5. Bill Senn, Chicago Bears, back

The New York Giants came out on top in '27 behind the play of fullback Jack McBride. The former Syracuse star led the NFL in scoring with 57 points and helped the Giants defense hold opponents to just 20 points and 10 shutouts. Rookie quarterback Benny Friedman took the league by storm by throwing for 11 touchdowns and guiding the Cleveland Bulldogs to an 8–4–1 finish.

1928 NFL

1. George "Wildcat" Wilson, Providence Steam Roller, back
2. Benny Friedman, Detroit Wolverines, back
3. Curly Oden, Providence Steam Roller, back
4. Ken Mercer, Frankford Yellow Jackets, back
5. Verne Lewellen, Green Bay Packers, back

Providence back George Wilson beats out Friedman in another close vote. Friedman finishes in the runner-up spot for the second year in a row by throwing for nine touchdowns as his Wolverines finished in third place in the standings. While "Wildcat" was the best player on the best team, Wilson scored five touchdowns and tossed six TD passes. He was named First Team All-Pro by the *Chicago Tribune* and the *Green Bay Press-Gazette.*

1929 NFL

1. Verne Lewellen, Green Bay Packers, back
2. Benny Friedman, New York Giants, back
3. Tony Plansky, New York Giants, back
4. Ernie Nevers, Chicago Cardinals, back
5. Len Sedbrook, New York Giants, back

For the first time in their history, the Green Bay Packers won the NFL championship, led by their dynamic halfback Verne Lewellen. In a two-man duel throughout the season, the New York Giants' quarterback Benny Friedman and Lewellen went neck-and-neck. Lewellen led the Packers in scoring with 48 points and earned First Team All-Pro honors from the *Chicago Tribune, Collyer's* and *Green Bay Press-Gazette.*

On November 24, in the biggest game of the year that decided the NFL title between the Giants and Packers, Lewellen outplayed Friedman with his rushing and punting to help Green Bay not only claim the title but also help Lewellen win the MVP award.

1930 NFL

1. Verne Lewellen, Green Bay Packers, back
2. Benny Friedman, New York Giants, back
3. Red Grange, Chicago Bears, back
4. Jack McBride, Brooklyn Dodgers, back
5. Cal Hubbard, Green Bay Packers, tackle

Tough voting again for Benny Friedman, coming in the runner-up position for the fourth year in a row! Not winning a championship would always haunt Friedman.

The Packers' Verne Lewellen continues his outstanding overall play by leading the NFL in touchdowns with nine and second in scoring with 54 points behind Jack McBride of the Dodgers with 56. But unlike McBride and Friedman, Lewellen guided the Packers to the NFL championship with a 10–3–1 record. Lewellen joins Paddy Driscoll as the only players to win back-to-back MVP awards.

1931 NFL

1. Johnny "Blood" McNally, Green Bay Packers, back
2. Dutch Clark, Portsmouth Spartans, back
3. Glenn Presnell, Portsmouth Spartans, back
4. Ernie Nevers, Chicago Cardinals, back
5. Red Grange, Chicago Bears, back

Nobody played better in 1931 than Johnny Blood. One of the key cogs of a Packers team that would win a third straight NFL championship (1929–1931), McNally scored a whopping 14 touchdowns to lead the NFL in scoring with 78 points. Spartans rookie back Dutch Clark finished runner-up but was setting himself up to be one of the best players of the two-way era.

1932 NFL

1. Dutch Clark, Portsmouth Spartans, back
2. Bronko Nagurski, Chicago Bears, back
3. Red Grange, Chicago Bears, back
4. Arnie Herber, Green Bay Packers, back
5. Cliff Battles, Boston Braves, back

After a runner-up finish the previous season, Dutch Clark captures the MVP award in 1932. Dutch finished the season sixth in the league in passing, fourth in rushing and was one of just eight players to catch at least 10 passes. As for scoring, Dutch finished first in the league with 55 points—on six touchdowns, three field goals and 10 extra points. Unfortunately, Dutch missed the season finale postseason game against the Bears—the famous "Indoor Game"—as his Spartans lost the title. But Clark establishes himself as the best player in the league.

Dutch Clark, halfback, Detroit Lions, ca. 1935 (courtesy Detroit Lions).

1933 NFL

1. Ken Strong, New York Giants, back
2. Glenn Presnell, Portsmouth Spartans, back
3. Bronko Nagurski, Chicago Bears, back
4. Harry Newman, New York Giants, back
5. John "Shipwreck" Kelly, Brooklyn Dodgers, back

Giants back Ken Strong had his best year as a pro in 1933. That season he finished the season third in the NFL in touchdowns with five—scoring three different ways, by rushing (two), receiving (two) and interception return (one), and his 64 points scored was tops in the league. Behind the play of Strong, the Giants compiled an 11–3 record and captured the Eastern Division. With Dutch Clark taking the year off, Spartans back Glenn Presnell had a career year tying Strong in points scored.

1934 NFL

1. Bronko Nagurski, Chicago Bears, back
2. Beattie Feathers, Chicago Bears, back
3. Dutch Clark, Detroit Lions, back
4. (tie) Harry Newman, New York Giants, back; Ken Strong, New York Giants, back
5. Arnie Herber, Green Bay Packers, back

The Bears finished the regular season undefeated at 13–0 behind the dynamic play of their two backfield stars—Bronko Nagurski and rookie Beattie Feathers. Although Feathers was the first back to gain 1,000 yards rushing in a season, Nagurski's lead blocking and defensive play was much better, especially down the stretch for the Bears. Feathers missed the last few games with an injury as Bronko held off Dutch Clark's Lions to win the Western Division and win the Retro-MVP for 1934.

1935 NFL

1. Dutch Clark, Detroit Lions, back
2. Ed Danowski, New York Giants, back
3. Ox Emerson, Detroit Lions, guard
4. Mel Hein, New York Giants, center
5. (tie) Arnie Herber, Green Bay Packers, back; Ken Strong, New York Giants, back

The great Dutch Clark was the best player on the best team—winning his second Retro-MVP award. Clark finished the season fourth in rushing yards and second in rushing touchdowns with four. He also led the NFL in extra points made (16) and scoring with 55 points. Clark's 42-yard weaving touchdown run in the championship game against the Giants was the signature play of a 26–7 victory, giving the

Lions their first ever world title. Ed Danowski of the Giants led the NFL in passing attempts (113), completions (57), passing yards (794) and touchdowns (10) and was consensus First Team All-Pro to finish in the runner-up position.

1936 NFL

1. Dutch Clark, Detroit Lions, back
2. Arnie Herber, Green Bay Packers, back
3. Ace Gutowsky, Detroit Lions, back
4. Tuffy Leemans, New York Giants, back
5. Cliff Battles, Boston Redskins, back

Dutch Clark wins back-to-back MVPs (joining Driscoll, Lewellen) and becomes the first player during the two-way era to win three Retro-MVPs. Clark led the NFL in scoring with 73 points and rushing touchdowns with seven. He was named First Team All-Pro by the NFL, *Chicago Daily News*, *Collyer's* and the UP as he led the Lions to an 8–4 record.

Dutch Clark (right) with NFL president Joe F. Carr at the 1936 NFL Owners Meetings (courtesy NFL Films Research Library).

1937 NFL

1. Sammy Baugh, Washington Redskins, back
2. Jack Manders, Chicago Bears, back
3. Cliff Battles, Washington Redskins, back
4. Mel Hein, New York Giants, center
5. Clarke Hinkle, Green Bay Packers, back

Redskins rookie quarterback Sammy Baugh couldn't have been better during his inaugural season in the NFL. Slingin' Sammy led the NFL in attempts, completions and passing yards, while guiding Washington to the Eastern Division title. He then went on to throw for over 300 yards and three touchdowns to win the NFL championship over the Bears, capping off a great rookie campaign.

1938 NFL

1. Mel Hein, New York Giants, center (JFC Trophy winner)
2. Ed Danowski, New York Giants, back
3. Clarke Hinkle, Green Bay Packers, back
4. Don Hutson, Green Bay Packers, end
5. Ward Cuff, New York Giants, back

The Giants and Packers were the best teams in the NFL in 1938, both meeting in the NFL championship game. But it was Giants center-linebacker, Mel Hein, who finished as the MVP, both our Retro and as the first Joe F. Carr Trophy winner. He led a Giants defense that led the NFL in points allowed by giving up just 79 points—the next closest was the Lions at 108 points.

1939 NFL

1. Mel Hein, New York Giants, center
2. Don Hutson, Green Bay Packers, end
3. Andy Farkas, Washington Redskins, back
4. Ward Cuff, New York Giants, back
5. (tie) Parker Hall, Cleveland Rams, back (JFC Trophy winner); Cecil Isbell, Green Bay Packers, back

Probably the weakest choice by the writers for the JFC Trophy was Rams back Parker Hall in 1939. Hall was solid but not the best player in the NFL. Although competitive, the Rams were just 5–5–1. Hard to choose an MVP from a team that was just .500 in the standings. Giants center-linebacker, Mel Hein, continues his great play for the Eastern Division champions. Hein beats out Packers end Don Hutson to win back-to-back MVPs.

1940 NFL

1. Sammy Baugh, Washington Redskins, back
2. Ace Parker, Brooklyn Dodgers, back (JFC Trophy winner)
3. Dick Todd, Washington Redskins, back
4. Dan Fortmann, Chicago Bears, guard
5. Don Hutson, Green Bay Packers, end

Sammy Baugh captured his second Retro-MVP award by holding off Dodgers triple-threat quarterback Ace Parker—the JFC Trophy winner. Parker was second in the NFL in passing touchdowns with 10; third in punting; first in extra points made (19) and was tied for first in interceptions on defense with six—while guiding Brooklyn to an 8–3 record, one game back of the Eastern Division champion Redskins. Baugh led the NFL in passing yards (1,367), touchdown passes (12) and completion percentage at 62.7 percent. He also led the league in punting average with a mark of 51.4. Unfortunately, Baugh would not finish the season with a championship, losing the famous 73–0 game to the Bears.

1941 NFL

1. (tie) Don Hutson, Green Bay Packers, end (JFC Trophy winner); George McAfee, Chicago Bears, back
2. Cecil Isbell, Green Bay Packers, back
3. Dan Fortmann, Chicago Bears, guard
4. Mel Hein, New York Giants, center
5. Ward Cuff, New York Giants, back

After a runner-up finish in 1939 and a fifth-place finish in 1940, the great Packers end Don Hutson made a yearly run at the NFL's MVP. In 1941 he shared the award with Bears back George McAfee. During the season the Packers and Bears played nearly perfect football as both teams finished with identical 10–1 records. Hutson won the triple crown in receiving with 58 catches for 738 yards and 10 touchdowns, while McAfee tallied 12 total touchdowns—scoring in five different ways (rushing, receiving, lateral, kickoff return, punt return). He also had six interceptions on defense. In the divisional playoff game, the Bears took it to the Packers, winning 33–14. A very close call, so Hutson (JFC Trophy winner) and McAfee tied for the MVP.

1942 NFL

1. Don Hutson, Green Bay Packers, end (JFC Trophy winner)
2. Clyde "Bulldog" Turner, Chicago Bears, center
3. Sammy Baugh, Washington Redskins, back
4. Sid Luckman, Chicago Bears, back
5. Bill Dudley, Pittsburgh Steelers, back

Don Hutson made it back-to-back MVPs with his greatest year as a two-way star. Hutson finished the season with 74 receptions for 1,211 yards and 17 touchdowns—all single-season NFL records. He also had seven interceptions on defense. Bears center "Bulldog" Turner led the NFL with eight interceptions while guiding the Bears to the NFL championship. He finished in the runner-up position.

1943 NFL

1. Sid Luckman, Chicago Bears, back (JFC Trophy winner)
2. Sammy Baugh, Washington Redskins, back
3. Don Hutson, Green Bay Packers, end

4. Bill Paschal, New York Giants, back
5. Tony Canadeo, Green Bay Packers, back

Sid Luckman vs. Sammy Baugh. Outside of the race in 1929 (Lewellen vs. Friedman), the MVP competition in 1943 between Luckman and Baugh was probably the tightest during the two-way era. Baugh put together a monster season, as he led the NFL in passing, punting and interceptions on defense with 11, which set an NFL record. Still, he did not win the NFL Carr MVP Award, which went to Luckman. The Bears signal caller led the league in passing yards with 2,194 and passing TDs with 28, both new single-season NFL records. In the championship game, Luckman beat Baugh's Redskins 41–21 by throwing five touchdowns and nabbing two interceptions on defense.

1944 NFL

1. Don Hutson, Green Bay Packers, end
2. Frankie Sinkwich, Detroit Lions, back (JFC Trophy winner)
3. Irv Comp, Green Bay Packers, back
4. Sid Luckman, Chicago Bears, back
5. Ward Cuff, New York Giants, back

Don Hutson won the Retro-MVP for 1944 over Lions back Frankie Sinkwich—who was given the JFC Trophy. Sinkwich led the Lions to a 6–3–1 record, finishing in second place behind Hutson's Packers. The great Hutson led the NFL in receptions (58), receiving yards (866) and touchdowns (nine). It was the fifth time in his career that he had led the league in all three categories. He helped the Packers win the NFL championship over the Giants. Hutson joined Dutch Clark as the only players in the two-way era to win three MVP awards.

1945 NFL

1. Bob Waterfield, Cleveland Rams, back (JFC Trophy winner)
2. Sammy Baugh, Washington Redskins, back
3. Steve Van Buren, Philadelphia Eagles, back
4. Jim Benton, Cleveland Rams, end
5. Roy Zimmerman, Philadelphia Eagles, back

Rookie quarterback Bob Waterfield of the Cleveland Rams took the NFL by storm in 1945. Waterfield led the NFL in touchdown passes with 14, extra points made with 31, and was second in the league in interceptions on defense with six. He guided the Rams to the Western Division title and in the league championship game he bested Sammy Baugh of the Redskins, 15–14, who finished runner-up in the voting to the fabulous rookie.

Introduction

Foundation

Professional football had been around since 1892, but an organized league would take nearly 30 more years to establish. It happened at the start of one of America's most fruitful and entertaining decades. From the beginning the Roaring Twenties lived up to the name. With the world safe for democracy after World War I, the United States discarded its battlefield persona and replaced it with an excess of fun and leisure. Prosperity fueled the celebration. Famed writer Paul Gallico wrote, "We had just emerged from a serious war and now wanted no more of reality but only escape therefrom into the realms of the fanciful." In 1920 prohibition went into effect, American women got the right to vote, Warren G. Harding was elected president, and on September 17, 1920, 10 professional football owners gathered in a Canton, Ohio, automobile showroom to organize the American Professional Football Association (APFA). Two years later in 1922 they renamed the league the National Football League (NFL).[1]

The NFL was established during the age of radio, flappers, jazz, the Charleston, Lindbergh, speakeasies, Capone, Chaplin, and sports of all sorts. For the first time the world of sports captured the public's eye and its pocketbook. In the words of one historian, "next to the sport of business, Americans enjoyed the business of sport." Most Americans enjoyed the economic boom following World War I and much of that was spent on sports tickets, as people flocked to stadiums and arenas in record numbers. Sport heroes emerged in every field of athletics. Names such as Jack Dempsey in boxing, Red Grange in college football, Lou Gehrig in baseball, Bill Tilden in tennis, and Bobby Jones in golf simply made this the Golden Age of Sports.[2]

Gallico, who followed all the sports giants of the 1920s as a columnist and sports editor of the *New York Daily News*, said that "sports and sports stories and sport characters who were almost magical in their performance provided much of that escape" for Americans to enjoy their free time. Throughout the 1920s, however, professional football was an ignored child in the family of American sports. Baseball was indeed the National Pastime. Baseball occupied the nation's conscience and the biggest stadiums and it had the biggest name in sports during the Roaring Twenties—Babe Ruth. And if baseball didn't fascinate you there was always college football. College football had its well-established traditions and its rah-rah attitudes that made front-page headlines. On the other hand, professional football and the NFL went mostly unnoticed. The sport was truly unloved.[3]

But what was it really like in the early days of the NFL, when the game was played in an era before television, million-dollar contracts, fantasy football leagues, domed stadiums, and field turf? What was the "Old Leather" era truly like, when professional football was fashioned from canvas and leather and the game was played on a dirt field? In *The Football Encyclopedia* football historian Jordan Deutsch explains, "Much of what we know about the early days of pro football has come from the pages of the newspaper of the day. Little is revealed from newsreels and photographs of games tantalize us with frames of action but cannot tell us of the pace of the game or what it was like to watch. All we have left is our imagination." Let's join Deutsch and attend an NFL game in the 1920s.[4]

We can get a front row seat for one dollar. If we're at Canton's Lakeside Park to watch the Canton Bulldogs, a mere 4,000 fans would pack the bleachers. A program would cost ten cents. There are no souvenir or beer stands. You could also make a friendly bet on the game with your neighbor sitting next to you. Usually, a dollar would do the trick. Other spectators would be wearing suits and ties, no outrageous costumes with team logos....

The field is your familiar 100-yards long, laid out in five-yard segments, with real grass, or more likely, real dirt. It has no hash marks. Not until 1933 will the ball be brought in towards the middle of the field when a play ends near the sidelines or out of bounds. The bench area is just that, a wooden bench. The goal posts are roughly 20 feet high and stationed at the front of the goal line....

There are only 16 players on each squad. By 1930 the league votes to expand the roster to 20. Both teams wear dark jerseys, giving fans a tough time telling them apart. The uniforms show little individuality, except for maybe a logo or letter on the front.

The trousers are made of canvas, worn with hip, thigh, and knee pads. Each player wears black high-top shoes with rectangular cleats and wool socks. The jersey was pulled over a flimsy set of shoulder pads that didn't seem to protect anything. The same could be said for the helmet. Some players didn't bother to wear one. No rule requiring a player to wear a helmet was passed until 1943....

Three [officials] govern the action. An umpire, a linesman, and a referee. The officials also keep the game clock on the field. From our bleacher seat we see that the ball is made of leather and is fairly round. Easy to drop-kick, but difficult to pass. By the end of the decade the ball is slimmed down, making passing easier.

We see a kickoff at the 40-yard line. All 22 men who were on the kickoff teams stay on the field, no substitutes. Each man plays both offense and defense. Most plays are called at the line of scrimmage instead of a huddle. The head coach doesn't send in plays and little time is spent in between plays. Most lineman weigh about 200 pounds, with most backs being much smaller.

Passing was restricted because of the rather fat ball. Some teams passed more than others, but the early pro game was built around the power running game.... Until 1933, the forward pass had to be thrown from five yards behind the line of scrimmage.

Punting was the key to the outcome of most games. The way to victory was not to possess the ball, but to give it to your opponent deep in their territory and let him make a mistake. An amazing number of punts occurred on third down, as teams played for field position. With defense so emphasized, low scoring games dominated the early days of the NFL.... The game usually lasted about two hours and ended with a gunshot from the referee.[5]

Representatives of pro teams were under the gun in 1920 when they met in Canton, Ohio, to organize what would become the National Football League. The pro game was beset with three major problems: salaries were skyrocketing; players hopped from team to team during the season to play for the highest bidder; and too many teams padded their rosters with moonlighting collegians playing under assumed names. A league needed to be formed.

They had good reason to meet in Canton, now the site of the Pro Football Hall of Fame. Ohio was the geographical center of professional football. Proximity was important in that era when teams traveled by train and team managers sought games with opponents in cities in Ohio and the Midwest that could be easily reached by rail. Thus, only a few East Coast teams played during the NFL's early years, and the too-distant West Coast would not be home to an NFL franchise until after World War II.

When the league was formed in 1920, the newly established organization elected the biggest name in pro football to help guide the league. His name was Jim Thorpe. But he was a great athlete, not an administrator, so in 1921 the young league elected Joe F. Carr—the long-time manager of the Columbus Panhandles—as its new president. Carr quickly established the building blocks that the league still sits on today: setting up a constitution and by-laws; creating the standard players contract, so players couldn't hop from one team to another; setting up territorial rights; establishing the rule where a college player couldn't come into the NFL until his class had graduated (Grange Rule); and keeping statistics. The NFL champion was the team with the best winning percentage in the standings. The league was now set up to succeed.

The Thirties

Once the stock market crashed in October of 1929, the NFL changed its business model. Over the ensuing few years, they left the small towns of the Midwest, such as Canton and Akron, to the big cities of New York, Chicago, Boston and Philadelphia. President Carr became the front man to help move the NFL to the big cities, and he worked hard to recruit financially capable owners to run these big city franchises. He recruited the likes of Tim Mara in New York, George Preston Marshall in Boston/Washington, Art Rooney in Pittsburgh, Bert Bell in Philadelphia, George A. Richards in Detroit and Charlie Bidwell to take over the Chicago Cardinals.

In the decade of the 1930s, the NFL began to look like Major League Baseball with just 10 teams in the league. The play on the field changed, too, mostly deriving from one of the strangest and most important games in NFL history. In 1932, for the first time two teams tied for first place in the league standings—the Chicago Bears and Portsmouth Spartans. The two teams, with the blessing of the NFL office, agreed to play a postseason game in Chicago. But because of a snowstorm the game was moved indoors to Chicago Stadium. Because of the constricted 80-yard indoor field,

Benny Friedman, quarterback, New York Giants, ca. 1926 (courtesy University of Michigan Athletics).

the teams agreed to use hash marks for the first time. In this altered space, the Bears pulled out a rather dull 9–0 win. After the game the NFL owners and President Carr could see that they had to open up the game to make it more fan friendly. They also could see the importance of having a game at the end of the season for a world championship title.

In 1933 the NFL adopted a few new rules to help separate themselves from the collegiate game for the first time, which established the league on its own. They agreed to get rid of the rule that you had to be five yards behind the line of scrimmage to pass; moved the field goal posts to the front of the end zone to encourage field goals; and then established hash marks for good. They also split the NFL up into two divisions and created the annual NFL championship game between the division winners. The NFL was now making its own mark in the sports world with one of the biggest events on the sports calendar.

As for the players, throughout the NFL's first 25 years, the league saw additional changes there. In 1920, players were free to sign with any team they wanted—there was no NFL Draft until 1936. The better teams and the wealthier owners usually got their man, although this hurt franchise stability as some owners eventually ran out of money to pay top players. Before the NFL was founded, rosters were filled with town players and the occasional college-trained football player—usually a hired gun brought in to win the bigger games. By the time the NFL got rolling in the '20s, most teams were played and coached by former college players. The level of play on the field improved dramatically throughout the decade.

From 1920 to 1933 the league did have some early Black players such as Fritz Pollard and Paul Robeson. However, an unspoken and unwritten rule appeared in 1934, and no Black players played on any NFL team again until 1946.

Getting players before the draft became a crapshoot with most NFL coaches using their connections to college coaches or local "scouts" to give them the low down on potential college players. "Most of my scouting information came from friends that were coaching or trainers," recalled Ray Flaherty, Boston/Washington Redskins Hall of Fame coach. "I loved to get the information from the trainers. They knew the injuries. They knew the attitude that the players had towards the game. Even better than the coaches. Then we had scouts. Bear Bryant was my scout in the southeastern conference. He sent me some very good football players, like Ed Cifers and Fred Davis, a number of fine players."[6]

In 1936, the NFL Draft started with the league's worst teams having a shot at the "top" college players, selecting them in reverse order of how the teams finished the year before. NFL rosters started to take shape, as roster limits increased from 16 players in 1925, to 20 in 1930, to 24 in 1935, to 30 in 1938, and to 33 in 1945. "Imagine, 33 players on one squad. Why, when I started on the Bears we had 15. You were hired to play a football game and you played it—all 60 minutes of it, brother," recalled George Trafton, Bears Hall of Fame center. "That [George] Halas used to come into the dressing room and say: 'Now boys, this half Trafton will replace Trafton, Hunk Anderson will replace Hunk Anderson, and [Ed] Healey, you'd better replace Healey.'"[7]

According to Steve Owen, Giants Hall of Fame tackle and coach, the average pay scale of players ranged from $50 to $75 for an average lineman and $100 for your "better" lineman while an average back was paid from $125 to $150 and your "better" backs would get between $200 and $400.[8]

But one thing that everybody did during this time period was play both ways. It was a true 60-minute game for most players ... they didn't know any different.

Playing Both Ways

When the NFL began, every player on a roster played both ways. They had to or they wouldn't be on the team. Each player had to have the skill set to play offense and defense. Most linemen had to know how to block and tackle, while most backs had to run, pass, kick, punt and tackle.

"It was a one-platoon game then," said Wellington Mara, Giants executive-owner, 1937–2005. "As Steve Owen used to say, men were men in those days. He was our great coach for so many years and he saw a lot of truly sturdy, talented sixty-minute men who played for and against us. Stamina played a great part of it in those days, and the players had to pace themselves. They couldn't go all out on every play, you just couldn't do that for sixty minutes of playing time. The player who played opposite you, however, was under the same handicap, but it still was grueling. The individual skills were not as refined as they are today either. Some were, like those of Don Hutson. But still he had to play defense even though his specialty was that of being a great pass receiver, probably as great as any receiver we have in the game today who only has to concentrate on catching footballs."[9]

Doc Elliott, a former All-Pro fullback for the Canton Bulldogs and Cleveland Bulldogs, who won three consecutive NFL championships from 1922 to 1924, told a reporter in 1959 his experience of playing both ways. "When I was playing we had to go all the way on both offense and defense. If the other club got a drive going you weren't sitting there on the bench with a blanket wrapped around you resting. You had to be out there backing up the line and making an effort to get a tackle on every play. You had to take the whole brunt of it…. I wouldn't say these kids are soft at all because you can see they play awfully rough football. But they don't have to play as long today as we did."[10]

The players of the two-way era knew what they signed up for. You weren't going to leave the field. "We had to play both ways when I started with the Redskins," said Sammy Baugh, Redskins Hall of Fame quarterback. "If you couldn't play both ways,

Duke Slater, tackle, Chicago Cardinals, ca. 1920 (courtesy University of Iowa Athletics).

you didn't play. A fellow could be good on offense and poor on defense, or vice-versa, and he'd be cut from the team."[11]

The two-way players during the league's first 25 years were coached by some of the greatest coaches in NFL history. Several coaches dominated the NFL during the two-way era. This list of coaches includes George Halas (Bears), Curly Lambeau (Packers), Guy Chamberlin (Bulldogs/Yellow Jackets), Jimmy Conzelman (Panthers/Steam Roller), Potsy Clark (Spartans/Lions), Steve Owen (Giants), and Ray Flaherty (Redskins). Their coaching styles helped shape the play on the field during this era.

Versatility was the name of the game; every player had to play more than just one position. "We didn't have a lot of players on the roster in those days, so you had to be ready to fill in wherever you were needed," said Bulldog Turner, Bears Hall of Fame center-linebacker, 1940–1952. "I can remember guys who never kicked the football trying to make extra points because the kicker had been hurt. In those days, we didn't carry a person just to kick, we'd just let someone take a swing at the ball for a couple of extra bucks."[12]

At the end of World War II, the pro game saw players start to hone their craft by playing just one position. In 1950, the NFL permanently adopted the two-platoon system. For current players, the NFL is an all-year, full-time job. Pre-war, it was not. Players had off-season and sometimes in-season jobs to make a living. The off season was spent working, or, for some players, participating in another sport such as baseball.

Strategy

Throughout the two-way era teams had different ways of trying to practice. In the '20s, most teams maybe practiced one time a week; usually that practice occurred on the day before the game or a few hours before kickoff. By the '30s, top teams such as the Bears, Giants, Lions, Packers, and Redskins would have daily practices. "Our preseason practices were probably a lot what they are like today," recalled Tuffy Leemans, Giants Hall of Fame halfback. "They were pretty tough. Of course, back then, you blessed the man that was helping you get into shape. You had to be in top condition to play those 60 minutes."[13]

When the NFL was organized in 1920, substitution rules permitted a withdrawn player to return only once during the game, at the beginning of a subsequent period. This rule was liberalized in 1922 to permit a player withdrawn in the first half to return at any time during the second half, but he was still limited to returning once. A player withdrawn in the second half could not return. Another change in 1932 permitted a withdrawn player to return at any time except in the quarter he was withdrawn, and a 1938 change permitted two players withdrawn during the fourth quarter to re-enter once. As a result, players participated on both offense and defense. Starters, if they left the game, were generally withdrawn in the middle of the second period, then returned in the middle or late in the third period.

On offense, most teams used the single-wing, the Notre Dame box, or a variation of these offenses. Generally, the tailback, who received the snap, was about five yards behind the center, with the fullback to his right and slightly ahead of or parallel with him. The wingback aligned a yard outside the right end and a yard in the backfield. The quarterback, who was a blocker, lined up just behind the gap between the right guard and tackle.

The first period during this era ran from 1920 to 1932 when passing was still limited with the "college rule" of passing that had to be five yards behind the line of scrimmage, and there were no hash marks on the field. When a play went to the sidelines or out of bounds, the next play had to be initiated right there. Most offenses punted or simply ran the ball back into middle of the field, wasting a play. After the famous "Indoor Game" in 1932, between the Spartans and Bears, the NFL decided to open up the "pro game" with new rules—passing from anywhere behind the line of scrimmage, hash marks and moving the field goal posts to the front of the end zone to encourage more field goals. All of this helped the pro game separate itself from the collegiate game and gave fans more excitement on the field on Sundays.

In the second period of this era (1933–1940), the single-wing was the predominant offense run by NFL teams—the two main exceptions were the Notre Dame box offense by Lambeau's Packers and the T-formation with man in motion by Halas' Bears. Starting in 1940–1941, the Bears' T-formation took off around the country.

Single-Wing

The single-wing formation depended on a center who was skilled both at blocking and at tossing the ball between his legs to the receiving back. The center had to direct the ball to any of several moving backs, with extreme accuracy, as the play started.

The direct snap or toss from the center usually went to the tailback or fullback; however, the quarterback could also take the ball. The tailback was very important to the success of the offense because he had to run, pass, block, and even punt. Unlike today, the quarterback usually blocked at the point of attack. As with his modern-day counterpart, a single-wing quarterback might also act as a field general by calling plays. The fullback was chosen for his larger size so that he could "buck" the line. This meant that the fullback would block or carry the ball between the defensive tackles. The wingback could double-team block with an offensive lineman at scrimmage or even run a pass route.

Double-Wing

The double-wing offense, with two halfbacks set wide and off the line of scrimmage, was also a very deceptive formation that could attack a defense from either the left or right and put fear in defenders who had to always be on guard for wing men running reverses. The development of the balanced wing set canceled the effectiveness of a defender over-shift to the strong side of the offensive formation in the single-wing and made the defense react to the two wings with a straight up and balanced front.

Notre Dame Box

The Notre Dame shift or Notre Dame box employed by Knute Rockne was a finesse formation in which teams could shift players around in the backfield to take advantage of their backfield players' respective strength, as well as the athletic skills required by a particular play. The four backfield players were arranged in a box-like pattern in the backfield and at the snap of the ball a veritable "fire drill" of counter motions, laterals, passes, fakes and hand-offs could wreak havoc with a defense not entirely focused. The Green Bay Packers under Curly Lambeau, a former Irish player for one year, used the Notre Dame box and were adept at both running and passing out of the set. "We had to pace ourselves to go the distance and still have something left at the finish," recalled Verne Lewellen, Packers All-Pro halfback. "We didn't throw too many passes, although Lambeau believed in the pass more than the other coaches of the time."[14]

According to Packers team historian Cliff Christl, Lambeau's Notre Dame box was not like the single-wing. There was no tailback, and the left and right halfbacks took direct snaps depending on whether the shift before the snap was to the left or right. Sometimes the fullback would take the direct snap as he was lined up directly behind the center.[15]

T-Formation

Predominately used by the Chicago Bears during the two-way era, this formation took off around the football community after the Bears 73–0 massacre of the Redskins in the 1940 NFL championship game. This formation had the quarterback under center to take the snap. The Bears added a man in motion to give the offense more flexibility and deception.

The tight T-formation, behind a balanced line of a guard, tackle and end on each side of the center, featured a quarterback behind center, a fullback behind the quarterback, and two halfbacks flanking the fullback. The tight T lent itself well to between-the-tackles dives, bucks, and cross-buck misdirection plays. This would be the predominate formation for George Halas and his Bears in the 1920s and '30s. Eventually, by the late 1930s, he would widen the line spacings and incorporate imaginative counter plays to open up his offense. "It made the entire country 'T' conscious," said George Halas, "and I believe it was the biggest reason for the influx of the T-formation in college and pro ball."[16]

The passing game's growth also occurred as this era progressed, although the NFL had good passers from the start. Throughout this era, the ball also changed. It

Ward Cuff, halfback, New York Giants, looking to pick off pass in front of Don Hutson, end, Green Bay Packers, ca. 1942 (courtesy NFL Films Research Library).

originally was between 22 and 22½ inches around the belly, which became between 21¼ and 21½ in 1934.

Defense

"You can't win a ball game with a million points if you let the other fellow score a million and one," wrote Potsy Clark in his coaching manual, *Football*, in 1935. On the other side of the ball, most defensive alignments saw eight- or seven-man fronts; that eventually turned into more six-man fronts, especially by the 1930s. The "Cup" defense had a seven-man front with four secondary players (LHB, RHB, QB, FB), while other teams could also use the 6-3-2 look or the 6-2-2-1 defense—where the center drops back into coverage to help the fullback in the secondary.

These were the most commonly used defensive schemes, especially in the '30s and early '40s.

During the seasons of 1943–1945, there was free substitution, but players continued to play on both offense and defense, and there was no extensive utilization of offensive and defensive platoons.

The next era from 1933 to 1944 would be the opening up of the pro game with passing legal from anywhere behind the line of scrimmage, hash marks on the field, and moving the goal posts from the back of the end zone to the front to encourage more kicking with field goals. These rules opened up the sport, scoring went up and the players took off.

Special Teams

During this era, one of the most important aspects of the game was punting and place kicking. Most backs had to punt and kick, even linemen such as Canton Bulldogs Hall of Fame tackle Pete "Fats" Henry kicked and performed very well. Some players performed the drop-kick in which the ball is kicked after it bounces off the ground, but that is now a lost art with the slimmed ball.

Punting was a huge part of strategy with maintaining field possession the number one priority. Most teams would punt on second and third down to pin their opponent deep in their own territory. The key was to force them to make a mistake deep in their own end to take over the ball and put points up on the scoreboard.

Positions

Quarterbacks

"Most of our quarterbacks called their own plays," recalled Ray Flaherty in 1985. "They had to because we couldn't send them in information. We had to go over our plays and game plan with the quarterbacks three or four days before the game. We had things pretty well figured out. They would go in and run the game on, pretty much on their own."[17]

The two-way era started out with mostly single-wing tailbacks/quarterbacks that transformed into the T-formation quarterbacks—starting around 1940. Early players who played the quarterback position were asked to block, throw passes, run the ball, go out on pass routes, punt and kick field goals and extra points.

Ace Parker, quarterback, Brooklyn Dodgers, ca. 1936 (courtesy Duke University Athletics).

When the T-formation came in, the quarterback became even more of a passing "weapon." "The most essential element of a pro quarterback is to be, number one, a great passer. Because no matter how smart you are, how great a leader, no matter what you know about football, if you can't throw under pressure, you're never going to be a great quarterback," said Sid Luckman, Bears Hall of Fame quarterback. The T-formation with quarterback under center changed the position into the quarterback position we see today.[18]

Because they were handling the football or lead blocking, toughness was always the calling card for players in the backfield. "When I came into the league, not only were helmets optional, but you could hit the quarterback until the whistle blew," said Sammy Baugh. "If I threw a short pass to a receiver and he zigged and zagged 75 yards for a touchdown, I had four sumbitches chasing me in the other direction. All defensive linemen were told to knock me in the dirt to get me out of the game. Another rule said that if you were injured and left the game, you couldn't return until the next quarter. If you could walk, you stayed on the field."[19]

Halfbacks-Wingbacks

Joining the quarterback in the backfield were usually two halfbacks. They would line up in the backfield or on the wing, as in the single- and double-wing formations. The halfback was usually the best athlete on the field or the most gifted. They would be asked to do a variety of roles, which in this era meant they had to do everything.

The halfback was given two major assignments: one was to advance the ball when his team had it and the other to stop the ball's advances when the other team had it. The wingback was predominantly a lead blocker and a pass receiver but still capable of running the ball on end-around plays. Two-way era halfbacks, like Red Grange, Fritz Pollard, Verne Lewellen and Dutch Clark, garnered all the headlines.

Fullbacks–Blocking Backs

The fullback's main job during this era was to be a lead blocker and goal-line threat. Big huskies like Bronko Nagurski, Ernie Nevers and Clarke Hinkle used their power and strength to their utmost advantage on offense. "We blocked below the hips," said Ernie Nevers, Hall of Fame fullback. "There was no just standing there brush blocking. Show me a good blocker, a man who doesn't flinch, who loves the game for itself and not only the money in it, and I'll show you a real football player who won't get hurt."[20]

On defense they backed up the line with an intimidation factor. Packers Hall of Fame fullback Clarke Hinkle once said about playing both ways during his era: "The offensive formation of our day spanned about 12 yards because we did not have flankers and split ends. In addition, our offensive linemen were not spaced as loose. Result, the defensive formations were tighter, so it was harder to find a hole…. In my time we went more for a touchdown inside our opponents' 20-yard line. Field goals were a last resort. We felt that a team which couldn't score a touchdown inside the opponents' 10-yard line was not a good team. Our game was more tiring because we stayed in there for sixty minutes. Our offense was only thirty minutes of the game. We also had to concentrate on defense. I backed up the line on defense, played fullback on offense, did the punting, kickoffs and long field goals, defended the pass, blocked for the pass and led the ball carrier when I wasn't carrying the ball."[21]

Ends

Ends of this era were usually tall, but solidly built. They had to be as well-rounded as any an athlete on the field. They had to have the skills to employ a variety of techniques and skills. "Today's football makes the end a combined lineman and back," wrote Potsy Clark in his coaching booklet, *Football*, in 1935. "Today's football means that the end must be strong defensively and offensively, must be able to block, tackle, catch passes, maybe throw 'em, run with the ball, recover fumbles, and be smart at all times."[22]

Catching passes was a special skill. "An end going down to receive passes uses all the tricks of a ball carrier to get himself in the open. He must have a good change of pace, change of direction, sidestep and pivot. These same qualifications are essential for him to free himself of a defensive back," wrote Ray Flaherty in the *1939 Official Guide of the NFL*.[23]

One of the most important aspects of an end was his ability to block and make tackles on special teams, especially covering punts. Some of the best ends in the two-way era would be the first man down on punts to make the tackle.

Tackles

"The name of the game for linemen is sacrifice. There isn't much glory in it for them, and there's a lot of pain," said Ed Healey, Bears Hall of Fame tackle, in 1975.[24]

Tackles of this era were usually the biggest men on the team, typically standing above six feet and weighing from 200 to around 250 pounds. Writing in his 1935 booklet, *Football*, Potsy Clark listed several coaching points for the perfect tackle:

1. Make him powerful enough in the legs to hold off opposing linemen while he sizes up the situation.
2. Make him strong enough to combine with his end in boxing the opposing tackle, or with his guard in boxing an opposing guard.
3. Make him shifty enough to vary his charge on offense and to meet the varied charge of the other fellow.
4. Make him durable enough to keep going 60 full minutes of each ball game and ready to give as much at the end as at the beginning.
5. Make him eager to charge into the opposing line on defense, pushing the other end in against his own tackle, meeting the interference behind the

opposing line, and charging strongly enough and high enough to make the tackle.

    6. And on top of it all put into him a flaming spirt that will never know defeat.[25]

"As the game is played today, linemen are called upon to shift their weight and power in the wink of an eye. They may 'feint' in one direction and drive through in another, to cover, momentarily, the direction of the ball carrier. That takes control. And to knock down a 230-pound lineman who is as tough as all-get-out, that takes power," said Bill Morgan, Giants All-Pro tackle.[26]

Guards

You can almost break down the guard positions into two different eras of play. An old-style guard (1920–1932) had to be tough and rugged, mostly called on to run, block and play hard-nose defense on a seven-man front. "He had to be strong enough not only to smash the opponents' charge between the tackles but also to help open holes down through the center for his own backs," wrote Potsy Clark.[27]

The new-style guard (1933–1945), when the game's use of passing, laterals and shifts increased, needed to not only be rugged, but "they also must know how to keep their feet under them as they charge, so that their opponents cannot drag them forward and out of the play. They must learn to hit hard enough to break through the opposing guard's defense. They must be able to make a quick opening hole and then charge for other types of plays," continued Potsy Clark. "It's a punishing position. It calls for strength and courage, as well as quick thinking and alertness."[28]

This new-style guard also had to be able to shift out of the line to run interference when his own team was sweeping around end or dashing off-tackle. He had to be fast and quick to be a lead blocker in front of fast halfbacks, as well as pass protect.

Centers

A pre–World War II center was asked to do a variety of jobs.

    1. Passing the ball accurately to the back who is to run-pass or kick it.
    2. Keeping his feet under his opponents' charge so that he will not be pushed back into his own players to spoil the play.
    3. Charging his opponent hard, either to open a hole or to get by and downfield to help clear the road in case the runner gets loose.

The pre–World War II center would generally do this out of single-wing, double-wing and T-formations. "A center should be, preferably, a fast man with a keen eye, quick judgment, iron courage, and exceptional tackling ability," wrote Potsy Clark.[29]

On defense, they usually backed up the line while playing a linebacker position. "Be jealous to the ball. Get to the man who is carrying the ball as quickly as possible.

By no means lose control of yourself and overrun the ball carrier. Keep your equilibrium, so carrier can't out trick you. It is better to have man gain two or three yards than miss him entirely," wrote Mel Hein in the *1939 Official Guide of the NFL*.[30]

The men on the following list of the NFL's 50 greatest two-way players put their heart and soul into playing these seven positions. They played a 60-minute game with all their blood and sweat. "It wasn't like today, when we played football, we played hard football," recalled Red Stacy, Detroit Lions tackle, 1935–1937. "There were few—very few—substitutions. You played the whole game, both offense and defense. No equipment. We played for the fun, the sport."[31]

The two-way era shouldn't be forgotten. The game was different, and the players played 60 minutes. However, the players were just like the players of today, especially the great ones: all they wanted to do was win. They did whatever they could to win games and, just like the Rams' Aaron Donald or the Bengals' Joe Burrow in Super Bowl LVI, they wanted to win a championship. For the two-way players, the stakes in 1930 were the same as they are in 2023. The Vince Lombardi trophy was still a few decades away, but the drive of the players to win a championship is eternal. Titles came easy for Bears Hall of Fame center-linebacker Bulldog Turner, who won four NFL championships during the 1940s. But with the emphasis on Super Bowl championships, sometimes it gets lost that the players during the two-way era also played for rings. "People ask me if I have any Super Bowl rings," said Bulldog Turner. "I say, 'No, but I have four championship rings. It's the same game.'"[32]

The greatest two-way players in NFL history deserve more attention. Their stories and accomplishments need to be told. With that said, let the countdown begin!

THE PLAYERS

No. 1

Dutch Clark

Halfback

Full Name: Earl Harry Clark
Nickname: "Dutch"
b: October 11, 1906 (Fowler, CO); d: August 5, 1978 (age 71; Canon City, CO)
High School: Pueblo (CO) Central; College: Colorado College
Height/Weight: 6-0, 185 pounds
Position: Halfback
Teams/Years: 1931–1932 Portsmouth Spartans; 1934–1938 Detroit Lions
Pro Football Hall of Fame: Class of 1963 (Charter Member)
Retro-MVPs: 1932, 1935–1936
All-Time Teams: C. Cagle (1937); B. Cahn (1943); J. Carr (1934); P. Clark (1947); G. Corbett (1938); G. Dorias (1952, 1954); R. Grange (1934, 1946–1947, 1955); G. Halas (1939); M. Hein (1944, 1968, 1974); B. Hewitt (1937, 1940); C. Hinkle (1940, 1942, 1986); C. Hubbard (1937, 1966); D. Hutson (1986); W. Keisling (1942); J. McMillen (1939); J. McNally (1944); M. Michalske (1982); G. Musso (1964); B. Nagurski (1939, 1944); S. Owen (1942); R. Richards (1944); C. Storck (1939); D. Tehan (1963)

The NFL's best player of the two-way era was Dutch Clark. Not just the best halfback, Clark was arguably the best all-around player in the NFL's two-way era. Nobody appreciated the Dutchman's skills more than his former head coach Potsy Clark. "He [Dutch] is one of the most intelligent men who ever played football. He knows the game thoroughly. But his main asset is an ability to gain the confidence of players. He makes them absolutely believe in him," said Potsy, coach of the Portsmouth Spartans/Detroit Lions.[1]

Born in the mountains of Colorado in 1906, little Earl Clark would be called by a different name for the rest of his life. In a 1969 interview Clark recalled how he got his famous nickname. "I came from Colorado, and although I'm called Dutch Clark, I'm not a Dutchman," said Dutch Clark. "Fact is, Clark is an Irish name. And my father was a Welshman. But I had two brothers and one of them didn't talk very plain when he was young, so an uncle named him Dutch. Then they started calling my other brother Big Dutch and they called me Little Dutch."[2]

Eventually, the Clark family settled in Pueblo, where Dutch realized that he had a special eye condition. "I'm kind of blind, I guess," said Clark. "When I was playing pro ball, I had 20/100 in the right eye and 20/200 in the left. But it didn't bother

Dutch Clark (no. 7), halfback, Detroit Lions, ca. 1936, against the Bears in Detroit (courtesy Detroit Lions).

me at all. I had bad eyes from the time I was in grade school, but in those days you didn't go buy a pair of glasses. You didn't have enough money to eat on. So I didn't get glasses till I was in college. But anyway, maybe the eye trouble helped me. Maybe I dodged quicker. But I do know it never bothered me at that time." The 20/200 in his left eye meant that he saw from 20 feet what a normal person saw at 200 feet. Most states today would consider 20/200 to be legally blind, but the vision problem never hindered Dutch in his ability to play football.[3]

Dutch learned how to be a hard worker during his high school days. "We didn't have anything. Times were bad. I quit school at fourteen to work for a year. When I went back to school, I'd work for the railroad from nine at night until six in the morning; then school; then football practice; then home to sleep. Mother would come in and wipe my face with a wet washcloth to get me awake for work," recalled Dutch Clark.[4]

Dutch became a star on the gridiron in Pueblo. His all-around skills flourished from an early age, especially his drop-kicking, which he learned from his high school coach, Ollie Herigstad, a former star at Colorado Agricultural College (now Colorado State University). "We'd bet malted milk shakes on accuracy and distance and even now I still must owe Dutch a couple hundred malts," said Ollie Herigstad in 1965. Dutch finished his prep career by scoring 262 points with 34 total touchdowns, and in 1981 the city of Pueblo built a statue at the high school field in his honor.[5]

After graduating from high school, Dutch stayed local to further his football career. He decided to attend Colorado College in nearby Colorado Springs. Here he became an even bigger star. Dutch would dominate the Rocky Mountain Conference as a triple-threat star where his rushing, passing, and kicking skills made weekly headlines.

After his junior year in 1928, Dutch was named First Team All-American by Alan Gould of the Associated Press, becoming one of the few players west of the Mississippi to be honored with a first team designation—as well as the first player from the state of Colorado. Just like in high school, Dutch finished with some impressive numbers at Colorado College—he scored in 21 of 23 varsity games, made first team all-conference three times and led the Rocky Mountain Conference in scoring twice (1928–1929).

At first, Dutch Clark didn't show much interest in playing pro football, accepting a job as assistant football and head basketball coach at his alma mater, Colorado College. But soon Dutch missed the competition of his favorite sport. He missed the contact. He missed the strategy and the ability to call his own plays. He soon wanted to prove he could play with the best football players. "So, I decided to try it. I kept telling myself it was financial, but I wanted to vindicate myself, or vindicate Alan Gould, to see if I could play. I felt I was a newspaper champion. The greatest satisfaction I got in professional football was proving myself ... to myself. That was the reason I went to play professionally," recalled Clark.[6]

In 1931, Potsy Clark was named head coach of the NFL's Portsmouth Spartans. Potsy's brother, Stu, coached basketball at Denver University and told his brother he needed to contact the best player he had seen on the gridiron in the Rocky Mountains. In the end, Potsy got Dutch to sign with the Spartans. Dutch recalled that he made $140 a game that first season. Playing professional football would be a decision that Dutch wouldn't regret.

The 6–0, 185-pound Clark played in 75 NFL games over seven seasons with the Portsmouth Spartans/Detroit Lions. During that time period, Dutch made first team consensus All-Pro *six* times in those seven years. He sat out the 1933 season to coach at the Colorado School of Mines, a season he probably would've made first team again. Usually listed in the lineup at the quarterback position, Dutch played halfback in Potsy Clark's single-wing offense. Dutch was the team leader and called all the plays on offense. He controlled a game like no other player during the two-way era. "I figure Dutch did everything with a football twice as good as any other player I saw. It's not his fault there isn't a page in the league record book where they measure a man's abilities in terms of his braininess on the field. Dutch's name would be all over it, just like he was all over a football field," said George Christensen, Lions All-Pro tackle, 1931–1938.[7]

Dutch took calling the plays seriously and consistently showed off his outstanding football I.Q., proving to his coach, Potsy, that he was the right man for the job. "He had confidence in me," recalled Dutch. "I used to put the plays in when I was playing. Potsy had nine runs and nine passes. He figured that was enough."[8]

Dutch also never called his own number unless it was the best play possible. "When I call signals, there are four men in the backfield. I look on Dutch Clark the same as I do Ace Gutowsky and Ernie Caddel," said Dutch. "I decided what play will get us over the line the quickest with the least handling of the ball. If I think Dutch Clark can do it I call his number, if someone else would do it better his number goes up."[9]

Dutch was equally gifted with the football in his hands. Teammates and opponents could see the specialness with which Dutch played the game. "Dutch was a very shifty runner," recalled Glenn Presnell, Spartans/Lions All-Pro halfback, 1931–1936. "He was an exceptional drop-kicker, which is a lost art today. But he drop-kicked extra points. He was a very shifty runner. He was very well-liked by all the players. He had a wonderful personality. He was very popular with the players."[10]

"Dutch Clark was a field general. He was a very smart quarterback. He could read defenses very well. He was a very good signal caller, a wonderful runner, just a very fine football player," recalled Ray Flaherty, Giants Hall of Fame end. "Dutch was outstanding. He was one of the most outstanding football players I ever played against," said Ralph Kercheval, Dodgers All-Pro back.[11]

In 1937, Packers Hall of Fame tackle Cal Hubbard was asked by Henry McLemore of the United Press to pick an All-Time team. Hubbard started naming his squad by saying, "I'll take that Dutch Clark with my first pick. I've been watching 'em a long time and he's the best backfield man I ever saw. Here's how good he is. That Detroit backfield he plays in has got some hot babies in it—Ernie Caddel, Ace Gutowsky, and Glenn Presnell. But when the going gets so tough they can't make a foot they gave the ball to Dutch and what does he do? He GOES."[12]

Dutch's triple-threat playing style made an immediate impact in the NFL. By his second year in the league in 1932, Dutch was the best player.

Retro-MVP: 1932 NFL Season

Dutch finished the '32 season sixth in the league in passing and fourth in rushing and he was one of just eight players to catch at least 10 passes. As for scoring, Dutch finished first in the league with 55 points—on six touchdowns, three field goals and 10 extra points. Dutch helped the Spartans play consistent football all season. In their opening game, Dutch's short touchdown run in the second quarter led to a 7–0 victory over the New York Giants. Three weeks later he caught a touchdown pass in the fourth quarter to force a 7–7 tie against Staten Island. Then Dutch put on a show over the next three games:

October 20—Clark had a 74-yard TD run to beat Staten Island again, 13–6.

October 27—Clark threw a TD pass to Father Lumpkin for the only score, a 6–0 win over the Giants.

November 6—Trailing 7–0, Clark caught a 65-yard TD pass (kicked the extra point), then kicked a 25-yard field goal in the fourth quarter to secure a 17–7 win over Brooklyn.

The biggest game of the year in the NFL was played on December 4 as the Spartans hosted the three-time NFL champion Green Bay Packers. The Spartans destroyed the Pack, 19–0, ending Green Bay's title hopes and tying the Spartans for first place with the Chicago Bears. The two teams asked the league to play a postseason game in Chicago. Unfortunately, Dutch would miss the NFL's first postseason game played on December 18. It was called the "Indoor Game" because a snowstorm in the Windy City moved it inside Chicago Stadium. The loss of Dutch was too much as the Spartans lost to the Bears, 9–0.

Dutch had arrived as a professional football player. "He can do anything with the football," wrote the United Press in 1932 about Dutch, "and I don't believe any coach, player or observer ever had a keener football brain."[13]

The following year Dutch decided to sit out the season. In 1933, the Depression was still roaring, and money was tight for the small-town Spartans. "After my second year at Portsmouth, I quit pro ball because it was so difficult to get my money. They were wonderful people in Portsmouth, but they just didn't have the money to operate it. It was still during the Depression and they had no money and it was hard to get your money. You had to fight for it, and wait for it, and maybe you got it and maybe you didn't. So I decided to take a job at the Colorado School of Mines. I was athletic director, and coached everything they had, football, basketball, and baseball. I got three thousand dollars for doing everything," recalled Dutch.[14]

After the 1933 season the Portsmouth Spartans were out of money. The team's board of directors decided to sell the franchise to Detroit radio mogul George A. Richards, whose first big decision was to get Dutch Clark back on the gridiron. "They moved the team from Portsmouth to Detroit. Portsmouth was a little difficult to get your money. So that was one of the reasons I quit. Then when they moved to Detroit the whole setup was different. It was high class and real first-class operation the night I signed to go back into it," recalled Dutch. Richards renamed the team the Detroit Lions with Dutch as the city's first superstar, nicknamed by the local press as the "Ty Cobb of football."[15]

Dutch's most impressive skill was his ability to not only lead, but to get his teammates to play at their highest level. The Spartans and Lions teams that he played on were just as competitive as any team in the two-way era. During his time with the Spartans/Lions, his teams won 66 percent of their games. Always a contender, Dutch guided the Lions to the 1935 NFL championship. In the championship game, he had the signature play, a 42-yard touchdown run in the first quarter that set the tone for the game to help defeat the New York Giants, 26–7. He finished the game with a team-high 80 rushing yards on just seven carries.

Besides being one of the NFL's best generals on the field, Dutch could do everything well and did most everything better than anybody. He could run, pass, catch, tackle, block, punt and kick. Watching game footage of Dutch, you can see that he has great feet and is always going forward. "He looked like the easiest man in the world to tackle. The first time I tried I thought I'd break him in two. But when I closed my arms, all I was holding was air," said Bronko Nagurski, Bears Hall of Fame fullback. In an era when most of the action was at the line of scrimmage and running plays dominated the game, Dutch always seemed to be going forward; rarely was he stopped in the backfield or for no gain. "Dutch is like a rabbit in a brush heap when he gets into the secondary. He has no plan but only instinct to cut, pivot, slant and run in any direction equally well," said Potsy Clark about his prize runner.[16]

Dutch's running style was purely instinctive. Something he was born with. It was a running style that couldn't be coached. "For me, running is like driving a car. I'd look down the field and see what was going on ahead of me. When people were close to me, I'd just let my instinct work for me," recalled Dutch. "And, oh, on a muddy field, I really killed them. For some reason, I don't know why, I didn't slip or slide like everyone else."[17]

Most defenses were set up to stop Dutch and the Lions' excellent running game. Usually the Lions had their way, even if the opponent thought they had an edge on the All-Pro back with bad eyesight. "We set up a defense against Dutch Clark, when we played the Detroit Lions," recalled Joe Kopcha, Bears All-Pro guard, 1932–1935. "Dutch Clark's left eye was a little bit receded, he was supposed to be blind in that left eye. Halas would say, 'Now, when we pass, we throw that pass over in Dutch Clark's area. Pass it, throw the ball over to his blind eye, the left eye.' Well, every time they'd throw that ball he'd intercept it. So, at halftime Halas says, 'My God, what would he do if he had two good eyes!'"[18]

Dutch excelled playing defensive halfback. Looking at game footage Dutch was never out of position and was a sure tackler in Potsy's regular 6-2-2-1 defense. And to top it off he was also the era's best kicker—usually by the drop-kick—who could score points in bunches. He led the NFL in scoring three times: 1932, 1935–1936. He also led the league in rushing touchdowns in 1934, 1936–1937. In the end, Dutch finished his career with 369 points and 42 career touchdowns (36 rushing, six receiving).

Clark was part of the Lions rushing offense that in 1936 set an NFL record for rushing yards in a season with 2,885 yards in 12 games, a record that stood until 1972 when the Miami Dolphins broke it in a 14-game season. He was also part of a Lions rushing offense that helped lead the NFL in rushing twice in 1936–1937 and finish second twice more in 1934–1935. In addition, Dutch was an accurate passer for this era, completing 45.6 percent of passes and 11 touchdowns. "He could run. Dutch could fake you out of your supporter, too. He was a good back, go one way and then go the other and so forth. He'd have you all tied up. He was hard to stop," said George Musso, Bears Hall of Fame lineman.[19]

Retro-MVPs: 1935, 1936 NFL Seasons

"He's the hardest man in football to tackle. His change of pace fools the best tackles," said Red Grange, Bears Hall of Fame back, about Dutch. Over the 1935–1936 seasons, Dutch played his best football. Just like in 1932, Dutch was the best player in the NFL in 1935. He finished the season fourth in the league in rushing with 427 yards, second in the league in yards from scrimmage with 551, and first in total touchdowns with six and points scored with 55, beating out the Packers' rookie end Don Hutson who had 43. To top it off he helped the Lions win the Eastern Division title and contributed mightily to the Lions win over the Giants for the NFL championship. Dutch wins his second Retro-MVP award.[20]

In 1936, Dutch called all the plays, but he called his number not as often as you would think. He rushed for 628 yards, third best in the NFL, but it was done on just 123 rushing attempts. His average was just behind Lions teammate Ernie Caddel's at 5.1 yards per carry, and his seven rushing touchdowns was tops in the league. Dutch was the best back in the Lions' crowded backfield. Detroit rushed for an NFL record of 2,885 yards in 12 games (averaging 240 yards per game). That record lasted for 36 years until the undefeated 1972 Dolphins rushed for 2,960 yards.

The 30-year-old Clark played the entire 1936 season at the highest level. He scored a point in every game, including an incredible stretch where the Lions played three games in eight days *twice* during the season. The Lions played games on October 11 (Philadelphia), October 14 (Brooklyn) and October 18 (Green Bay) and again later in the year on November 25 (Green Bay), Thanksgiving Day on November 29 (Bears) and December 2 (Bears). He was never better than those three late season games. He scored a touchdown in all three games, kicked one field goal and four extra points. Against the Bears on Thanksgiving Day, he sprinted 51 yards for the deciding touchdown in a 14–7 victory, sending Lions fans home happy on Turkey Day.

Dutch held up throughout the season by putting together a remarkable resume, leading the NFL in scoring with 73 points, finishing third in rushing with 628 yards, and topping the circuit in passing percentage with a mark of 53.5 percent. Although he only completed 38 of 71 passes, for 467 yards and four touchdowns, he was highly efficient throwing the ball. He only had six interceptions, which paled in comparison to the massive interception totals of the other quarterbacks who threw. Dutch wins back-to-back Retro-MVP in '35 and '36 and his second and third overall.

Dutch Clark was simply the best player in the NFL for the 1935 and 1936 seasons. From November 17, 1935, and going through October 31, 1937, Dutch scored a point in 24 consecutive games. In those 24 games he tallied 150 points, averaging nearly a touchdown a game. He scored 17 touchdowns and kicked 33 extra points and five field goals. The Lions posted a 16–7–1 record including winning the 1935 NFL championship. It was simply a terrific run of great football.

Besides winning those three Retro-MVPs (1932, 1934–1935), Dutch was a consensus First Team All-Pro six times during his seven NFL seasons.

First Team All-Pros

NFL: 6 times (1931–1932, 1934–1937)
United Press: 6 times (1931–1932, 1934–1937)
Collyer's: 6 times (1931–1932, 1934–1937)
Green Bay Press-Gazette: 3 times (1932, 1934–1935)
Brooklyn Times-Union: 2 times (1932, 1934)
I.N.S. and *New York Daily News*: once (1937)

Dutch was a player-coach with the Lions for two seasons in 1937–1938, going 14–8, preparing himself for a future in coaching. After the 1938 season, Dutch retired for good as a player. Bears owner-coach George Halas commented: "My All-Time set of backs would include Jim Thorpe, Paddy Driscoll, Red Grange, Bronko Nagurski, Ernie Nevers—and last but far from least, the brilliant Dutch Clark. In the football world, there will be deep regret when Dutch ends his playing days, but there will be no regrets among the Bears.... This elusive back had been in our hair too often, too long and too much. Even so, there has never been a finer, cleaner sportsman on the football field than Dutch."[21]

In 1939, Dutch left Detroit to become the head coach of the Cleveland Rams, going 16–26–2 in four seasons (1939–1942). Clark then was an assistant with the independent Seattle Bombers (1944) and the Los Angeles Dons (1949) of the AAFC. Later, Clark would go on to be an assistant, head coach and athletic director for the University of Detroit (1950–1954), winning Missouri Valley Conference coach of the year in 1952.

After stepping away from coaching, Dutch retired to his home state of Colorado. On August 5, 1978, Dutch Clark passed away of cancer at the age of 71.

In 1963, Dutch was honored as a Charter Member of the Pro Football Hall of Fame, joining the likes of Jim Thorpe, Don Hutson, Sammy Baugh, Red Grange, Cal Hubbard and Mel Hein. He was one of just 11 players in the first Hall of Fame class that totaled 17 charter members. He was an obvious selection. Jack McDonald, sports columnist for the *San Francisco News Call-Bulletin*, was one of the original members of the selection committee who recalled the easier choices. "Bronko Nagurski was one of the enthusiastically accepted. Three others—Sammy Baugh, Don Hutson, and Dutch Clark—were unanimous choices."[22]

At the induction ceremony in Canton, Ohio, Dutch gave a humble speech when he accepted this prestigious honor: "This is the most wonderful thing that ever happened to me and to be able to be a part of these ceremonies today in

Canton are things that I'll cherish the rest of my life, and for those who are responsible, for coaches, and players, and sports writers, I shall be forever grateful. Thank you."[23]

Dutch was selected to the NFL 1930s All-Decade Team and the Detroit Lions retired his number 7 jersey. But what separated Dutch Clark from the other players of the two-way era? Why is he number one? Let's look at the resume. Awards and All-Pro honors? Check. Leadership and playing abilities on offense, defense and special teams? Check. NFL championship? Check. Testimonials from opponents and teammates? Check.

When researching the All-Time teams for this project, I found that Dutch was listed on 23 teams including squads selected by the era's greatest two-way players: Red Grange, George Halas, Mel Hein, Clarke Hinkle, Cal Hubbard, Don Hutson, Mike Michalske, George Musso, and Bronko Nagurski. The 23 All-Time teams do not include any of his teammates or coaches, just opponents. Giants Hall of Famer Mel Hein, when selecting Clark in 1968 for his All-Time team, said, "Then there was Dutch Clark, the last of the great drop-kickers. If Dutch had played with a New York team, he might have been better known. But he was inducted into the Hall of Fame in 1963 and no one deserved it more. He was a fine runner, a superb defensive back, and also a great drop-kicker.... He was in my opinion the greatest triple-threat back of his era. He could be classified as one of the greatest, if not the greatest all-around back of all-time."[24]

Two more reasons why Dutch Clark is number one on our list. First, in 1940 the Associated Press voted a Football Man of the Decade for the 1930s. For the decade of the 1920s they selected Red Grange. For the 1930s they voted Dutch Clark over fellow two-way stars such as Don Hutson, Mel Hein, Bronko Nagurski, Clarke Hinkle and Sammy Baugh. The AP writer, Dillon Graham, wrote: "In this era of gridiron specialists all-round football players are rare. Versatile perfectionists who can successfully match the best kickers, runners, and passers come seldom. Earl [Dutch] Clark was one.... Many call him the greatest player modern football has produced. And since football today is much more demanding and complex than in earlier years it might not be an exaggeration to rank Clark as the best all-around performer of all-time. Dutch is our selection for football's Man of the Decade.... Sammy Baugh, Mel Hein and Don Hutson were others who belong in everyone's who who's.... But Clark is our man. He could do everything. An accurate punter, a great drop-kicker, a sure tackler, and a skillful, hard blocker, he was also one of the National League's better passers and had few equals as a runner. As a quarterback he was virtually a coach on the field."[25]

Second, in 2019 Dutch was named to the NFL 100th Anniversary Team, the greatest honor of his career. A blue-ribbon panel that included the likes of Bill Belichick, Tony Dungy, Dick LeBeau, John Madden, Ozzie Newsome, Bill Polian, Art Shell, Don Shula, and Ron Wolf could see the greatness of Dutch Clark. "Dutch is one of the great two-way players and really one of the most versatile players to ever play the game," said Bill Belichick, Patriots head coach, in 2019. "He was a very elusive runner, and he could also run with power."[26]

Dutch Clark is the greatest two-way player.

"I have no regrets about playing. And I hope I attained one goal—vindicating Alan Gould [AP writer] for that selection he made of a player from a small college many years ago," said Dutch Clark.[27]

No. 2

Don Hutson

End

Full Name: Donald Roy Hutson
Nickname: "Alabama Antelope"
b: January 31, 1913 (Pine Bluff, AR); d: June 26, 1997 (age 84; Rancho Mirage, CA)
High School: Pine Bluff (AR); College: Alabama
Height/Weight: 6–1, 183 pounds
Position: End
Teams/Years: 1935–1945 Green Bay Packers
Pro Football Hall of Fame: Class of 1963 (Charter Member)
Retro-MVPs: 1941–1942, 1944 (Joe F. Carr MVP Trophy, 1941–1942)
All-Time Teams: S. Baugh (1949, 1957, 1999); B. Cahn (1943); D. Clark (1942); P. Clark (1947); E. Cuneo (1973); G. Dorais (1952, 1954); P. Driscoll (1956); R. Flaherty (1990); M. Gantenbein (1966); R. Grange (1947, 1955); M. Hein (1944, 1968, 1974); A. Herber (1946); C. Hinkle (1940, 1942, 1986); W. Kiesling (1942); C. Lambeau (1946, 1948, 1955); T. Leemans (1953); V. Lewellen (1946); F. Lumpkin (1937); J. McMillen (1939); J. McNally (1944, 1963); G. Musso (1964); B. Nagurski (1944); S. Owen (1942, 1952, 1955); D. Slater (1949); J. Stydahar (1951, 1952)

The greatest of all the two-way ends and the runner-up to Dutch Clark on our list of the NFL's greatest two-way players is the incomparable Don Hutson. The 6–1, 183-pound Hutson had the perfect combination of size and speed for an end in the early days of the NFL. "The only real superman I ever saw was Don Hutson. You can't cover him and that goes for any team in the country. Day in and day out Hutson can't be covered," wrote Jimmy Conzelman, Hall of Fame coach, in the *St. Louis Post-Dispatch* in 1940. Hutson played 116 games over 11 years, all with the Green Bay Packers, and was the main offensive weapon for pass-happy Curly Lambeau.[1]

Don Hutson was born on January 31, 1913, and was raised in Pine Bluff, Arkansas. His only claim to fame during his boyhood days was the finest collection of rattlesnakes in the state. This was an early sign that Hutson was truly a different breed. Besides his rattlesnakes, Hutson was a gifted athlete known more for his baseball skills than his football prowess. As an outfielder for his high school team, he showed enough promise for a shot at professional ball, but before his senior year he made a decision that changed his sporting career.

Football held no interest for him in high school. He awakened to it only because the kid across the street, Bob Seawell, was about to go to a preseason training camp in the Ozarks in August of his senior year. Despite playing some the year before, Hutson went out for the team merely to qualify for the trip to the Ozarks—definitely a breed apart. "I wasn't that good a football player in high school," recalled Don Hutson. "I'd just started as a junior and hadn't really gotten going yet." Hutson continued, "Well, I reported that fall, more to satisfy Bob than anything else. I only weighed about a hundred and fifty pounds, and I never expected to amount to anything." However, Hutson did indeed amount to something.[2]

Don Hutson, end, Green Bay Packers, ca. 1942 (courtesy Green Bay Packers).

Hutson's senior year in high school showed enough promise that Alabama awarded him a scholarship to play baseball and football. At 6-1 and 160 pounds, Hutson didn't put any fear into opposing defenders, but his sprinter's speed and instinctive moves caught the coach's attention. While at Alabama Hutson played with a fellow end named Paul "Bear" Bryant, who would go on to be the all-time winningest coach in college football history. "Don had the most fluid motion you've ever seen when he was running," recalled Bryant. "It looked like he was going just as fast as possible when all of sudden he would put on an extra burst of speed and be gone. Don had great hands and excellent moves, but the thing that made him most dangerous was his ability to run in the open field. He could really move, with an excellent change of pace." By his senior year Hutson was still unproven and unknown. All of that was about to change in 1934.[3]

That fall the Crimson Tide went through the regular season 9-0, with a 13-6 win over Tennessee as the only close contest, during which Hutson scored the winning touchdown. Alabama was then invited to play in the prestigious Rose Bowl against West Coast power Stanford. Before a "frightful" crowd of 85,000 Hutson responded with the game of his life by catching seven passes for 165 yards and two touchdowns to lead Alabama to a 29-13 upset. Hutson was a national hero and pro scouts started to recruit the star receiver.

His outstanding Rose Bowl game attracted NFL teams. In the days before the NFL Draft, any team had the right to sign any player they wanted. Hutson became involved in a bidding war. Both Curly Lambeau of the Green Bay Packers and John "Shipwreck" Kelly of the Brooklyn Dodgers wanted Hutson. Because there was no college draft, each coach was determined to sign him, and Kelly assured Hutson that he would top any offer Lambeau might make.

After the game Lambeau mailed a contract to Hutson in Tuscaloosa, Alabama. The new "phenom" sent a collect wire to Kelly in Brooklyn, so that the bidding might begin. Kelly was vacationing in Florida, however, and by the time word from Hutson finally reached him Hutson already had signed the Green Bay contract and sent it to Lambeau. Kelly flew directly to Tuscaloosa and talked Hutson into signing a Brooklyn contract as well. Kelly told Hutson that Lambeau's contract was null and void, because at the time he signed it, he hadn't heard his offer. He told Hutson to sign his contract for $500 a year more and leave the rest to him. Hutson signed the contract and Kelly sent it to the league office.

A couple of days later NFL president Joe Carr was amazed when he opened his mail and found that Hutson had agreed to play for both Green Bay and Brooklyn—at slightly different salaries. Carr's ruling: the earlier contract to arrive would be valid, the other invalid. Lambeau's letter, forwarding the signed contract and sent special delivery, had been stamped at 8:30 a.m. Kelly's had been stamped at 8:47 a.m. Seventeen minutes is all that separated both teams. Lambeau later thanked the postal service for landing Hutson and bringing the Packers back to power for the next decade.

The special delivery letter was also a blessing for Hutson. Had he gone to Brooklyn, he might not have been in the league very long. The Dodgers had no quarterbacks and Lambeau was the only coach at the time using the pass as his primary weapon. The recruitment of Hutson and other college stars convinced the league to finally adopt a system to allocate players, thus the college draft was born in 1936.

"I didn't really know much at all about pro football before I got to Green Bay," said Hutson. "I never followed it while I was in college. In fact, they never even carried the scores or standings of the professional teams in the newspapers down in Alabama in those days. So when I got there it was a whole new world, a far cry from the college game. But I got into it pretty quick."[4]

Initially Hutson had some doubts about himself playing professional football and didn't know how well he could play at this high level. He was still only 6-1 and weighed about 180 pounds; he knew the pro game was much faster and bigger. Lambeau had tremendous confidence in Hutson and knew what he could do when given the chance to play. After the 1935 season opener against the Chicago Cardinals in which Hutson played sparsely, he was ready to tackle the Packers chief rival, the Chicago Bears. Hutson voiced his concern to Packers Hall of Fame lineman Cal Hubbard in the dressing room. "I'm scared to death," he confessed to Hubbard. "I did all right in college, but these fellows are so much bigger and better. I'm not even sure I belong." "Don't worry kid," growled Cal. "You belong." On the very first play from scrimmage, Hutson proved he belonged and never worried again.[5]

The opening kickoff was returned by the Packers to their own 17-yard line. The first play from scrimmage was a designed pass play to Hutson. He ran a slow, deliberate pattern to lure the defensive player, then took off with his great speed. Eighty-three yards later, Hutson had a touchdown on his first play as a pro. The Packers went on to upset the Bears 7–0 on Hutson's big play. "We used one man to defend against Hutson. We used two men. Finally, we used three men. It never did any good," said George Halas, Bears coach.[6]

During his time learning from Lambeau, Hutson refined pass patterns and was routinely double- and triple-teamed. Hutson would work on his craft in practice. "For every pass I caught in a game, I caught a thousand passes in practice," Hutson once said to the *New York Times*.[7]

Watching game film, we see Hutson showing an uncanny knack of getting open. He displayed an array of moves and faints that combined with his deceptive cuts to lift him above all other ends in the NFL. And to top it off he was one of the fastest players during this era, too. "I got to where I could run the 100 in 9.7 consistently and that was pretty good in those days," recalled Hutson. An unstoppable combination of athletic ability, the man nicknamed the "Alabama Antelope" was going to be used as the number one offensive weapon in Green Bay. "He would glide downfield, leaning forward as if to steady himself close to the ground," said Lambeau. "Then, as suddenly as you gulp or blink an eye, he would fake one way and go the other, reach up like a dancer, gracefully grab the ball and leave the scene of the accident."[8]

Hutson's ability to run pass routes and his great work ethic rubbed off on his teammates. When Hutson joined the Packers, they hadn't won a title since 1931. He would team up with quarterbacks Arnie Herber and then Cecil Isbell to form two lethal passing combinations. They could see his greatness. "Don weighed about 178 pounds. He didn't run with his knees up under his chin, so his speed was deceiving. No one man could cover him. It took two men, either one to hold him up on the line of scrimmage and then the cornerback take him as he came down in the secondary. He had just great moves," recalled Clarke Hinkle, Packers Hall of Fame fullback. "He was a pretty good blocker. He played thirty minutes of defense also. So, he turned out to be a pretty good cornerback. He ran pass patterns. Of course, a lot of times [Arnie] Herber and [Cecil] Isbell threw to spots. Put the ball to spot and Hutson was always there. But he had a particular pass pattern to run. He just didn't go out there and run his own route. But he had such great speed and such beautiful moves. I've often said, 'If a person could see a gazelle running through a secondary defense on the football field today that would be Don Hutson. Nobody could cover a gazelle.'"[9]

Hutson's ability to run after the catch, track passes and make the acrobatic catches was duplicated by more than his teammates. Baseball Hall of Famer Willie Mays used to emulate the great Hutson. Mays admitted to watching game films of Hutson to play centerfield. "I watched the way he caught a football," Mays once said in 1975. "He would catch a ball and stop real fast, go one way, go the other way. I watched what he did. I said if he can do that with a football why can't I do it with a baseball."[10]

Cecil Isbell, Packers quarterback, recalls Hutson's greatness: "He wasn't afraid of anybody, but they were afraid of him," said Isbell. "All week long the other coach would tell his team how Hutson was likely to beat them. The man who was supposed to cover Don would probably lie awake nights while Hutson got his sleep."[11]

Isbell continues: "I never threw to a spot. All our pass plays depended on how Don got position on the defensive man. He could catch the ball high or low and many times, to cut down the chance of interception on passes to the flat or button hooks, I'd fire the ball low and ahead of him. He'd make a diving catch for the first down and the [defensive] halfback wouldn't have a chance. He'd charge off the line with his head down like a bull out of a chute. He had great eyes and fine judgment and could see what was going on around him all the time. Most teams would try and beat him up on the line, not letting him get out, but he was tough to box in, too."[12]

Hutson would practice and practice to improve his craft. He would use everything to his advantage, like wearing eye black. "It was just a glare thing, that's all," recalled Hutson. "The same reason that people wear dark glasses in the sun. It helps cut the glare out when you're in a position. We used to play in the Polo Grounds in New York, there was a time during that game where I don't know which was north and which was south. But at one end of the field the ball was directly in the sun. As far as trying to catch it was concerned. And that was the idea of the eye black."[13]

Or using small shoulder pads. "I had some very small and very light shoulder pads that I used probably 75 percent of the time with no hip pads," recalled Hutson. "It's just a question of mobility and speed, as far as I was concerned. Getting a feeling of being loose and going up for the ball and so forth. The other side of it is your chance of being hurt. Maybe I was just fortunate, but in playing 11 years I was never hurt. So that didn't bother me about not using the pads."[14]

Hutson was the most difficult receiver to cover during the two-way era. Over the years numerous opponents raved about Hutson's ability as an all-around player, not just as a receiver. "Don Hutson, Green Bay would split him out. He had these little bitty shoulder pads, little bitty hip pads so he could run. We put three men on top of Hutson. We had me on the outside as a halfback. Pug Manders on the inside and Ralph Kercheval on safety. He scored two touchdowns on us. He just went up and took it away from us," recalled Ace Parker, Dodgers Hall of Fame quarterback. "If you didn't see that guy play, you can't imagine how good he was. He didn't weigh much. He played safety on defense. He was a hell of an athlete, but he was just quicker, had better hands, had jumping ability and things like that it took to be a receiver."[15]

"On defense, they put him in at defensive end and they moved Don back to safety," recalled Ray Flaherty, Redskins Hall of Fame coach. "He was an excellent safety because he was used to feeling that ball. He had great speed and could cover the field well. So it was really a perfect setup for him. Hutson was by far the best pass receiver of our day. He had exceptional speed. He had very good hands. If there was a ball near him he'd catch it. He had very good moves. He would fake those defensive men out of position. We always played Don, played him from the inside to make him go to the sidelines. That's the way we played him. But he was, by far, the best pass receiver that had been in football up to my time."[16]

Teams' whole defensive game plans would be built around trying to stop Hutson, but usually it was to no avail. "There is no defending Hutson," said Steve Owen, Giants Hall of Fame coach. "We put two men on him, just as every other team in the league does, and two men aren't enough. He's a genius."[17]

"He could really turn it on. Hutson had a lot of changes of pace. He could outmaneuver almost anybody and he had speed," recalled Johnny Sisk, Bears halfback, 1932–1936. "Besides that, he made all sorts of sensational catches with opponents hanging all over him, and he could elude people after he caught the ball. He was a rare football player, a once-in-a-lifetime guy. He'd be great in any season."[18]

"I'd read and heard a lot about Hutson and it sounded like fiction," recalled Bill Osmanski, Bears fullback, 1939–1943. "Nobody could be that good. Then I played against him. The guy is unbelievable. He fakes you silly! He can practically tell you what he's going to do and still can't stop him."[19]

Hutson's greatness was defined on his ability to catch a football. He finished his career with 488 catches for 7,991 yards and 99 TD catches—all NFL records at the time. He had 31 games where he caught two or more touchdowns; led the NFL in receiving eight times; receiving yards seven times; and receiving touchdowns nine times. For over a decade he put up ridiculous numbers for receivers during his era.

"He was the greatest receiver in football. There's no doubt about that. Don could catch the ball going full speed and jump in the air. It seemed like two or three yards and catch the ball and never break stride. He had glue hands. He had great moves. He could change direction, it was tough for any defensive man to cover him. It was almost impossible to cover him. I know when he played the Giants he was the left end. If I was back up the line on the right side I'd cover him short. Then our halfback would cover him long. That's the only way we could cover him and do a good job," said Mel Hein, Giants Hall of Fame linebacker.[20]

Hutson was named First Team All-Pro a whopping nine times by the *New York Daily News,* seven times by I.N.S. and the United Press, six times by the NFL and the Associated Press and five times by *Collyer's.* He played in four Pro Bowls from 1939 to 1942. "Oh gosh, that guy would tear your nerves all to pieces," recalled George McAfee, Bears Hall of Fame halfback. "We had two, three different defenses for him when he was in there. When he went out, we resorted to an old, normal defense. But he was great. He really was."[21]

In 1942, Hutson showed how dominant he could be. Despite it being the first war year, his numbers were so much better than the next guy it is hard to fathom. All four marks set were new NFL single-season records.

- 74 Receptions (2nd—Pop Ivy with 27) (broken in 1949 by Tom Fears with 77)
- 1,211 Receiving Yards (2nd—Ray McLean with 571) (broken in 1951 by Elroy Hirsch with 1,495)
- 17 Receiving TDs (2nd—Ray McLean with 8) (broken in 1984 by Mark Clayton with 18)
- 138 Points Scored (2nd—Ray McLean with 54) (broken in 1960 by Paul Hornung with 176)

During Hutson's career he captured back-to-back Joe F. Carr MVP Awards in 1941 and '42, and in 1944 he's our Retro-MVP winner—beating out Lions back Frankie Sinkwich who won the Carr Award. In his last year Hutson received $15,000 a year from the Packers, making him one of the highest paid players in the league. Later that fall, Hutson might've had his best game in the NFL. In 1945, at the age of 32, Hutson put on a show in the second quarter of the October 7 game against the Detroit Lions. In that quarter alone he caught four touchdowns of 56, 46, 17 and six yards and kicked five extra points, giving him 29 points scored in a single quarter of the 57–21 victory.

Hutson contributed to a Packers team that won three NFL championships—1936, 1939, and 1944. He played in five playoff games, catching 10 passes for 163 yards and one touchdown—which came in the 1936 NFL championship game, a 48-yard reception to help the Packers defeat the Boston Redskins, 21–6.

As noted, Hutson also kicked field goals and extra points for the Packers, and he finished his career with 825 points and leading the NFL in scoring five straight years from 1940 to 1944. On defense Hutson started out as a defensive end, but his lack of size hindered his effectiveness on that side of the ball. "I played defensive end the first few years in Green Bay until we drafted a boy named Larry Craig, who was a fine blocking back and a helluva defensive end. He took over at that position and I moved back to safety," said Hutson. It was at safety that Hutson flourished, where he had 30 career interceptions, including leading the NFL once in 1940 with six. "He had great hands, big hands. He also was a great pass defender. He could cover a lot of ground," recalled Tony Canadeo, Packers Hall of Fame back. "We played a 5–4 defense and he played like a free safety does today. He was a great, great football player. It was just a thrill to be on the same field with him."[22]

For many two-way players, Hutson was the best they had seen. "Without hesitation my pick would be Don Hutson. He was so much better than the rest that he could dominate a game. And I consider him an all-around star because he was a great defensive back when he wasn't catching passes, scoring touchdowns and kicking points," said Dan Fortmann, Bears Hall of Fame guard.[23]

Hutson went on to establish 19 NFL records, the 19th being holding the most records. Although many of Hutson's records have been broken, nobody can take away his impact on the way professional football was played. His ability to run precise patterns and the great attention he drew from opposing defenses as an end was unseen before Hutson. Hutson combined his great athletic talent with a sterling work ethic. The attitude and work habits of Hutson bring up modern day images of Jerry Rice. "He was the Jerry Rice of my day," said Bernie Scherer, Packers end, 1936–1938.[24]

After retiring from the Packers after the 1945 season, Hutson became a successful businessman, operating a bowling alley and a car dealership. Hutson has received his share of accolades. He was a Charter Member of the Pro Football Hall of Fame in 1963.... Named to the NFL 1930s All-Decade Team.... Named to the NFL's 50th Anniversary, 75th Anniversary and 100th Anniversary All-Time Teams.... Packers retired his no. 14 jersey.... Elected to Packers Hall of Fame in 1972. Taking a look at the list of All-Time teams we found, Hutson appears on 26 of them.

Don Hutson passed away on June 26, 1997, at the age of 84. Ron Wolf, Packers general manager at the time, said: "I speak for the entire Green Bay organization when I say that we are extremely saddened to hear of Don Hutson's passing. He most certainly was the greatest player in the history of this franchise."[25]

"Football is the greatest game in the world," said Don Hutson. "I have a lot to thank football for. It gave me an education at Alabama and it gave me enough money to go into business for myself. I wouldn't give anything for the experience I've had in football and for the things it has done for me."[26]

No. 3

Sammy Baugh

Quarterback

Full Name: Sam Adrian Baugh
Nickname: "Slingin' Sammy"
b: March 17, 1914 (Temple, TX); d: December 17, 2008 (age 94; Rotan, TX)
High School: Sweetwater (TX); College: TCU
Height/Weight: 6–2, 182 pounds
Position: Quarterback
Teams/Years: 1937–1952 Washington Redskins
Pro Football Hall of Fame: Class of 1963 (Charter Member)
Retro-MVPs: 1937, 1940
All-Time Teams: C. Brock (1986); D. Clark (1942); G. Corbett (1938); M. Gantenbein (1966); R. Grange (1947); M. Hein (1944, 1968, 1974); C. Hinkle (1942); W. Kiesling (1942); T. Leemans (1945, 1953); J. McNally (1944, 1971); S. Owen (1942, 1952, 1955); C. Storck (1939); J. Stydahar (1952)

Sammy Baugh was simply the best quarterback of the NFL's two-way era. Nobody threw a better pass nor threw from more angles than the former TCU star. Just like Dutch Clark (#1) and Don Hutson (#2), the versatile Baugh impacted games in multiple ways, including as a punter and defensive back.

Sam Baugh was born in the dust town of Temple, Texas, in 1914, the son of a railroad worker. From there the Baugh family moved to Sweetwater, where young Sammy became engrossed in playing several sports, baseball and especially football. His spindly body made it difficult to find the right position. But soon he would play the position that was destined to make him a legend. "I started out as an end but when I was a freshman in high school we had such a sorry team that our coach kept changing people around to different positions. He found out I could throw the ball better than any of our backs, so I ended up as our passer. And I stayed in the backfield ever since," recalled Sammy Baugh.[1]

From an early age, Baugh found the best way to throw the ball by teaching himself to grip the football. "We threw the ball off the seam," said Baugh. "I could finesse a ball better off the seam than I could off the string. If it was a muddy day, we threw off the string." To practice his throwing style, Baugh found creative ways to improve his technique. "I used to practice by throwing a football at a tire hung from a tree in our backyard," recalled Baugh. "You really need to throw it to somebody who is

Sammy Baugh, quarterback, Washington Redskins, ca. 1940 (courtesy Washington Commanders).

moving, not just some tire swinging back and forth. But I did spend a lot of time throwing at one when I was a boy."[2]

Baugh also worked on other aspects of the game, not just throwing. "I worked at punting a lot, too. Every day in the summer I used to go over to our football field for an hour or so and I'd just kick the ball from one end of it to the other. I'd punt, trot down and get the ball, and then punt it back. I spent a lot of time working at kicking the ball out of bounds, too, angling it so I could get it out of bounds inside the 10-yard line. I was usually by myself when I practiced kicking but sometimes, I could talk a friend into coming along," recalled Baugh.[3]

Despite his slender build of 6-2 and 182 pounds, the young Texan became one of the greatest two-way players in the Lone Star State, even though his path to a professional career in sports was on a different field. "Everybody thought I was a better baseball player growing up," said Baugh. "I thought I was going to be a big-league baseball player." In the end, Baugh's pro career was going to be on the gridiron not the ball diamond.[4]

Nicknamed "Slingin' Sammy" for his ability to throw the ball, Baugh became a Texas legend at Texas Christian University (TCU). Coached by Dutch Meyer, Baugh was taught the ins-and-outs of playing the tailback position in the single-wing. "He was like hundreds of other Texas kids—forward-pass conscious," said Dutch Meyer. "He had a nice pair of hands, and he could make that ball travel, but he was crude as college passers go. No deception, no finesse, and he didn't know exactly when to turn the ball loose. But he learned plenty fast. When he began having some luck with those short flips, he was satisfied. But he became a great forward passer because he had kind of a sixth sense. He was a good passer instinctively."[5]

Baugh quickly became a star under Meyer, using the pass to keep his undersized Horned Frogs in every game. "Most teams—even in the pros—would try and pound at you with the running game, and then, in desperation, throw on third and long," said Baugh. "Then they would just try to throw it as far as they could. Dutch taught us the short passing game, and it was a revolutionary thing for that day and time. We would just move the ball down the field hitting short passes—with little risk of an interception—and nobody could figure out how to stop it."[6]

In his three years with the varsity Baugh led TCU to a record of 29-7-2 and wins in the Sugar Bowl over LSU and Cotton Bowl over Marquette. "He was the greatest passer I ever saw. And in all the years since, I don't remember ever seeing anyone better. In all my life, I never saw another passer like Sam Baugh," said Dutch Meyer. Baugh had put TCU on the national map. It was now time to see if he could play with the big boys in pro ball.[7]

When Baugh was drafted by the Washington Redskins in the first round of the 1937 NFL Draft, Redskins head coach Ray Flaherty saw his dreams come true. Flaherty recalled: "I didn't have any idea we'd land him. Five other clubs had choices of the college crop before it was the Redskins' turn. I'd have bet they all would put in for Baugh…. By the time three or four clubs passed Baugh up, I began to hope, but

I still didn't think it was possible. Then five clubs passed Baugh up. Then they asked Steve Owen of the Giants what player he wanted. He said, 'Widseth, of Minnesota.' Then it was my turn to pick. With Baugh not yet drafted, I thought I was dreaming. Anyway, the league president said, 'Flaherty, who is the Redskins' choice?' Well, by gawd, I think I bellowed Baugh so loud that it must have been heard downtown, and we had him."[8]

Baugh was drafted sixth overall by the Redskins. Once selected, Baugh talked to Redskins owner George Preston Marshall about his rookie contract. The first offer was for $5,000. Baugh talked to Meyer who told him that was good money. Baugh thought he was worth a little more and with the threat of him playing Major League Baseball with the St. Louis Cardinals, Baugh upped the offer. "So, Marshall called me the next time, and I told him, 'What would you think about $8,000?'" said Baugh. "He thought a minute, and said, 'All right. Are you ready to sign?' I said, 'Yes.' He said, 'All right. It'll be $8,000.' Hell, I got more money than I was thinking he'd give me. To me that looked like a million bucks." Baugh was worth every penny as one of the highest paid players in the NFL as a rookie.[9]

Baugh was used as the single-wing tailback guiding the Redskins under the coaching of Ray Flaherty, a former All-Pro end for the New York Giants. "Single-wing was a good offense. I hated to get out of it to tell you the truth. You could do a few things that you can't do in the T [formation] really. Because you always had a chance to quick kick some of the time and gain about thirty or forty yards," said Baugh. Baugh became an instant star in Washington, their first year playing in the nation's capital after leaving Boston.[10]

His coach could see the potential of his newest recruit. "Sammy Baugh was the best short passer I've ever seen," said Ray Flaherty in 1983. "He couldn't throw the long ball as well as some of these fellows today, but we didn't throw the long ball as much. Sammy had a quicker release than anybody in football today."[11]

Flaherty continued: "Baugh would have been great in any era because he could throw the football. He threw short passes better than anybody I've ever seen. He couldn't throw long as well as Otto Graham and some of those guys, but nobody ever threw a short pass better. He would get back there in the shotgun, or double-wing as we called it, and he had everybody in front of him and could get the ball to them quickly."[12]

During his rookie season, Baugh's talent took over most games. The NFL had seen some passers before Baugh, but nobody played the position at this level. He learned how to get the pass off quickly in the NFL as the pass rush got to him much faster in pro ball. "A passer had to learn to throw and move," said Baugh. "You would never see him just throw and stand there looking. You had to throw and start protecting yourself, because those linemen were going to lay you flatter than the ground every time."[13]

Baugh developed a reputation of hitting his receivers in the perfect spot. "When you're out there and break into the open—look out! The ball'll be on top of you in a second. Boom! Like that," said Wayne Millner, Redskins All-Pro end. "He could hit his receiver while lying on his stomach," said Cliff Battles, Redskins All-Pro halfback.[14]

Behind the play of Baugh and fellow All-Pros Battles and tackle Turk Edwards, the Redskins won the 1937 Eastern Division title, setting up a championship matchup with the Western's Chicago Bears. In the title game played on a frozen field in Chicago, Baugh lit up George Halas's Bears, going 18 of 33 for 335 yards and three touchdowns in a 28–21 upset win. His touchdowns covered 55 and 78 yards to Millner and 35 to Ed Justice. It was Baugh's performance that encouraged Halas to find his passing quarterback—which in 1939 he found with Sid Luckman.

After winning the 1937 NFL championship Baugh, who had played in just 12 league games, was praised by the whole NFL world. "It was a perfect exhibition of passing, and as great a one-man performance as I've ever seen," said Ray Flaherty. "He's a wonder. His ability to set up deceiving pass plays had the Bears secondary half crazy. They couldn't tell where he was going to throw next," said Cliff Battles. Baugh never forgot that first championship. "That game was my biggest thrill—bar none," said Baugh. "Remember I was just a green kid from Texas and this was my first year with the big, tough pros."[15]

"I've seen and played against [Ernie] Nevers, [Benny] Friedman, [Harry] Newman, and Baugh is the greatest passer of them all," said Lou Gordon, Cardinals-Packers tackle, 1930–1938. Besides being the best passer during the two-way era, Baugh was maybe the best punter, too. From his single-wing position in the backfield, Baugh often used the quick kick to his advantage, dictating field position like no other player. "I could punt all of my life," said Baugh. "I worked on punting more than I did passing, to tell you the truth."[16]

Baugh's punting and quick-kicking skills out of the single-wing made him a perfect weapon during this era. Baugh finished his career with a punting average of 45.1—which was an NFL career record for over 60 years. He led the NFL in punting average four times and helped decide many Redskins games with field possession.

Baugh went on to earn First Team All-Pro honors seven times in his career. Everybody who played against him seemed to be mesmerized by his all-around skills. "They don't come any greater than Baugh. He's the greatest passer I've seen," said Dutch Clark, Lions back. Opponents were in awe of Baugh's talents. On game footage Baugh shows the skills and techniques of a modern-day quarterback, as well as the athletic abilities to punt and play the secondary. "He was the best passer I ever saw. He could do everything. He could pass, he could play defense, and he was the best punter," said Ace Parker, Hall of Fame quarterback.[17]

"Baugh was the best as far as I'm concerned. He could not only throw the ball, he could play defense, he could punt the football, he ran it when he had to. He knew football, played it, and everybody had confidence in him," said Bill Dudley, Hall of Fame back. "Sammy Baugh, oh, he was brilliant. One of the best quarterbacks that ever played," said Ralph Kercheval, Dodgers All-Pro back.[18]

"[Baugh] would cock the ball, bring it down, and drift off as if about to run, cock again, make a mock throw to one side, and shoot a touchdown to the other. I have seen him make bullet-like throws with his tremendous wrist action as he was nailed by a hard tackle and falling," recalled Steve Owen, Giants Hall of Fame coach.[19]

One of the Redskins biggest rivals was the New York Giants. The two teams battled for first place in the Eastern Division for most of Baugh's 16-year career. "Nobody could touch him as a passer and as a punter," said Tuffy Leemans, Giants All-Pro back. "When Sammy was young, he wasn't a bad ball carrier. Every now and then, when he had to do it, Baugh could block. In fact, he was expert at it. As for kicking, he was terrific. There aren't any words left to describe his passing. Sammy was all by himself in this field."[20]

"If I were starting a team, he'd be my first man," said Mel Hein, Giants Hall of Fame center. "People don't realize that when Baugh was at his peak, which was 1937 and 1938, he could run as well as pass, he was the best quick kicker who ever lived, and he was a great defensive player who led the league in pass interceptions [two years in a row]."[21]

Opponents always tried to game plan around stopping Baugh. They also knew they had to avoid him on the defensive side of the ball. Baugh's natural athletic abilities made him a very good defensive back. He had a knack of coming up with interceptions. He officially finished with 31 career interceptions from 1940 to 1952. The tall Texan was very difficult to throw over, coming up with numerous passes broken up. "When I went up there, it was a damn defensive game, you had to play defense," said Baugh. "That's all there was to it. I've seen a lot of good running backs get cut because they couldn't play defense. Everybody had to be able to play defense."[22]

"You must remember we used to use Sammy on defense," recalled Turk Edwards. "He was one of the finest defensive backs I've ever seen and there never was anybody better at pass interception. He had a wonderful instinct for snaring the other guy's passes." "A lot of people think of Baugh only as a great passer. I think of him as a great all-around football player. He was as good a defensive safetyman as I ever saw. Seldom did a ball carrier get by him. And how about those punts of his?" said Wayne Millner, Redskins Hall of Fame end. "You'll never find a football player as good as Baugh who doesn't love it," said Dan Fortmann, Bears Hall of Fame guard.[23]

Besides all of the physical skills on the football field, Baugh's leadership was obvious to all of his teammates in Washington. "When you're on the field, you've got to feel like you're the best son of a bitch that's out there. That's what you're thinking. That nobody's no damn better than I am," said Baugh. Baugh was always the man in charge, whether on offense or defense. He always looked out for his teammates, regardless of how they were playing.[24]

"I recall one vital Bears game when I was all alone in the end zone but dropped a perfect pass from Sam," recalled Wayne Millner. "When we got back in the huddle, Baugh said, 'Forget that one, Wayne. Anybody can drop one.' Two plays later, he threw me another and that time it meant six points. Sam was always that way with a guy who missed a tackle or block. 'Get 'im next time,' was all he'd ever say."[25]

"I'd never chew a player out on my team," said Baugh. "He dropped four passes, I'd tell him, 'Well, I had it a little too hard. I led him too much, or he had to turn and try and catch it.' In other words, I'd try to make him feel good and not run him down."[26]

Physical abilities combined with great leadership make it clear why Baugh is considered one of the best two-way players of all time. "I'd say he's the greatest I've ever seen," said Turk Edwards, "and that goes for Sid Luckman or any of them. Sammy has accuracy, first of all. It's his ability to throw from any angle that makes him so great. The other passers must be planted. But Sammy can throw from anywhere."[27]

Continued Edwards: "A lot of people think the Redskins always have given Baugh elaborate protection. He never got any more blockers than any other passer, but he certainly has been a lot smarter. He maneuvers better than any man I've ever seen. He helps his protection by moving around. He watches the blockers from a pocket which he sets up. Baugh is the point of the pocket, deep—very deep. Usually, when he fades back to pass, Baugh knows exactly where he's going to throw the ball, but he never watches his receiver until a spilt second before he lets fly."[28]

Baugh's worst moment on the field came in 1940 when the Redskins lost the famous 73–0 game to the Bears in the NFL championship. Early in the game, the Redskins end Charley Malone dropped a sure touchdown. In the locker room, Baugh was asked what Malone's catch would've made the score. Baugh famous quote was, "73–6!" Two years later Baugh got his revenge by helping defeat the Bears in the 1942 NFL championship, 14–6, to spoil Chicago's undefeated season.

Baugh's best season might have been in 1943. He led the NFL in passing, punting and interceptions on defense with 11, which set an NFL record. Still, he did not win the NFL Joe F. Carr MVP Award, which went to Sid Luckman. Sammy had perhaps the greatest two-way single-game quarterback performance in league history that season. On November 14 in a 42–20 win over the Detroit Lions, Baugh fired four touchdown passes, intercepted four passes and got off an 81-yard punt, the longest of the year in the NFL. He guided the Redskins to the Eastern Division title with a 6–3–1 record. Once again, he would be outdone by Luckman in the NFL championship game, losing to the Bears, 41–21. "Sammy Baugh is the best player ever. He was so automatic that he hardly ever looked at his receivers. He was the nearest thing to perfection," said Sid Luckman, Bears Hall of Fame quarterback.[29]

In the end, Baugh played 167 games over 16 seasons, all with the Redskins. He dominated his position, playing mostly out of the single-wing before switching to the T-formation in the 1944 season. It took him awhile to master it. With his typical low-key Texas attitude, Baugh took the transition in stride. "The easiest position in football to play is quarterback in the T-formation," said Baugh. "All you do is hand the ball off or pass. If they had had the T when I started to play pro ball, I could play until I was forty years old." In 1945, while playing mostly out of the T-formation, Baugh led the Redskins to the NFL championship game against the Cleveland Rams but lost to the Rams hotshot rookie signal caller Bob Waterfield, 15–14. It would be the last championship game in which Baugh would play. He finished with a record of 2–3 in title games.[30]

Baugh played and passed often in his 16 NFL seasons. Baugh retired following the 1952 NFL season and he held every career NFL passing record including attempts (2,995); completions (1,693); passing yards (21,886); and touchdown passes (187). To show how his legacy has endured, his 187 touchdown passes in 167 games is still a Washington franchise record—ahead of Sonny Jurgensen (179 in 135 games) and Joe Theismann (160 in 167 games)—even though Sammy has not thrown a touchdown pass in 70 years.

Retroactively, Baugh led the NFL in passing rating six times—a record tied by Steve Young, while he led the league in completions five times; passing yards four times; and passing touchdowns twice in 1940 and 1947. Twice, he set an NFL record for completion percentage for a single season, in 1940 with 62.7 percent and again in 1945 by completing 70.3 percent, a record which lasted until 1982 when Ken Anderson bested it with 70.6 percent.

Baugh stayed close to the game after he retired by going into coaching. He was the head coach for five years from 1955 to 1959 at Hardin-Simmons and compiled a 23–28 record. He next coached the New York Titans for two years to a 14–14 mark from 1960–61, and finished his head coaching career in 1964 with the 4–10 Houston Oilers. "I never liked coaching like I liked playing the game," said Baugh. "Coaching took up most of the damn year. I liked playing the game in the season, then going back home and ranching the rest of the year." Baugh retired from coaching to run his ranch in Rotan, Texas, which he bought with his Redskins salary in 1941.[31]

Baugh was always considered one of the greatest to ever play in the NFL, regardless of era. He was named to the NFL 1940s All-Decade Team, Charter Member of the Pro Football Hall of Fame in 1963, NFL 75th Anniversary All-Time Team and NFL 100th Anniversary Team.

While living on his ranch after his playing and coaching days were over, Baugh continued to follow the game. "I love to watch pro football, too. I still love the game," said Baugh. "But I don't like crowds. You can't find a better seat than right in front of my television." The tough Texan simply loved the game of football. It's what made him one of the greatest two-way players of all-time. "I don't think anybody can be very good at football unless he really likes to play. There have been guys in this league who had a lot of mechanical ability, in addition to size and strength, but they didn't like to play very much," said Baugh.[32]

On December 17, 2008, Sammy Baugh passed away at the age of 94.

No. 4

Mel Hein

Center

Full Name: Melvin Jack Hein
Nickname: "Old Indestructible"
b: August 22, 1908 (Redding, CA); d: January 31, 1992 (age 82; San Clemente, CA)
High School: Burlington, Fairhaven (WA); College: Washington State
Height/Weight: 6-2, 225 pounds
Position: Center-Linebacker
Teams/Years: 1931–1945 New York Giants
Pro Football Hall of Fame: Class of 1963 (Charter Member)
Retro-MVPs: 1938, 1939
All-Time Teams: S. Baugh (1949, 1957); C. Brock (1986); D. Clark (1942); P. Clark (1947);
    G. Dorias (1952, 1954); R. Flaherty (1990); M. Gantenbein (1966); B. Hewitt (1937, 1940);
    C. Hinkle (1942); C. Hubbard (1937, 1947, 1966); D. Hutson (1986); W. Kiesling (1942);
    C. Lambeau (1955); T. Leemans (1953); J. McMillen (1939); J. McNally (1944);
    M. Michalske (1986); B. Nagurski (1939, 1944); S. Owen (1942, 1952, 1955); R. Richards
    (1944); C. Storck (1939); J. Stydahar (1951, 1952)

    In 1938, Mel Hein achieved something that has not been accomplished in the NFL since, a center winning the NFL MVP. Hein was the first, and he is still the only center to win the league's most prestigious award. His outstanding play as a center-linebacker in 15 years with the New York Giants from 1931 to 1945 has landed him at number four on our list.

    Melvin Hein was born in 1908 in Redding, California, before moving with his family to the Pacific Northwest near Bellingham, Washington, a small town about 15 miles from the Canadian border. Hein's father operated a power plant near Mount Baker, teaching his three sons how to work hard. Here Hein learned the game of football. "I remember getting in it at Lowell Grammar School, that had to be about 1920. We had uniforms and a league. It was well-organized, but we did not have turf fields back in those days. We played on dirt fields, with rocks and gravel. It would tear up our shoes, socks, pants, and kind of drive our parents crazy, but we all loved football anyway. It was painful playing on fields like that," recalled Mel Hein.[1]

    Mel learned the techniques of the game while playing with his brothers, especially his older sibling, Lloyd. Hein became a center from the beginning. "I started in high school, throwing the ball back," recalled Mel Hein. "I had an older brother that was a back. He was [also] a punter, [and] I used to practice all the time between seasons. He wanted to punt, and I wanted to pass the ball. So, it became automatic for me to throw the ball back. In the single-wing, well our tailback might be four and half yards, five yards back, our fullback about four yards. You had to get the back there accurately."[2]

Hein continued: "And according to the type of play that they were going to run, whether it was going to be an end run where the tailback was carrying the ball, you'd have to lead him a yard. If it was a fullback bucking up into the line, he may hang that ball right in front of him so he could run into it. So, it became like an automatic thing. You'd practically do it without looking. But I always did look, then get that head up fast as I could, so I wouldn't get a beat off."[3]

Mel Hein, center, New York Giants, ca. 1930 (courtesy Washington State University Athletics).

Hein followed his older brother Lloyd to Washington State to play football for Babe Hollingberry. Hein had a growth spurt, peaking at 6-2 and 225 pounds, a perfect size for a center-linebacker during the two-way era. His body was built up working the summers for the forest service at Mount Baker. For a few months Hein built trails and patrolled the mountains, always running the course, as much as five miles uphill. "Trudging over those ranges out there in Washington gave me a good pair of legs. I work all the time to keep in shape and in the evenings, I go out and toss a football with my kid brother who was in high school," recalled Hein.[4]

Hein became a starter his sophomore year, an all-conference performer his junior year, then an All-American his senior year. He played during the glory years at WSU, playing on the same line with Turk Edwards, future All-Pro tackle for the Washington Redskins. After his senior season in 1930, Hein and the Huskies played in the Rose Bowl but lost 24–0 to Alabama. Despite playing out west where there were no NFL teams, Hein's name was on the wish list of several NFL teams.

After he graduated from college, Hein was totally interested in playing pro football. He heard from the Portsmouth Spartans, Providence Steam Roller and the New York Giants. Hein liked the offer from Providence but held out to hear a final offer from the Giants. "Well, Jimmy Conzelman was the Steam Roller coach, and he was pushing me, so I signed with Providence for a hundred and twenty-five dollars a game, which was a pretty good salary for a lineman in those days," recalled Hein. "After I signed the contract, I went down to Spokane for a basketball game, another sport I played at Washington State. We were playing Gonzaga and Ray Flaherty, the captain of the Giants at that time, was coaching there during the off-season. He came down to the dressing room after the game and asked me if I'd received a contract from the Giants yet.

'No, I haven't,' I said. 'But if one is on the way it's too late now. I signed one with the Providence Steam Roller and mailed it back to them yesterday.' Ray said, 'Oh, no. How much are they paying you?' I told him, and he said, 'The Giants contract is a better offer, one hundred and fifty dollars a game.' A little later he came back to me and said, 'Why don't you go down to the postmaster when you get home and see if he won't send a telegram to the postmaster in Providence to see if he would intercept the letter?' So, I sent a telegram myself and, sure enough, the letter with the contract came back and in the meantime the Giants [contract] for one hundred and fifty dollars a game had arrived. I signed with the Giants and tore up the other contract with Providence."[5]

With his contract situation taken care of, Hein got married right before he took his bride on a cross-country ride to New York to start his career with the Giants. Hein quickly developed a passion for playing football. His hard work in high school and college already had him well ahead of some of the players in the NFL, because he had practiced the techniques needed to play the center position.

In New York, Hein was coached by the great Steve Owen, who knew he was coaching a special player. "I've been around this league a long time and I've never seen a player who made fewer mistakes than Mel. He has a feel for football, an instinctive understanding and grasp of it that allows him to command every bit of action on the field ... teaching him was like teaching Babe Ruth. Mel was a dynamic offensive blocker, a most accurate snapper, and a genius at backing up the line. Hein could discourage the most accomplished attacking stars who ever lived," recalled Owen.[6]

In 1931, Hein easily made the squad, backing up veteran center Mickey Murtagh. When Murtagh got hurt in the second game of the year, Hein took over and became the starting center for the next 15 years. "You learned about the pro game pretty quick in those days," recalled Hein. "It was very rough in the line, a lot of punching and elbowing and forearms and that sort of stuff. You had to stand up for yourself or you would be walked all over." Nobody walked over Hein.[7]

During his first few years with the Giants, Hein had the look of a great player. Owen could see he was going to be a leader on a team that was going to win a lot of games. Hein took his leadership role very seriously. "During the early days the veterans had ignored me. After I made the team, I was sure that it would be different. But it wasn't. When they organized a group to go to a show or have a party, they didn't invite us. I felt bad about this, and I vowed that if I ever had anything to say about policy on the team, I would make sure that the rookies were invited to all social events. When I was elected captain in my third year, I was able to make good on the promise," recalled Hein. For the next decade and half Hein was the leader of the Giants.[8]

By 1933, Hein was nearly the best center in the league. Opponents saw his skills. "Hein is the perfect center—that's all. He does everything right and he seems to do everything instinctively. He has a genius for diagnosing plays and he's always where he can do the most harm," said Curly Lambeau, Packers Hall of Fame coach.[9]

Film study confirms Hein was one of the best athletes to ever play his position. Very mobile at 6-2, 225 pounds, Hein was tough at the point of attack, equally good at run and pass blocking, and flawless on snaps in Steve Owen's single-wing and A-formation offenses. "He's never made a bad pass. He's impossible to fool. He's so darn good that you can't even get mad at him," said Potsy Clark, Dodgers head coach.[10]

On defense, he was always around the ball and made many of his tackles at the line of scrimmage, not down field. Hein, because of his size and agility, was a perfect fit at right linebacker in Owen's 5-3-2-1 defense, or in the 6-2-2-1 defense. "Mel Hein was one of the greatest defensive players I ever ran against," recalled Cliff Battles, Redskins Hall of Fame halfback. "He never hurt you. He tackled securely but high. He had a remarkable ability for diagnosing plays and he was so big you just couldn't get away from him."[11]

"There were some other great ones, we the Bears had some great ones, but Mel Hein was the greatest linebacker that I played against…. He had the ability to analyze plays and where the play was going to develop. He was always in the right spot at the right time. He was a deadly tackler once he got his hands on you," recalled Bronko Nagurski, Bears Hall of Fame fullback.[12]

"The first time I saw him he looked like a giant back there backing up the line. As soon as I got through the line of scrimmage, he knocked me back into it. But Mel was a hog on defense, and a tremendous pass defender, and still took care of the linebacking duties. On offense he was a tremendous blocker, so he was an all-around great football player," said Clarke Hinkle, Packers Hall of Fame fullback.[13]

To show how good he was in coverage he had 10 career interceptions, returning one for a score—a 50-yard return against the Packers on November 20, 1938, to seal a 15-3 win. Many opponents challenged Hein to see if he was as good as the newspaper headlines said he was. One of those teams was the Chicago Bears. "He could center a ball from 50 yards and hit a needle in its eye. Even as a rookie [1931] there was no one like him. Usually, you look for the rookies on another team and try to take advantage of them. We tried working on Hein from the beginning, he was too smart. Even as a rookie, there was no one like him," recalled George Halas, Bears Hall of Fame coach.[14]

Giants teammates were equally in awe of Hein. "He was a very strong 60-minute football player," said Red Badgro, Giants Hall of Fame end and teammate. "Hein was outstanding," recalled Jim Lee Howell, Giants end, from 1937 to 1942. "He was a good blocker as a center, and bear-hugged the runner on defense. He'd wrap his arms around the ball carrier and then slam him to the ground."[15]

After losing the NFL's first ever championship game in 1933, Hein and his Giants were ready the following year. They would shock the undefeated Chicago Bears, 30–13, in the famous "Sneakers" game. "Everybody was slipping and sliding all over the place and Chicago was winning simply because they were bigger and stronger than us. They were actually a better team than us but that didn't matter that day, not with those field conditions. Their size gave them an advantage in the first half but the advantage we got from the traction provided by the sneakers in the second half was much greater and that's why we were able to outscore them 27–3 in that period," recalled Hein.[16]

Hein was now an NFL champion. He was more impressed with the extra money he earned.

"The winner's share of that 1934 championship was $621 per player, a far cry from all the money a Super Bowl winner takes home today," said Hein in 1984. "But we thought it was a lot of money, that we were suddenly wealthy."[17]

Retro-MVP: 1938, 1939 NFL Seasons

But the highlight of Hein's career was winning the 1938 NFL MVP Award (Joe F. Carr Trophy), still the only center to win the NFL's most prestigious award. That season Hein played his best football. Every week he was the best on both sides of the ball, leading the Giants to the Eastern Division crown with an 8–2–1 record. He led a Giants defense that paced the NFL in points allowed by giving up just 79—the next closest team was the Lions at 108 points.

In the NFL championship game, Hein helped the Giants defeat the Packers, 23–17, in capturing the title. Hein was named First Team All-Pro by the NFL, I.N.S., *New York Mirror, New York Daily News* and the United Press. Before the championship game, Hein was given a wristwatch by NFL President Joe F. Carr for winning the NFL's first ever MVP award. That season Hein made $275 a game as one of the highest paid players in the NFL. He seemed to be on top of the world. "1938 was a pretty big year for me," said Hein. "I got $150 for endorsing Mayflower Doughnuts and another $150 for doing the same for Rheingold Beer. When I won the MVP some pipe company sent me a set of pipes. Free."[18]

Winning the NFL championship over the Packers was a tough chore for the Giants and in particular Mel Hein. He was asked to help defend the most dangerous weapon in the league—Don Hutson. Once while playing against the Packers, Hein's play mystified his coach, Steve Owen, because he was giving up some short gains without performing his usually forceful play at the line of scrimmage. Owen called Hein over for him to explain himself. "Don't worry, Steve," barked Hein. "I'm giving them the short gains. I'm letting them commit themselves before I commit myself. Then they won't be able to pass over my head to Don Hutson for a touchdown."[19]

"Well, Mel Hein, of course, all football so-called experts will tell you he was one of the great players, especially on defense, of all-time. I spent many interesting afternoons in the Polo Grounds in New York trying to get away from him on many pass patterns," recalled Don Hutson.[20]

Owen always thought that Hutson had a flaw. "We discovered that if we could make Hutson break to the outside when he got through the line, he found it difficult to cut back inside where he might run for a touchdown," wrote Steve Owen in his book, *My Kind of Football*. "Hutson, although he was setting all kinds of records at the time, did not score a touchdown on us in the first five games we played. We double-teamed him to keep him outside. Mel Hein, at backer-up, was the key man in turning Hutson toward the sideline. Then the halfback would take over to make sure the great Packer end at best was limited to a medium gain on a fan pass to the side line."[21]

From 1935 to 1940 the Packers played the Giants seven times including two NFL championship games. In those seven games Hutson had *zero* touchdowns. The Giants went 4–3 in those games and split the two title games. From 1941 to 1945 the Packers played the Giants five more times and Hutson scored four touchdowns—with two each in two separate games—as the Packers came out on top with a 4–1 record. But Hein made a difference in trying to shut down the era's greatest receiver.

In 1939, Hein would repeat the feat by winning the Retro-MVP as the Giants won the Eastern Division again. This time they were defeated by the Packers, 27–0, in the title game. Hein was the best player in the league during this time, besting out the likes of Sammy Baugh and Don Hutson. "He was the finest player in the league," said Wellington Mara, Giants owner. "He was a very quiet person, very reserved. He was very strong. It was amazing how strong he could be without the training. He was also a natural leader without trying to be. The others would gravitate toward him. He was still there at the end. You weren't really aware of him losing a significant amount of his physical ability. He had such knowledge and intuition, anyway."[22]

After the 1940 season Hein was once again honored. For the eighth straight year, he was voted First Team All-Pro by multiple newspapers and coaches including the NFL, Associated Press, I.N.S., *New York Daily News* and the United Press. Nothing seemed to harm Old Indestructible. On December 7, 1941, Hein took a shot to the face just as Pearl Harbor took a shot from the Japanese. "My worst injury was a fractured nose against the Brooklyn Dodgers on Pearl Harbor Day," recalled Hein.

"I was able to play two weeks later in the championship game against the Bears by wearing a mask. I never even lost a tooth playing, and I played against some pretty tough customers."[23]

After the 1942 season, Hein retired … or so he thought. During World War II, Hein accepted a job as the head coach at Union College in New York. He was ready to move on from playing pro football, but then he got a call from his old coach. "After the 1942 season I retired from professional football—or so I thought. I had been offered the job as head coach of Union College in Schenectady, New York, and I took it. In 1943, because of the manpower shortage, Union dropped football, but I stayed on to help train the Naval V-12 men on campus. Just before the football season started, I had a call from Steve Owen. Steve wanted me to be a Sunday center for the Giants. I would come down and play on Sunday in New York. Then I'd spend the rest of the week in Schenectady. This may sound like a precarious arrangement for Steve but I had played under him so long I knew the system inside and out. And my work at Union kept me in shape."[24]

During 1943 Hein would do double duty, teaching at Union College during the week and playing for the Giants on Sundays. Although his career seemed to be winding down, Hein had a major impact on the game and, especially, the position he played. "Mel Hein, the great New York Giants center, was my idol. I went to the Giant games and never took my eyes off him. Many times there would be only six, seven, maybe ten thousand people at the Giants games, and most weeks Fordham would outdraw the Giants four to one or at least two to one, but I always went to the Giants games because I wanted to get all the pointers I could and Mel Hein was my man," recalled Alex Wojciechowicz, Eagles Hall of Fame center, 1938–1950.[25]

After the 1945 season, Hein finally retired. He played 15 seasons—170 games in all—with the Giants, all at a high level, while earning the nickname "Old Indestructible." Along with winning two NFL championships, Hein won two Retro-MVP awards and played in four Pro Bowls. "I'll nominate Mel Hein as the greatest football player I ever saw," said Steve Owen in 1945. "He has an instinctive sense of what to do under all conditions. As a football player, Mel Hein is something out of this world—a sixty-minute player after 20 years. Try to match that." The only sour statistic on his resume was going 2–5 in NFL championship games.[26]

In 1946, Hein was head coach at Union, going 3–5 in his one year at the helm. Hein then continued his coaching career in the AAFC as an assistant with the Los Angeles Dons (1947–1948) and New York Yankees (1949). After the AAFC folded, Hein returned to the NFL and the West Coast by joining the Los Angeles Rams as an assistant coach in 1950. The following year, Hein moved across town to join the football staff at USC under Jess Hill and stayed at USC for 14 years from 1951 to 1965. While at USC in the late 1950s, Hein became a close confidant with a future Hall of Famer also working as a USC assistant—Al Davis—who would give him an opportunity to become more involved in the game of pro football again.

In 1966, Davis reached out to his old coaching friend to join him in the AFL office as supervisor of officials with the AFL. Hein took the job. When Davis left the AFL office to return to the Oakland Raiders, Hein stayed on the job. Once the AFL-NFL merger occurred, Hein continued as the supervisor of officials for the AFC from 1970 to 1974. "[Learned] quite a bit in my new job. Naturally, as a player and coach, I had contact with the officials. So, I feel that I understand their problems as well as those of the players and coaches. I am aware of how they all think—and that's been most helpful in this job," said Hein.[27]

After spending many years living in California, Hein returned to New York, working in the NFL office for commissioner Pete Rozelle. "You can believe that many times when I walk around our new offices on Park Avenue, I remember that day I left for New York with a bride and the remnants of a $100 advance to try out for a job that would pay $150 a game," recalled Hein. In the spring of 1974 Hein officially retired. After 47 years in college and pro football, he finally stepped away from the game.[28]

In 1963, Mel Hein was one of the 17 Charter Members selected to the Pro Football Hall of Fame. He was an easy choice like Dutch Clark (#1), Don Hutson (#2) and Sammy Baugh (#3). Hein has received every post-career football award there is, as he was selected to the NFL 1930s All-Decade team, to the NFL's 50th as the runner-up at center and the 75th Anniversary Team as one of only two centers with Mike Webster. The Giants deservedly retired his number 7 jersey. Hein is on the short list of the greatest centers to ever play in the NFL—regardless of era. In 2019, he was named to the NFL 100th Anniversary Team as just one of four centers on the team—joining Jim Otto, Dwight Stephenson and Mike Webster.

Mel Hein passed away from stomach cancer on January 31, 1992, at the age of 82. "He was truly a football legend and a giant among men," said Al Davis. "Mel was one of the greatest football players who ever lived."[29]

"I always thought it was an advantage to play two ways. Playing center, I ran up against a lot of those big, tough, ornery guards who liked to take a few free shots as I snapped the ball," recalled Mel Hein. "But when the ball changed over, then I was on defense, and they were on offense. So, if a guy had tried something a little crude on me, now I could show him how it was on the receiving end. Usually, after a couple of licks, those types became a lot more gentlemanly."[30]

Nobody played any better on the front line during the two-way era than Mel Hein. For nearly 15 years his play at center and linebacker was unmatched. "I don't ask myself if I should have played 30 years later for the big dough. I ask myself if I would do it again in my own time," said Hein in 1974. "And the answer is yes. I'd do it all over again."[31]

No. 5

Guy Chamberlin

End

Full Name: Berlin Guy Chamberlin
Nicknames: "Guy"; "Champ"
b: January 16, 1894 (Blue Springs, NE); d: (age 73; Lincoln, NE)
High School: Blue Springs (NE); College: Nebraska
Height/Weight: 6-2, 196 pounds
Position: End
Teams/Years: 1919 Canton Bulldogs (pre–NFL); 1920–1921 Decatur/Chicago Staleys; 1922–1923 Canton Bulldogs; 1924 Cleveland Bulldogs; 1925–1926 Frankford Yellow Jackets; 1927 Chicago Cardinals
Pro Football Hall of Fame: Class of 1965
Retro-MVPs: 1922
All-Time Teams: J. Conzelman (1941); P. Driscoll (1956); R. Grange (1934, 1946); G. Halas (1940–41); S. Owen (1952); D. Slater (1949)

Rounding out the top five is Guy Chamberlin, who played one year of pro football with the Canton Bulldogs in 1919 before the NFL was founded, and then went on to play eight seasons in the NFL with the Decatur/Chicago Staleys (1920–1921), Canton Bulldogs (1922–1923), Cleveland Bulldogs (1924), Frankford Yellow Jackets (1925–1926) and Chicago Cardinals (1927). Altogether he appeared in 92 games in the NFL.

What made Chamberlin special was that he performed the dual role of player-coach better than anybody in the first decade of the NFL. He was a player-coach for six of his eight years, amassing an unsurpassed coaching record of 58-16-7 and would win four NFL championships over a five-year period with the 1922–1923 Canton Bulldogs, 1924 Cleveland Bulldogs and the 1926 Frankford Yellow Jackets, earning the nickname "Champ."

The man they called "Champ" was actually born Berlin Guy Chamberlin in 1894 in Blue Springs, Nebraska. His mother was of German descent, so she named him after the famous city in Germany. But nobody called him Berlin. He would go by his middle name, Guy, for most of his life.

Guy was one of six children and the son of a farmer. He grew up playing in pickup games with the neighboring children. Blue Springs didn't have enough boys to field a proper team, so Chamberlin had to wait to fully participate in football.

After high school he first attended Nebraska Wesleyan where he played organized football for the first time. Chamberlin played end and halfback while his body filled out to 6–2 and 196 pounds. The *Omaha World Herald* once wrote: "Chamberlin is almost in a class by himself. He is a fierce and aggressive runner and adopts the system of bowling over the opposing tacklers in much the same style as the famous Coy of Yale. Chamberlin rarely used a stiff arm, and yet many times it was next to impossible to stop him."[1]

After two seasons Chamberlin transferred to the University of Nebraska, where he again played end and halfback. In his senior season of 1915, Chamberlin was one of the best players in the country. He scored 15 touchdowns and led the Cornhuskers to an undefeated 8–0 season, including a 20–19 victory over Notre Dame, where he scored two touchdowns.

Guy Chamberlin, end, Canton Bulldogs, ca. 1922 (courtesy NFL Films Research Library).

After graduating from Nebraska, Chamberlin did some teaching and coaching, while also helping out on his father's farm. During World War I, Chamberlin joined the Army, earning the rank of second lieutenant and served from 1918 to 1919. When he came back home in the fall of 1919, Chamberlin was recruited by Jim Thorpe to play for the Canton Bulldogs—the best team in pro football in the time before the NFL was founded. Thorpe was Chamberlin's football hero. Once he was asked who the greatest player he ever saw. "Jim Thorpe," Guy replied without a hesitation. "He was the best of them all. He could do everything. And I ought to know. I played with him and against him. There has never been another like him."[2]

The following year he was recruited by George Halas to play for his Decatur Staleys. There he not only made money playing football but made a living working in the Staley starch factory. Playing end for Halas was a lesson in strategy and organization. He picked up all he could from Halas. The Staleys competed hard in the

NFL's first season (APFA) but came up short behind the Akron Pros (8–0–3) with a 10–1–2 overall record. In the end Chamberlin was the highest paid player on the team. According to Halas' biography he claims that Guy received $1,650 for the season, roughly $137 per game, slightly more than Dutch Sternaman and George Trafton who each received $1,618. Halas would always say that Chamberlin was worth every penny.

In 1921, Chamberlin became a force on the field as the best two-way end in pro football, helping the Staleys win the NFL championship and giving Halas his first pro football title. Throughout the season he made big play after big play. On December 4 he had a huge 75-yard interception return for a touchdown against Buffalo to help his team win 10–7. Then the following week he scored the only touchdown in a 10–0 win over the Canton Bulldogs to secure the title. "Guy Chamberlin was a great football player. But he didn't look like he was working. But boy when something happened, he was always in the right spot. He'd block a kick, he'd catch a pass or make a real good tackle when some guy was breaking loose. He was a wonderful player," said Paddy Driscoll, Cardinals Hall of Fame back.[3]

In 1922, he assumed the role of player-coach for the Canton Bulldogs. The "Champ" got a nice raise. "I was paid $7,000 the two years I was at Canton. That was quite remunerative," recalled Chamberlin about his salary. Although Halas had lost his best player, he could see how special Chamberlin was. He was the best end and the best player during the NFL's first decade. "The best two-way end I've ever seen was [Guy] Chamberlin. He was a big, tall boy and very fast.... He was a tremendous tackler on defense and a triple-threat performer on offense," said George Halas about his former teammate.[4]

While his coaching helped his squads win championships, Chamberlin's play on the field was equally impressive. From his usual end position, he had a knack for scoring touchdowns, scoring 17 career TDs. He also had a flair for the dramatic. As an example, in 1926, Chamberlin scooped up a fumble for a TD late in the fourth quarter to help his Frankford Yellow Jackets defeat the Detroit Panthers, 7–6. "Often, I was lucky enough to be there at the right time. It boils down, I believe, to give your best at all-time," said Chamberlin to the *Canton Repository* in 1965.[5]

Chamberlin's main goal as player-coach was to win the game. He would not only drill his team during practice, but he would also make sure they were prepared for everything. Even the NFL president, Joe F. Carr, could see the great leadership of Guy Chamberlin. "Chamberlin had ability, tact, athletic understanding and the confidence of his players as well as being an inspirational leader," wrote Carr.[6]

But you can't overlook his play on the field too. He impacted the game from his end position, whether it was on offense or defense. He was greater than other player-coaches of his era—better than the likes of George Halas, Curly Lambeau and Jimmy Conzelman. Check the box scores; when Chamberlin scored, his team was unbeatable.

Chamberlin's Career TDs

Receiving = 8 TDs
Rushing = 3 TDs
Interceptions = 3 TDs
Blocked Punt Returns = 2 TDs
Fumble Recovery = 1 TD

Total = 17 career TDs

*Win-Loss Record

*His teams were 15–0 in games he scored in.

Retro-MVP: 1922 NFL Season

In his best season in 1922, Chamberlin scored seven TDs with the Canton Bulldogs while coaching them to an unbeaten 10–0–2 season and an NFL championship. His touchdowns came four different ways—three by rushing, two by interception returns (both in the same game vs. Cardinals), and one each on a reception and a blocked punt return. He wins our 1922 Retro-MVP award.

"Chamberlin was our best end. We had this play where he came around on an end-reverse, and sometimes he would get the ball on an end sweep or we'd fake it to him and hand it to the fullback up the middle. Other times, our fullback Louie Smyth would drop back and hit me on a tackle-eligible play down the field. We would average a touchdown a game with Guy coming around from his end position. They couldn't stop it," said Link Lyman, Hall of Fame tackle and former Bulldogs teammate, 1922–1923.[7]

The following season Chamberlin and his Bulldogs continued their winning ways, going unbeaten again at 11–0–1. That squad outscored its opponents 246–19, giving up just one touchdown all season—to Cleveland on November 25. The Bulldogs were the first team in NFL history to win back-to-back titles. Over those couple of seasons Chamberlin's squad also set the NFL record for Most Consecutive Games Without a Defeat with 27 straight games (24 wins, three ties)—a NFL record that still stands today!

While coaching in Canton, Chamberlin coached two Hall of Famers, tackles Pete "Fats" Henty and Link Lyman, as well as other All-Pro caliber players such as Doc Elliott, Duke Osborn, Wooky Roberts and Harry Robb. Following the back-to-back titles, the Bulldogs were sold to Cleveland Indians owner Sam Deutsch who moved the franchise to Cleveland. Guy followed the team there and they never missed a beat. Playing and coaching with many of the same players who were in Canton, the Cleveland Bulldogs captured the NFL title with a 7–1–1 record—giving Chamberlin a third straight NFL championship.

With Cleveland having money issues, Chamberlin moved on in 1925 to coach the Frankford Yellow Jackets, who had joined the NFL the year before. Chamberlin the coach taught the Yellow Jackets his winning system. "We only had a dozen plays. A couple of off-tackle runs and sweeps. Four or five passes, including a screen. That was it, but we practiced those plays over and over until we could run them in our sleep," said Bill Hoffman, Yellow Jackets guard, 1924–1926. "Chamberlin didn't have any assistant coaches, but he didn't need any. He was a taskmaster like [Vince] Lombardi. He kept us on the field for hours, even in the bitter cold. We couldn't complain, though, because he was out there practicing with us [as a two-way end]." Continued Hoffman, "As a player, Chamberlin was outstanding. He had unusually large hands so he could catch any ball that came near him, and he had a knack for coming up with the big play when we needed it."[8]

After going 13–7 in 1925, Chamberlin had his squad ready to contend for a title. Holding off the 12–1–3 Chicago Bears, the Yellow Jackets secured Chamberlin's fourth NFL title in five seasons as a player-coach, with a 14–1–2 record. The man they called "Champ" was living up to his nickname. His coaching and play as the league's best end impressed everybody he competed against. "I didn't know when I went off to the pros I was going to see the winningest end I ever knew in my life. Guy Chamberlin, who played for the Canton Bulldogs and later coached the Frankford Yellow Jackets. In every close game I saw Chamberlin play he was the guy who caught the pass, picked up the fumble, or recovered the blocked punt for the decisive score. The way he could change a game with his speed and alertness was uncanny," wrote Steve Owen in his book *My Kind of Football*.[9]

He left Frankford to coach the Chicago Cardinals in 1927, but just didn't have enough talent in Chicago and suffered his only losing season with a 3–7–1 mark. After that season, he decided to retire as a player and coach. His overall record of 58–16–7 is one of the NFL's all-time best, a winning clip of 78 percent.

Chamberlin was named to the NFL 1920s All-Decade Team as one of three ends to make the team, joining George Halas and Lavvie Dilweg of the Packers. In 1965, he was elected to the Pro Football Hall of Fame—the Hall's third class. Nobody handled the dual role of player-coach better than Guy Chamberlin. Not George Halas. Not Curly Lambeau. His accomplishment of winning four NFL championships in a five-year span was not duplicated during this era.

Chamberlin passed away from a heart attack on April 4, 1967, at the age of 73.

"I love the game," said Guy Chamberlin to the *Philadelphia Public Ledger* in 1926. "That's why I play it. I might make more money in some other line of endeavor, so it is not the 'sugar' that keeps me at it."[10]

No. 6

Bronko Nagurski
Fullback

Full Name: Bronislaw Nagurski
Nickname: "Bronko"
b: November 3, 1908 (Rainy River, Ontario); d: January 7, 1990 (age 81; International Falls, MN)
High School: International Falls (MN), Bemidji (MN); College: Minnesota
Height/Weight: 6–2, 226 pounds
Position: Fullback
Teams/Years: 1930–1937, 1943 Chicago Bears
Pro Football Hall of Fame: Class of 1963 (Charter Member)
Retro-MVPs: 1934
All-Time Teams: S. Baugh (1949, 1957); C. Cagle (1937); B. Cahn (1943); J. Carr (1934); D. Clark (1942); J. Conzelman (1941); G. Corbett (1938); E. Cuneo (1973); P. Driscoll (1956); M. Gantenbein (1966); R. Grange (1946, 1947, 1955); G. Halas (1939, 1940, 1941); M. Hein (1944, 1968, 1974); B. Hewitt (1937, 1940); C. Hinkle (1942, 1986); C. Hubbard (1937, 1966); D. Hutson (1986); W. Kiesling (1942); T. Leemans (1953); V. Lewellen (1936); J. McMillan (1939); J. McNally (1944, 1971); M. Michalske (1982); G. Musso (1964); E. Nevers (1932); S. Owen (1942, 1952, 1955); C. Storck (1939); J. Stydahar (1951)

At number six is the first fullback on the list. The man whose evocative name sounds like the perfect football player of the two-way era—Bronko Nagurski. The 6–2, 226-pound Nagurski played 97 games over nine years, all with the Chicago Bears. His career was broken up by a six-year retirement after quitting pro football following the 1937 season to make more money as a professional wrestler. Then, Bronko came back during World War II in 1943 to play mostly as a tackle for the Bears.

Born Bronislaw (*Bron-is-law*) Nagurski in Ontario, Canada, in 1908, his family soon moved across the border to make their home in International Falls, Minnesota. Family records indicate the baby didn't have a middle name, making him unique from the start. Soon the baby would be known by just one name. A unique moniker.

The healthy baby quickly became the family's pride and joy. However, when little Bronislaw was introduced to the other children by his birth name, Bronislaw, one thing began to puzzle his parents. Because of their Ukraine accents, and unique first name, most of the neighborhood parents and children had trouble pronouncing his first name. This frustrated his mother. She thought it was a beautiful name, preserving the family's Ukraine history, but something had to be done, because nobody could pronounce it. She compromised. "Bronko is a common name in that part of Ukraine from which we come and as far as I know it has no particular meaning," said Bronko's mother, Michelina, in 1937 to a United Press reporter. Not wanting to see their boy struggle with his new playmates, they decided to call him Bronko for short.[1]

It was here in the land of winters that Nagurski first picked up a football. "I started playing football right after kindergarten. We'd throw the ball around the sandlots. There wasn't much else to do in town during your spare time. In a way, my parents sort of wished I didn't play—they thought their little boy would get hurt. But they didn't raise [any] serious objections," said Bronko Nagurski.[2]

Bronko Nagurski, fullback, Chicago Bears, ca. 1929 (courtesy University of Minnesota).

Young Bronko developed his body into a well-oiled athletic machine. He filled out to be 6–2 and over 220 pounds. His passion for the game led him to further his education and playing career at the University of Minnesota under coach "Doc" Spears. In his three years of varsity play, Nagurski played end, tackle and, of course, fullback. He was the best in the country at all three positions, so much that in his senior year he was named to a few All-American teams at both tackle *and* fullback.

Near the end of his college career Nagurski had thought long and hard about playing pro football. "It probably wasn't till my senior year, that I started thinking pro football," recalled Nagurski. "And so I pushed myself and proved myself because that would be a means to an end."

The result would be Nagurski playing pro football as well as anybody had during the two-way era, under a man who helped organized the NFL—George Halas. "I played in the East-West game in San Francisco after my senior year at Minnesota. We practiced and had press conferences in Chicago," recalled Nagurski. "George Halas showed up at the practices looking for players for the Bears."[3]

Despite playing pro ball himself, Doc Spears didn't seem approachable to give Nagurski some advice on his offers to play pro football. He turned to another coach on the staff for help. "Dutch Bergman, he was from Notre Dame, he was an assistant coach that was easier to talk to than Spears was," remembered Nagurski. "He had a good friend in Chicago who kind of steered me to this good friend who also was closer to pro football and also knew the owners. There were two owners at that time, George Halas and Dutch Sternaman. So, he kind of steered me to this fellow and this fellow's my advisor. But for those times I think I got a good contract which was double the amount of what they offered me. But we had to do quite a bit of negotiating."[4]

At first, Halas thought dealing with Nagurski would be no problem. He didn't know how stubborn and driven the young man from the Falls was. Eventually Halas, like always, would get his man—even if he had to spend more money to get him. "I signed with the Bears for $5,000 in 1930 and almost didn't get that. George Halas offered me $3,500 and I said, 'Wait here, I'll be back.' I had Coach Bergman outside and he told me to ask for $6,500. When I told that to Halas, he compromised and I got $5,000 for 12 or 13 league games."[5]

The high-priced rookie quickly earned his stripes with his new Bears teammates. They could see how special the quiet and talented Nagurski was. Nagurski was different than any other fullback in the NFL. They also noticed that he had a unique running style that oozed "power." "There was something strange about tackling Nagurski," recalled Red Grange. "When you hit him, it was almost like getting an electric shock. If you hit him above the ankles, you were likely to get killed."[6]

The reserved Nagurski didn't hear the chatter going on about his play, he just showed up every day to play football. "Oh, you know how they say things like that. But I always used my strength in football. I liked to meet a guy head-on when I was carrying the ball. Then I drop my shoulder, and catch him with that, and then brush him off with my arm. It worked most of the time," explained Nagurski.[7]

Nagurski took the NFL by storm with his unique combination of size and speed. He impressed opponents throughout his career. "Bronko just naturally ran low, with his head up. You never in your life saw 235 pounds carried so low," recalled Benny Friedman, Hall of Fame quarterback. "When Nagurski broke through the line it was a frustrating sight. All you could see was his helmet and those white shoe lacings he wore ... and that shoulder dipped to hit you. When he came at you, Nagurski dipped that inside shoulder and let you have it. Nobody taught him. It was a natural move."[8]

"He was so big they never should have let him play," recalled Cliff Battles, Redskins Hall of Fame halfback. "It was a good thing Bronko was good natured because they were always giving him a rough time. If he really got upset he would have killed someone. He wasn't the type of fullback that Jimmy Brown and Jim

Taylor are. He was pure powerful. Once he got under way he was almost impossible to bring down."[9]

"I still got some headaches from running into Bronko Nagurski," recalled Ray Flaherty, Giants All-Pro end, in 1985. "He was a great football player and exceptional blocker. When he was running interference for Beattie Feathers, who was a very clever runner, they were a good combination. Bronko, I think ran the football just about as hard as anybody that was ever in football."[10]

Over his entire career with the Bears Nagurski was part of some of the greatest teams in NFL history. The Bears became winners, capturing three NFL championships, 1932–1933 and 1943, and winning 70 percent of their games (79-21-12) with Nagurski on the roster.

Nagurski became the era's best power runner and lead blocker. "Bronko was a great blocker, as well as a powerful runner. He was one of the really great linebackers. He could have been an All-Pro defensive star today as a linebacker, or a fullback if he played. I compare him to Dick Butkus as a linebacker and Larry Csonka as a fullback," said Red Grange in 1973.[11]

No other player defined the two-way era of 60-minute men as well as Bronko Nagurski. He often displayed unreal toughness during a time when every player had to demonstrate they could take a hit or deliver a hard tackle. "Nagurski was the toughest," said Sammy Baugh, Redskins Hall of Fame quarterback. "He was big, strong and powerful. He had a way of dipping his shoulder so you couldn't get a big lick on him. He'd use his arm or turn his body a certain way. When the field was frozen, I just tried to run up and hit him like I was blocking him, and I always hoped I could knock him off balance. If you tried to tackle him, he'd knock the living hell out of you. Hell, I used to get hurt more on defense than offense."[12]

"Bronko was the toughest guy to tackle I ever hit in my 15 years. What many people don't realize is that Bronko had great speed in addition to his weight. At his prime, though, I think he weighed only about 225. He ran so low. As a linebacker, I would meet him head on, but he had the fine knack of using his shoulders perfectly. Then he had such great balance, too," said Mel Hein, Giants Hall of Fame linebacker.[13]

"Bronko was one of the greatest all-around football players. He could do so many things well. He was much faster than people thought, and when he got into the clear, he could break away from the pack. He could play any position on the team. The defenses had to respect him so much that they would leave holes in the defense that other people took advantage of," recalled Cal Hubbard, Packers Hall of Fame tackle.[14]

"I always had the greatest respect for Nagurski. He was a wonderful person and the cleanest player you'd every play against. He was extremely strong and fast. I played safety on defense and he always got to me at least three or four times a game. I was always happy when those big guys up front got him down but sometimes he got to me.... Bronko ran in sort of a bent-over slant and he would kill you if you tried to tackle him around the knees or body. The only way I could stop him was to just hit the ground right at his ankles," said Dutch Clark, Lions Hall of Fame back.[15]

Nagurski's unselfishness as a lead blocker made him popular with his Bears teammates. He never complained about doing the grunt work. But when it was time to play the most important games of the year Nagurski would show up willing to do his part. He became a big-time performer in postseason games. He threw the game-winning touchdown pass to Red Grange to win the 1932 title—in the famous "Indoor Game"—over the Portsmouth Spartans, 9–0. "Nagurski was not the greatest passer in the world," recalled Red Grange about the game-winning play in the Indoor Game. "He threw me a great end-over-end pass. I had blocked, or tried to block for someone and Bronk went for a jump pass. He threw me the ball."[16]

The following year in 1933 he was even better, throwing two touchdown passes to help defeat the New York Giants, 23–21, including the game-winning pass late in the fourth quarter that was lateraled by Bill Hewitt to Bill Karr, to win the NFL's first ever league championship game. "The greatest offensive football game I ever played in or ever hope to be in," said Nagurski after the game. In the 1943 title game he moved from tackle to fullback and scored on a short touchdown run to help defeat the Redskins, 41–21. He also scored on a touchdown run in the 1934 championship game—also known as the "Sneakers Game"—but the Bears lost to the Giants, 30–13. The bigger the game, the better Bronko played.[17]

Nagurski's best season came in 1934. That fall he was the lead blocker for the NFL's first ever 1,000-yard rusher—rookie halfback Beattie Feathers, who finished the year with 1,004 rushing yards. But Nagurski was more valuable than Feathers when it came to performing in all aspects of the game. He was a better blocker, a better defensive player and was just as good a passer as Feathers. He was more durable too as Feathers missed the last two regular season games and the championship game that season.

The definition of MVP is pretty self-explanatory. If you miss the two most important games of the year and your team still wins, you might not get the vote. Nagurski played in all 13 Bears games and was the heart and soul of an undefeated team. He finished fourth in the NFL in rushing with 586 yards; tied for third in rushing TDs with seven; and was ninth in the league in rushing attempts per game behind Newman, Feathers, Strong and Dutch Clark with only 9.5 carries a game. Plus, he was the lead blocker for Feathers and a Bears team that rushed for an NFL high 2,847 yards.

Nagurski helped guide his team to back-to-back wins against the tough Lions in the season's final two games—just three days apart, too—while having no Feathers in the backfield. In the end, his production on the field, as well as his defensive play and blocking prowess, gives him the edge over Feathers in a close, close vote. Bronko Nagurski is your 1934 NFL Retro-MVP.

Nagurski finished his career with 633 carries for 2,778 yards, a 4.4 average, and 25 touchdowns. He led the NFL in rushing TDs in 1932 with four. He was very effective as a passer, throwing seven career TDs and only nine interceptions, in an era where interceptions were fairly common. Although he didn't do any kicking, Nagurski's overall play during this era was as good as anybody's. His spot as one of the greatest two-way players places him just outside of the top five players on our list. "Bronko ran his own interference. He was hard to tackle because he would lower his arm and if you went to tackle him he'd just block you off with his arm. He was so big and strong, he weighed 230. He was one of the fastest boys on the Bears team. He was really hard to tackle," recalled Glenn Presnell, Spartans/Lions All-Pro halfback, 1931–1936.[18]

Nagurski played in same era as fellow Hall of Famer fullbacks Ernie Nevers and Clarke Hinkle but claimed his share of First Team All-Pro honors.

First Team All-Pros

Collyer's: 5 times (1932–1934, 1936–1937)
United Press: 4 times (1932–1934, 1936)
Green Bay Press-Gazette: 3 times (1932–1934)
NFL: 3 times (1932–1934)

Nagurski was also selected as a Charter Member of the Pro Football Hall of Fame in 1963; picked for the NFL 1930s All-Decade Team; chosen in 1969 to the NFL 50th Anniversary All-Time Team Fullback Runner Up, behind Jim Brown; the NFL 75th Anniversary Team in 1994; and he had his number 3 Bears jersey retired in 1949.

While he was playing pro football, Nagurski also became a professional wrestler. In 1937, he won the world heavyweight championship. That fall he wrestled and played a full season with the Bears, a double duty that hasn't been replicated. After his wrestling career finished, Nagurski owned and operated his own gas station in his hometown of International Falls. "I joined the Bears in 1930, it was a different game we played and in rough times, but was the fulfillment of a lifetime dream. My first year with the Bears was tough, but I loved to play football," recalled Bronko Nagurski.[19]

Bronko Nagurski died on January 7, 1990, at the age of 81.

No. 7

Verne Lewellen

Halfback

Full Name: Verne Lewellen
Nickname: N/A
b: September 29, 1901 (Lincoln, NE); d: April 16, 1980 (age 78; Rockville, MD)
High School: Lincoln (NE); College: Nebraska
Height/Weight: 6–1, 182 pounds
Position: Halfback
Teams/Years: 1924–1932 Green Bay Packers; 1927 New York Yankees
Pro Football Hall of Fame: No
Retro-MVPs: 1929, 1930
All-Time Teams: A. Herber (1946); C. Hinkle (1942); C. Lambeau (1946, 1948); J. McNally (1963)

One of the most underrated players of the two-way era, regardless of position, is halfback Verne Lewellen. He is the highest ranked player on this list NOT in the Pro Football Hall of Fame, although he should be. The 6–1, 182-pound Lewellen played nine seasons with the Green Bay Packers (102 games total) from 1924 to 1932. As a halfback in the two-way era, he comes in just below the number one player on the list—Dutch Clark.

Lewellen picked up football in his hometown of Lincoln, Nebraska, eventually making his way to the University of Nebraska. Lewellen was the best player on a Nebraska team that would give Notre Dame and Knute Rockne their only losses in 1922 and 1923, shocking the country and putting the Cornhuskers' all-around halfback on the football map.

It looked like Lewellen would play Major League Baseball with the Pittsburgh Pirates, but a case of smallpox changed the course of his athletic career. In 1924, Lewellen signed with the Green Bay Packers. One Green Bay reporter claimed that Lewellen made about $200 a game. He played his entire pro career under Hall of Fame player-coach Curly Lambeau, who built his offense around Verne—although Lewellen did play three games with Red Grange's New York Yankees at the end of the 1927 NFL season after the Packers' schedule was completed. Looking at his career the overlooked Lewellen was one of the best all-around halfbacks to play during the NFL's two-way era (1920–1945), leading the Packers to three straight NFL championships in 1929–1931.

Lewellen was also an excellent runner and receiver in Lambeau's Notre Dame box offense. He wasn't asked to throw as often as his teammates Red Dunn and Lambeau himself but could be effective when asked to pass. Playing in the secondary, Lewellen was an equally adept defensive player and tackler. "I don't recall many spectacular incidents involving Lewellen—probably because he was always spectacular," said Guy Chamberlin, Pro Football Hall of Fame player-coach. But what separated Lewellen from some of the other two-way halfbacks at his position was that he was one of the best at performing the two most important aspects of the two-way era: punting (field position) and scoring!¹

Verne Lewellen, halfback, Green Bay Packers, ca. 1929 (courtesy Green Bay Packers).

Arguably, he was the era's best punter for the first three decades—perhaps only surpassed by Sammy Baugh. When researching the newspaper accounts and game play-by-plays, one can see that his punting skills truly affected the outcome of games. Accorded to the stats published in *The Football Encyclopedia*, Lewellen averaged nearly 40 yards a punt from 1926 to 1931. He often punted on 1st and 3rd downs as much as he did on 4th down, and routinely kicked inside his opponents 45-yard line for field possession. Looking at his 1929 season, one can see how Lewellen was a weapon punting on any down. According to play-by-plays from the Packers and the *Green Bay Press-Gazette,* Lewellen punted 84 times in 1929. The breakdown was: 1st down (24 times); 2nd down (8); 3rd down (27); and 4th down (25).²

"[I did] hours of practice. Dropping the ball right was the biggest thing. I had a few kicks between 80 and 90 yards, but darn few of those, and with a strong wind," said the modest Lewellen in 1948.³

He also had a knack for the coffin corner kicks. "Lewellen was the greatest punter I ever saw. I never saw Jim Thorpe punt, but I saw a lot of others. I don't think they kept any stats when he was punting, but I saw him punt 80 yards. I saw him punt the ball out on the five, the three, the 10," said Mike Michalske, Packers Hall of Fame guard, in 1980.⁴

"Best kicker [punter] I ever saw was Verne Lewellen. In 10 years, I never saw him make a bad kick. One of the reasons is that he had a size 13 and a half shoe—big enough for a lifeboat. Then, too, he had a great line—one of the best ever. It was so strong and unyielding that he could take a five-yard run 'into his leg lift,'" said Cal Hubbard, Packers teammate.[5]

Besides punting, Lewellen also excelled in putting points on the scoreboard. In an era (1920–1932) where the average points scored per game was 10, Lewellen was one of the all-time best at putting points on the scoreboard. (Note: In his time, offense was limited and the NFL had passing restrictions pre–1933 such as having to pass the ball behind LOS 5 yards and an incomplete pass in the end zone turned the ball over.) In his nine seasons, Lewellen scored 51 total touchdowns. During the two-way era, from 1920 to 1944, *no other back* scored more total touchdowns than Lewellen. Out of the *23 Hall of Fame backs* who played during the two-way era, Lewellen scored more TDs than all of them. If you count the seven two-way ends, only Don Hutson scored more touchdowns.

Verne Lewellen's 51 total touchdowns included 37 rushing; 12 receiving; one fumble recovery; and one INT return.

Touchdowns, Hall of Fame Backs Who Played 1920–1945 (Halfbacks, Quarterbacks, Fullbacks Who Played Two-Way Era, 23 Players)

Verne Lewellen—51 TDs (105 games)
Johnny Blood—49 (137 games)
Bill Dudley—44 (90 games)
Clarke Hinkle—44 (113 games)
Dutch Clark—42 (75 games)
George McAfee—39 (75 games)
Ernie Nevers—38 (54 games)
Ken Strong—34 (131 games)
Red Grange—32 (96 games)
Cliff Battles—31 (60 games)
Paddy Driscoll—31 (118 games)
Tony Canadeo—31 (116 games)
Jimmy Conzelman—26 (104 games)
Bronko Nagurski—25 (97 games)
Tuffy Leemans—20 (80 games)
Ace Parker—20 (68 games)
Benny Friedman—18 (81 games)
Fritz Pollard—12 (49 games)
Joe Guyon—10 (46 games)
Curly Lambeau—12 (77 games)
Sammy Baugh—9 (165 games)
Arnie Herber—7 (129 games)
Jim Thorpe—6 (52 games)
Sid Luckman—6 (128 games)

Lewellen was a scoring machine:

- When he retired, he held NFL record for touchdowns scored with 51—broken by Don Hutson in 1941.
- Led Packers in scoring for five straight years, 1926–1930 (307 total points).
- Twice led the NFL in TDs scored, 1928 (nine) and 1930 (nine).

Another special part of Lewellen's impact was helping Green Bay win games. Because he scored touchdowns and help win the field possession battle, Lewellen guided the Packers to three straight NFL championships, 1929–1931. During those three seasons the Packers went an incredible 34–5–2. Over his nine seasons the Packers went a combined 79–26–10, winning 75 percent of his games, and he never had a losing season. Just as impressive was the games where he scored a touchdown.

Games Scoring a Touchdown

His 51 total TDs came in 43 different games (26 of those TDs were go-ahead TDs). The Packers went 36–5–2 in those games. During the three-year championship run (1929–1931) the Packers were almost unbeatable when Lewellen scored, going 19–1 (1929: 7–0; 1930: 7–1; 1931: 5–0)! Lewellen's best years were during the three-year championship run.

He wins our Retro-MVP award for both 1929 and 1930 as the best player in the NFL. Not too many players of the two-way era played as well as Lewellen, especially as an offensive weapon, only Dutch Clark (#1) and Don Hutson (#2) were on par with Lewellen as a triple-threat star.

To be expected, Lewellen was one of the most decorated halfbacks in the two-way era, earning First Team All-Pro honors from several media outlets during his time. He was named four times by the *Green Bay Press-Gazette* (1926–1929) and three times by the *Chicago Tribune* (1927–1929).

In 1970, he was elected to the Packers Hall of Fame. The only honor he didn't receive was the NFL's All-Decade Team for the 1920s, which is unfortunate, because Lewellen was equal to or better than the players they selected. Halfbacks chosen were Red Grange, Jim Thorpe, Curly Lambeau, and Joe Guyon—mostly on name recognition. Thorpe's best years were not in the 1920s.

Lewellen also had a signature moment in his career that showed off his special skills. Late in 1929, on November 24, the undefeated Packers (9–0) played the unbeaten New York Giants (8–0–1) for first place in the NFL. Although there wasn't an NFL championship game at this time, essentially the winner of this game was going to be the champion, and 25,000 fans showed up at the Polo Grounds to watch.

Lewellen went beyond the call of duty in the game. Due to an injury, starting quarterback Red Dunn missed the game, so Lambeau moved Lewellen to quarterback, Johnny Blood played halfback with Hurdis McCrary, while Bo Molenda was at fullback. The Packers didn't miss a beat with Lewellen guiding the team.

Lewellen's punting was the key to the game as he kept the ball away from Giants Hall of Fame quarterback Benny Friedman who Lewellen outplayed in a matchup of the NFL's two best players. Friedman threw for an NFL record 20 TDs in 1929, including one in this game, but was outshone by Lewellen throughout this contest. In the game film, Lewellen was very impressive with his directional punting, considering the Polo Grounds field was very muddy. Lewellen's punting stats:

- Seven punts, 354 yards (average of 50.6 yards per punt)
- Yards per punt: 70, 63, 43, 65, 41, 40, 27

In the first quarter Lewellen threw a four-yard TD pass to Herdis McCrary for the game's first score (7–0). Later in the fourth quarter, with the Packers leading 7–6, Lewellen helped Green Bay on a scoring march of 80 yards on 15 plays. He accounted for 59 of the 80 yards (14 rushing, 15 receiving, 30 passing) that led to a touchdown and a 14–6 lead. The Packers would add another score to close out the 20–6 victory in the most important game of the 1929 NFL season.

The Packers would go on to win the 1929 NFL championship—the franchise's first ever NFL title. The following day newspapers in New York wrote mostly about the play of Lewellen.

> *New York Daily News* (C.A. Lovett): "Lewellen distinctly outshone Friedman, both at passing and ball carrying.... Lewellen annoyed Giants throughout game with his passing, end runs, punts and tackling."[6]
>
> *New York Evening World*: "Verne Lewellen was a potent factor in the Packers' stunning triumph. Punts of 60 and 70 yards that spiraled from Lewellen's shoe gave the visitors a decisive edge."[7]
>
> *Brooklyn Daily Eagle* (Harold Burr): "Lewellen kicked mighty spirals with a rain-soaked, heavy ball that boomed over Giants safety man's head repeatedly. His passes were mostly perfection. If his foot wasn't driving the Giants back, his arm was doing it."[8]

After the 1932 Packers season Lewellen retired from pro football. He served as the Packers general manager from 1954 to 1958, resigning right before the team hired Vince Lombardi, eventually staying on as Packers business manager until 1967. Shorty after announcing his retirement, then–NFL commissioner Pete Rozelle wrote Lewellen a letter.

> Dear Verne:
>
> It was with interest that I read Oliver Kuechle's [newspaper] recent column pointing out the injustice resulting from records not being kept when you were doing such a fine job of punting.
>
> You have, however, left your stamp on the growth of the Nationa5l Football League in many other ways—as a player, an executive and as a fine representative of the league.
>
> The best of luck and good health to you in retirement.
>
> Sincerely,
> Pete[9]

Lewellen passed away on April 16, 1980, at the age of 78.

Looking back at Verne Lewellen's NFL career, one can only wonder why his name isn't mentioned with some of the all-time greats of the two-way era. The Packers have a number of Pro Football Hall of Famers, but Lewellen isn't one of them. "Defensively, offensively—of the players we had in the old days, Lewellen was No. 1. And I'm not alone in saying that. Any of the old-timers I've talked to say the same thing. The reason he is so often mentioned as a punter is because his equal hasn't shown up yet. From 60 yards, if he aimed to put it out of bounds on the 5-yard line, he'd generally make it. He had almost dead accuracy. He was way ahead of his time in ability. I don't think there are too many players of that time who could have made it today, the caliber is so far advanced, but Verne Lewellen could have made it any time from that day to this.... There hasn't been a punter in all these years who could kick like Lewellen could. But he not only was a great punter, he was a fine defensive player and a fine offensive player," said Charlie Mathys, Packers quarterback, 1922–26.[10]

"Many times, [Lewellen] pulled us out of a hole—not only with his kicking, but by slashing through the line. We could call on him practically any time.... He turned out to be a sensational punter, which is one of the things Curly was looking for, because in those days you tried to kick the ball out of bounds.... And he was a great football player, and should be in the Hall of Fame. And I'm sure the day will come when he will be in there," said Jug Earp, Packers center, 1922–32, in 1967.[11]

He was arguably the greatest halfback of the Packers during that time and one of the all-time greats on any team. "Verne Lewellen should have been in there in front of me and Hubbard. Lewellen should be in the Hall of Fame just on his punting ability. He'd be an All-Pro punter if he played today. But, remember, he did everything else, too, and he did it all well. He was an excellent runner, a good passer, a good receiver, and a hell of a defensive back," said Johnny Blood, Packers Hall of Fame halfback.[12]

His overall play at halfback puts him just below Dutch Clark, which is saying a lot. He deserves to be in the Pro Football Hall of Fame.

No. 8

Sid Luckman

Quarterback

Full Name: Sidney Luckman
Nickname: N/A
b: November 21, 1916 (Brooklyn, NY); d: July 5, 1998 (age 81; Aventura, FL)
High School: Erasmus Hall (NY); College: Columbia
Height/Weight: 6-0, 197 pounds
Position: Quarterback
Teams/Years: 1939–1950 Chicago Bears
Pro Football Hall of Fame: Class of 1965
Retro-MVPs: 1943 (Joe F. Carr MVP Trophy)
All-Time Teams: S. Baugh (1949); C. Brock (1986); P. Driscoll (1956); R. Grange (1947); D. Hutson (1948, 1986); G. Musso (1964); J. Stydahar (1951)

The perfect signal caller for the T-formation during this era was Sid Luckman. He comes in five spots below our first quarterback and chief rival Sammy Baugh (#3). The 6-0, 197-pound Luckman played 128 games over 12 NFL seasons, all with the Chicago Bears, winning four NFL championships (1940–1941, 1943, 1946). His six-season peak in this era was as good as any player, regardless of position.

In 1916, Sidney Luckman was born to Jewish parents in Brooklyn, New York. His faith was a big part of his identity. "We had the Temple a block and half away, and we used to go there when we were younger," recalled Sid Luckman, "and it's never left me."[1]

Young Sid gravitated to playing sports in his Jewish neighborhood. "Where I grew up in Brooklyn, we used to play football, stickball, and baseball all the time. But football was my favorite," said Luckman. "We played right out there on the city streets. We used to wait for the cars to pass, then we'd start playing. It was in Flatbush by a place called Erasmus Hall High School."[2]

Luckman was the main man with his group of friends. He had something they didn't have. "Mostly, I was a big man in the gang because I owned the only football on the block," recalled Luckman. "My father gave me one when I was eight years old. He saw how much I liked the game and he decided I should have my own ball. That fixed things so the kids couldn't leave me out of a game even if they wanted to." Luckman would usually be the best player on the sandlots.[3]

Luckman's father was involved in organized crime, but he would take his boys to see the New York Giants play. "He worked odd jobs during the week then on Sundays he would drive my older brother Leo and myself over to the Polo Grounds where the New York Giants played," wrote Luckman in his book *Luckman at Quarterback*. "The pro game was still comparatively undeveloped, and the boys played a pile-up game, except when a fellow like Benny Friedman got hold of the ball for the Giants. He appeared mighty tricky in the eyes of a youngster, throwing forward passes high over the heads of burly tacklers who would have loved to tear him apart."[4]

Sid Luckman, quarterback, Chicago Bears, ca. 1940 (courtesy Columbia University Athletics).

From the beginning Luckman had a passion for football. He became a standout on the gridiron at Erasmus Hall High School in the city. His high school coach helped Luckman with the proper technique to pass. "[Coach] Paul Sullivan corrected my natural way of throwing," recalled Luckman. "If I had a flaw in the way I placed my hands on the ball, or if I took a step in to pass, or if I was throwing off balance, or if I was spiraling the ball too much, he would work on those things with me for many hours. We also practiced my signal calling. After all that work, I learned a lot about the game."[5]

"In those days the balls were much rounder, not as pointed as they are now," continued Luckman. "You had to place your hands on the laces to get a good spin on the ball. In those days, they didn't have movies of any of the teams, so the only times you could see someone else throw was to watch the pros play.... I learned to pass just from working at it, from many, many thousands of hours and throws. I would have to get down on one knee, spread my knees, and pass the ball 10 yards to someone. It was known as a snap pass if you could do it right."[6]

His playing ability was noticed widely, making him a local legend, even at a young age. His high school play attracted the attention of Lou Little, head coach at Columbia. Luckman was more than happy to continue his football career as well as get an Ivy League education.

At Columbia Luckman learned even more football techniques from Little, the future College Football Hall of Fame coach. "As a football coach, Lou Little was tremendous," said Luckman. "It was very difficult for him. Admissions were very strict at Columbia. He couldn't get the players that other schools outside the Ivy League could. I was the biggest back he had, and I weighed only about 178 pounds then. Our line averaged only about 170 pounds. I was the tailback in the single-wing. But I called the signals."[7]

Playing football on the East Coast gave Luckman the opportunity to been seen by many football experts who saw the potential in young Sid. "Luckman stands head and shoulders above the rest of the passing crowd today," said Benny Friedman, All-Pro quarterback and Luckman's boyhood hero. "And that's because of his poise. He's never rattled, and I like that in a passer."[8]

Luckman's senior year didn't see too many victories as Columbia went 3–6 overall, but Luckman was one of the best players in the country. He was almost a one-man machine, so much so that he finished third in the 1938 Heisman Trophy voting behind TCU quarterback Davey O'Brien and runner-up Pittsburgh halfback Marshall Goldberg. Luckman appeared on the cover of *Life* magazine; he was a star.

Despite the success at Columbia, Luckman wasn't too keen on playing professional football. He grew up watching the New York Giants play, but thought he was too small to play with the big boys. One man who saw Luckman at Columbia would change his mind and his life forever. "I saw him play a game in the rain in Baker Field," recalled George Halas, owner of the Chicago Bears. "And he did so many tricks with the ball I said, 'We have to have this man.'" "George Halas wrote me a letter, saying he might like to have me play for him in Chicago. I answered it saying I didn't have any desire to play professional football. I'd taken a lot of punishment as a tailback in college, and I knew how rough the pro game was."[9]

Halas wanted Luckman so bad he made a trade with the Pittsburgh Steelers, sending them veteran end Eggs Manske, to nab the second overall pick in the 1939 NFL Draft. The Bears selected Luckman number two overall, two spots ahead of Heisman winner Davey O'Brien. Eventually, George Halas got his man. "It was a hunch more than anything else," recalled Halas. "Maybe it was a question of size. Sid was at least 3 inches taller than Davey, and that advantage in height means an awful lot when you're under the center."[10]

Halas signed Luckman to one of the richest rookie deals. "When he gave me the contract, and I signed it, he said, 'You and Jesus Christ are the only two that I would pay $5,000.' I said, 'Coach, you put me in some pretty good company,'" recalled Luckman.[11]

First, Luckman would have to learn how to play quarterback in the T-formation, which the Bears used as their primary offense. "From the way I called signals, threw passes and handed off the ball for Columbia, he saw a potential T-formation quarterback for Chicago. At the time, only Halas used the formation that would revolutionize football and make the quarterback most critical to its success. Now, it's the norm for every high school, college and professional team," said Luckman in 1994.[12]

"It was a very difficult transition from playing tailback at Columbia to quarterback for the Bears," continued Luckman. "The signal-calling was diametrically opposite. The spinning was very difficult because you had to be so precise and so quick. They don't do it today like we had to do it. We had counterplays and double-counters and fakes. It was very hard for me to adjust, to get my hand under the center, and to get back and set up."[13]

But one thing Luckman brought with him that Halas didn't have to instill—a relentless work ethic. Combining hard work with his gifted athletic abilities, Luckman became a star with the Bears. He was not the pure passer that Baugh was, but he could make all the throws, was very good throwing deep and was an able ball handler and faker. "I've never seen a player who worked as hard as Luckman. When everyone else left the practice field, he stayed on. He practiced pivoting and ball-handling by the hour. When he went to his room at night, he stood before a mirror and practiced still more. He became a great player simply because he devoted about 400 percent more effort to it than most athletes are willing to do," said Halas about Luckman.[14]

Learning the Bears playbook would be a challenge, even for an Ivy League graduate.

"When I first reported to Chicago, Luke Johnsos [assistant] took me aside, gave me the Bears playbook, and told me to study it. There were about 500 plays in it and I was sure I could never master them all," said Luckman.[15]

Halas was impressed by Luckman's commitment to the game. "We coaches would work until 11 p.m. on our plays for the next game. Then I'd call Sid at home and tell him the plays. The next morning I'd ask him to repeat the plays and have to say, 'Wait a minute … go a little slower,'" said Halas.[16]

Luckman became a pure winner, from 1939 to 1944 his Bears teams went 51–11–2, as part of one of the NFL's greatest dynasties. "Still, the secret weapon was the team spirit," said Luckman. "It's hard to believe when you look back, but this team was the most unselfish bunch I've ever known. Nobody thought about the headlines. No one worried about being the star. No one said 'I,' it was always 'we.' The team always came first and I would say the results bore that out."[17]

In his second season in 1940, Luckman guided the Bears to the top of the mountain. He also helped usher in the T-formation as the predominant offense in the NFL. Besides Halas, Luckman was also tutored by Clark Shaughnessy, who was head coach at Stanford at this time. "Shaughnessy worked with George Halas a lot and he was a genius," said Luckman. "He went to his room at night and studied 20 hours, then he would take a nap and go back at it. He was very instrumental in developing the T-formation. At training camp, he would be there after lights out at 11 p.m., working with me. I tried to pick Shaughnessy's brain as best I could, because he had more time to spend with me than Coach Halas."[18]

Luckman had not only become one of the NFL's best quarterbacks, but also he was about to unleash the Bears T-formation attack in one of the league's most famous games. On December 8, 1940, the Bears made history by destroying the Washington Redskins, 73–0, in the NFL championship game. "It was just one of those incredible games. We were perfectly prepared for it. Halas had seen it. We were motivated. And we won 73–0," recalled Luckman.[19]

Luckman only completed three of four passes for 88 yards and one touchdown in the game, but he directed an offense that piled up 519 yards that day. "To this day I thank the good Lord that I was part of the team that played one of the greatest games in the history of football. It's something you can never forget," recalled Luckman in 1969. It was the Bears' T-formation offense that grabbed the attention of the country, especially the high school, college and NFL coaches everywhere. For the next few years Luckman was hired to show coaches and football teams the proper way to run the T-formation. He was very popular while doing these football clinics. "The whole nation wanted to know more about it, so Halas had some of his players go to different places. They didn't know what to do with it," recalled Luckman.[20]

The following year, Luckman's Bears won another NFL championship by going 10–1 and defeating the New York Giants 37–9 in the championship game. After winning back-to-back titles, Luckman cemented his legacy as one of the greatest quarterbacks of the NFL's two-way era during the 1940s and World War II.

Throughout his career Luckman continued to get better, especially as a passer. "I didn't have a quick release," recalled Luckman. "I wound up before I threw the ball. I didn't have what I'd call a great arm. If there was a reason for my success it was the hours and hours of work I would put in after practice with my receivers. We'd go over and over their routes and our timing until we had them down perfectly."[21]

Luckman continued: "I knew that Ken Kavanaugh liked to have the ball come in high. George Wilson was famous for his hook across the middle and I would study his steps so I knew exactly when to throw the ball. It was hard work plus the fact that I was with a great team. No quarterback can throw the ball sitting on his fanny."[22]

Luckman's leadership and great work ethic was always apparent to his coaches and teammates. He seemed to be the perfect player to guide the Bears through World War II. "He kept money in my pocket," said Bulldog Turner, Bears Hall of Fame center and teammate. "I thought he was the greatest. He didn't throw the ball as well as Baugh. In fact, lots of times his passes didn't look very good. But they always got there. You thought he was lucky at first, but when it kept happenin' year after year, you knew it wasn't luck." "He was certainly a great quarterback as we all know," recalled Hamp Pool, Chicago Bears end. "He was a fine passer, but he was also an excellent signal-caller as well. He did everything with perfection."[23]

Luckman, like so many other greats from the two-way era, strived to be the best player that he could be. He dedicated himself to being the best on the field at all times; it didn't matter what side of the ball he was playing. "We played offense and defense in those days. It was very different from today. You couldn't today, not with the kind of players you go up against who are fast, so big, so strong. I as a defensive back couldn't compete with them," said Luckman. "In those days there weren't any substitutions like now, if they took you out of the game you couldn't come back during that quarter. It was a 15-yard penalty if a play was sent in from the bench, so I had to call the plays myself. It was truly different."

Luckman continued: "I mean I had to cover as a defensive back a receiver like Don Hutson or Jim Benton of the Rams. It was a problem. And while you were doing that you were also thinking about what you were going to do as soon as you got the ball: what kind of plays you would call, what kind of series you would plan. In other words, your mind had to be functioning all the time. You had to stay a little bit ahead of the game."[24]

Luckman's best year came in 1943, where he beat out Sammy Baugh and Don Hutson to win the Joe F. Carr NFL MVP Award. He led the league in passing yards with 2,194 and passing TDs with 28, both new single-season NFL records—the TD mark lasted until 1959 when Johnny Unitas threw 32. He was the first player in NFL history to throw for seven touchdowns in a game against the Giants in 1943—a day when he also set a single-game record for passing yards with 433 yards. Luckman became the first quarterback in NFL history to throw for over 400 yards in a single game. (Five years later, Sammy Baugh broke single-game record with 446 yards against Boston on October 31, 1948.)

Luckman threw five touchdown passes in the 1943 championship game and had two interceptions on defense. He got the best of Sammy Baugh, including knocking out the tough Texan. "My knocking Baugh out was entirely unintentional," recalled Luckman. "I took his punt near the sideline and they had one man coming at me from one side and another from the other side. There was nothing left for me to do but go straight through. I saw Baugh ahead of me. He was running full speed. I got my knees pumping as hard as I could. So, going full speed, we came straight at each other. He dove at me, head on, and as my left knee went down, my right knee hit him on the forehead and he fell back and I went on over him."[25]

Not as good a punter as Baugh or as good a kicker as Dutch Clark, the versatile Luckman did contribute as a defensive back. From 1940 to 1944 Luckman had 16 career interceptions on defense. On film, Luckman showed great range and excellent toughness. "During my whole career my nose was always broken because we played without face guards," said Luckman. "You can't play football without something getting injured. Getting hit didn't bother me, because I didn't think about it. I knew I was standing out there ready to be hit. If you think about it you are never going to do anything. You just get yourself conditioned to be hit."[26]

He was one of the few quarterbacks of his era who had more touchdowns (137) than interceptions (132); in the postseason he had a 7–4 ratio. Luckman finished his 12-year NFL career (128 games) with 904 completions on 1,744 attempts for 14,686 passing yards and 137 touchdowns. Seven decades later only Jay Cutler has more passing yards and touchdowns than Luckman in Bears history. Luckman led the NFL in passing yards and passing touchdowns three times (1943, 1945–1946).

His honors were plenty. He was named to the NFL 1940s All-Decade Team and the Pro Football Hall of Fame in 1965. His number 42 jersey was retired by the Bears. "I was at the right place at the right time. And I have to thank Mr. Halas for that," recalled Luckman. "If I'd have been a tailback or signed with another team, which I probably would not have done, I don't think I would have been able to stay in the league for twelve years as I did with the Bears. As a quarterback in the T-formation, however, I was able to stay."[27]

Luckman's passion for playing pro football and with the Bears lasted his entire life. "There isn't anything like it in the world," remembered Sid Luckman. "The crowd, the smell of the grass, the people, the scoring, and winning and losing. The greatest thrill, the greatest feeling a human could ever have, was to walk out on the field and say, 'I'm a Chicago Bear.'"[28]

Sid Luckman passed away on July 5, 1998, at the age of 81.

No. 9

Cal Hubbard

Tackle

Full Name: Robert Cal Hubbard
Nickname: "Cal"
b: October 31, 1900 (Keytesville, MO); d: October 17, 1977 (age 76; St. Petersburg, FL)
High School: Keytesville (MO); College: Centenary, Geneva
Height/Weight: 6–2, 253 pounds
Position: Tackle (End)
Teams/Years: 1927–1928, 1936 New York Giants; 1929–1933, 1935 Green Bay Packers; 1936 Pittsburgh Pirates
Pro Football Hall of Fame: Class of 1963 (Charter Member)
Retro-MVPs: No
All-Time Teams: B. Bell (1940); C. Cagle (1937); J. Carr (1934); D. Clark (1942); P. Clark (1947); J. Conzelman (1941); G. Corbett (1938); P. Driscoll (1956); M. Gantenbein (1966); R. Grange (1934, 1946–1947); M. Hein (1944, 1968, 1974); A. Herber (1946); B. Hewitt (1940); C. Hinkle (1940, 1942, 1946); W. Kiesling (1942); C. Lambeau (1946); V. Lewellen (1946); J. McNally (1944, 1963); B. Nagurski (1939, 1944); S. Owen (1942, 1952, 1955); J. Stydahar (1951)

At number nine is the first tackle on the list, the great Cal Hubbard, considered the most feared lineman of his time. The 6–2, 253-pound Hubbard played nine years of pro ball, appearing in 105 games with the New York Giants (1927–1928, 1936), Green Bay Packers (1929–1933, 1935) and Pittsburgh Pirates (1936).

In 1900, Robert Hubbard was born on a farm in Keytesville, Missouri, the son of a successful farmer. Named after his father, young Robert was called "Cal" for the rest of his life. Growing up on the farm, he became enamored with playing sports, especially baseball, and learned how to play from his father. But deep down he yearned to play football. "I guess it was born in me," said Cal Hubbard.[1]

Hubbard's only high school football experience was at nearby Glasgow because his town didn't have a football team. "I didn't know much about the game," recalled Hubbard. "I didn't know what they meant by third down and three or anything like that. I guess they put me at tackle or something like that. I just wanted to run over somebody."[2]

Despite the lack of playing in high school, Hubbard held out hope to play college football. He enrolled at Chillicothe Business College, a prep school in Missouri, in 1918. Hubbard began to learn the game he desperately wanted to play, even if it meant roughing it up some. "I played hard and rough. But I made only one dirty play in my life," recalled Hubbard. "When I was playing for Chillicothe Business College against Kemper Institute, they had a fine player named Art Coglizer who later went on to the University of Missouri. He came through the line and I tried to hit him and I did. And he said, 'You dirty son of a bitch.' And I didn't say anything because I was ashamed of what I did and kind of agreed with him."[3]

After spending some time at Chillicothe Business College, Hubbard caught a break. Always the biggest player on the field while growing up in Missouri, Hubbard's boyhood idol was a diminutive All-American quarterback at tiny Centre College in Kentucky named Bo McMillin. Blind luck occurred when Hubbard ran into McMillin at a track meet he attended in Columbia, Missouri. Seeing Hubbard's massive size and enthusiasm for playing football, McMillin convinced the young man to play for him at Centenary College in Louisiana, where he was just named football coach in 1922.

Cal Hubbard, end-tackle, Green Bay Packers, ca. 1929 (courtesy Green Bay Packers).

"Bo was the best one-man coaching staff I ever saw. He could tell the guards and tackles how to play just as well as he could the halfbacks," said Hubbard. Taught by McMillin, Hubbard learned how to play end and tackle. He instantly became a starter for McMillin. During their time together the coach frequently had to ring in his prized pupil. "I was rough as a cob," recalled Hubbard. "I liked to hit people so much that Bo McMillin wouldn't even let me play in our scrimmages."[4]

"Cal was an outstanding tackle right from the start, an agile giant, a great competitor with a passionate love for football," said Bo McMillin. Hubbard's dedication to McMillin became even more apparent when McMillin left Centenary for Geneva (PA) College in 1925. Hubbard didn't hesitate to follow his coach up north. Hitting his peak physically, Hubbard's athletic body filled out to be 6–2, 250 pounds. At Geneva in 1926, Hubbard played well enough to be named to a few All-American squads, including first team by the *New York World News Service* and a third team selection by Red Grange who was writing for *Universal News Service*. His play made his mentor proud. "In my opinion Hubbard was the greatest lineman of all-time. I've never seen anybody equal to him," recalled McMillian in 1950.[5]

Several NFL teams, including the Frankford Yellow Jackets and Providence Steam Roller, contacted Hubbard about playing pro football. After seeking advice from McMillin—who had played in the NFL for the Milwaukee Badgers and Cleveland Indians—Hubbard choose to play for the New York Giants.

As a 27-year-old rookie in 1927, Hubbard played end for the Giants. He joined a team that included All-Pros Al Nesser (guard), Steve Owen (tackle) on the line, and Jack McBride, Hinkey Haines, Mule Wilson, and Doug Wycoff in the backfield. On offense Hubbard fit in well. The Giants would often use him on screen passes, where Hubbard would take two steps, then turn slightly to be ready for a bullet pass. The play usually would gain positive yards or a first down.

Hubbard quickly became a player to be reckoned with in the early days of the NFL. "I faced the best players in Princeton, Yale, Harvard, Penn and other colleges," said Gus Sonnenberg, former All-Pro tackle. "But the first game I played with the Providence Steam Roller [NFL] was against the New York Giants. Hubbard gave me the worse beating that I received in all my football, east or west. He was the greatest lineman I ever saw."[6]

Big "Cal" also impressed his new teammates. "A giant of a man who could outrun any back in the league for 30 yards…. Cal, with his combination of speed, weight, and timing, was a devasting blocker. On defense he made them run the other way," recalled Steve Owen, former Giants tackle and head coach. "We once had a halfback named Mule Wilson," continued Owen. "Mule was a sprinter who was beaten only by a yard by Charlie Paddock, then the 'World's Fastest Human.' But for a short burst of 30 yards Hubbard could outrun Wilson."[7]

Hubbard played his first two years in the league as an end for the Giants, making All-Pro both years and helping the Giants win the 1927 NFL championship. That season he helped anchor a hardnosed defense that surrendered just 20 points all season. "In my day we thought it was sissified to pass the ball, we'd rather run over them," said Hubbard. Little did Hubbard know that his next NFL team was the league's best at tossing the pigskin.[8]

Early in the 1928 season Hubbard traveled with the Giants to Green Bay to face the Packers. The team from the Big Apple played in Chicago the next week, so they spent a few extra days in Green Bay to prepare, giving Hubbard time to fall in love with the small Wisconsin town. "In 1928 we played a game in Green Bay and stayed the week to practice for our next game with the Bears in Chicago," recalled Hubbard. "I'd already decided I didn't want to live in New York any longer. I liked the town of Green Bay and I asked Dr. Harry March, who was sort of the business manager of the Giants, to trade me there. I told him I wasn't going to play any more if he didn't."[9]

Hubbard's arrival in Green Bay coincided with the beginning of the Packers first dynasty. The squad already had All-Pro backs Verne Lewellen and Red Dunn as well as All-Pro end Lavvie Dilweg. Along with Hubbard two other future Hall of Famers joined Green Bay that season: back Johnny "Blood" McNally and guard Mike Michalske.

In 1929, he moved to tackle when he joined Curly Lambeau's Green Bay Packers. Although excellent at end, Hubbard was an even better tackle. He excelled as a blocker on offense and backed up the line on defense (sometimes standing up like a linebacker). Hubbard loved playing a 60-minute game. "Let's say you're on offense and the guy you're playing opposite is handing you a beating, there's no chance to get even," recalled Hubbard. "Now, when that happens you're out of luck because the other guy trots off the field when the ball changes hands. Where's the fun in that?"[10]

Hubbard continued: "We played six- and seven-man lines, mostly—five men up front only when we knew they would be throwing the long pass. Otherwise, we thought the best pass defense was to rush the passer and we really went out to get him."[11]

Hubbard adjusted to Lambeau's coaching style, especially on defense. "Starting out as a pro with the Giants I was a linebacker in the 7-diamond or 6-2-2-1 defense," said Hubbard. "I was all right as long as we were playing zone. But when I got to Green Bay they played man-to-man, and I couldn't keep up with those fast little guys coming out of the backfield. I told Curly, 'I'm not fast enough, you better put me at tackle.'" Once he got settled in at tackle, Hubbard was one of the best players in the NFL.[12]

Throughout his career with the Packers Hubbard was an enforcer on the field. He gained a reputation as being a "policeman." He would not back down from anybody, especially the bitter rival Chicago Bears. "I never played harder than I did against the Bears. I can still hear Halas hollering from the sidelines for me to lay off his center, George Trafton. Trafton was a mouthy guy. He was always lipping off. So, I knocked the hell out of him every chance I got," said Hubbard in 1976.[13]

During the two-way era, few players at his position earned greater respect from his opponents than Hubbard. His name consistently comes up in selecting an All-Time team from the two-way era. "Hubbard is the best tackle I've seen. He's six-foot-two, weighs 250 and believe it or not, he's very fast. I've tried to block him out, and it can't be done. I've seen him on defense start through the line and shove it entirely out of position. He must be 35 now, but he is all man, and I've never seen a better football player," said Dutch Clark, Hall of Fame halfback.[14]

"The greatest tackle I ever seen or been pulverized by was Cal Hubbard," said Red Grange, Bears Hall of Fame halfback. "Probably the greatest tackle I ever played against was Cal Hubbard of the Packers. Hubbard was the left defensive tackle and he stopped everything," said Mel Hein, Giants Hall of Fame center-linebacker.[15]

"Green Bay had the most brutal lineman in the game, Cal Hubbard," said Harry Newman, Giants All-Pro quarterback. "He played tackle and was about 6 feet 2 inches and maybe 270 pounds. He played with the same kind of intensity that Dick Butkus did later. We used to say of Cal that even if he missed you he still hurt you. When he tackled you, you remembered it. I do to this day."[16]

Hubbard was a dynamic force on winning teams throughout his career. Besides the '27 Giants, Hubbard was a key member of the Packers who won three straight NFL championships, 1929–1931. Hubbard was at his peak with the Packers during the championship run. Hubbard was known for his ferocious blocking from his tackle position, leading the way for several All-Pros such as Lewellen, Red Dunn, Johnny "Blood" McNally and Dilweg. While on defense he anchored a unit that was hard to score on. He played like a linebacker on some plays, standing up.

The Packers compiled an overall record of 34–5–2 during their three championship seasons. "I never saw a better lineman, either on offense or defense," said his coach, Curly Lambeau of the Packers. In 1929, the Packers finished the season unbeaten at 12–0–1, scoring 198 points and surrendering only 22 points all season; they gave up just three touchdowns in 13 games. The following season Hubbard scored his first ever touchdown by catching a pass from Red Dunn in a 37–7 victory over the Staten Island Stapeltons.[17]

Hubbard became the Packers team leader. He was someone that everybody knew was a great teammate. "He was a very good friend, but then, he didn't have many enemies, until he put his uniform on, that is," recalled Mike Michalske, Packers Hall of Fame guard. "And he loved to play the game, not for the sustenance. I think he was the best tackle Green Bay ever had in the Iron Man era, if not the best in the league. He was a bone-cruncher at linebacker. He wasn't that fast, but he had great instincts, great reactions. Sometimes his head knew what he'd do before his feet."[18]

Hubbard might've been the smartest tackle to play during the two-way era. "He's forgotten more about line play than most players ever know," recalled Lon Evans, Packers guard, 1933–1937. "Cal was the smartest football player on the rules I ever encountered. Hubbard would disagree with a ref, they'd look up the rule, and Hubbard would be right," recalled Red Grange, Bears Hall of Fame back.[19]

Being a stickler for rules, Hubbard picked up another occupation during the off-season that would lead him to a spot in another Hall of Fame, this time on the baseball diamond. "We got maybe $220 to $225 a game," said Hubbard. "I needed something to do in the off-season to make money to support my family and that's why I went into umpiring. No, we didn't make the big money but I'll say this—we sure enjoyed the game. I can remember some championship teams of my time that had only 18 men on the squad. But if the coach took you out of the game, you'd want to fight him."[20]

Despite his age, Hubbard's play at the end of his football career didn't slow down. In 1933, he was named First Team All-Pro by the NFL, *Chicago Daily News*,

Collyer's, Green Bay Press-Gazette and the United Press. In 1934, he took a job as line coach at Texas A & M under Homer Norton. But the following year, he came back to play with the Packers. That season against his old team, the Giants, Hubbard picked off a fourth quarter pass and returned it eight yards for a touchdown to clinch a 16–7 win. It was his second and last touchdown in the NFL.

At this time, he thought he was done. But he wasn't quite through with the game of football yet. In 1936, he played one game with the Pittsburgh Pirates, before calling it quits. Then suddenly Hubbard got a call to play for his first team and Hubbard couldn't say no. Helping out the New York Giants and Steve Owen, he only planned to play one game; instead, he played in six. "I reported on a Friday night," recalled Hubbard, "and they used me Sunday against Detroit. I was to be a sub, but both tackles got hurt and I played 56 minutes. I made tackles all over the field. It was one of my best days I've ever had." For the second time in 1936, he called it quits. "I was 36 and I had enough bruises on my body," said Hubbard.[21]

Since he had already been umpiring while playing football, Hubbard had a good idea what he was going to do next. "Back home," said Hubbard, "I did a lot of umpiring of sand lot games. I was so big that the other fellows were afraid to argue with me." Hubbard became a great umpire, reaching the major leagues. He was an umpire in the American League from 1936 to 1951, then worked as the AL's umpire supervisor until his retirement in 1969. The well-respected Hubbard had now conquered two sports. "I always hated to throw a guy out of the game. But sometimes it is necessary to maintain discipline," said Hubbard. "An umpire owes it to the fans and players to understand the nuance of every rule."[22]

Since his retirement from the NFL, Hubbard consistently has been recognized as one of the greatest players in NFL history—not just as a two-way player. He was elected as a Charter Member of the Pro Football Hall of Fame in 1963. In 1969, he was named to the NFL 1920s All-Decade Team and was selected the NFL's All-Time Tackle for the 50th Anniversary All-Time team. In 1970, he was elected to the Packers Hall of Fame.

In 1994, he was named to the NFL 75th Anniversary All-Time Two-Way Team and in 2019 was named to the NFL 100th Anniversary Team as one of just seven tackles selected. But his most impressive honor to date came in 1976 when he was elected to the Baseball Hall of Fame as an umpire. He is the *only* man to be elected to the Pro Football and Baseball Halls of Fame, an achievement that will be hard to match. On the day he was selected to the Baseball Hall of Fame, the Pro Football Hall of Fame wired Hubbard: "Congratulations on your baseball Hall of Fame election. We are proud we named you first in 1963. You have been a credit to the entire sports world and your dual elections are a just reflection of your exceptional accomplishments in both sports."[23]

On October 17, 1977, Cal Hubbard passed away from cancer at the age of 76. "There never was a better lineman than that big umpire," said George Halas, Bears Hall of Fame coach.[24]

No. 10

Paddy Driscoll
Quarterback

Full Name: John Leo Driscoll
Nickname: "Paddy"
b: January 11, 1895 (Evanston, IL); d: June 29, 1968 (age 73; Chicago, IL)
High School: Evanston (IL); College: Northwestern
Height/Weight: 5-11, 160 pounds
Position: Quarterback
Teams/Years: 1919 Hammond Pros (Pre-NFL); 1920–1925 Chicago Cardinals; 1920, 1926–1929 Decatur Staleys/Chicago Bears
Pro Football Hall of Fame: Class of 1965
Retro-MVPs: 1925, 1926
All-Time Teams: J. Carr (1934); G. Halas (1939–1941); R. Grange (1947)

You can make an argument that the best all-around back that played in the 1920s was Paddy Driscoll. He comes in one spot below Cal Hubbard (#9) at number 10.

The son of Irish immigrants, Driscoll's father was a stone cutter in Evanston, north of Chicago, near the campus of Northwestern University, where little Paddy made a name for himself playing with the bigger boys. He learned all he could about the game, playing daily at the playground at St. Mary's Catholic grammar school. Paddy quickly learned the game and mastered early football formations such as the single-wing and T-formation. Even at a young age he was almost a coach on the field. He absorbed everything he could. "Heck, the T-formation isn't new," said Paddy Driscoll in an interview in 1947. "When I was a kid in the west end of Evanston we used to run plays every night on Davis Street from Florence Street to Ashland Avenue, and we didn't have one [play] where the quarterback didn't take the ball from center and hand it to the back who was carry it."[1]

Driscoll grew up to stand 5-11 and weigh just 160 pounds, but he would dominate his opponents. At Northwestern he was the best player in the Western Conference—the precursor to the Big Ten. Walter Eckersall of the *Chicago Tribune* and a former All-American back at the University of Chicago once wrote: "Driscoll was among the first to use the pivot in dodging, and he ran with his knees kicking nearly as high as his chest. He was absolutely reliable in handling punts, always waiting a few yards back so that he caught the ball on a dead run." In his senior year of 1916, Driscoll was named First Team All-Conference and Third Team All-American by the Father of American Football, Walter Camp, who was so impressed with Driscoll that he once said he was "the greatest quarterback I have ever seen."[2]

With his college eligibility over, Driscoll turned to his second favorite sport. In the summer of 1917, Driscoll played Major League Baseball with the Chicago Cubs. In 13 games with the Cubs as a utility infielder, Driscoll only had three hits and batted .107. That fall, he turned his attention to pro football, playing with the Hammond Clabbys (1917), where Driscoll led the Clabbys to a 7–3 record.

Paddy Driscoll, quarterback, Chicago Cardinals, ca. 1924–1925 (courtesy Arizona Cardinals).

Soon Driscoll's playing abilities took a back seat to the battle across the seas. Joining the Navy, Driscoll was assigned to Great Lakes Naval Station located off Lake Michigan. During World War I, he would reach the rank of petty officer. While at Great Lakes he played football alongside future two-way era Hall of Famers George Halas and Jimmy Conzelman as the Bluejackets finished with a 6–0–2 record and played in the 1919 Rose Bowl against the Mare Island Marines. In that game, he kicked a field goal and threw a touchdown pass to Halas in the 19–0 victory. Later that year, Driscoll was discharged from the Navy, returning to pro football.

At the end of the 1919 season, Driscoll played a few games for the Hammond All-Stars. On Thanksgiving, he lined up at halfback against the Canton Bulldogs and Jim Thorpe. Over 10,000 fans showed up at Cubs Park to watch the big matchup. A first quarter touchdown by Thorpe is all the Bulldogs needed in the tough 7–0 victory. By now Driscoll was sold on the sport and would dedicate the next decade to playing in the NFL. He went on to play 118 games in 10 seasons in the league with the Chicago Cardinals (1920–1925) and the Decatur Staleys/Chicago Bears (1920, 1926–1929).

When the APFA-NFL was founded in 1920, Driscoll signed for a whopping $300 a game to play for the Chicago Cardinals. From 1920 to 1922 Driscoll was also the

Cardinals head coach. He guided the Cardinals to an overall record of 17–8–4. His best year on the field during this time was in 1922 when he scored 40 points (two TDs; eight FGs; four XPs) and guided the Cardinals to a 8–3 record—good for third place in the NFL.

A smart, intelligent player, Driscoll was always a coach on the field. A triple-threat player on offense and a flawless defender, Driscoll's best trait was his ability to kick the ball. "He was the greatest athlete I ever knew," said Halas about Driscoll. He was so passionate about sports that while he was playing in the NFL, Driscoll also helped coach football and basketball at St. Mel's High School in Chicago, something he would do for a decade. The following year in 1923, he gave up coaching to Arnie Horween, which allowed him to flourish on the field. He scored seven total touchdowns, four extra points and a league-high 10 field goals. His 78 points led the NFL, as the Cardinals finished with an 8–4 record.[3]

Driscoll went toe-to-toe with all the early greats in the 1920s, including Jim Thorpe. "I liked to run back those kickoffs," said Driscoll to the *Chicago American* in 1965. "Because you could dodge around, but this day I didn't zig when I should have and that Thorpe and Doc Spears got me in a vise. I had never stopped so fast in my life, and I haven't since."[4]

Throughout the 1920s, the gifted Driscoll was a leader in scoring points; like Dutch Clark and Verne Lewellen, Driscoll could put points on the scoreboard on a regular basis. His excellent kicking skills allowed him to finish his career with an NFL record 402 points, broken by Don Hutson in 1942. He also set an NFL record with 51 career field goals, broken by Bob Waterfield in 1952, and points in a season with 78 in 1923. Three years later, he broke that record by scoring 86 points, exceeded by Hutson in 1941 with 95 points. To top it off he was the first player in NFL history to kick four FGs in a game on October 11, 1925, against Columbus, a 19–9 Cardinal victory.

In his 10 years in the NFL, he unofficially scored 34 total touchdowns (28 rushing; four receiving; one punt return.; one fumble recovery). Because of his all-around play Driscoll goes down as one of the greatest two-way quarterbacks of all time. He finishes on this list just behind Sammy Baugh (#3) and Sid Luckman (#8). "Another great back of that time who should also be remembered was Paddy Driscoll," recalled Red Grange, Bears Hall of Fame halfback. "Paddy was a runner, a passer and a great drop-kicker. He could drop-kick it through the uprights from anywhere from 50-yard line in. And he was a good defensive player as well."[5]

Driscoll had a special knack for drop-kicking—once booting one from 50 yards in 1924 against the Milwaukee Badgers—and could convert field goals and extra points at ease. "You know, it wasn't just because they slimmed down the football that the drop-kick became obsolete," said Driscoll. "The place-kick was faster to get off, and more certain in sloppy weather because you had someone holding the ball stationary. Another factor, we used to keep a football quite a while, even for several games. The ball would expand and become rounder as it was booted around. Easy to drop-kick!"[6]

In 1925 and 1926 Driscoll would play his best football.

Retro-MVPs: 1925, 1926 NFL Seasons

A member of the 1925 Chicago Cardinals that won the NFL championship, Driscoll finished second in the league with 67 points to Charlie Berry who scored 74 points with Pottsville and led the league in field goals made with 11. (Although if Pottsville is ineligible for the NFL title then Driscoll would've led league in points.) Driscoll easily captures the 1925 Retro-MVP with his outstanding play.

The following year (1926) saw a pro football war with Red Grange and his agent, C.C. Pyle, starting a new league—the American Football League (AFL). They placed a team in Chicago—named the Bulls—to challenge the Bears and Cardinals, who were in financial disarray despite winning the championship. Cardinals owner Chris O'Brien was approached by George Halas about his star player Paddy Driscoll. Halas didn't want Driscoll going to the rival Bulls (AFL), so he offered O'Brien $3,500 for Driscoll. O'Brien said yes and sent his best player across town to the Bears. "I hated to let Driscoll go," said Chris O'Brien to the press in 1926. "But his value had become so great, that I could not afford to pay him what he deserved and hated to see him take less."[7]

When Halas began negotiating with Driscoll on his new contract, Paddy had the leverage.

"He had long wanted to play with the Bears," wrote Halas in his autobiography. "He and I had played together most happily on the Great Lakes team. He admired the Bears. In the end, he decided to play with the Bears for $10,000." The pricey salary made Driscoll one of the highest, if not the highest, paid players in the NFL.[8]

In 1926 with the Bears, Driscoll didn't miss a beat. He scored an amazing 86 points which led the NFL. Playing in 16 games, he scored seven TDs, 14 XPs and 12 FGs, helping lead the Bears to a second-place finish in the NFL with a 12–1–3 record. He wins his second consecutive Retro-MVP, this time with a new team. "There is no more intelligent player in pro football than Paddy. He handles punts unerringly, excels at the aerial game, and his accuracy in punting and drop-kicking has never been surpassed. He is the final word as a triple-threat performer," wrote Wilfred Smith of the *Chicago Tribune* in naming Driscoll First Team All-Pro in 1926.[9]

Driscoll played the next three years with the Bears and was named First Team All-Pro by the *Chicago Tribune* in 1927–1928. Driscoll's competitive spirit still flowed through his body. "I suppose I'll keep on playing until Father Time gets out his scythe and mows me down," said Driscoll to the Associated Press in 1929. "Every year I think I'll quit, but when the football season opens and I hear the thud of leather, I can't resist the urge and I don moleskins again. I guess it's just in my blood." Driscoll finally called it quits after the 1929 NFL season. "It was a pleasure to have such a charming model gentleman and great athlete with us. Driscoll was a terrific ballplayer, a real competitor," recalled Ed Healey, Bears Hall of Fame tackle.[10]

Driscoll stayed close to the game by becoming a coach. He was head coach at Marquette from 1937 to 1940, compiling a record of 10–23–1, before joining the Bears as an assistant under his good friend George Halas. He spent the next 27 years with the Bears as an assistant (1941–1955), head coach (1956–1957), vice president (1958–1962) and director of planning and research (1963–1968). "Rapidly developing techniques in professional football have heightened the importance of game preparations to the point where a single coordinator should spend all of his time on that job," said Halas in 1963. "Study of game films and scouting charts has taken on an added dimension, which is the need for translating information into concise, meaningful reports. Paddy will concentrate on this phase of the game."[11]

Decades before analytics became fashionable, Driscoll studied games films, wrote out spreadsheets, and crunched football statistics on a routine basis for the Bears. He was a football lifer. In 1963, he helped his mentor and friend George Halas win the 1963 NFL championship by defeating the New York Giants, giving Halas his last NFL title at the age of 68.

It didn't take Driscoll long to achieve football immortality when the Pro Football Hall of Fame opened its doors. Driscoll was elected to the Hall of Fame in 1965 as part of the third class. "It's inconceivable that a fellow like myself weighing 128 pounds playing fullback in high school, would come up here to get these high honors. I've had many great days on the football field both at Northwestern and with the Bears and Cardinals, but this is my greatest honor, and we'll have to move the furniture around to find a good place for that bust. Thank you," said Paddy Driscoll at his Pro Football Hall of Fame induction. A few years later Driscoll was named to the NFL 1920s All-Decade Team, joining Jimmy Conzelman as the only two quarterbacks selected. In 2006, Driscoll was inducted into Cardinals Ring of Honor.[12]

Paddy Driscoll died from complications of a leg ailment on June 29, 1968, at the age of 73.

No. 11

Pete "Fats" Henry
Tackle

Full Name: Wilbur Francis Henry
Nicknames: "Fats"; "Pete"
b: October 31, 1897 (Mansfield, OH); d: February 7, 1952 (age 54; Washington, PA)
High School: Mansfield (OH); College: Washington & Jefferson
Height/Weight: 5-11, 245 pounds
Position: Tackle
Teams/Years: 1920-1923, 1925-1926 Canton Bulldogs; 1927 New York Giants; 1927-1928 Pottsville Maroons
Pro Football Hall of Fame: Class of 1963 (Charter Member)
Retro-MVPs: 1923
All-Time Teams: G. Dorias (1952, 1954); P. Driscoll (1956); J. McNally (1937, 1944); P. Robeson (1941)

Nicknamed "Fats," mainly for his odd body shape of 5-feet-11, 245 pounds, Pete Henry was just as fast and athletic as any back in the NFL during his era. A 60-minute performer at tackle, Henry played in 86 games over eight years in the NFL with the Canton Bulldogs, New York Giants and the Pottsville Maroons.

Wilbur Henry was born in 1897 in the small town of Mansfield, Ohio, located just 60 miles west from Canton—the area called the "Cradle of Pro Football." Fats was the only child of Ulysses and Bertha Henry. While growing up, the name Wilbur didn't stick for very long and the Ohio kid was called "Pete" for the rest of his life. Pete gained a big appetite for food while living on the family farm and the rotund boy would use his size to become a great athlete.

As Henry entered Mansfield High School he weighed 215 pounds and attracted the attention of the football coach. Henry was large enough to stop any ball carrier, but his surprising speed and quickness really separated him from his teammates and opponents. Instead of playing on the line like most big kids of his era, Henry was moved to fullback for his entire high school career. Henry enjoyed a solid high school career, including being named captain of the team during his senior year, when the team finished with an 8-1 record—losing only to nearby Wooster. Colleges around the country started to notice the big kid from Mansfield.

Because of his size and unique shape, Henry filled out to 5 feet, 11 inches and tipped the scales at 245 pounds. He was not a slow-footed fat guy, he was an athletic football player who made plays on the football field. His swift feet next took him to Washington & Jefferson College located near Pittsburgh.

In the fall of 1915, Henry enrolled at W & J, where Bob Folwell was the head coach; Folwell would go on to become the first head coach of the New York Giants in 1925. Although Henry played fullback in high school, Folwell quickly looked at Henry's size and moved him to tackle. Folwell left after the season and was replaced by Sol Metzger who coached Henry for two seasons (1916–1917). He helped Henry reach Honorable Mention All-American both seasons.

In 1918, the W & J football season was interrupted by World War I, and the team played only two games all season. Because of the shortened season Henry was given an extra year of eligibility in 1919. Besides playing football Henry competed in track, baseball and basketball while at W & J. He became the first player at the school to letter in four major sports—earning 11 total letters.

The 1919 season would be Henry's finest year and maybe his most difficult. After leading the Presidents to a 4–0 start rumors started to swirl about Henry playing professional football. In early October there was a report that he played a game with the Massillon Tigers. Henry responded with a quote that was printed in the October 8 edition of the *Canton Daily News*, with the headline, "Big Tackle Denies Massillon Connection." "Apparently someone has tried to put me in the wrong at Massillon," said Henry to the press. "Not only did I not play with Massillon last Sunday, but I have no intention of playing professional football before I am through my college course. I will admit that flattering offers have been made to me to play on a number of professional teams, but I have rejected all of them and certainly will maintain my amateur standings while I am in college."[1]

Walter Camp, the father of American football, once said, "Henry was the

Pete "Fats" Henry, tackle, Canton Bulldogs, ca. 1919 (courtesy Washington & Jefferson Athletics).

finest lineman I ever saw." Henry was named to Camp's First Team All-American squad. Henry also stuck to his guns even after the football season ended. Several pro football teams made an offer to him when the college football season was over, but he turned them all down so he could be eligible to participate in track during the spring. Henry stayed at W & J and graduated from the school in June of 1920.[2]

As the summer went by, Henry was finally ready to sign and play professional football. He decided to play for the best team, the Canton Bulldogs, and be a teammate with the great Jim Thorpe. On the same day Henry signed his contract it was announced that a new league was being formed for professional football. On September 17, 1920, the American Professional Football Association (APFA) was formed in Canton, Ohio, at the automobile showroom of the Bulldogs' owner, Ralph Hay. Two years later the league was re-named the National Football League. The organizational meeting took place late in the day, but the main headlines in the Canton sports page the next day was the signing of Wilbur "Pete" Henry. On page 26 of the *Canton Repository*, under the headline "Bulldogs Land Big Wilbur Henry, 235-Pound Tackle, From W-J, All-American," the article read:

> Buck of Wisconsin, Edwards of Notre Dame, Kellison of West Virginia Wesleyen, Smith of the Michigan Aggies and Lowe of Fordham are all good tackles corking good ones, but they haven't a thing on the husky youngster just signed up for the Canton Bulldogs of 1920—Wilbur Henry of Mansfield.
> The signature of Henry to a Bulldog contract was announced Friday morning after Manager Hay had received a telegram to that effect. He is the most notable addition to Jim Thorpe's crew of professionals and commands a fancy salary but will be worth it in playing ability and drawing power. Henry plans to come to Canton for the season and practice with the rest of the champions.[3]

Now that Henry had signed a professional contract, he was ready to play, but the first two seasons with the Bulldogs were transition years. Henry played at a high level from the start. "I think that Henry was the greatest tackle I ever saw," said Lou Little, Buffalo All-Americans tackle, 1920–1921. "I'll never forget the day he proved it to me. He was playing with the Canton Bulldogs. I was a tackle on the Buffalo club. The first play was directed at Henry. 'Fats' met it head on. Using his huge hands and active body, Henry telescoped himself over me, Henie Miller [end] and Swede Youngstrom [guard] and he threw us all into Lud Wray, our center. Then he plowed through and hit [Tommy] Hughitt of Michigan, the ball carrier. Suffice to say the remainder of the game we left Henry alone."[4]

After the 1920 season—when the Bulldogs finished 7-4-1—Thorpe left the Bulldogs and a new leader was needed to take charge of the team. After a 5-2-3 finish in 1921 under Cap Edwards, the Bulldogs found their leader by hiring former Nebraska All-American Guy Chamberlin, who had played the previous two seasons with George Halas and the Staleys. He was the perfect man for the job. In 1922, Henry was paired with Link Lyman at tackle to form the greatest tackle duo during the two-way era. Chamberlin made sure his team was ready to contend behind his great line.

Besides his great play on the line, Henry was one of the better kickers and punters in the NFL. "You were allowed special toes in those days. Fats would boot the kickoffs so high in the air that I can never recall a runback by the receivers," recalled Harry Robb, Bulldogs back, 1921–1923.[5]

The Bulldogs' 1922 season started off with a bang, as the team went unbeaten in their first six games (4-0-2), including a 7-6 victory over Halas's newly-named Chicago Bears. On November 12, the Bulldogs won a hard-fought 3-0 victory over the tough Buffalo All-Americans and the Canton papers praised Pete Henry for his performance. "[Henry's play] marked the greatest game he ever has played for Canton, and it came close to being the most remarkable performance ever given by a lineman on a local field."[6]

The Bulldogs finished the season by winning the NFL title with a 10-0-2 record and the defense yielded just 15 total points in 12 league games. Henry was becoming one of the best tackles in pro football, being named First Team All-Pro by the *Buffalo News* and George Halas. Using his big body to his advantage, Henry moved on the gridiron as easy as a "bounding deer." The round-faced Henry might have played hard and tough on the field, but he never took it out on his opponents. He was known to never lose his temper or use foul language. What would the Bulldogs do for an encore in 1923? For Henry, he would have his best year ever.

The Bulldogs kept the team intact with such stars as Harry Robb, Doc Elliott, Duke Osborn, Link Lyman, Tex Grigg, and Bird Carroll all returning. With the coaching and playing of Guy Chamberlin, the Bulldogs looked to have another great season. After winning their first six games of the season by a combined score of 104–6, the Bulldogs faced their biggest test yet. With the unbeaten streak at 19 games, the Bulldogs played on the road in front of 10,000 fans against the Buffalo All-Americans on November 11. After Buffalo kicked a first-quarter field goal, the Bulldogs saw themselves trailing 3–0 late into the fourth quarter. With under a minute to go Guy Chamberlin blocked a punt and Henry recovered at the 11-yard line. One play later Henry drop-kicked a 25-yard field goal to give the Bulldogs a 3–3 tie and kept the Bulldogs undefeated. Once again Pete Henry claimed the headlines in the local paper. "The World Champions can thank their lucky stars that Wilbur Henry was with them Sunday. The big fellow not only turned defeat into victory when the case seemed hopeless, but played a wonderful game from the start until his spectacular climaxing act in the last few seconds of play. Canton deserved a victory."[7]

After the Buffalo game the Bulldogs would go on to win their last five games by a combined score of 139 to 10 to claim another NFL championship. For the year, they scored 246 points to just 19 by their opponents. They also were unbeaten in their last 25 games, setting an NFL record that still stands today, as Most Consecutive Games Won Without Defeat (27 total with two wins in 1925).

Retro-MVP: 1923 Season

The 1923 NFL season was also the finest year for Pete Henry. He finished second in the NFL in scoring with 59 points, behind the Chicago Cardinals' Paddy Driscoll's 78, including nine field goals and a league high 26 extra points. To show how dominate Henry was, just consider the month of October when Henry led the Bulldogs with his stellar play.

> October 7—Henry caught a rare touchdown pass from his tackle position in a 37–0 victory over the Louisville Brecks.
> October 14—Henry kicked three field goals and three extra points in a 30–0 win over the Dayton Triangles.
> October 21—Henry kicked two field goals, scoring Canton's only points, in a big 6–0 victory over the Chicago Bears. The Bears would go on to finish in second place behind the Bulldogs with a record of 9-2-1.[8]

Henry was the best player in the NFL in 1923. Henry wins our Retro-MVP for the 1923 season. "He was a smiling, laughing, jolly kind of guy, the stereotype of the jolly fat man," said Johnny "Blood" McNally, Green Bay Packers Hall of Fame back. "But on the football field he could be ferocious. And he was surprisingly quick and fast. Underneath that layer of blubber, there was a lot of pretty good muscle."[9]

The Canton Bulldogs were now two-time NFL champions but financially the Bulldogs were in trouble. Ralph Hay wanted to devote his money for his automobile business and the city of Canton didn't want to finance the team. Thus, in 1924 the Bulldogs were sold to Sam Deutsch, owner of the NFL's Cleveland Indians, who moved the Bulldogs to Cleveland. Henry couldn't come to an agreement to play for Cleveland, so he decided to play for the Pottsville Maroons, a very good non–NFL team, who were playing games in the Pennsylvania coal region.

The following year Pete Henry and several former Canton teammates—including Link Lyman, Rudy Comstock, and Ben Jones—bought back the Bulldogs franchise and returned it to Canton. But the 1925–1926 Bulldogs teams didn't have the same success as the earlier teams. After a solid 4-4 season in 1925, Henry and co-coach Harry Robb seemed to field an old and slow team in 1926, finishing with a woeful record of 1-9-3. The only win was a 13–0 victory over the Louisville Colonels, when Jim Thorpe, who had returned to play for the Bulldogs as a 38-year-old halfback, scored both touchdowns. Pete Henry would go down as one of the best ever to play for the Canton Bulldogs.

"Pete Henry was the most unusual specimen you ever saw. He was fast and could run all day. You hit him and your head would go in clear up to your neck. How he could play," recalled Cal Hubbard, former teammate with the Giants (1927).[10]

After six seasons playing with the Bulldogs, Henry thought about retirement, but he decided to play a bit longer. In 1927, he split time with the New York Giants (four games) and the Pottsville Maroons (nine games). He then finished his career by being the player-coach for the 1928 Maroons. They finished with a 2–8 record in NFL games, and Henry was finally done with professional football. At 31 years of age, Henry retired from the sport he loved.

Henry had a hard time quitting the game. "Now that football's over, I don't know what to do," he would be quoted as saying. If he felt that way, he didn't stay idle for very long. In the fall of 1929, Henry was hired by his alma mater, Washington & Jefferson, to be an assistant coach for both basketball and football. Two years later on August 16, 1931, Henry was named athletic director—a position he would hold for the next 21 years.[11]

The school became like a second family to Henry, and he would eventually need their support. After Henry turned 50 years old his body started to fail him. A leg injury that hampered him for years and a case of diabetes would eventually take his life. The school publication, *The Red and Black*, detailed the last few years of Henry's life as he struggled with his health problems. "In 1949 the diabetes ailment which had been threatening to catch up with Henry for some time laid him low and people, for the first time, began to realize that the splendid Henry physique was susceptible to the ravages of disease. He became critically ill and finally had one leg amputated to prevent the spread of the infection. He was fitted with an artificial leg, but was always reticent to use it because the use of such helps did not seem consistent with the Henry saga." In December of 1951 tragedy came again, and Henry lost in his final scrimmage. He was hospitalized with a diabetic infection setting in his other leg. Just before Christmas, the famous Henry fighting spirit showed itself and he said, "I'll be home for Christmas." He was, returning home the day before Christmas, but in the final week in January, he suddenly took another turn for the worse. "On Thursday February 7, 1952, the beloved Pete died in his home on East Wheeling Street."[12]

Wilbur "Pete" Henry was only 54 years old when he passed away.

In 1962, when the Pro Football Hall of Fame had its groundbreaking ceremony in Canton, Ohio, George Halas compared Henry and Cal Hubbard, the two great tackles of the two-way era. "Yes, Henry was the best. That big umpire was awfully good, too," said Halas. "In a way, though, Hubbard was more of a linebacker, a position he invented. He was able to wreck destruction from anywhere behind the line of scrimmage. Fats was orthodox and, as such, I never saw his equal. As an end for the Bears, I played directly opposite him on hundreds of plays. Only once in all that time was I able to block him out."[13]

In 1963, the Pro Football Hall of Fame opened its doors for the first time. The Hall of Fame selected 17 charter members as the first class inducted and Henry was included in that first group. Henry would join the likes of Red Grange, George Halas, and his former Bulldogs teammate Jim Thorpe as immortals of the game. Henry's former teammate with Canton, Harry Robb, accepted the honor for him. "I consider it a great honor to have this privilege of receiving this plaque [bust] for Pete Henry from the Hall of Fame. My only regret is that Pete is not here to receive it in person. Pete, in my estimation, is the greatest lineman that ever played football."[14]

Henry was also selected to the NFL 1920s All-Decade Team and NFL 75th Anniversary All-Time Two-Way Team (1994). "Fats was the most happy and ever-smilingest guy you ever saw on a football field," recalled Lou Little. "And he would knock you the length of the football field without ever losing that smile. He was the best for my money."[15]

"He was a man I would love to have my children be like," said Russ Stein, college teammate and NFL tackle, 1922 and 1924–1926. "He loved life and he loved everybody."[16]

No. 12

Dan Fortmann
Guard

Full Name: Daniel John Fortmann
Nickname: N/A
b: April 11, 1916 (Pearl River, NY); d: May 24, 1995 (age 79; Los Angeles, CA)
High School: Pearl River (NY); College: Colgate
Height/Weight: 6–0, 210 pounds
Position: Guard
Teams/Years: 1936–1943 Chicago Bears
Pro Football Hall of Fame: Class of 1965
Retro-MVPs: No
All-Time Teams: S. Baugh (1949, 1957); B. Cahn (1943); D. Clark (1942); G. Dorais (1954); P. Driscoll (1956); M. Gantenbein (1966); R. Grange (1946–1947); M. Hein (1944, 1968, 1974); C. Lambeau (1955); T. Leemans (1953); J. McNally (1944); S. Owen (1942, 1952); J. Stydahar (1951)

At number 12 on the list is the first guard on the countdown—Dan Fortmann.

Dan Fortmann had brains from the beginning. He was a Phi Beta Kappa scholar at Colgate who graduated with the intention of going to medical school. After his collegiate career he was a ninth-round pick (78th overall) by the Chicago Bears in the NFL's first ever draft in 1936. Since scouting in the NFL's early days wasn't a science, a well-known story came out about how Fortmann got chosen by the Bears. During that ninth round, Bears coach George Halas looked at the remaining names on his scouting sheet. He noticed Fortmann from Colgate. "I like that name, I'll take him," yelled the Bears coach as he made the selection. Fortmann was now a Chicago Bear. He was just 19 years old.[1]

When Halas heard about Fortmann's plans to become a doctor, he didn't hesitate to help. He would do whatever he could to make sure Fortmann got his degree from the University of Chicago Medical School. That first year Fortmann made $1,700.

Dr. Dan Fortmann played 86 games over eight years with the Chicago Bears. Halas would always say that Fortmann was "one of the finest linemen I ever coached." In that same 1936 draft, Halas selected West Virginia tackle Joe Stydahar in the first round and placed him next to Fortmann. The two future Hall of Famers would play mostly side-by-side for the next several years, forming a dynamic duo.[2]

Fortmann was modestly built at just 6–0, 210 pounds, but nobody could move him off his guard spot. On offense, Fortmann was known to call signals at line and was a battering ram on blocks. Game film shows him to be very powerful at the point of attack, and difficult to get around or beat man-to-man; Fortmann always came off the ball first and delivered a hard blow. The Bears loved to run behind him. "He was quick. He weighed 210 pounds and he was quick. He could pick up the play in a hurry and he did a wonderful job [for us]," said George Musso, Bears teammate and Hall of Fame lineman.[3]

Dan Fortmann, guard, Chicago Bears, ca. 1935 (courtesy Colgate Athletics).

Fortmann was part of an offensive line that helped the Bears led the NFL in rushing four straight years from 1939 to 1942 and finish second another three times (1936, 1938, 1943). Making an immediate impact, he made First Team All-Pro in 1938 and 1939 and quickly became the best guard in pro football. "That Danny Fortmann of the Bears was really something," said Pete Tinsley, Green Bay Packers Pro Bowl guard, in 1962. "An afternoon of trying to stay with him physically and mentally is something to remember. Danny gets a lot of all-time mention. He'd get my vote any time."[4]

On defense, he was described as a "genius at diagnosing plays" and was a deadly tackler. On film he doesn't stay blocked for long and rushes the passer very well. "You'd look at Danny and wonder how he'd ever compete. Check old movies and you'll see Fortmann all over the field. I'll bet he made 40 percent of the tackles in some games. I honestly never remember him missing a tackle. He practiced 100 percent full speed. He never quit in practice, or when the score was heavy in our favor," said Sid Luckman, Bears teammate.[5]

Showing off Fortmann's smarts, Halas put a lot on his plate. Heading into games he would have to maneuver into 20 different alignments or checks. While on defense from his guard—and sometimes linebacker position—he would make the defensive checks. For example, against the Green Bay Packers he had to know and direct 15 separate defensive calls for Don Hutson alone. On defense, Fortmann had a chance to play linebacker. "The 6–2–2–1 defense was standard and almost without exception, the center and fullback became the linebackers on defense," said Aldo Forte, Bears Pro Bowl lineman. "Hunk Anderson was the coach, and it was his scheme. In addition to the center, Danny Fortmann dropped back from his guard position to be a third linebacker. He was maybe the best linebacker of his day."[6]

Fortmann loved the game and playing both ways made it extra special. In an interview with *Pro! NFL Magazine* in 1973 he said: "The game was more fun because we played both ways. I mean, taking nothing away from the specialist of today, how can you have any fun playing offensive tackle? At least when we go through making our precise blocks, we got to move over the other side and tackle somebody!"[7]

After acquiring Sid Luckman in 1939, the Bears turned their attention on offense full-time to the T-formation. In 1940, the T became a hit as the Bears won the Western Division title for the first time since 1937. They went on to play the Washington Redskins for the NFL championship in a game that ended with the Bears winning 73–0. On the train ride home a Pullman passenger noticed with interest the rainbow decorating Fortmann's left eye. "My, my," said the passenger, "that's a terrible black eye you have there." "Yes," Fortmann agreed. "But it will disappear in a day or two. Think of the Redskins, that 73–0 score is in the record books for all-time." Fortmann always got enjoyment from playing in that historic game. "I believe I got more satisfaction out of that one game than any other I played," said Fortmann.[8]

"Fortmann is super-fast, shrewd enough to tip off his quarterback on opponents' line weakness, powerful enough to spearhead ground attacks and strong enough to discourage the enemy from trying the left side of the Bear line," wrote the *New York Daily News* in 1940 after naming Fortmann First Team All-Pro.[9]

By this time Dan Fortmann was the best guard in the NFL. Some might say he was the best player, regardless of position, in the NFL, challenging the likes of Sammy Baugh, Sid Luckman and Don Hutson. "In all the years I played him I never got a good block on him. Danny was one of the quickest and most versatile men I ever played against. He was not like some other linemen, big and slow. You could get a good shot at them, but not with Danny. He was never in one place long enough to lay a real hard block on him. He was also good at fading back for a pass. I really think he could have been a great defensive back. He was a truly great guy," said Charles "Buckets" Goldenberg, Packers All-Pro guard, 1933–1945.[10]

In 1941, he almost proved it. Fortmann played his best ball as a pro in 1941. On offense he played his usually tough minded, hard-nosed style of football. With the help of center Bulldog Turner, tackles Lee Artoe and Joe Stydahar were on the line as he helped lead the Bears to number one in the NFL in rushing and total offense. On defense he dominated from his defensive line position as he was the best lineman in the league at stopping the run. He also dropped back into coverage with three interceptions, second on the team behind George McAfee's six.

Dan was named consensus First Team All-Pro by the NFL, Associated Press, United Press, *New York Daily News*, *Collyer's Eye* and *Chicago Herald-American*.

"Fortmann played guard at 208 pounds, but he could move much larger men because of his quickness and skill," said George Halas in 1975.[11]

When it came time to vote for the league's MVP, the Joe F. Carr Trophy, Fortmann finished runner-up behind Packers end Don Hutson, who had a monster year, and ahead of quarterbacks Sid Luckman, Irv Comp (Packers) and Sammy Baugh (Redskins). The voting committee consisted of nine sportswriters including Grantland Rice, Arthur Daley (*New York Times*), Irv Kupcinet (*Chicago Times*), Ray Pagel (*Green Bay Press-Gazette*), Dale Stafford (*Detroit Free-Press*), Franklin Lewis (*Cleveland Press*), Harry Keck (*Pittsburgh Sun-Telegraph*), Ross Kaufman (*Philadelphia Bulletin*) and William Dismer (*Washington Star*). Almost winning league MVP was one of the highlights of Fortmann's career. He was at the top of his profession, all the while attending medical school. There was nothing he couldn't accomplish.

In 1942, Fortmann made First Team All-Pro again as the Bears just steamrolled the rest of the NFL, going undefeated at 11–0. They were first in points scored (376) and points allowed (84). Although the perfect season was ruined by the Washington Redskins in the championship game, Fortmann made consensus First Team All-Pro. "How about that guard, Danny Fortmann. I can't think of a better guard in history," said Jimmy Conzelman, Hall of Fame coach, in 1942. "He's big, he's fast, he's strong—and what's more he's smart."[12]

That season the future doctor did something in an NFL game for the first and only time in his career. He scored a touchdown. In the final regular season game against the crosstown Cardinals, Fortmann scooped up a fumble and rumbled 69 yards for a score to help the Bears win 21–7. "As I remember it, there were about four inches of snow on the field that afternoon and I picked up a fumble and ran about 50 yards for the touchdown," recalled Fortmann. "A dentist in Chicago wrote me that he had taken a movie of that play and we got together one day and he gave me the film. I'll show that to my youngster when he grows and prove to him that his dad scored a touchdown!"[13]

Heading into his eighth season with the Bears in 1943, Fortmann was now making roughly $6,000, a far cry from the $1,700 of his rookie year. In what would be his last NFL campaign, Fortmann continued to play at an elite level, making First Team All-Pro for the sixth straight year. "Fortmann is the fastest-thinking lineman in football," said Bears line coach Hunk Anderson to the *Detroit Free Press* in 1943. This time the Bears finished the season as champs by defeating the Redskins, 41–21, giving Fortmann his third NFL championship in eight seasons.[14]

In his career Fortmann made three Pro Bowls while being selected First Team All-Pro six times by the NFL (1938–1943), five times by the United Press, and four times by the Associated Press (1940–1943), as well as a whopping seven times by the *New York Daily News* (1937–1943). "Danny Fortmann, the Chicago Bears guard, was like a cat. He had all the moves in the world," recalled Alex Wojciechowicz, Eagles Hall of Fame center.[15]

After the 1943 season, he entered the Navy. When he returned after World War

II ended, it was time to turn to medicine. He had finished his playing days at just 27 years old. After retiring from the Bears, Fortmann practiced medicine as a surgeon at Saint Joseph Medical Center in Burbank, California, from 1948 until his retirement in 1984. He was chief of staff in 1965. During this time, he also served as the team doctor for the Los Angeles Rams.

He was selected to the NFL 1930s All-Decade Team and was named runner-up at guard for the NFL 50th Anniversary team, behind Jerry Kramer (Packers). He was elected to the Pro Football Hall of Fame in 1965—the Hall's third class. Fortmann was also named to the NFL 75th Anniversary Two-Way Team (1994) and in 2019 achieved the greatest honor by being named to the NFL 100th Anniversary All-Time Team.

Dan Fortmann died on May 24, 1995, at the age of 79.

"I wanted to play pro football but I was also determined to go to medical school. Except for the fact that the summer quarter overlapped two weeks into the Bears' summer training period, I could substitute the summer quarter for the fall quarter at med school and proceed on a normal course toward my medical degree," recalled Dan Fortmann. "But George allowed me to miss two weeks of summer practice each year while I finished up my school. Of course, I practiced on weekends. But without George's understanding and cooperation, I could never have prepared for my future."[16]

No. 13

Clarke Hinkle

Fullback

Full Name: William Clarke Hinkle
Nickname: N/A
b; April 10, 1909 (Toronto, OH); d: November 9, 1988 (age 79; Steubenville, OH)
High School: Toronto (OH); College: Bucknell
Height/Weight: 5–11, 202 pounds
Position: Fullback
Teams/Years: 1932–1941 Green Bay Packers
Pro Football Hall of Fame: Class of 1964
Retro-MVPs: No
All-Time Teams: S. Baugh (1999); B. Bell (1940); B. Cahn (1943); M. Gantenbein (1966);
  A. Herber (1946); C. Lambeau (1946, 1948, 1955); V. Lewellen (1946); J. McNally (1937,
  1963); M. Michalske (1982); B. Nagurski (1944); C. Storck (1939); J. Stydahar (1951, 1952)

One of the fiercest player rivalries between players during the two-way era was Bronko Nagurski vs. Clarke Hinkle. These two powerhouse fullbacks took turns knocking each other out. The debate was always, who's the best fullback in the NFL? On our list Bronko appears slightly higher at number six, but Hinkle wasn't too far behind.

William Hinkle was born in Southern Ohio in 1909 and went by his middle name of Clarke. The son of a steel mill worker, Hinkle was raised to do everything with a purpose, and do it well. Young Clarke took that attitude to the football field. "My first experience with playing football was as kid in Boomtown in Toronto, Ohio, on the banks of the Ohio River, when I was about seven years old," recalled Clarke Hinkle. "When I was about seven I played with my brothers. They liked sports, especially football, and I naturally followed them. My mother was very supportive of we boys playing athletics. In those days, we used to play on a back lot near our house. We had to learn all parts of the game: running, passing, kicking, tackling. So we were [playing] pick-ups and we just kind of taught ourselves how to do it. When I went to high school, I could kick a football pretty good and I just kept after it from then on. I wanted to be a back and a kicker, so I really worked at both."[1]

Not as huge as Bronko, but equally as powerful and tough was the 5-11, 202-pound Hinkle, who played in 113 games over 10 years with the Green Bay Packers. In the years before the NFL Draft, Hinkle was free to sign with any team. After he played his final game for tiny Bucknell against Fordham on November 21, 1921, he stayed in New York to watch the New York Giants face off against the small-town Green Bay Packers. Giants owner Tim Mara was interested in signing Hinkle, who was very much interested in playing pro football. But this proved to be a mistake as the Packers defeated the Giants 14–10. Hinkle recalled: "One of the Maras who owned the Giants invited me to stay over in New York after my last college game, to see the Giants play the Packers. That game really convinced me to go to Green Bay. They had a huge team and they looked awesome. They had a guy playing tackle named Cal Hubbard who stood six-foot-four or six-five and weighed about 265 pounds. As I watched the game, I thought to myself, 'By God, I believe I would rather be on his side than play against him.'"[2]

Clarke Hinkle, fullback, Green Bay Packers, ca. 1932–1933 (courtesy Green Bay Packers).

Shortly after that game Packers coach Curly Lambeau talked to Hinkle about joining Green Bay—if the price was right. Little did the Hall of Fame coach know that he could've had Hinkle for nothing. Shortly after that visit Hinkle played in the East-West Shrine game. After the game he had visitor. "Curly came to my hotel room to talk to me about playing for the Packers," recalled Hinkle. "I didn't hesitate, I remembered that game in New York and Lambeau offered me $125 a game. The Giants offer was only about $85 a game but I believe I would have played for almost nothing."[3]

During his rookie year of 1932, Hinkle fit in well with the three-time defending champions. He was as good as anybody on the Packers roster. Although they didn't win the championship that season, Hinkle was satisfied with his choice at playing pro football. "One hundred and twenty-five dollars a game and it was easy, just for playing football, which was something I loved to do," said Hinkle.[4]

Hinkle ran as hard as any fullback ever had. He was productive in the running game and was probably a better defensive player, even slightly better than Nagurski was on that side of the ball. "The greatest all-around fullback to ever play in the National Football League was Clarke Hinkle. Hinkle runs the middle, runs wide, and blocks and tackles viciously. He punts and place-kicks with the best. He can do a good job as a pass receiver. And in defense against aerial attack, Hinkle has no superior in professional football," said Curly Lambeau, Packers Hall of Fame coach.[5]

Coming from a small school out of college, Hinkle played with a chip on his shoulder, trying to prove that he belonged. His opponents knew that he had the goods to play pro football, especially the rival Chicago Bears. "Hinkle was one of the three greatest players I ever faced in all my years in the league. His style of running made him very difficult to bring down and when you did get him you knew it," said Dan Fortmann, Bears Hall of Fame guard.[6]

Film shows that Hinkle loved to punish defenders when carrying the ball. He always wanted to be the first one to make impact. If he was mad and upset you would know it, because that is how he ran. "I'd rather run into tacklers than use a little finesse, you know, so I lost a lot of yards that way," once said Hinkle. "But I felt I wanted to be tougher than the next guy. If they were going to tackle me, they were going to pay for it."[7]

Playing within Lambeau's Notre Dame box formation, Hinkle could block with the best of them, a skill he never took for granted. "Usually I wasn't faking or carrying the ball, I was the lead blocker for the ball carrier on the Notre Dame shift. One blocker down. It might give the ball carrier a chance to break loose," recalled Hinkle. "I put out 1,000 percent [into] blocking, that I did the other phases of my game. My idea was to not brush-block him or shadow-block him, but stop him and put him out of the play."[8]

Hinkle took pride in being a complete player. On film he blocked savagely, and his protection of the passer was an important part of the Packers aerial success. But he could run the ball with the best of fullbacks. "When he runs past you, you can feel the suction," said Baby Ray, Packers All-Pro tackle.[9]

Hinkle's clashes with Bronko Nagurski were legendary although Hinkle gave up about 25 pounds. "I learned a lot from watching Nagurski play," recalled Hinkle. "He taught me how to use my shoulders. He never played dirty, but if you had to play against Nagurski you had to use the same tactics he did." "They said I was hard to tackle, but here's a guy who didn't have too much trouble," said Bronko Nagurski.[10]

By 1936, Hinkle was at the top of his game. That season he made First Team All-Pro by the NFL and United Press. He led the Packers in rushing and rushing touchdowns with 476 yards and five scores, all while helping lead the Packers to the Western Division title. In the NFL championship game against the Boston Redskins, he led a defense that slowed down the league's best running back, Cliff Battles, to just eight yards rushing, as the Packers won the game 21–6. He led the Packers that day in rushing with 59 yards on 16 carries. Hinkle was now an NFL champion.

He would go on to win another NFL championship in 1939. Playing with the likes of Don Hutson, Arnie Herber, Cecil Isbell, Buckets Goldenberg and Baby Ray, Hinkle was part of Green Bay teams that won 67 percent of their games (80–35–4). "He was one of the greatest competitors I ever saw. He shut out everything else. And he was tough. He got such a kick out of hitting people, and getting hit, too," said George Sauer, Sr., Packers back and teammate.[11]

As good a runner and blocker as he was on offense, Hinkle might've been even better on the defensive side of the ball. He was great at backing up the line from his (linebacker) position while being the best tackler on the team. He was a vicious hitter that used all of his body to make the tackle. "No one in the whole league bruised me more than did Hinkle," said John Sisk, Bears back. "After we had played the Packers, I'd be black and blue down to my toenails. All I'd want is peace and quiet. Hinkle had a lot of leg action. I broke my shoulder twice tackling Mister Hinkle!"[12]

Green Bay Packers opponents regularly praised Hinkle's toughness. "When he hit you," said Ken Strong, Giants Hall of Fame back, "you knew you were hit. Bells rang and you felt it all the way down to your toes." "Clarke Hinkle was a great football player," recalled Ray Flaherty, Redskins Hall of Fame coach. "Not only a great offensive player, he was a great defensive football player. He backed up the line for Green Bay. He could, from that linebacking position he could cover a wingback as good as anybody I've seen."[13]

Hinkle was the most competitive player on the Packers during his time with the team. He didn't take losing well. "He didn't know how to lose," said Cecil Isbell about Hinkle. "He'd get so fired up before a game he'd be glassy-eyed. If we lost, he wept."[14]

After that championship season in '36, Hinkle played maybe his best season in 1937. He rushed for a career-high 552 yards, second in the NFL, and led the league with five rushing touchdowns and seven total touchdowns, tying teammate Don Hutson. He was named consensus First Team All-Pro by NFL, I.N.S., UPI, *Collyer's Eye*, and *New York Daily News*.

Usually not a threat as a passer in Lambeau's offense—he threw no touchdown passes and five interceptions—but his kicking skills were used often by Lambeau. Over his career he had a punting average of 40.8 yards per punt and was a very productive field goal kicker, leading the NFL in field goals made in 1940 and 1941 and in points in 1938 with 58 points. He finished his career with 379 points. "I always kicked at least twelve yards back from the line of scrimmage. I kicked from way back there because I always took three steps to get power. Everything I did, I had to do with force. That's just the way I was built," said Hinkle.[15]

In the end, Hinkle finished his career with 1,171 carries for 3,860 yards and 35 TDs and was the NFL's all-time leading rusher at the time of his retirement. He was a capable receiver with 49 catches for 537 yards and nine TDs. Hinkle retired after the 1941 season, leaving a lasting impression on everybody he played. "Clarke Hinkle was near the end of the line when I first played him," recalled Bulldog Turner, Bears Hall of Fame center. "But he was still the hardest runner I ever tried to tackle. He didn't bend over. He run just about straight up. And when you hit him it would just pop every joint all the way down to your toes."[16]

After 10 NFL seasons and 113 games Hinkle called it quits. The two-way star loved his time playing pro football. "When I give a speech on occasion I usually tell 'em that I played 20 years of pro football—10 years on offense and 10 years on defense," said Hinkle in 1964. Hinkle was elected to the second class of the Pro Football Hall of Fame in 1964, was selected to the NFL 1930s All-Decade Team and added to the Packers Hall of Fame in 1972. In 1997, the Packers named one of their two practice fields after Hinkle—Clarke Hinkle Field sits next to Ray Nitschke Field.[17]

The tough fullback wore his emotions on his sleeves, appreciating his time playing the game he loved. "We were in the same boat. They were a great bunch of guys. There wasn't any dirty playing. We were all out there making a living. We played hard. It was our livelihood and we were honest. We trained loyally. You had to get in shape for sixty minutes," said Clarke Hinkle in a 1983 interview.[18]

Nagurski vs. Hinkle

Historians have a debate about who was the best fullback during the two-way era. Nagurski vs. Hinkle turned out to be closer than expected. Let's take a closer look. Both players were the standard for their position. Both players made their respective teams' running game go, although the Bears with Nagurski were clearly better in the running game. During these years the Bears consistently ran the ball more than the Packers, who in turn threw the ball more. "Clarke Hinkle was the greatest all-around player of all-time," said Charles "Buckets" Goldenberg, Packers All-Pro guard. "He didn't hit as hard straight on as Nagurski and he didn't have Bronk's size. But he could do so many things well."[19]

The two fierce competitors always had a great respect for each other, becoming close friends later on in life. Hinkle always knew he was the toughest opponent he ever played against. "My greatest thrill in football was the day Bronko Nagurski announced his retirement," said Clarke Hinkle in 1990 when Nagurski passed away. "There's no question he was the most bruising fullback football has ever seen. I know because I've still got the bruises."[20]

In 1986, Hinkle told the *Green Bay Press-Gazette* his five greatest players of his era. He listed in order Bronko Nagurski, Dutch Clark, Don Hutson, Cliff Battles, and George McAfee.[21]

Clarke Hinkle died on November 9, 1988, at the age of 79. Along with Bronko Nagurski, nobody played the fullback position better during the two-way era than Clarke Hinkle. "Hinkle was one of the greatest fullbacks I've ever seen," said Paddy Driscoll.[22]

No. 14

Roy "Link" Lyman
Tackle

Full Name: William Roy Lyman
Nickname: "Link"
b: November 30, 1898 (Table Rock, NE); d: December 28, 1972 (age 74; Barstow, CA)
High School: McDonald Rural (KS); College: Nebraska
Height/Weight: 6–2, 233 pounds
Position: Tackle
Teams/Years: 1922–1923, 1925 Canton Bulldogs; 1924 Cleveland Bulldogs; 1925 Frankford Yellow Jackets; 1926–1928, 1930–1931, 1933–1934 Chicago Bears
Pro Football Hall of Fame: Class of 1964
Retro-MVPs: 1924
All-Time Teams: B. Bell (1940); B. Cahn (1943); G. Halas (1940–1941); B. Hewitt (1937, 1940); C. Hinkle (1940); Cal Hubbard (1937); C. Lambeau (1955); V. Lewellen (1936); J. McMillian (1939); S. Owen (1942, 1952, 1955)

    The third tackle and number 14 on our list is Link Lyman.

    Lyman played 11 years and 133 games with four different franchises—Canton, Cleveland, Frankford and three stints with the Chicago Bears (1926–1928, 1930–1931, 1933–1934). Very agile for his size at 6-2, 233 pounds, Lyman is often given credit for pioneering more sophisticated defensive play on the line by shifting and sliding, forcing opponents to adjust to his tactics with new blocking strategies. A dominant force on defense, and almost unblockable at times, Lyman changed the game.

    William Roy Lyman was born in Table Rock, Nebraska, in 1898. He didn't play football in high school because there were only eight boys in the whole school. His lack of experience didn't hinder Lyman when he tried out for the football team at the University of Nebraska. Tipping the scales at over 230 pounds, Lyman loved to hit. He used his size to his advantage often in his career in Lincoln and earned numerous honors.

    After graduating from college, Lyman was recruited to play pro ball with the Canton Bulldogs coached by former Cornhuskers All-American Guy Chamberlin (#5). "After my senior year I was contacted by Guy Chamberlin, who was an All-American at Nebraska a few years before me and he wanted to know if I wanted to play pro football. He was about to take charge of the Canton Bulldogs of the NFL and he offered me a spot on the team, so I took it. I heard a lot about Chamberlin

Link Lyman, tackle, Canton Bulldogs, ca. 1922 (courtesy NFL Films Research Library).

while at Nebraska, he was a hero there so I thought playing for him would be great," recalled Link Lyman.[1]

Lyman was an impact player from the start. Bulldog opponents could see that Lyman was a special player. "Lyman was the first lineman I ever saw who moved from his assigned defensive position before the ball was snapped. It was difficult to play against him because he would vary his moves and no matter how you reacted, you could be wrong," said Steve Owen, NFL lineman and Giants Hall of Fame coach. "I often quizzed Link about his invention. He said he had struck on it almost unconsciously, as an instinctive move to fool a blocker. His style and innovations impressed me so much that a seed of an idea was planted in my mind. This finally led to my own device, the A-formation attack which the Giants used to win the world title in 1938."[2]

Lyman performed at a high level for over a decade with plenty of battles with the Packers' Cal Hubbard, ranked number nine, our highest ranked tackle. "[Link] Lyman was a linebacker and was the best all-around lineman I ever played against," said Cal Hubbard in 1976. Lyman routinely showed quick footwork for a man his size, by stepping back and forth from one side to the other after members of the offensive line had set themselves and couldn't move. Lyman then would "shot the gap" and arrive in the backfield as the back took the handoff.[3]

Lyman always felt that he had to be in motion to get an explosive start, making the most of his bulk. This made it tough to block him and made the opposing line employ new strategies to block him, such as cross-blocking, trapping and using assignment-switching signals. Lyman also made many of his teammates better, whether with Canton or the Chicago Bears. "The greatest football player, college or pro, I ever saw was Link Lyman. If it hadn't been for Lyman, nobody ever would have heard of poor Bill Hewitt at all. He taught me more about football than I ever learned in my life before," said Bill Hewitt, Bears Hall of Fame end.[4]

The next two seasons saw Lyman and the Bulldogs dominate the NFL. Like in previous chapters with Chamberlin and Pete Henry (#11), no team in the NFL defeated the Bulldogs in 1922–1923. Lyman at one tackle and Henry at the other made it hard for any team to either run the ball or stop the run when playing the Bulldogs.

Just like with Pete Henry, newspapers constantly pointed out the outstanding play of Lyman when recapping the games. On November 18, 1923, Lyman scored his first ever NFL touchdown. You might think it would be on defense, but you would be wrong. Lyman caught a 40-yard scoring pass from Lou Smyth against Jim Thorpe's Oorang Indians in a 41–0 victory.

Retro-MVP: 1924 Season

As we mentioned before, the Canton Bulldogs struggled with money to finance the team after winning the NFL title in 1922–1923, so the club was sold to Cleveland owner Sam Deutsch. Lyman followed the squad there and produced his best year as a pro. Anchoring the line, this time without Pete Henry at the other tackle, Lyman completely dominated his opponents. His tackling was the best in the league. "I call them right and left 'busters' because that describes their work better than does the word tackle. Actually, tackling is about the last thing they do. It's much more important that they strip the ball carrier of his interference and never trade themselves for less than two men on the opposition," said Link Lyman. "After all, blocking is nothing more than getting position on the other fellow. Sort of a war of movement."[5]

The Bulldogs outscored their opponents 229–60, leading the NFL in scoring. Individually Lyman had a spectacular season. He made First Team All-Pro by *Collyer's Eye* while scoring four touchdowns! He had two on fumble recoveries, one on a blocked punt return, and one on a 50-yard touchdown catch from Hoge Workman against the Dayton Triangles on November 2 to help the Bulldogs win 35–0.

Lyman played the best on both offense and defense for the 1924 season and was named that year's Retro-MVP. After three seasons Lyman was the best player in the

NFL. "I love it. You can't play the game, as a matter of fact, if you don't love it. Of course, the cash is a consideration too. But I don't know any more pleasurable way of making money," said Lyman about playing pro football.[6]

Just like the previous year, Cleveland had money problems that led them to sell the team back to Canton. But this time Lyman and a few former Bulldog players were the ones buying the team, as Lyman, Pete Henry, Rudy Comstock and Ben Jones became NFL owners. But Canton in 1925 wasn't a very good time for Lyman as an owner or a player. "We had two beautiful Sundays and made enough to pay all the rest of the players for the season," recalled Lyman in 1964. "But every other Sunday we played in the rain and mud, and the five of us ended up playing for nothing. We were so disgusted at our misfortune that we gave the franchise back to the league for nothing." That fall the Bulldogs went 4–4 to finish in 11th place in the 20-team NFL.[7]

After the Bulldogs 1925 season ended, Lyman hooked up with Guy Chamberlin's Frankford Yellow Jackets to play a few games against Red Grange and the Chicago Bears during the famous barnstorming tour. This led him to become a member of the Chicago Bears (1926–1928, 1930–1931, 1933–1934) where he would continue his fine play on both sides of the line. Consistently earning First or Second Team All-Pro honors for the next several years, Lyman was highly thought of by his opponents. Once All-Pro quarterback Benny Friedman was asked to name the three greatest lineman he saw in his time. "They were Link Lyman, Mike Michalske and Cal Hubbard," replied Friedman. "They were all great, but Link Lyman was the toughest man who ever set foot on a football field."[8]

Even when he was older, Lyman could dominate at the line of scrimmage. In 1933, at the age of 35, he made an impression on hot-shot rookie Bears end Bill Hewitt. "I've seen 'Link' bust thru, no slicing, but straight ahead and take that end and wingback coming to block him with just two motions. He'd sweep with one elbow and down would go the end. He'd wave the other, and boom! The back would be stretched. And there'd be Lyman, standing up, ready for the ball carrier."[9]

In 1933, he helped the Bears reach the first ever NFL championship game against the New York Giants by continuing to make big plays, especially on defense. "Link Lyman, the old bald eagle of the Bears, now retired from pro football, was a master at the art of tackling the ball," said Harry Newman, Giants All-Pro quarterback in 1936. "Many a ball carrier found himself not only stopped by Lyman but divested of the ball as well." Lyman would get another NFL title when the Bears defeated the Giants 23–21 in that '33 title tilt.[10]

After the 1934 season, Lyman called it quits. His last game as an NFL player was the 1934 NFL championship game, the famous "Sneakers Game." Despite the presence of Turk Edwards of the Redskins and George Christensen of the Lions at tackle, Lyman at 36 years old was named First Team All-Pro by United Press, *Green Bay Press-Gazette* and *Collyer's Eye*.

"Link Lyman, ranked head and shoulders above any other tackle in Joe Carr's 'cash and carry' gridiron wheel.... Lyman's comeback was most remarkable and some coaches claim Link's work on this placed him on a higher plane than Cal Hubbard, former Packers lineman, who was considered the peer of all tackles in the land. It was next to impossible to take Lyman out of a play and he would cut holes a mile wide for the Bears backs," wrote G.W. Calhoun of the *Green Bay Press-Gazette* when naming Lyman First Team All-Pro in 1934.[11]

Speaking to Francis Powers of the *Chicago Daily News* after the 1934 season, Red Grange said that Lyman "was the best lineman. I don't believe there ever was a smarter player than Lyman. At 36 he still is the best tackle I can mention." After over a decade of pro football, his passion for the sport was still evident. "I think I had as fine a career as anybody could want in pro ball," recalled Lyman in 1964. In the end Lyman was a member of four NFL championship teams: Canton (1922–1923), Cleveland (1924) and Bears (1933). He never played for a losing team in 11 NFL seasons.[12]

Somehow overlooked for the NFL 1920s All-Decade Team—he should've been selected over tackle Steve Owen—Lyman was not overlooked when the Pro Football Hall of Fame opened. He was elected to the Hall in 1964 in just the second class—when he was called "the cleverest tackle of his time on defense."[13]

Lyman went into coaching after his playing career ended and spent seven years at his alma mater as line coach. Later in life he was asked often about his opinion of the current game as the popularity of the NFL grew. "Everybody played 60 minutes back in my day," said Link Lyman. "All this talk about the old teams not being able to keep up with the present day boys is a lot of malarky. The coaches say everybody is a lot better now, but we had boys who weighed 220 and 230 and could run 100 yards in 10 seconds. And they were not only fast but quick. I used to run four or five miles every night in the summer just to get in condition. And I worked with cattle and in the harvest fields. I was bound to be in better shape than some guy riding a block in his dad's car to get a malted milk."[14]

Link Lyman died of complications from an auto accident on December 28, 1972, at the age of 74.

No. 15

Bill Hewitt

End

Full Name: William Ernest Hewitt
Nickname: "Offside Kid"
b: October 8, 1909 (Bay City, MI); d: January 14, 1947 (age 37; Sellersville, PA)
High School: Central Bay City (MI); College: Michigan
Height/Weight: 5–9; 190 pounds
Position: End
Teams/Years: 1932–1936 Chicago Bears; 1937–1939 Philadelphia Eagles; 1943 Philadelphia/Pittsburgh Steagles
Pro Football Hall of Fame: Class of 1971
Retro-MVPs: No
All-Time Teams: S. Baugh (1999); B. Bell (1940); B. Cahn (1943); D. Clark (1942); P. Clark (1940, 1947); G. Corbett (1938); M. Gantenbein (1966); R. Grange (1946–1947, 1955); G. Halas (1940–1941); M. Hein (1944, 1968, 1974); C. Hinkle (1942); C. Hubbard (1937, 1947, 1966); D. Hutson (1948); R. Lumpkin (1937); B. Nagurski (1939); S. Owen (1942); D. Slater (1949); J. Stydahar (1951)

Nicknamed the "Offside Kid" for his explosive first step on defense, the 5–9, 190-pound Bill Hewitt might've been the best defensive end during the two-way era. He never stopped moving, especially on defense. With a motor that didn't stop, he often has been compared to former Giants linebacker Lawrence Taylor. Hewitt developed the technique of playing off ball a few yards and sprinting to the line of scrimmage to time the snap of the ball. His style was aided by his powerful upper body, barrel chest, and muscular arms to dish out punishment. "Bill Hewitt, of the Chicago Bears, was as tough on defense as he was agile on offense," said Mel Hein, Giants Hall of Fame center.[1]

Hewitt played eight seasons with the Bears and Philadelphia Eagles from 1932 to 1939. Then after a three-year hiatus during World War II, he returned for his ninth season to play for the merged Pittsburgh Steelers-Philadelphia Eagles team called the Steagles, 101 games in all. "Hewitt was big enough and strong enough to hold his own physically with anyone. He had the best ear on offense and the quickest eye on defense I ever have seen. He always outcharged his opponent … the criticism that Hewitt usually was offside was unfair. He was so fast off the mark, that it appeared as if he were," said Potsy Clark, former coach.[2]

Bill Hewitt was born in 1909 in Bay City, Michigan, near Lake Huron. The son of a mason contractor, toughness was in his blood, but size wasn't. Hewitt didn't play football until his senior year in high school at Central High. Since he weighed just 100 pounds at 14 years old, Hewitt was reluctant to put his body at risk. When he turned 17, he was up to 150 pounds. "I liked football, but at that time basketball was my game. I didn't play football until the fall of 1926. And when I did make the Bay City high school team at left end in my senior year, I was no whirlwind," said Bill Hewitt to the *Chicago Tribune* in 1933.[3]

Hewitt's high school coach was Garlan "Chief" Nevitt, who was a former grid star at Haskell Institute School. Hewitt slowly picked up the game, learning from Nevitt.

Bill Hewitt, end, Chicago Bears, ca. 1931 (courtesy University of Michigan Athletics).

His most common trademark was his all-out effort, never taking a play off. "Hewitt was one of the greatest boys I ever coached," recalled Coach Nevitt. "Although Bill was handicapped in size and lacked experience, his aggressive, untiring play, and finally his sheer power and will to succeed made him one of the finest competitors I have seen. Bill loved to win and he delivered when the going was toughest."[4]

After graduating from high school, Hewitt took a year off from school, working odd jobs around his hometown. Soon, Hewitt got the itch to play football again. He went down south to attend the University of Michigan. "By this time I was anxious to play football again and I also knew that a college education wouldn't hurt my chances of success," recalled Hewitt. "The one year that had elapsed since graduation from high school proved to me that unless I did something about it, I might wind up wrestling with the well-known wolf on my doorstep for the remainder of my life. The reasons I started for Ann Arbor with a lot of hope and few dollars was the encouragement my father gave me. He urged that I go and pointed out that if I had to come home, I wouldn't be any worse off than I was right then."[5]

At Michigan, Hewitt quickly became a star at left end. He continued his all-out effort on both sides of the ball. He played three years of varsity ball for Harry Kipke. Over those three seasons the Wolverines went a combined 21–4–3, winning back-to-back Big Ten championships in 1930–1931. Teaming with quarterback Harry Newman, Hewitt earned All-American honors. His play attracted the attention of NFL teams and coaches, especially one from the Windy City.

After his stellar career at Michigan, Hewitt signed with the Chicago Bears, joining a loaded squad with the likes of All-Pros Bronko Nagurski, Red Grange, George Trafton, Joe Kopcha and Luke Johnsos. Despite his size at just 5-9 and 190 pounds, Hewitt made an immediate impact for the Bears in his rookie year of 1932, becoming a starter at end.

Hewitt learned the pro game from Halas who tried to rein in his prized pupil. He had to play within the defensive scheme. "I had a tendency to play what we call a floating end. This is all right if you can sift through the interference and nail the runner and of course, they'll never get around you if you go wide. But in professional football if an end floats all the time he will find himself on his back most of the afternoon," said Bill Hewitt in 1933.[6]

Combining his God-given talent with Halas' coaching, Hewitt became a force on both sides of the ball. Teams would try new ways to block the disruptive Hewitt. "He was so fast getting into the backfield, that we always thought he was offsides," said Wellington Mara, Giants owner in 1971. "[Coach] Steve Owen finally put Ken Strong out as a flanker and had him block back on Hewitt, which was something very new in those days."[7]

Hewitt never seemed to stop working at his craft, whether in practice or during the game. His teammates loved him for that. "Never saw a guy play as hard as that guy," said Red Grange in 1937. "After every game he's covered with bruises from head to foot, but they never get him hurt enough to leave the game."[8]

Hewitt's motor never stopped on either side of the ball. "He was a good pass receiver and fast on his feet," said George Halas in 1947. "Other teams might knock Bill down, but he would get up and wind up making the tackle 20 yards down the field. He had a flaming spirit." Once Halas explained how Hewitt played his position: "Hewitt is not offside any more than anybody else. He follows three plans of action. First, he nearly always lines up at least one yard behind the line of scrimmage. He is in motion forward, but not across the line of scrimmage until the ball is snapped. He goes out three or four yards wider than the average end and runs toward center. This sometimes makes it look as if he is offside. Bill watches the center's hands closely and as he sees fingers clutch the ball he moves forward. Thus he actually goes at the same time as the ball. No other end in football makes such a specialty of his play as does Hewitt. That's why he's the best there is."[9]

That rookie season Hewitt helped the Bears reach the top of the standings. He played in the famous "Indoor Game" against the Portsmouth Spartans that decided the NFL championship. Playing his usually carefree style, the Bears defeated the Spartans, 9–0, to claim the title.

Hewitt followed up his rookie year with an even better campaign in 1933. That season he threw three touchdown passes on end-around plays specially designed for him. They would be the only touchdown passes of his career. Also that season, with passing legal from anywhere behind the line of scrimmage, the Bears fully developed a play where the fullback—usually Bronko Nagurski—would charge the line, stop short and throw "pop pass" to an end who would slant in the middle of the field to catch the pass. Sometimes the end, especially Hewitt, would then lateral to the other end who trailed the play. This play was used by Hewitt—who lateraled to Bill Karr—for the winning score in the first NFL championship game in 1933 to help the Bears defeat the Giants, 23–21. Hewitt had won back-to-back NFL championships in his first two pro seasons.

In 1933, Hewitt was a Consensus First Team All-Pro by the NFL, UPI, *Green Bay Press-Gazette*, *Chicago Daily News* and *Collyer's Eye*. "Bill Hewitt of the Chicago Bears, hawk-like end, was named as the greatest player in the league by coaches. His inspired play brought the Bears from behind to win several of their games in the last few minutes of play. He has no superior in football in smashing down interference and breaking up the opposition's attack before it gets to the line of scrimmage," wrote George Kirksey of the United Press in naming Hewitt First Team All-Pro. He would repeat this feat in 1934 as the Bears went undefeated in the regular season, before losing in the championship game in the famous "Sneakers Game" against the Giants.[10]

Halas always held Hewitt in high esteem. In 1941, Papa Bear named Hewitt one of two ends on his Chicago Bears All-Time Team. "Hewitt was absolutely fearless. He was a happy-go-lucky guy until he stepped onto the field—and then he was a terror on offense and defense. He asked no quarter nor gave any," said Halas.[11]

Hewitt enjoyed his time being coached by Halas. "The college player is told what to do. He accepts the decision of the coach, because he doesn't know enough to question it. George Halas, in coaching our team, is always willing to listen to what we players have to say. If we tell him that such and such a play can best be accomplished in this fashion, well, we try it and see. That's impossible in college," said Hewitt in 1933.[12]

The Offside Kid was also known to be an excellent player on special teams, racing down on kickoffs and punts. He also was one of the best at blocking kicks and punts. A perfect example of his special teams play came in a game against the Packers on September 24, 1933. The Bears, trailing 7–0 late in the fourth quarter, had their fortune change when Hewitt blocked a field goal kick that led to him throwing a touchdown pass to Luke Johnsos to tie the game. Then minutes later he blocked a punt that he scooped up and returned for the game-winning score in a 14–7 win.

Hewitt was very popular with fans during his playing career because he was one of the last players to play without a helmet. Many game films show Hewitt crashing off the edge on the Bears defensive line without a helmet to make the tackle or get into the quarterback's face as he tries to throw the ball. He was simply fearless on the gridiron. "The man who bothered me most was Bill Hewitt," recalled Tuffy Leemans, Giants Hall of Fame halfback, "whom they say was the greatest end ever in the pro league. He can have my vote. He snorted like a bull, and it was the worst sound I used to hear in the pro league."[13]

In 1937, Hewitt was traded from the Bears to the Philadelphia Eagles in exchange for Nebraska fullback Sam Francis who was drafted number one overall by the Eagles. He played all three seasons with the Eagles under Bert Bell. Hewitt's last productive year was in 1938, making First Team All-Pro in the United Press, *Collyer's Eye* and *New York Daily News*. After the 1939 season, Hewitt retired.

Hewitt came back to play in 1943 with the World War II combined team called the Steagles. Bert Bell offered him $400 a game. With the Steagles, Hewitt struggled on the field after not playing for three years. He also hated wearing a helmet. "He'd take that helmet off and he'd throw it into the sidelines and Greasy [Neale] would pick it up and tell him, 'Put this on! You gotta wear it!' He hated that helmet," recalled Tom Miller, former Steagles end. After playing in just six games, Hewitt retired again to spend more time with his war job. His disappointing play on the field made the decision easier.[14]

Hewitt started his career the same year that the NFL started keeping official statistics. He finished his career with 103 catches for 1,638 yards, 23 touchdown catches and 26 total TDs. He also led the NFL in TD catches in 1934 with five and was second in 1936 when he caught a career-high six. Hewitt was easily named to the NFL 1930s All-Decade Team. In selecting his All-Time team, Giants center Mel Hein always chose Don Hutson (#2) and Bill Hewitt as his two ends. So well thought of by teammates and opponents, he was named to numerous All-Time teams, routinely being on them next to the great Hutson and ahead of Guy Chamberlin (#5).

Unfortunately, Hewitt died tragically in a car accident in 1947 at the age of 37. In 1949, the Bears retired his number 56 jersey alongside Nagurski (no. 3) and Grange (no. 77). In 1971, Hewitt was honored by being elected to the Pro Football Hall of Fame, joining a class of football legends that included Jim Brown, Frank "Bruiser" Kinard, Vince Lombardi, Andy Robustelli, Y.A. Tittle and Norm Van Brocklin. Accepting for him was his daughter, Mary Ellen (Hewitt) Cocozza, who never knew her father and never saw him play. At the podium on the steps of the Hall of Fame she said, "Thank you very much. It's a great privilege and honor to be here in Canton accepting this award on my father's behalf. He is recognized with such great men that have made football the American tradition it is today. My only regret is that my father cannot be here to reap the harvest of his efforts, but I know he is here in spirit. Thank you so much."[15]

For the next four and half decades the name of Bill Hewitt seemed to get lost until 2019 when the NFL celebrated its 100th season. During that campaign, a 26-member blue ribbon panel went about choosing an All-Time team. The panel selected seven defensive ends for the squad. Because of his standout play on the defensive side of the ball, Bill Hewitt was selected as one of the seven defensive ends. Over 75 years since he last played a snap in the NFL, Hewitt was given one of the greatest honors any former NFL player could achieve—a spot on the league's 100th Anniversary All-Time Team. "He was a little undersized but fast and tough. Helmet or no helmet, Bill Hewitt is a tough football player, that's easy to see," commented Bill Belichick when announcing Hewitt made the NFL's 100th All-Time Team.[16]

In 1944, Bill Hewitt wrote an article for *Saturday Evening Post* titled "Don't Send My Boy to Halas." Within that article he wrote, "I love football. I'd like to say my experience in the game helped me in other fields. In one sense that may be true. A lot of what I am today and hope to be in the future is due to the discipline of competition. You learn things in football: that a timeout is costly … forget the hurt … cooperate as one of the team … don't bother the quarterback unless you can really help … control your nerves … rise above the situation … be alert; you can score even though the other fellow has the ball … he can fumble … he surely will, if you keep the pressure on him…. Yes, football taught me all this."[17]

No. 16

Mike Michalske
Guard

Full Name: August Mike Michalske
Nickname: "Iron Mike"
b: April 24, 1903 (Cleveland, OH); d: October 26, 1983 (age 80; Green Bay, WI)
High School: West Tech (OH); College: Penn State
Height/Weight: 6–0, 210 pounds
Position: Guard
Teams/Years: 1926–1928 New York Yankees (AFL-NFL); 1929–1935, 1937 Green Bay Packers
Pro Football Hall of Fame: Class of 1964
Retro-MVPs: No
All-Time Teams: B. Bell (1940); C. Cagle (1937); J. Conzelman (1941); R. Flaherty (1990); M. Gantenbein (1968); R. Grange (1934, 1947, 1955); M. Hein (1944, 1968, 1974); B. Hewitt (1940); C. Hinkle (1940, 1942); C. Hubbard (1937, 1966); W. Kiesling (1942); C. Lambeau (1946, 1948, 1955); J. McMillian (1939); J. McNally (1944, 1963); B. Nagurski (1939, 1944); E. Nevers (1932); S. Owen (1942, 1952, 1955)

Next on the list is Mike Michalske, who is the second guard ranked, coming in four spots behind Dan Fortmann (#12). The 6–0, 210-pound Michalske was the best guard during his era—an old-style guard, combing superior strength, perfect balance and relentless determination.

Michalske grew up in Cleveland in the heartland of football country. After a successful prep career at West Tech, Michalske went east to play his college ball at Penn State, where he played everywhere for coach Hugo Bezdek, lining up at end, fullback, tackle and guard. In the fall of 1926, after his Penn State career was over, Michalske joined Red Grange's New York Yankees in the rival American Football League (AFL). The man they called "Iron Mike" played 11 seasons in pro football with two different teams, the New York Yankees and the Green Bay Packers, in 132 career AFL-NFL games.

From his guard position with the Yankees, Michalske blocked for the Galloping Ghost as well as halfback Eddie Tryon. He would earn First Team All-Pro honors in 1927 and 1928. After playing three seasons with the Yankees, Michalske then signed with the Green Bay Packers. "I didn't want to play in New York any longer, I couldn't save any money. Spent it all on bright lights and pretty girls," said Michalske with a chuckle. "I had played a half a year with Jug Earp barnstorming with the Yankees [in

Mike Michalske, guard, Green Bay Packers, ca. 1929 (courtesy Green Bay Packers).

1927]. He had joined Green Bay and he recommended me—I think that's how I happened to catch on there." More likely is that Curly Lambeau knew that Michalske was one of the best guards in pro football. In 1929, he joined a team that would dominate the NFL for the next three seasons. That first year Michalske was in a starting lineup that usually included All-Pros tackle Cal Hubbard, end Lavvie Dilweg, and backs Red Dunn, Johnny "Blood" McNally and Verne Lewellen. Coached by Lambeau, the Packers were loaded and took over the NFL standings.[1]

Michalske's first year with the Packers not only saw them win an NFL championship, but he earned himself consensus First Team All-Pro honors. His new teammates were very impressed by how he played. "Let me tell you about Mike," said Eddie Kotal, Packers back and teammate in 1929. "I was a right half for the Packers and I enjoyed the work. But I don't think I would have enjoyed it as much if it hadn't been for Mike. In the old days, Mike opened many a hole for me. I've always said that if I had ever been a head coach somewhere, Mike would have been my first assignment…. What made him such a great player? A lot of things. He was a great pursuit man. He had those big hands. He had all of that strength. But that wasn't really it. His story is that he has always had tremendous desire. That's made him a great player."[2]

After the 1929 season Ernie Nevers told the press, "The classiest player of the year is Michalske of Green Bay. He isn't a flashy back, he's a guard and a wonder. There's nobody like him on the college or professional field today."[3]

The Packers went on to win two more titles in 1930–1931. Over those three championship years Michalske was the best guard in the NFL, continually earning First Team All-Pro honors. "He was a tremendous football player. He was as great as any football player Green Bay ever had. He had very fast reflexes. He would start moving before his opponent. He was a fierce competitor and an indispensable member of the three championship teams," said Johnny "Blood" McNally, Packers teammate.[4]

Michalske was a 60-minute workhorse who specialized in "blitzing" on defense. One technique he used was "stunting," combining with tackle Cal Hubbard to form a dominant front line. "Our target was the man with the ball, especially the passer. It may not have been exactly ethical, but it was legal in those days to rough the passer, even after he got rid of the ball. We worked him over pretty good," recalled Michalske. "Hubbard and I used to do some stunting in the line to find an opening for a blitz-through. We always figured the best time to stop them was before they got started."[5]

"On defense, he was always one step ahead of the offense. As a blocker, he always gave me 110 percent. He was all muscle. In our day, you had to be a knockdown blocker, not a standup blocker like today. He was a fine man," said Clarke Hinkle, Packers Hall of Fame fullback.[6]

"Iron Mike" never left the field and never got injured. "I just didn't get hurt, not until my last season of pro ball when I injured my back. The players used to kid me. They used to say I must been getting paid by the minute," recalled Michalske.[7]

From his guard position he scored two career touchdowns, including a fantastic 80-yard interception return in a 6–2 victory over the Bears on November 1, 1931. Although they wouldn't win another title in his remaining years with the Packers, Michalske was always considered the best guard in pro football. His play was highly thought of by his teammates and opponents. "I would put him down in my book as the best guard—bar none—I ever saw. That was Mike Michalske of the Green Bay Packers," said Benny Friedman, Giants Hall of Fame quarterback. "Mike weighed about 215 pounds and was one of the fastest and most agile of linemen. He was smart, alert, aggressive and, in general, a severe pain in the neck to the opposition. Mike was never mouse-trapped, never out of position. He was always in the right place at the right time and a deadly tackler."[8]

Throughout his career, Michalske had a great mind for the game. He had played for nearly a decade, picking up different kinds of football strategy on both offense and defense. In 1935, while still playing, Michalske was tapped by Lambeau to help coach the defensive line with Cal Hubbard helping the offensive line. "[Mike] was a great player. He was like our coach. If you really wanted to know something he was the guy you went to," recalled Herm Schneidman, Packers blocking back, 1935–1939. "He was on our board of strategy. If you had trouble with something and wanted to know how to handle it, he'd be the guy you'd go to. Lambeau would say we need a couple of new plays and Mike would suggest something. They wouldn't say much about it. But when we started practicing on Tuesdays, the things Mike would suggest would be put in by Lambeau." It looked like coaching would be in Michalske's future. That season Michalske earned his final First Team All-Pro with the Packers.[9]

Since he experienced being a fullback at Penn State, he could see the advantage of those type of players being able to play the guard position in the NFL, so recommending players to switch positions to guard was not a hard choice for Coach Lambeau. "Few men could start faster or charge harder from a standing start, and could move laterally too," said Buckets Goldenberg, Packers teammate and All-Pro guard. "Mike was not only a smart player, but he had a fine mind for football and a great interest in the game from all stand points. He sold [Curly] Lambeau quite a few of his ideas, including the value of a former fullback at guard. Not an accident that a few of the Packers guards like Russ Letlow and Pete Tinsley, and myself, had played fullback in college."[10]

In 1936, Michalske retired from the Packers to go into coaching. He was hired by Ernie Nevers to be an assistant coach at Lafayette College in Pennsylvania. After a disappointing 1–8 season, Michalske returned to the Packers for one more season in 1937. He only played in six games because of a back injury, before finally calling it quits at the age of 34. "It was in Detroit, about four or five games left in the [1937] season," recalled Michalske in a 1979 interview. "I got hurt unnecessarily. Somebody jumped on my back after the play. They cut my shirt off and I told them to throw it away. I wasn't gonna play again. I put one on to coach after that, but never to play."[11]

After his playing days were over Michalske began a coaching career that would last for two decades. "[Mike] had a great spirit of leadership," said Lon Evans, Packers All-Pro lineman and teammate. "Mike was real fast, but not big. No one knows more football than Mike." He had stops as line coach with the Chicago Cardinals (1939), St. Norbert College (1940), Baltimore Colts (1949), Baylor University (1950–1952), Texas A & M (1953) and Texas (1955–1956). In between those stops he was also head coach at Iowa State for five seasons (1942–1946), compiling an overall record of 18-18-3.

Named to the NFL 1920s All-Decade Team, Michalske was the first guard ever elected to the Pro Football Hall of Fame in 1964. He was elected to the Packers Hall of Fame in 1970. We have him ranked just a few spots down from Dan Fortmann as the top guard of the two-way era. Both Fortmann and Michalske were picked together on Mel Hein's All-Time team (1944, 1968, 1974); Johnny "Blood" McNally's team (1944) and Steve Owen's All-Time team (1942, 1952). In 1955 when Curly Lambeau selected an NFL All-Time team, he choose Michalske and Fortmann as his two guards as well. "The people who really enjoyed his ability were other players. He was a football player's football player," said Don Hutson, Packers Hall of Fame end.[12]

Michalske passed away on October 26, 1983, at the age of 80.

No. 17

Benny Friedman

Quarterback

Full Name: Benjamin Friedman
Nickname: "Benny"
b: March 18, 1905 (Cleveland, OH); d: November 23, 1982 (age 77; New York, NY)
High School: Cleveland East Tech (OH), Glenville (OH); College: Michigan
Height/Weight: 5–10, 183 pounds
Position: Quarterback
Teams/Years: 1927 Cleveland Bulldogs; 1928 Detroit Wolverines; 1929–1931 New York Giants; 1932–1934 Brooklyn Dodgers
Pro Football Hall of Fame: Class of 2005
Retro-MVPs: No (Four straight runner-up finishes; 1927–1930)
All-Time Teams: E. Cuneo (1973); R. Grange (1934); J. McMillian (1939); J. McNally (1937)

The first pure passing quarterback star in the NFL two-way era was Benny Friedman. "No football team can be successful in these days without a good forward passer. The time when a ground attack could carry a team to successive victories has gone forever. To make a running attack successful a passing attack is needed to spread the defense," wrote Benny Friedman in his 1931 book *The Passing Game*.[1]

Benjamin Friedman was born in 1905 in the Jewish neighborhood in Cleveland. His father was a successful tailor and his mother a housewife, but neither knew anything about football, except that it was violent. Passing time in school, Friedman found time to help build his hands into a great passer. "I'd stretch my hand and stretch my hand till I could get it all the way across [the desk] so that I was able to make a 180-degree spread between my thumb and my little finger and have this big spread between my first finger and thumb," recalled Friedman.[2]

Friedman first attended Cleveland East Tech High and then transferred to Glenville High, mainly to play football. He became a prep star who attracted the attention of the University of Michigan, where he became an All-American quarterback. Friedman made a name for himself throwing all types of passes for the Wolverines. He quickly became one of the most sought out pro prospects.

Well-traveled, the 5–10, 183-pound Friedman ended up playing 81 games in eight seasons with four different NFL teams—Cleveland, Detroit, the New York Giants and the Brooklyn Dodgers. In 1927, after a brilliant All-American career at

Michigan, Friedman signed with his hometown NFL team, the newly formed Cleveland Bulldogs, becoming one of the league's biggest attractions. Benny didn't disappoint, leading the Bulldogs to an 8–4–1 record and a fourth place finish in the NFL. Behind the guidance of coach Leroy Andrew, Benny finished the year with 11 TD passes, as the Bulldogs led the NFL in scoring with 209 points. "Until Friedman came along, the pass was used as a desperation weapon in long-yardage situations on third down—or when your team was hopelessly behind. Benny demonstrated that the pass could be mixed with running plays as an integral part of the offense," said George Halas, Bears Hall of Fame coach. "The time to pass is on first and second down. Why wait until third down, when the defense is looking for it?" said Benny Friedman.[3]

Benny Friedman, quarterback, New York Giants, ca. 1926 (courtesy University of Michigan Athletics).

Friedman was well equipped to play 60 minutes of pro football despite his slight 180-pound body. Learning how to protect his body while throwing at Michigan under Fielding Yost paid off when he played pro ball. "You couldn't get hurt and we, of course, didn't get hurt," recalled Friedman. "And we had to go 60 minutes. I remember playing in Frankford on Saturday because in Pennsylvania, with their Blue Laws, you couldn't play on Sunday. We then played [them] in Cleveland on Sunday. I would say we were rugged. On defense I would play either safety or halfback.... We all played 60 minutes. We didn't wear [face] masks in those days, yet I never had my nose busted."[4]

Despite the Bulldogs' success on the field, and Benny's strength as a gate attraction, the Cleveland Bulldogs lost a ton of money. The following year in 1928, Friedman moved on to the Detroit Wolverines. Again, using the passing game as a weapon under Coach Andrew, he tossed nine touchdown passes—which was tops in the NFL—to lead Detroit to a 7–2–1 record, good for third place in the NFL. Once again, his team led the league in points scored with 209. And once again the team lost money.

At this time Giants owner Tim Mara wanted a star attraction to get fans out to the games in New York. He wanted Friedman. So, in 1929, he bought the entire Detroit franchise to get Benny to play for his Giants. Friedman claimed to have been given

$10,000 a year to play with the Giants. "He made us believers. He was a natural leader who came to us with a great reputation, someone we were able to respect right away because he had already proven himself," said Steve Owen, Giants Hall of Fame coach.[5]

Friedman adapted well in the Big Apple, both on and off the field. "Benny Friedman made a great contribution to pro football in New York, off the field as well as on it. Several times a week he would go around to high school assemblies in the mornings and give tickets away to promote the game. He really did make an enormous contribution," recalled Wellington Mara. "He was also, of course, a fine player and a durable one. I don't think he ever missed a game because of an injury. Friedman was one of a kind."[6]

That first season in New York Friedman went off using his great passing skills to make weekly headlines in the media capital of the world. Even despite the stock market crash that fall, Friedman continued to fire bullets. He set an NFL record with 20 TD passes that season, which would not be broken until 1942 by Cecil Isbell with 24, and he led the Giants to the top of the standings. But once again Benny fell short of winning an NFL championship. He guided the Giants to a 13–1–1 record, but lost out to the Packers (12–0–1) by one game.

Friedman was an artist throwing the football and the first pure passer during the two-way era. "When I finished throwing the ball, I was always on balance and ready to cover. And I was accurate. Back to my early days we were conservative. Of course, we had other handicaps. The ball was very fat. Not good for passing but good for drop-kicking. When they streamlined the ball to make it easier to pass, the sharp point practically did away with drop-kicking," said Friedman.[7]

In 1930, Friedman also helped out coaching at Yale under Mal Stevens. "I was living in Brooklyn that year," recalled Friedman. "I'd get up at dawn, rush to the Polo Grounds for practice with the Giants, catch the noon train to New Haven, coach at Yale in the afternoon and get home late at night."[8]

Friedman led the NFL in passing touchdowns for four consecutive years, 1927–1930, and his 66 career TD passes set an NFL record that would be exceeded by Arnie Herber later in the decade. "They talk about great passers today, but remember that the football has been changed three times since the early 1930s, and each time it has been made narrower and the axis pulled in. Anybody could throw today's football. You go back to Benny Friedman playing with the Giants in the late 1920s and early 1930s. He threw that old balloon. Now who's to tell what Benny Friedman might do with this modern football. He'd probably be the greatest passer that ever lived," said Red Grange, Bears Hall of Fame halfback.[9]

Retro-MVPs: 1927–1930

Friedman had a great four-year run from 1927 to 1930, finishing in second place all four years in the Retro-MVP voting. Not winning a championship hurt the most, as well as coming up short in some of the bigger games, such as when Verne Lewellen outplayed him in the late 1929 showdown with the Packers. "Friedman was the first pro I was conscious of strictly as a passer. The pass in those days was a third down play. Friedman, who was probably ahead of his time, would throw on first down and was criticized for it," said Wellington Mara, Giants Hall of Fame owner.[10]

After the 1931 season, Friedman talked to Tim Mara about becoming part owner of the Giants. Mara declined the offer, leaving Friedman somewhat bitter. He left the Giants to join the crosstown Brooklyn Dodgers. He was a player-coach in 1932, leading the Dodgers to a disappointing 3–9 record. He then would only play eight games over the next two seasons with the Dodgers, finally calling it quits after the 1934 NFL season in which he appeared in just one game.

The versatile Friedman could also run and kick. When he had to, Friedman could tuck the ball under his arm to run. He had 18 career rushing touchdowns, including six in 1928. In 1928, he led the NFL in scoring with 55 points and in extra points with 19. He converted 71 career extra points.

Friedman would rank higher if he had won an NFL championship. He came closest in 1929. In seven seasons from 1927 to 1933, Friedman had an overall record of 56–30–5, winning 65 percent of his games. "Maybe the best passer I saw was Benny Friedman," said Ken Strong, Giants Hall of Fame back.[11]

After his NFL career was over, Friedman went into coaching, making a stop at Yale as an assistant while he played with the Giants in 1931, before becoming head football coach at City College of New York from 1934 to 1941 with a 27–31–4 record and then Brandeis University from 1950 to 1959 with a 34–32–4 record. In 1964, he opened a summer camp for boys, mainly teaching the quarterback position, called the Kamp Kohut Football School for aspiring quarterbacks in Oxford, Maine.

After several decades, Friedman was finally elected to the Pro Football Hall of Fame in 2005. "Although Sammy Baugh of the Washington Redskins is every bit as good as stories about him indicate, I still think he cannot compare to Benny Friedman as a passer," spoke Tommy Hughitt, Buffalo All-Americans All-Pro back, in 1938.[12]

The sad part is that Friedman did not live to see his induction. Because of severe health issues, Friedman committed suicide on November 23, 1982. He was 77 years old.

No. 18

Ernie Nevers

Fullback

Full Name: Ernest Alonzo Nevers
Nickname: "Blonde Blizzard"
b: June 11, 1903 (Willow River, MN); d: May 3, 1976 (age 72; San Rafael, CA)
High School: Superior Central (MN), Santa Rosa (CA); College: Stanford
Height/Weight: 6-0, 205 pounds
Position: Fullback
Teams/Years: 1926–1927 Duluth Eskimos; 1929–1931 Chicago Cardinals
Pro Football Hall of Fame: Class of 1963 (Charter Member)
Retro-MVPs: No
All-Time Teams: J. Carr (1934); J. Conzelman (1941); E. Cuneo (1973); R. Grange (1934);
   G. Halas (1939); C. Hubbard (1937, 1947, 1966); V. Lewellen (1936); M. Michalske (1982);
   B. Nagurski (1939, 1944); P. Robeson (1941); D. Slater (1949); C. Storck (1939)

Number 18 is the man they called the "Blond Blizzard."

Fullback Ernie Nevers played just five NFL seasons with two teams—the Duluth Eskimos and Chicago Cardinals. Despite playing just 54 NFL games Nevers was one of the best all-around fullbacks to have played during this era. His peers, like Bronko Nagurski, put Nevers at the very top of their list of "best player to have played against." On our list he comes in just a notch below two previous fullbacks, Nagurski (#6) and Clarke Hinkle (#13). Not winning a championship hurts his case.

Ernie Nevers was born unexpectedly in Willow River, Minnesota, in 1903. His parents came to Minnesota from Nova Scotia and were well into their 40s when Ernie arrived. When Ernie was seven years old his father moved the family to Moose Lake, Minnesota, where he bought a small hotel. In 1913, the hotel structure was leveled by a raging forest fire. George Nevers then moved his family to Superior where he bought an inn.

In the fall of 1917, a 14-year-old Nevers decided to try out for the Central High School football team, never mind that he "didn't know a football from a squash," as he admitted later. Standing 5 feet, 7 inches, and weighing 155 pounds, he had size but no clue how to play. Teammates picked up on how green he was and urged Nevers to "go back to the farm," and turn in his jersey. But Nevers, joined by his good friend Ole Haugsrud, persisted. His first role in practice was as a tackling dummy. "I used to stand in the sawdust pits and let the other kids tackle and block me,"

Nevers recalled. Haugsrud also recalled those drills: "I stood on one sawdust pit and Ernie on the other.... We just stood there, and one by one every other guy on the team took his turn at banging into us. Eventually though, Ernie's size and ability as a football player showed through and he was put on the first team."[1]

Nevers' high school coach first put him at tackle. As a sophomore, things started to look up for Ernie, who grew to 170 pounds. Nevers also excelled on the hardwood; in fact, basketball was probably his best sport in high school. Nevers became a three-sport prep star when he added baseball to his resume. Just prior to Nevers' senior year, his father sold the inn and moved his family to a ranch in Santa Rosa, California. His new high school had launched a football team for the first time. He quickly realized he knew more than the coach and designed the offense, putting himself at fullback. "You see, I wanted every chance to carry the ball and kick," recalled Nevers.[2]

Ernie Nevers, fullback, Chicago Cardinals, ca. 1929 (courtesy Arizona Cardinals).

After high school, Nevers enrolled at Santa Rosa Junior College where he helped organize the school's first football team. After one year at Santa Rosa, he transferred to Stanford University where playing fullback changed his football destiny. "Brick Muller [All-American back] had been an idol of mine, and I got to know him," recalled Nevers about choosing a college. "So, I was all set to go to Cal, but at the last minute I picked Stanford. But if I had gone to Cal I probably would have stayed a lineman and nobody would have given me much of a chance. I was a terrible tackle. I did much better at fullback."[3]

Arriving at Stanford, Nevers was quickly dubbed the "Blonde Blizzard" because of his size and sun-washed hair. Quiet off the field, Nevers was ferocious and intense between the lines. Nevers quickly became a legend out west. With his broad shoulders, he could do everything—running, passing, kicking—and was a phenom who excelled in all phases of the game. While at Stanford, Nevers competed in four sports (football, basketball, baseball, and track) and earned 11 varsity letters.

In 1924, Pop Warner arrived at Stanford. The man who had coached the great Jim Thorpe at Carlisle would now build his squad around the skills of Ernie Nevers. "You're going to be the deep man in my double-wing," Warner told Nevers. "Brush up on your passing and kicking. You'll be doing about all of it."[4]

From 1923 to 1925, Nevers led Stanford to 22 wins against five losses and one tie. But his greatest performance, that clinched his stardom, was on the biggest stage against the sport's greatest team. On New Year's Day 1925 in the Rose Bowl, Nevers had his greatest performance. Playing against undefeated University of Notre Dame and their famous Four Horsemen backfield, Nevers ran the ball 34 times for 114 yards, passed for 138 yards, and seem to make every tackle on defense, while playing all 60 minutes. Better yet, he did this while healing two broken ankles he suffered early in the season against the University of Washington. Although Stanford lost, 27–10, Nevers was honored as the game's MVP.

During the 1925 season, Red Grange signed with the Chicago Bears and barnstormed across the country, becoming the biggest star in football. However, Nevers wasn't too far behind. The 6-0, 205-pound bulldozer was the big man on campus throughout his tenure on the West Coast. His coach, Pop Warner, who had Jim Thorpe at Carlisle, said Nevers was the best back he ever coached, the greatest all-around man in football he had ever known, "and a player without a fault.... Nevers could do everything Thorpe could do and he always tried harder. Ernie gave sixty minutes of himself every game."[5]

After leaving Stanford, Nevers signed to play pro football for a promoter in Jacksonville, Florida. He was paid $25,000 up front to play at least six exhibition games, including one against Grange. The press hammered Nevers for signing to play pro ball. "But I needed the money," said Nevers explaining why he signed. "All we got at college in those days was a side job. I got a little help on the tuition, [but] I was still in debt. And so was my father. Those exhibition games took the mortgage off my family's ranch."[6]

On January 2, 1926, in Jacksonville in front of 6,700 spectators, Nevers outrushed Grange 46–29 yards, had two interceptions on defense and averaged 53 yards on six punts. But the Galloping Ghost hogged the headlines by throwing a touchdown pass in a Bears 16–7 victory. Nevers ended up only playing two exhibition games in Florida but received his full $25,000. "I felt like a robber since I already had $25,000 safely in the bank back home," said Nevers.[7]

After the exhibitions were completed, Nevers signed a contract to play Major League Baseball with the St. Louis Browns. He received a $10,000 bonus and a yearly salary of $7,000 as a right-handed pitcher. Nevers would go on to play three seasons from 1926 to 1928 with the Browns but went just 6–12 with a 4.64 ERA. His dubious claim to fame was serving up two of Babe Ruth's 60 home runs in 1927. Later in one of those games Nevers struck out Ruth; as Ernie headed to the dugout, Ruth gave him a pat on the shoulder. "You've got great speed kid," the Bambino said. "For my sake, I hope you stick with football." A year later, Nevers would do just that.[8]

In the fall of 1926, the NFL and the rival American Football League—established by Grange and his agent C.C. Pyle—began a war for players. The biggest free agent out there was Ernie Nevers. Reports came out that the Blonde Blizzard would sign a contract with the AFL for a reported salary of $15,000. But the NFL's Duluth franchise had an ace in the hole—Ole Haugsrud.

Haugsrud assumed ownership of the Duluth franchise in 1926 and came up with a plan to make the Duluth football team one of the best and most popular teams in the league. He was going to sign Ernie Nevers. Haugsrud had reason to be optimistic about wooing Nevers to Duluth, the NFL's most-remote venue, since they had been friends in high school. That summer Nevers was playing pro baseball with the Browns. Haugsrud made the trip to St. Louis to visit his former classmate.

Inside the apartment he shared with his wife, Nevers showed his friend the letter from Pyle of the AFL promising to pay Nevers $15,000 for the 1926 season. He had not signed it yet. "Ole, if you can meet the terms Pyle is offering in this letter, it's OK with me. I'll play for Duluth," Nevers said. Haugsrud agreed to Nevers' terms, adding 10 percent of the team's larger gate receipts. "I had the money to do it," recalled Haugsrud. "I had various holdings—buildings and things like that. I had inherited a little money."[9]

He hadn't brought much cash with him to St. Louis, however. Nevers inked his name on the Duluth contract without a signing bonus. "Oh maybe I gave him a dollar to make it legal, but really a handshake was all Ernie wanted," said Haugsrud. "A handshake with an old friend was good enough for Ernie."[10]

That fall, Duluth played more than 25 games, counting exhibitions, and nearly all their games were played with a roster of only 13 men. Thus, the team was tagged "The Iron Men of the North." Nevers was the highest-paid NFL player. On the field, Nevers lived up to his "One-Man Team" reputation. The Eskimos lined up in a double-wing formation, similar to a modern shotgun, with Nevers as the only deep back. He called signals, handled the ball on every play, did most of the running, and all of the passing and kicking. On defense, he seemed to be in on every tackle. "Ernie Nevers was playing in a formation where we had 2 wingbacks," said Johnny "Blood" McNally, Duluth back, 1926–1927. "He was the fullback. He got the snap on every play and so forth. He passed. He ran. He did the whole thing. He called the signals…. For that offense he was perfect. Absolutely perfect. He was a great football player." "Ernie Nevers was the Lawrence Taylor of the backs," recalled John Alexander, Giants tackle, 1926. "Nevers could take the ball, and he did against the Giants on his ten-yard line and rush it down the field against us. He rushed the ball right over the goal line. It took him 10 or 12 plays, but you couldn't stop him."[11]

However, despite Nevers' heroics the Eskimos were only an ordinary team, winning against weak foes and losing to all their strong opponents. The Eskimos NFL record was 6–5–3.

In 1926, Nevers added to his base salary of $15,000 with a share of the gate receipts that totaled him more than $65,000 for the season. That's about $750,000 in today's dollars. Of his guaranteed $15,000, Nevers once joked, "The only mistake I made was that I forgot to ask how long the season was going to be."[12]

As much as the 1926 Eskimos was a success, the 1927 version was a downright failure. After losing their opener to the Green Bay Packers, the Eskimos played their best game. Nevers threw four touchdown passes in a 27–0 pounding of the

Pottsville Maroons. It was the Eskimos last win. The following week Nevers scored three touchdowns, but his team lost 21–20 to Benny Friedman's Cleveland Bulldogs. A week later Nevers' squad played before 15,000 fans in New York against the Giants, losing 21–0 to the future NFL champions. The team's last five games were all losses as the Eskimos were outscored 72–21. On December 11 at Wrigley Field Nevers threw two touchdowns, but it wasn't enough as the Chicago Bears came away with a 27–14 win. The Eskimos would play only nine league games and finish 1–8.

Nevers returned to the baseball diamond in the summer of 1928. After the baseball season Nevers, instead of returning to the pro gridiron, headed west to be an assistant coach for Pop Warner at his alma mater Stanford. Nevers needed a break from the demands and injuries of pro football.

When the Eskimos folded other teams quickly moved in to sign its talented players. But in 1929, Ole Haugsrud and partner Dewey Scanlon were asked to help run the Chicago Cardinals. They brought the old gang back, including Nevers. Ten former Duluth players played for the Cardinals in '29. Nevers quickly got back into form. He began a streak of three straight All-Pro seasons with the Cardinals. After three straight losing seasons, the Cardinals became relevant with Nevers leading the charge. Although they didn't win an NFL title, they did play competitive football with two winning seasons in the three years with Nevers starting at fullback. "[Nevers] could do it all—run, block and kick. Then he'd turn around and stop you on defense ... his tackle rattled the bones. He made you ache," said Cal Hubbard, Packers Hall of Fame tackle.[13]

At the end of the 1929 season Nevers had his greatest game ever, one for the record books on Thanksgiving Day against the Bears. The week before, Nevers scored all of his team's points in a 19–0 victory over the Dayton Triangles. But that performance paled in comparison to what Nevers did on Thanksgiving.

In front of about 8,000 shivering fans at Wrigley Field, Nevers put on a one-man show for the ages. Just six minutes into the game, Nevers plowed ahead for a 20-yard touchdown, but then missed the extra point. With time running out in the first quarter, Nevers plunged into the end zone again, this time from three yards out and this time he converted the point after. In the second quarter Nevers continued to have his way on the field as he powered through the line for another short touchdown run. The extra point was good again. Three touchdowns and two extra points. Not a bad day's work, but Nevers was only halfway done.

Early in the third quarter the Bears finally lit up the scoreboard when Walter Holmer threw a touchdown pass to Garland Grange, younger brother of Red. But the Cardinals and Nevers went back to work. The Blonde Blizzard plunged in from one yard out to score his fourth touchdown and added the extra point to make the score 27–6. Ten minutes into the fourth quarter Nevers scored his fifth touchdown of the game on another one-yard plunge. To end his day, he scored his final touchdown from 10 yards out. He converted one of his last two extra points. The *Chicago Tribune* wrote: "Then Ernie left the game, and how those south-siders cheered. Forty points plus nineteen points against Dayton last Sunday gave him fifty-nine in a row. Which is some kind of record, but the south side didn't care. For the Cardinals had defeated the Bears."[14]

The Cardinals defeated the Bears 40–6, but Nevers' performance was one for the ages. Forty total points was the most ever in an NFL game for an individual player—and now 93 years later the record *still stands*! Nevers called the game his greatest moment in sports.

For the next two seasons Nevers became the Cardinals player-coach (1930–1931), guiding the team to an overall record of 19–9–2. "Ernie Nevers was the greatest of them all. He could pass, kick and run. The fellow had everything, including a great desire to play. He was emotional, and he played his heart out in every game," said Duke Slater, Cardinals teammate and Hall of Fame tackle. After the 1931 season Ernie Nevers, who finished second in the NFL in scoring with 66 points to Johnny Blood's 84, announced his retirement from pro football. He was 28 years old.[15]

After retiring from the NFL, Nevers became an assistant coach in the college ranks with Stanford from 1933 to 1935 and Lafayette in 1936. In 1939, he decided to give the NFL one more try, coming back to the Chicago Cardinals as head coach. It was disaster, as Nevers' squad finished with the worst record in the league, going 1–10. After helping form the Chicago Rockets of the AAFC in 1946, Nevers finally stepped away from football for good.

In 1963, Nevers was named a Charter Member of the Pro Football Hall of Fame. He later was selected to the NFL 1920s All-Decade Team at fullback and the NFL 50th Anniversary All-Time Team as a kicker runner-up in 1969. "Ernie Nevers was the best all-around football player I've ever seen," recalled Ray Flaherty, Giants Hall of Fame end, in 1985. "Ernie Nevers could do anything. He could pass, he could punt, he could kick points after touchdowns, kick field goals. He was a very good linebacker, and he was an excellent fullback. If you wanted to put him back at the halfback position, he could run it through the middle."[16]

Nevers' NFL career is a tough one to evaluate. He played on some bad teams that won only 39 percent of their games (23–29–6), and he never won a championship, which hurts him overall. But he usually was a one-man team when he played. "I never saw anyone who epitomized the idea of a will to win more so than Ernie. He was a tremendous football player, tremendous leader, both on offense and defense. And you always knew you were in a battle when you played against one of his teams," said Benny Friedman, Hall of Fame quarterback.[17]

He scored 38 career touchdowns in his 54 career games. His teams went 15–8 when he scored a touchdown, but he was a tough-luck loser. A perfect example came in 1927 playing with Duluth. He scored three touchdowns with two in the fourth quarter, against Benny Friedman's Cleveland Bulldogs, but his team lost 21–20.

Nevers was an excellent passer from his fullback position, tossing 24 career

TDs, much better than Clarke Hinkle and on par with Bronko Nagurski. "Ernie shoots bullet-like passes on a flat trajectory that leads a receiver just right. He also analyzes enemy plays so well and makes more tackles than any other man on the field," said Jimmy Conzelman. He was very good on defense, although a notch below Nagurski and Hinkle in this department.[18]

Ernie Nevers died on May 3, 1976, at the age of 73.

Nevers was the definition of a two-way player. He wanted nothing more than to show up, hit everything he saw, and play the game hard on both sides of the ball. In 1969, Nevers was asked if he would enjoy playing in the NFL right now. "I wouldn't care of it," Nevers said. "All the clubs have two teams—one for offense, the other for defense. In my day, eleven men were about enough. No, I wouldn't like it. I couldn't stand to spend half the time on the bench."[19]

Two-Way Era Fullbacks Comparison Chart

The "Big Three" fullbacks were clearly ahead of the rest of the pack. Below is a closer look at the numbers, stacking Nagurski (#6) vs. Hinkle (#13) vs. Nevers (#18).

Fullbacks Comparison Page

(Note: Official NFL statistics didn't start until 1932)

Seasons Played
Clarke Hinkle: 10
Bronko Nagurski: 9
Ernie Nevers: 5

Games Played
Clarke Hinkle: 113
Bronko Nagurski: 97
Ernie Nevers: 54

Championships Won
Bronko Nagurski: 3
Clarke Hinkle: 2
Ernie Nevers: 0

Overall Team Record
Bronko Nagurski: 79–21–12 (112 games; 70%)
Clarke Hinkle: 80–35–4 (119 games; 67%)
Ernie Nevers: 23–29–6 (58 games; 39%)

Postseason Record
Bronko Nagurski: 3–2
Clarke Hinkle: 2–2
Ernie Nevers: 0–0

Hall of Fame Enshrinement Year
Bronko Nagurski: 1963 (Charter Member)
Ernie Nevers: 1963 (Charter Member)
Clarke Hinkle: 1964

Total Touchdowns
Clarke Hinkle: 44
Ernie Nevers: 38
Bronko Nagurski: 25

Rushing Touchdowns
Ernie Nevers: 38
Clarke Hinkle: 35
Bronko Nagurski: 25

Points Scored
Clarke Hinkle: 379
Ernie Nevers: 301
Bronko Nagurski: 154

Yards Per Rush
Bronko Nagurski: 4.4 avg.
Clarke Hinkle: 3.3 avg.
Ernie Nevers: N/A

Passing Touchdowns/Interceptions
Ernie Nevers: 24 TDs/ N/A
Bronko Nagurski: 7 TDs/9 INTs
Clarke Hinkle: 0 TDs/5 INTs

No. 19

Cliff Battles

Halfback

Full Name: Clifford Franklin Battles
Nickname: "Gip"
b. May 1, 1910 (Akron, OH); d. April 28, 1981 (age 70; Clearwater, FL)
High School: Kenmore (OH); College: West Virginia Wesleyan
Height/Weight: 6-1, 195 pounds
Position: Halfback
Teams/Years: 1932–1937 Boston Braves-Redskins/Washington Redskins
Pro Football Hall of Fame: Class of 1968
Retro-MVPs: No
All-Time Teams: B. Bell (1940); B. Cahn (1943); J. Carr (1934); D. Clark (1942); R. Grange (1934, 1946–1947, 1955); M. Hein (1944, 1968, 1974); C. Hinkle (1940, 1942, 1986): D. Hutson (1948); T. Leemans (1945, 1947, 1953); B. Nagurski (1939, 1944); C. Storck (1939); J. Stydahar (1952)

Coming in at number 19 is Cliff Battles, the third halfback on the list behind Dutch Clark (#1) and Verne Lewellen (#7).

Athletic, fast and instinctive, the 6-1, 195-pound Battles was the first superstar player for the Boston/Washington Redskins franchise before the arrival of Sammy Baugh (#3). He played in 60 games in six seasons, all with the Redskins. Battles wasn't asked to kick or punt like Clark or Lewellen, leaving him a notch below those two as an all-around player. He also didn't pass all that well, throwing just one career TD and 15 career interceptions. But as a ball carrier, he was as skilled as Clark, Lewellen and Red Grange.

Battles grew up in Akron, Ohio, the birthplace of the Firestone tire company where his father worked. "My father, who was a laborer with Goodrich and Firestone and then in the saltworks, took a dim view of athletics. He was the one who had put me and my sister into music. But in my junior year of high school, I began to play football, and my mother covered for me. She signed the permission papers. My old man probably would have refused to," recalled Cliff Battles. "He had no idea I was playing football. He never read the sports pages. Of course, word got around, but when my father would hear something about my playing ball, we would pretend that people were talking about my cousin Roy, who also played on the team. At school I had a nickname—'Gip'—Battles. What little publicity I received, we pretended that

Gip Battles was Roy. My senior year, we figured that maybe I would receive more prominence than I had, so we decided to make a clean breast of it. Tearfully, I got my father's consent to play."[1]

Battles had enough talent that he attracted the attention of West Virginia Wesleyan, a small school south of Akron. There he played under Coach Cecil Ross and made his mark as one of the most talented backs in the country. Despite his playing at a small college, several NFL teams recruited Battles hard. The Portsmouth Spartans, New York Giants and Boston Braves all made offers. West Virginia native George Preston Marshall, who recently founded the Boston Braves and was born in West Virginia, wanted Battles to anchor his new NFL franchise. He told the scout to go sign Battles: "If you don't sign him, keep going south and don't come back."[2]

Cliff Battles, halfback, Washington Redskins, ca. 1937 (courtesy Washington Commanders).

Battles wasn't entirely set on playing pro football, but his love for the game made the decision clearer. "This was the time of the Depression and there were very few jobs around. And so while the pros were not offering much, they were offering more than private industry was. Besides I loved football and was curious to see how I'd do with the big boys," recalled Battles. "I signed for about $175 a game, as I recall, or something like $2,500 a season. If somebody handed you almost a couple hundred dollars a week for doing something you enjoyed, why, it seemed like a pretty good thing."[3]

Playing for Coach Lud Wray in his rookie year, Battles became an instant star. He led the NFL in carries with 148 and rushing with 576 yards. He became the first star attraction for the new Boston franchise. He was even better in 1933, rushing for 737 yards—second in the league behind teammate Jim Musick's 809 yards. On October 8, 1933, he became the first player in NFL history to rush for over 200 yards in a game, with 215 against the Giants, setting a single-game record that stood until 1950 when Gene Roberts of the Giants rushed for 218.

Known to be one of the fastest backs in the NFL during this era, on film Battles consistently shows good elusiveness in running around the ends and toughness between the tackles. "Cliff Battles was a superstar. He had great speed and all the moves any back would need. He could run like a deer, and once he got past the line of scrimmage, you could say goodbye to him. He was gone for a touchdown," said Mel Hein, Giants Hall of Fame linebacker.[4]

Despite playing just six seasons he was named on more than a dozen All-Time teams, routinely selected with the likes of Dutch Clark, Red Grange, Clarke Hinkle and Tuffy Leemans. "The best all-around back I saw in my time was Cliff Battles," recalled Tuffy Leemans. "I never saw the day I could run with him. Name the assignment and he would carry it out."[5]

Taking on Battles was no easy job for any NFL tackler. In 1933, Giants All-Pro quarterback Harry Newman said about tackling Battles, "All that I got for my fine tackle was a split lip. He kicked loose and one of his heels hit me in the mouth, splitting my lip. Battles is the best running back in the league and the hardest back in the country to bring down."[6]

Battles had a running style that was hard to duplicate. "Cliff Battles was the best I saw," once said Dutch Clark. "I think he was the hardest runner." Battles used his entire 195-pound body when he carried the ball. He never went down easy. "A good ball carrier never gets hurt by a tackler he can see. He can anticipate the impact and relax his body or sideslip so that he absorbs only part of the jolt. What I used to worry about was tacklers I couldn't see, fellows who would come up from behind or from the side," explained Battles. "Speed is not a great asset in a player unless it is controlled speed, there is such a thing as running so fast you lose maneuverability and are not able to take advantage of interference or defensive openings."[7]

After hiring three coaches—Wray, Lone Star Dietz, Eddie Casey—in four years, Marshall made a great decision in 1936 by hiring Ray Flaherty as his head coach. The former Giants All-Pro end brought a fresh vision to Washington, and winning became a habit. He built his offense around Battles. "Flaherty put in the box formation and we did well with it," recalled Battles. "In the box formation the tailback and fullback would switch off throughout the game. The idea of that was to disguise intent. This meant that I was often in the fullback spot and the person checking the records and finding I was 6–1 and weighed 195 pounds might wonder what I was doing as a running back."[8]

Boston soon found success under Flaherty, with Battles leading the way. He finished with a career-high 176 carries for 614 rushing yards and five touchdowns. The Redskins won the Eastern Division but generated no fan support in Boston. Marshall felt so slighted by the local fans and press that he asked for the NFL championship game to be moved from Boston to New York to ensure a bigger crowd. The NFL agreed. The Packers, led by Hutson and Herber defeated Boston, 21–6, stopping Battles, who had just two carries for eight yards.

Although they had success in 1936, the Redskins could be one-dimensional with no true passing threat. "We had a good ground game and could move the ball almost at will between the 20-yard lines," recalled Battles. "But we didn't have a real passer on the club and when we got near the 20 the other club could pretty well concentrate on our running game."[9]

That all changed in 1937 when Washington drafted Sammy Baugh out of TCU. Battles knew the rookie signal caller was special, and the team became more balanced with the all-around skills of Baugh. Battles' favorite play was a weakside reverse or counter play around end, against a defensive front that would over-shift to one side. "It was a counter play against an over shifted defense which was used against the more popular strong side plays," said Battles. "By faking across on some of Sammy Baugh's pass plays, we put additional pressure on the defense and were able to catch the other team by surprise."[10]

The counter play run by Battles would become a staple in 1937 when the Redskins won the Eastern Division title for the second straight season. Early in the championship game against the Bears, Battles ran his favorite play to perfection to score the first touchdown of the game. However, Baugh was the star for the rest of the game, throwing three TDs to help defeat the Bears, 28–21. In that game Battles had 17 carries for 53 yards and one touchdown, while catching three passes for 80 yards for a total of 133 yards from scrimmage.

Over his six-year career, Battles led the NFL in yards from scrimmage three times: 1932 with 636, 1933 with 922 and 1937 with 955. In his final season of 1937, he led the NFL in rushing for the second time with 874 yards on an NFL high of 216 carries, setting a league record.

Playing 60 minutes was easy for the flash from the Mountaineer state. "Many people will say that the playing conditions in those days were bad," recalled Battles. "Actually they weren't so bad. We were all in better condition than today's players because we were playing all the time. There was none of this sitting down, getting up, then sitting down again. If you were healthy, you played both ways all the time."[11]

Battles was considered an electrifying athlete who scored many different ways. "Red Grange and Cliff Battles were the best runners when I played. They could really break games open. They were a lot like Walter Payton today," said Red Badgro, Giants Hall of Fame end, in 1979. He scored 31 career touchdowns in five different ways: rushing 23; receiving four; punt return two; kickoff return one; interception return one. He could score from anywhere on the field and flashed big-play ability with 11 TDs of 40 or more yards. Battles could take over a game. A perfect example was in 1937 when Battles scored three touchdowns from long distance to defeat Pittsburgh, 34–20. He returned an interception 65 yards and had runs of 60 and 62 in the fourth quarter to seal the win. "Battles had the long stride and he had the change of pace. He was fast, too. Maybe not like the sprinters of today. But he could turn it on," said Jim Lee Howell, Giants end.[12]

He finished his career with 4,057 yards from scrimmage, 3,511 rushing and 546 receiving, showing toughness every time he took the field. "Cliff is the best running back I have ever seen and I've seen plenty of good backs. I never saw Red Grange, but he couldn't have been better than Battles," said Riley Smith, Redskins back, 1936–1938. "Many times, I've seen Cliff come in from practice, fill the tub with all-but-scalding water, empty a box of Epsom salts in the water and sit there hoping the pain would leave his legs. Nobody knows what Battles went through to play football."[13]

Despite Battles' heroics in the 1937 NFL championship, George Preston Marshall refused to raise Battles' salary above $3,000. Rather than play for the same contract, he retired as a champion. He was just 27 years old.

Battles took a job as an assistant coach for Lou Little at Columbia from 1938 to 1943, coaching for $4,000—more than his NFL contract. Following a stint with the Marines during World War II, Battles was named head coach of the Brooklyn Dodgers of the All-America Football Conference, but he didn't do all that well, going just 4–16–1 over two seasons in 1946–1947. After leaving the Dodgers, Battles stepped away from football, eventually working for General Electric.

Battles was honored by being named to the NFL 1930s All-Decade Team and being selected to the Pro Football Hall of Fame in 1968. "I thought Red Grange was a runner until I saw Cliff Battles. Red wasn't even in Battles's class," said Benny Friedman, Hall of Fame quarterback. "Cliff Battles was a truly poetic runner. He had speed, perfect rhythm, and a hair-trigger sense of timing. You merely had to watch Battles walking down the street to realize that he had perfect balance."[14]

Cliff Battles died on April 28, 1981, at the age of 70. "We would have lasted longer in years and been better late in games if we hadn't had to play 60 minutes," said Cliff Battles in 1958. "I think this free substitution has made football much better. I wish we could have played in these times."[15]

No. 20

Ken Strong
Halfback-Fullback

Full Name: Elmer Kenneth Strong, Jr.
Nickname: "Ken"
b: April 21, 1906 (West Haven, CT); d: October 5, 1979 (age 73; New York, NY)
High School: West Haven (CT); College: NYU
Height/Weight: 6-0, 206 pounds
Position: Halfback-Fullback
Teams/Years: 1929–1932 Staten Island Stapletons; 1933–1935, 1939, 1944–1947 New York Giants; 1936–1937 New York Yanks (AFL)
Pro Football Hall of Fame: 1967
Retro-MVPs: 1933
All-Time Teams: C. Cagle (1937); J. Carr (1934); G. Corbett (1938); E. Cuneo (1973); C. Hinkle (1942); B. Nagurski (1939); D. Slater (1957)

At number 20 is Ken Strong.

Big and athletic, Strong played in 131 games over 12 seasons for two NFL teams, the Staten Island Stapletons (1929–1932) and the New York Giants (1933–1935, 1939, 1944–1947). He also played two seasons in the rival AFL in 1936–1937 with the New York Yanks. His career saw him retire for four seasons (1940–1943), then come back to play for the Giants until 1947—mainly as a kicker. He usually bounced from fullback to halfback during his time in professional football.

Born in West Haven, Connecticut, Strong grew up the son of an egg and dairy inspector. The headstrong Strong gravitated to sports to find his passion. He became a star baseball and football player in high school. The two-way star took his skills into the Big Apple to New York University.

In 1928, Strong led the nation in scoring with 162 points and also had over 3,000 yards from scrimmage in his time at NYU and made numerous All-American squads. He was the best player in the nation that fall. Carnegie Tech coach Walter Steffen said of Strong's performance: "This is the first time in my career that one man was good enough to run over and completely wreck an exceptionally good team. I can tell you he is better than [Willie] Heston or [Jim] Thorpe." Famed sportswriter Grantland Rice wrote: "He [Strong] was like a runaway deer but with the speed of a deer. He ran all over a big powerful team, smashed its line, ran its ends, kicked 50 and 55 yards, threw passes and tackled all over

Ken Strong, halfback-fullback, New York Giants, ca. 1934 (courtesy New York University Athletics).

the lot. He was the best running back I've seen in years—and that includes Red Grange."[1]

After his stellar collegiate career at NYU, Strong was recruited to play pro ball by two NFL teams in New York, the Giants and the Staten Island Stapletons. Dan Blaine, owner of the Stapletons, made a generous offer to Strong, paying him $300 a game. Strong wanted to hear what the crosstown rivals would offer. The Giants sent head coach Leroy Andrew to sign him, but the coach fumbled the ball. Giants owner Tim Mara told Andrew to offer the NYU star $4,000 for the year, but Andrews thought he could get Strong for less, offering him only $3,000. Strong quickly refused knowing he was worth more. He went back to Blaine and signed with the upstart Stapletons who had just joined the NFL. Mara fumed not getting his man. He would have to wait a few years.

In 1929, Strong was the whole Staten Island team. The squad was built around his skills at halfback, and in his four years with the Stapletons he usually delivered a great effort. Because of the lack of other skillful teammates around him, the Stapes came up short on the scoreboard more times than not. Over his four years with Staten Island they compiled an overall record of 14–22–9, never finishing higher than sixth place in the league standings.

Strong was almost a one-man show for the Stapes. He played in 44 games over the four seasons (1929–1932), scoring 160 points, nearly half of the team's points during those four seasons. In 1931 alone he scored 53 of the team's 79 points—by scoring seven of the Stapes 11 touchdowns all season.

While playing in the fall with the Stapletons, Strong also played some minor league baseball. In 1930, while playing for the Hazleton (PA) Mountaineers of the New York–Pennsylvania League, he played in 117 games and hit .373 with 31 doubles, 16 triples and a whopping 41 home runs. Later that fall for Staten Island Strong scored seven touchdowns (two rushing and five receiving) and kicked eight extra points and one field goal, totaling 53 points. The Stapes ended up with a 5–5–2 record (sixth place, NFL), which would be Strong's best record during his four years with Staten Island. He was named First Team All-Pro by the *Green Bay Press-Gazette* and *Collyer's* in the same backfield with the likes of Benny Friedman, Red Grange and Ernie Nevers.

In 1931, Strong was off to a strong start on the baseball diamond with Toronto of the International League until tragedy struck. Strong ran full speed into the outfield wall, hurting his wrist. The injury left him unable to throw a baseball correctly, thus ending his baseball career. The wrist injury didn't hamper him on the gridiron, though, as he made All-Pro again in 1931 despite the Stapes' losing record of 4–6–1.

The following year, in the midst of the Depression, the Stapes lost too much money to stay alive. Strong had his worst year as a pro, scoring only two touchdowns as he guided his team to a terrible 2–7–3 record. After the 1932 season, the Stapletons went out of business. Strong was left to sign with another team.

This time the Giants would sign the former NYU star. While Strong was negotiating with the Giants, owner Tim Mara questioned Strong's yelling at players who may not have blocked well. "That's right," Strong told Mara. "I know I'm paid to run with the ball. I can't run with the ball unless someone does some blocking. So, I yell at them when they don't block. I play to win. If you don't want a winner, you better not hire me." Well Mara hired Strong, who instantly made the Giants better.[2]

In 1932, the Giants suffered a losing season, going 4–6–2 under Steve Owen. In 1933, it was a different story. Strong joined a team that had All-Pros at several positions, such as center Mel Hein, ends Ray Flaherty and Red Badgro, fullback Jack

McBride, as well as adding rookie quarterback Harry Newman. With all that talent, Strong was the best player on the team. He also would be the best player in the NFL.

Retro-MVP: 1933 NFL Season

Strong had his best year as a pro in 1933. That season he finished the season third in the NFL in touchdowns with five—scoring three different ways, by rushing (two), receiving (two) and interception return (one). His 64 points scored was the top in the league. Behind the play of Strong, the Giants compiled an 11–3 record and captured the Eastern Division title. "It was still a 60-minute game for all the regulars and when we substituted, we weakened the team, but not to the degree that we did at Staten Island," recalled Strong.[3]

Strong was never better than in a November 5 game against fellow MVP candidate halfback Glenn Presnell and the Portsmouth Spartans. Heading into the game, the Western Division Spartans were 5–1 and one game back of the undefeated Bears (6–0). At the Polo Grounds, Presnell started fast with an 80-yard touchdown run and a 20-yard field goal to give the Spartans a 10–0 lead heading into the fourth quarter. Then Strong took over the game. He caught a 12-yard scoring pass from Harry Newman and capped the comeback off with a short two-yard scoring plunge to give the Giants a 13–10 victory.

Led by Strong, the New York Giants would not lose another game the rest of the regular season—winning six straight. Two weeks after the Spartans win, Strong once again showed why he was the best player in the NFL. In front of 22,000 fans at the Polo Grounds, Strong's 21-yard field goal was the difference as the Giants defeated the Chicago Bears 3–0 in a hard-fought battle of the NFL's two best teams. The two teams would eventually meet in the NFL's first championship game with the Bears pulling out a 23–21 last-minute victory.

After the season, Strong was named First Team All-Pro by *Green Bay Press-Gazette*, United Press, *Collyer's*, *Brooklyn Times-Union* and *Chicago Daily News*. "Ken could not only do everything well—he could do everything brilliantly. There never was a greater all-around back," said Steve Owen in 1943. Strong wins the 1933 Retro-MVP award.[4]

The versatile Strong could do everything. His teammates knew the value he brought to the Giants. "[Strong] was not only a great power runner with speed, but he was an excellent defensive halfback ... after Ken's defensive days with the Giants ended, he became the Giants' all-around kicker. He was recognized as the greatest kicker of his era," said Mel Hein, Giants Hall of Fame teammate. A very versatile player from the halfback or fullback position, Strong was also one of the era's best kickers.[5]

After the heartbreak loss in the '33 title game, Strong and his Giants came back to win the NFL championship in 1934. In the championship game, Strong played a huge part in the Giants' comeback to win the famous "Sneakers Game" against the undefeated Bears, 30–13. In the game, he rushed nine times for 94 yards and two touchdowns; he also had two catches for 17 yards and kicked one field goal and two extra points, accounting for 17 of the Giants 30 points. "When I hit the hole, I was knocked backwards. I spun around and I saw a bit of daylight and went through it. For some reason, Brumbaugh and the other defensive backs were nowhere near me. I went all the way for a touchdown," recalled Strong about his 42-yard run in the Sneaker Game.[6]

In a shocking upset, Strong had won his first ever NFL championship. He always believed the magic "sneakers" weren't what won the game. "Actually, the sneakers weren't that much of a factor. By the end of the third quarter and through the fourth quarter they didn't make much difference. The Bears had started with new pointed cleats made of bakelite, I believe. By the end of the first half, they were nubs. That did make a difference. If they had new cleats for the second half, they would have walloped us," recalled Strong.[7]

Strong had a habit of playing big in the most important games the Giants played during his time in New York. He would score touchdowns in three straight NFL championship games from 1933–1935. In the 1935 NFL championship game, Strong had a 42-yard touchdown catch against the Lions, although the Giants would lose that game, 26–7, but it was proof that Strong played very well in some of the biggest games he ever played.

After the 1935 season, Strong left the Giants to play for more money in the rival American Football League (1936–1937). But it wasn't the same. He didn't receive all the money he was guaranteed, and he sat out the 1938 season before rejoining the Giants in 1939 when he played just nine games and suffered a broken back before retiring after the season.

Then with World War II in full tilt in 1944, Strong was asked by the Giants to come back and kick for them. He agreed. Over the next four seasons, Strong was one of the best place-kickers in the NFL, once leading the league in field goals made in 1944. "We had kickers, like Ken Strong," said Mel Hein, Giants Hall of Fame center. "He may stay out half an hour, forty-five minutes after practice and work on kicking that ball out of bounds, within the fifteen-yard line and the goal line, which would really put a team in the hole if you get in position like that."[8]

After the 1947 season, Strong retired for good at the age of 41. "Ken Strong is one of our all-time greatest stars in the history of the National Football League. He is a wonderful credit to sports and football in particular," said Bert Bell, NFL commissioner.[9]

Strong finished his career with 484 points, and his 324 points with the Giants was a team record, broken by Frank Gifford. He scored 34 total touchdowns with 24 rushing, seven receiving, two punt returns, and one interception return. He was one of the few fullbacks that would return kicks, scoring two career punt return TDs. He made 38 career FGs and was 111 of 166 on XP kicks. Strong led the NFL in points in

1933 (66) and in FGs made in 1931 (two) and in 1944 (six). He finished third in scoring in 1930 and fourth in 1931. Five times he finished in the top five in field goals made in 1933–1935, 1939, and 1944.

Strong played for 12 seasons in the NFL, playing against some of the two-way era's best. Who was the best he played against? "I'd have to go with Bronko Nagurski," said Strong in 1967. "But there were so many great ones, Mel Hein, Cal Hubbard and others. It's tough choosing one, but Bronko could do everything."[10]

Strong stayed around football as a kicking coach for the New York Giants for three seasons from 1962 to 1965, before becoming a liquor salesman near his home in Queens. Strong picked up several nice honors following his playing days. He was named to the NFL 1930s All-Decade Team, was the runner-up kicker on the NFL 50th Anniversary All-Time Team, and his number 50 jersey was retired by the New York Giants. Strong achieved the ultimate honor by getting inducted into the Pro Football Hall of Fame in 1967. "One of the greatest [Giants] of them all was Ken Strong. He was a fabulous all-around player, and he truly deserved to go into the Hall of Fame.... Strong was a great blocker, great punter, great runner and could pass with the best of them until he broke his hand," said Wellington Mara, Giants Hall of Fame owner.[11]

Ken Strong passed away from a heart attack on October 5, 1979, at the age of 73.

No. 21

Johnny "Blood" McNally
Halfback-Wingback

Full Name: John Victor McNally
Nicknames: "Blood"; "The Vagabond Halfback"
b: November 27, 1903 (New Richmond, WI); d: November 28, 1985 (age 82; Palm Springs, CA)
High School: New Richmond (WI); College: St. John's (MI), Notre Dame
Height/Weight: 6-1, 188 pounds
Position: Halfback-Wingback
Teams/Years: 1925–1926 Milwaukee Badgers; 1926–1927 Duluth Eskimos; 1928 Pottsville Maroons; 1929–1933, 1935–1936 Green Bay Packers; 1934, 1937–1938 Pittsburgh Pirates
Pro Football Hall of Fame: Class of 1963 (Charter Member)
Retro-MVPs: 1931
All-Time Teams: M. Gantenbein (1966); A. Herber (1966); C. Hinkle (1942); C. Lambeau (1946); V. Lewellen (1946); D. Tehan (1963)

The man they called "Blood" played in 137 games over 14 seasons for five different NFL franchises—Milwaukee, Duluth, Pottsville, Pittsburgh and most notably the Green Bay Packers. Because of his traveling nature he also was known as the "Vagabond Halfback."

John Victor McNally grew up the son of a mill factory manager father and a schoolteacher mother. Johnny would balance the outdoor, adventurous life—which he embraced—and the academic life throughout his entire life. While growing up in Northwest Wisconsin, McNally participated in a neighborhood game called Run, Run, Forward. "There was a lot of tackling, that sort of thing," recalled Johnny "Blood" McNally. "This was around 1910. I was very young when I got into it…. I went around with boys who were always two or three years older than I was, played with them and tried to compete in their games. I wasn't as physically developed as they were and consequently got knocked around a lot. No one ever considered that I would wind up being an athlete back then."[1]

Despite his skinny frame, McNally loved to play sports. His mother had different plans, expecting her son to get his education. He graduated high school early—14 years old—then went off to college at nearby River Falls. After one year there McNally went to St. John's University (MN), his father's alma mater. While at St. John's, McNally played organized football for the first time. "I'd never played football in my life," said McNally. "This guy thought I looked the right size to be a football player, I guess, so he chose me."²

After three years at St. John's, McNally took a step up by attending Notre Dame in the fall of 1923 and learning from the great Knute Rockne. McNally found his true spot on the field. "A tackle's job is to seek contact. A halfback's job is to avoid contact. I think my talent, if I have any, lies in avoiding contact," said McNally to one of the Irish coaches. Very soon, McNally's heart and wandering spirt got the best of him, and he left Notre Dame.³

During one summer away from football,

Johnny "Blood" McNally, halfback, Green Bay Packers, ca. 1935–1936 (courtesy Green Bay Packers).

McNally found himself back in Minneapolis to learn the newspaper trade from his uncle. At this time, he helped one of his St. John's buddies, Ralph Hanson, get a job at the paper. One day at work, McNally saw an item in the newspaper that caught his attention. It was an ad for "able-body young men" to play semi-pro football with a local team called the East 26th Street Liberties. Five other teams were looking for men and they would form a citywide league for play that fall. Since the Liberties were the team closest to the newspaper's office, McNally and Hanson decided to head over to the Liberties practice field after work one day. Both of them had one year of college eligibility left that they wanted to protect. The two agreed to use fake names to protect their eligibility. But what names to use?

After work, Hanson hopped on the back of McNally's Ace motorcycle to head over to the practice field. Seven blocks later, McNally swung the motorcycle east, passing the Garrick Theatre, and he looked up at the marquee sign. It read, "Rudolph Valentino, Star of *Blood and Sand*." McNally stopped the bike and told Hanson, "That's it! I'll be Blood and you be Sand…. If Olsen and Johnson had been playing, I guess we would have been John Olsen and Ralph Johnson," said McNally many years later.⁴

That fall "Blood" and "Sand" made the team and helped the Liberties win the league championship. "About twenty guys came out—cops, truck drivers, a couple of kids just out of high school, a few guys like Ralph and me, who'd played some college ball and just wanted to keep playing," said McNally. Play football he did. He was even paid $6 a game. McNally had missed playing football. Despite his vagabond travels and his indecision of a career, he definitely loved to play football.[5]

After his success with the Liberties, McNally was recruited to play pro ball the following fall with the Ironwood Miners who played in a league in the Iron Range of Michigan's Upper Peninsula—an area known for its toughness. McNally was offered a whopping salary of $60 a game. He jumped at the opportunity, upsetting his whole family. McNally explained: "I wanted to be able to something I enjoyed and something that would leave me enough leisure time to do other things that I enjoyed. The family, I'm sure, thought I was being lazy, being afraid of work. But that wasn't it. I've worked hard at a lot of jobs. What I wanted was freedom, and freedom meant, to me, being allowed to choose what I wanted to do."[6]

McNally joined the Miners for the 1925 season. He earned his $60 a game the hard way, both on and off the field: "This was quite a training ground. The games were rough as hell, but the parties after the games were even rougher. Both teams would usually go over to Hurley to drink, and the brawls that started during the game would resume right where they'd been left off," said McNally.[7]

After just three games with the Miners, McNally was contacted by the Milwaukee Badgers of the NFL to come play for them. They offered $75 a game. He took the money and left the Miners behind. McNally was joining the big leagues, but not a good team. The Badgers finished the 1925 season not winning a single game, going 0–6. The Badgers were no longer in the NFL and McNally didn't have a team.

The following fall McNally was recruited to play halfback for the Duluth Eskimos who had just signed former Stanford All-American fullback Ernie Nevers to play as a full-fledged traveling team. Between September 6, 1926, and February 5, 1927, the Eskimos played 29 games (15 exhibitions and 14 league games). The squad rarely had more than 16 players at one time and during one eight-day stretch, the team played five games in five different cities. The Eskimos logged over 17,000 miles that season and finished with a 19–7–3 record.

While on the tour McNally impressed Eskimos team manager Ole Haugsrud with his pass catching abilities: "He always kept his body between the ball and the defensive man, and he used his body, his elbows, his shoulders, everything to protect the ball, just like a good rebounder does," recalled Haugsrud. "We knew, even if he was covered, we could throw him an alley oop pass—we didn't call it that, but that's what it was—and he'd probably come down with it." Haugsrud also had to deal with the zany side of Blood. "[John] was clearly the most colorful character on the Eskimos squad. Truly brilliant, both physically and mentally, but a trifle unpredictable."[8]

The following year McNally returned to the Eskimos. This time the season wasn't as fun as the team finished in last place in the NFL standings with a 1–8 record. The novelty had now worn off. It was time for the Vagabond Halfback to move on. McNally ended up signing with the Pottsville Maroons who were on the downside of being a competitive team. After winning seasons in 1925 and 1926, the Maroons limped to a 5–8 season in 1927. They looked to get back on track in 1928 and signing McNally was a good start. However, he was all they brought in. The Maroons were old with former Canton Bulldog star Pete Henry and fullback Tony Latone, both 31 years old. The Maroons went a disappointing 2–8 and then folded.

After playing for five different professional teams in five seasons, Johnny Blood would finally find a home in the NFL. Curly Lambeau, the head coach of the Green Bay Packers, wanted to improve his roster to help compete for an NFL championship. From 1921 to 1928 the Packers had eight straight winning seasons but no NFL titles. The flamboyant coach used the passing game as his number one weapon to win games. In 1928, the Packers played the Pottsville Maroons where McNally scored two touchdowns against Lambeau's boys in a 26–0 upset win. Curly was impressed by McNally's pass catching abilities that day, so he brought the free agent to Green Bay.

Very quickly Lambeau found out that McNally would be a handful. In his initial letter to McNally stating his contract terms, Lambeau wrote, "Dear John, I'll give you a hundred dollars a game or a hundred and ten if you won't drink from Wednesday until after the game." A few days later John replied, "I'll take the hundred." Eventually, the two agreed on $110 per game, with McNally still being able to drink on Wednesday.[9]

Over the long haul, the tradeoff for Lambeau dealing with Johnny Blood was worth it. While Lambeau, the coach, might not have appreciated Blood's off-field antics—drinking, breaking training rules, missing curfew—Lambeau, the manager, knew that his notoriety and on-the-field heroics would bring in paying customers. The resulting cash flow kept the Packers football machine alive in small-town Green Bay, while the Johnny Blood party train kept moving forward.

In 1929, McNally helped the Packers achieve greatness on the football field. At this time McNally was considered one of the game's best pass receiving backs. He could also throw the ball with accuracy and was a serviceable punter. Lambeau used his new weapon in the passing game that he pioneered, helping the Packers to back-to-back NFL championships. Over those two seasons McNally scored 10 total touchdowns and was named Second Team All-Pro by the *Green Bay Press-Gazette* in 1929 and by *Collyer's* in 1930.

But 1931 would be a season for the ages. Johnny Blood was the best player in the NFL, scoring 14 touchdowns in 14 games and an NFL-best 84 points. The next closet total was 66 by Ernie Nevers of the Chicago Cardinals. Twice that season he scored three TDs in a single game. He earns our Retro-MVP for 1931. The 14 touchdowns in 14 games set an NFL record for a single season that was broken in 1942 by Don Hutson's 17. "Johnny was a wonderful receiver," recalled Ray Flaherty, Giants Hall of Fame end. "Johnny Blood was probably as good a receiver as anyone in football until Don Hutson came along."[10]

Behind the play of McNally, the Packers won the NFL championship for the third straight season. Over those three seasons the Packers compiled an overall record of 34–5–2. Blood was convinced the pro game was the best place to play. "There is no room for loafers in the National Professional Football League," said McNally to the *Minneapolis Tribune*. "The club owners have had little trouble with their players during the past two years with the result that our patrons are treated to high-grade exhibitions. If you ask me, the professional teams play football that comes as near being perfect as humanly possible."[11]

The 6-1, 188-pound McNally played his best football during his seven years with the Packers, helping them win four NFL championships, from 1929 to 1931, and in 1936. McNally was a very versatile player, who had a knack for the big play. He was an excellent receiver, one of the best to come along in the NFL's first decade. McNally flourished in Lambeau's passing offense by combining his great speed and outstanding football instincts to regularly come up with the acrobatic catches. In his career he caught an amazing 37 touchdowns, which was the NFL record until Don Hutson came along.

McNally also had the skills to make the big play, especially in crunch time. He scored 18 touchdowns in the fourth quarter and had 21 TDs of 30 or more yards. His flair for the dramatic was evident in 1930 when he caught a 70-yard TD in the fourth quarter to beat the Giants 14–7, and even later in his career in 1937, with the game tied in the fourth quarter against the Eagles, McNally ran back a kickoff 92 yards and caught a 44-yard TD to seal a 27–14 win for Pittsburgh.

After winning the 1936 NFL championship with the Packers, Blood could see his time in Green Bay was done and a $3,000 offer from Art Rooney to coach and play for the Pirates was too good to pass up. McNally would coach the Pirates for three seasons but retired as a player after the 1938 season. Despite having a great football mind, it didn't translate into victories, and over three years McNally won just six games (6–19 overall record). "I like him. I think he was a great football player," recalled Art Rooney, "and I think he could have been a great coach because of his intelligence. Unfortunately, he just wasn't disciplined enough to do it."[12]

After the first three games of the season in 1939, all losses, McNally turned in his resignation to Rooney. Johnny Blood the football star was done with football. Despite his off-the-field antics and unique personality, McNally was a tremendous football player in the NFL's two-way era. A much better offensive player, he scored 49 career TDs (297 career points). Only former Packers teammate Verne Lewellen (#7) scored more (51). He showed flashes of brilliance on defense, scoring five touchdowns on interception returns and was an aggressive tackler. But McNally's lack of discipline and consistency are what hurt him. He would sometimes disappear from games and not be a factor, other games his play would decide the outcome.

McNally was highly thought of by his peers and the press. He was a Charter Member of the Pro Football Hall of Fame in 1963, made the NFL 1930s All-Decade Team and was elected to the Packers Hall of Fame in 1970.

Johnny "Blood" McNally died on November 28, 1985, at the age of 82.

No. 22

Red Grange
Halfback

Full Name: Harold Edward Grange
Nicknames: "Red"; "Galloping Ghost"; "The Wheaton Iceman"
b: June 13, 1903 (Forksville, PA); d: January 28, 1991 (age 87; Indian Lakes, FL)
High School: Wheaton (IL); College: Illinois
Height/Weight: 6-0, 180 pounds
Position: Halfback
Teams/Years: 1925, 1929–1934 Chicago Bears; 1926–1927 New York Yankees (AFL-NFL)
Pro Football Hall of Fame: Class of 1963 (Charter Member)
Retro-MVPs: No
All-Time Teams: C. Cagle (1937); J. Carr (1934); E. Cuneo (1973); G. Halas (1939, 1940, 1941); C. Hubbard (1966); V. Lewellen (1936); J. McMillen (1939); G. Musso (1964); E. Nevers (1932); S. Owen (1952, 1955); R. Richards (1944); C. Storck (1939)

The legendary Red Grange. The "Galloping Ghost." It's hard to believe that he's only ranked number 22.

The NFL's first superstar, the 6-0, 180-pound Grange played 96 NFL games over nine seasons of professional football with two teams—his own New York Yankees and the Chicago Bears. The game's greatest open field runner coming out of the University of Illinois, Grange was more of an all-around player in the NFL after suffering a major knee injury in 1927 that caused him to miss the entire 1928 season. Not only was he productive as a runner in the NFL, but he was also one of the game's premiere defensive players during this era.

Born in central Pennsylvania in 1903, Grange lost his mother when he was six years old, prompting his father to move the family west to Wheaton, Illinois, to be near his siblings. It was here that Grange learned the game of football. It was football in the fall that got his blood going more than anything else. "We used to play football in a vacant lot near the edge of town. None of us had uniforms but improvised by cutting off the pant legs of our oldest trousers and added padding where needed most. The lot we played on was convex in shape, with fifty yards of the field on one side of a hill and fifty yards on the other. On a kickoff the ball would sail up and over the top of the hill, seemingly coming from nowhere. By the time a player tucked the pigskin under his arm and started up the field behind his interference, the opposition would suddenly swarm over the top like

Red Grange, halfback, Chicago Bears, ca. 1925 (Library of Congress).

'The Charge of the Light Brigade.' It was enough to scare the daylights out of a kid."[1]

Grange was a gifted athlete from the beginning. He was an unstoppable force during his prep career in Wheaton, usually scoring three or four touchdowns a game. He also gained his first nickname. While in high school Grange got a job delivering ice around town, earning the moniker "The Wheaton Iceman." Besides making some extra money during the summer, Red quickly learned that delivering ice could benefit his athletic career—especially in football. Years later, Red would recall how the job helped him physically:

> It is an accepted fact the most important parts of a football player are his legs. Keeping those legs in shape represents the biggest single responsibility of a boy interested in playing football. While working on a road gang, laboring in the coal mines or steel mills is good for general muscle development, it contributes nothing toward keeping a player's legs in condition. One stands still when working at those jobs and doesn't use his legs. Delivering ice, which required my walking miles every day up and down stairs, kept me in all-around fine trim and provided the best possible off-season training for my legs.
>
> The most important thing for a player to remember is that football isn't a game that can be played just three months in the fall. In order to excel in the sport, one must constantly work at keeping his body and, especially, his legs strong the other nine months of the year.
>
> Reporting for football in the fall after a summer on the ice truck, I would be tough as nails and at least four weeks ahead of the other boys in conditioning. My iceman duties made my

arms, shoulders and legs strong and developed my wind. It was, in effect, my own private brand of "spring training."[2]

Grange used his outstanding athletic ability not just to dominate his high school opponents, he also used his great open field running skills to become a national sensation at the University of Illinois. Mainly running out of the single-wing, Grange became a three-time All-American halfback under the coaching of Bob Zuppke. His signature game was as a junior in 1924 when he scored four touchdowns in the first 12 minutes against mighty Michigan, putting his name in every newspaper across the country. At Illinois he was given the nickname the "Galloping Ghost."

After the Michigan game, Grange was in the short conversation of being the greatest college football player of all time. He had maximized his time at Illinois. "You know, you can't beat the training you receive on a university football squad to prepare you for the hard knocks of the future when you go forth to earn a livelihood. That training makes real men of the boys. It puts you in the very best physical condition so there isn't any reason for whimpering when you are nailed hard by an opposing tackler," said Red Grange in 1925.[3]

Because of his success, the football world and the rest of the country were very curious to see what Grange would do once he finished his senior year at Illinois. In the end, Grange chose to do the most unpopular thing he could do: he chose to play professional football. That caused a firestorm when he left school after his final collegiate game. Grange went on to join the Chicago Bears of the NFL and went on the famous 1925–1926 Barnstorming Tour that elevated the pro game nationally. Excellent on end runs in the Bears offense on tour, he scored 17 touchdowns in 17 games on the tour. Throughout the tour Grange attracted sold-out crowds in Chicago, Philadelphia, New York (70,000), Tampa, Los Angeles (75,000) and San Francisco. It was the first time the NFL became national news.

After tour ended Grange formed his own league, the rival American Football League (AFL), and operated his own team, the New York Yankees. For the next two years he played for the Yankees. Although he was the main target in the Yankees offense, Grange had a solid year in 1926. He finished third in the AFL in scoring with 50 points as the Yankees finished in second place behind the Philadelphia Quakers.

The following year, the AFL disbanded and the Yankees joined the NFL. Grange suffered a horrible knee injury against of all teams—the Chicago Bears. In the fourth game of the year, Grange went high to catch a pass and was tackled hard by former teammate George Trafton. When he came down, he had torn ligaments in his right knee. He would never be the same runner again.

Grange sat out the 1928 season, thinking his football career was over. But one man wouldn't give up on the Galloping Ghost. George Halas thought Red still had a few more good years of playing ahead of him. Plus, he could still put fans in the stands. Rejoining the Bears in 1929, Grange tried to recapture his glory days of running with the ball. "There have been faster runners than Grange, and probably more elusive ones," recalled Benny Friedman, Hall of Fame quarterback, "but he ran naturally knock-kneed. His gait baffled tacklers…. Unless you had seen Grange carrying the ball you wouldn't appreciate how deceptive his manner of running was. It set up a lot of ineffective tackles against him."[4]

By this time Grange knew he was just another ball carrier. Instead of accepting his limitations, Grange focused on the other parts of his game to become one of the best all-around players in the NFL. He started on the defensive side of the ball. Underrated for his intelligence, Grange was excellent in pass coverage, being able to read pass plays very well. He never seemed to be out of position. After his injury, he knew his own strengths and leaned on them. "What many people don't realize is that Grange was outstanding as a defensive player. He had the ability to smell out plays and was great," said George Musso in 1964. "In addition to being one of the greatest open field runners in football history, Grange was also tops when it came to breaking up passes on the defense. A completed pass in his territory was as rare as an 80-yard punt. The crowds only saw his spectacular running, but you can bet that the men that played with him knew what he could do," wrote Cliff Battles, Redskins Hall of Fame halfback, in 1938.[5]

"Red Grange was a great football player. Unfortunately, he hurt his knee and was never the great offensive player that he was before. But when Grange left the New York Yankees and went out for the Chicago Bears he usually played left halfback and I was usually playing right end. He was covering me. I think that he was probably the best defensive back in the league," recalled Ray Flaherty, New York Giants All-Pro end, in 1985.[6]

Once he got over his knee injury Grange became a better, more all-around player, not just a breakaway threat. He played a key role in the revamped offense by often going in motion before the snap. "He was shifty. Red had a way of faking people out of position. He'd make you think he's going one way and the other. You never knew where he was going. He just faked you out of your supporter," said George Musso, Bears Hall of Fame lineman. "He was just a good offensive running man. Not only that, he was a good blocker too. Because he used to run interference too for ballplayers when he wasn't carrying the ball. What made him clever was how he could handle his body. And shift it from stopping. People just didn't know how to tackle him. You'd tackle him, you'd get an armful of air. Try to tackle him and he wasn't there. He was just a good running back."[7]

Some of his best games came against the Green Bay Packers, the best team in the NFL for three straight years from 1929 to 1931. "Grange was better than anyone ever gave him credit for. Not only could he run but he might even have been a better blocker than he was a runner. And his defensive skills were superb. At Green Bay, we had a pretty good passing team but whenever we got ready to play the Bears, we'd steer our attack away from his area," said Cal Hubbard, Packers Hall of Fame tackle. "Today Grange is the best blocking back in the league. That shows you what a great natural player he was from the start. It's comparable to changing Lefty Grove over into a home run slugger," said Curly Lambeau, Packers Hall of Fame coach, in 1932.[8]

Grange became a key member of the Bears team that won back-to-back NFL championships in 1932–1933. He made big plays in both postseason games. He caught the game-winning touchdown pass from Bronko Nagurski in the fourth quarter to defeat the Portsmouth Spartans, 9–0, to win the '32 championship. He followed that up the next year by making a late game-saving touchdown tackle to preserve a 23–21 win over the Giants in the NFL's first ever championship game. "That play Grange made was the greatest defensive play I ever saw," said George Halas.[9]

His statistics seem "small" considering his status as one of the NFL's all-time greats. He scored 194 points and had 32 career touchdowns (21 rushing; 10 receiving; one interception return) in 96 NFL games. He finished fifth in the NFL in scoring in 1930 and 1931, and second in 1932 with 42 points, when Dutch Clark led with 55. For three straight years from 1930 to 1932, Grange made First Team All-Pro. His superb all-around play in the NFL, especially in his later years from 1929 to 1934, earned him number 22 on the list. After the 1934 season, Grange retired for good at the age of 31.

Once retired, Grange received almost every post-career honor. He had his Bears number 77 jersey retired in 1949; he was named to the NFL 1920s All-Decade Team; he was the NFL 50th Anniversary All-Time Team's second halfback behind Gale Sayers and was a Charter Member of the Pro Football Hall of Fame in 1963.

Opponents and teammates never failed to praise the Galloping Ghost. For nearly 100 years Grange's name has always been at the top of the list as one of the game's earliest stars. "He was one of the best blockers I ever faced, and he was simply terrific as a defensive back. At 180–185 pounds, Red had everything as a runner: speed, shiftiness, and power," said Steve Owen, Giants Hall of Fame player-coach.[10]

"Greatest player I ever saw? [Ernie] Nevers was a great back ... he's a dandy all right and may be the greatest of them all, but you've asked my opinion and I've given it. It's Red Grange," said Verne Lewellen in 1936. "I'd like to get in a word about 'Red' Grange," said Bronko Nagurski in 1944. "For my dough, 'Red' was the greatest team player in pro football history. He always went out of his way to make plays go when he himself was not supposed to figure in them prominently. He had a wonderful spirit. His work on pass defense was particularly brilliant.... And even when he was far past his prime, we were able to recognize his great ability when he turned on the stream for occasional spurts. Yes, you must class 'Red' Grange as one of the greatest football players of all time. He'll always be tops in my book."[11]

Grange served as an assistant coach with the Bears from 1935 to 1940 and then became the first former player to broadcast football games for college and pro football on radio and television. He worked NFL games until his retirement after the 1963 season and was a pioneer in football broadcasting.

Red Grange died on January 29, 1991, at the age of 87.

No. 23

Fritz Pollard

Halfback

Full Name: Frederick Douglass Pollard
Nickname: "Fritz"
b: January 27, 1894 (Chicago, IL); d: May 11, 1986 (age 92; Silver Spring, MD)
High School: Lane Tech (IL); College: Brown (Bates)
Height/Weight: 5–9, 165 pounds
Position: Halfback
Teams/Years: 1919–1921, 1925–1926 Akron Pros/Indians; 1922 Milwaukee Badgers; 1923–1924 Gilberton Cadamounts (Independent team); 1923, 1925 Hammond Pros; 1925 Providence Steam Roller
Pro Football Hall of Fame: Class of 2005
Retro-MVPs: 1920
All-Time Teams: P. Robeson (1941)

One of the game's greatest pioneers, halfback Fritz Pollard appeared in 49 games over six seasons in the NFL for four different teams—Akron, Milwaukee, Hammond, and Providence. He's mostly known for being the first Black head coach in NFL history with the 1921 Akron Pros, but along with his historical significance in league history, Pollard goes down as one the more dynamic halfbacks during the two-way era, coming in as our seventh greatest halfback.

Fredrick Douglass Pollard, born on January 27, 1894, grew up in Rogers Park, a quasi-suburban, mostly white neighborhood on the northern fringe of Chicago. His father, a Civil War veteran and successful barber, named him Frederick Douglass, after the abolitionist. But his German and Luxembourger playmates shortened that to Fritz. While growing up in the Windy City, the younger Pollard idolized his older brothers, Luther, Leslie and Hughes, who looked after their younger sibling.

Fritz attended Albert Grannis Lane Manual Training High School, also known as "Lane Tech," where he excelled in many sports. In high school Pollard was an all-around athlete, excelling as a running back, a three-time Cook County track champion, and a talented baseball player. In his first football game for Lane Tech, Pollard was being abused by a Hyde Park tackle named Butch Scanlon. His big brother, Hughes, asked for the ball and flattened the Irish kid. "I was real excited about playing organized football," recalled Fritz Pollard. "I used to play a lot of pickup games with my brothers during my grammar school days.

Fritz Pollard, halfback, Akron Pros, ca. 1915 (courtesy Brown University Athletics).

They made sure I got a chance to play despite my size. They taught me a lot about the game. I remember my first game in high school against Hyde Park. They tried to massacre me. But my brother Hughes told them, 'That's my kid brother,' and because they had so much respect for him, they didn't give me any trouble from then on."[1]

Even for the early days of football, Pollard was small, peaking at 5-9, 165 pounds. But he quickly learned how to protect himself. "Being Black never really affected me on the playing field. I was taught early on by my father and my brothers not to pay any attention to anything negative," recalled Fritz Pollard. "I would forget the color of my skin when I played, and if anything happened to me physically, my brothers taught me how to protect myself. See, opposing players would try to hit me hard, one on top and one below. But my brothers taught me to spin out of it, so I wouldn't get caught in a pileup where they could get me. After that, some players would say, 'Well you little Black so-and-so, I'll get you the next time.' So the next time they'd tear into me again, but after the tackle I would spin away from them. That was a way of protecting myself against any rough play."[2]

The family thought Pollard might attend nearby Northwestern or Ivy League Dartmouth, where his brother Leslie attended. But Fritz went east to another Ivy League school—Brown University. Now, teams like Brown, Yale and Harvard might not be college football powers today, but they were the USC, Alabama and Florida of their era. Of course, they were basically all white, so when Pollard ran all over a team like Yale, it attracted a lot of attention.

In 1915, Brown went 5-3-1 but was chosen to play Washington State in the Rose Bowl after Syracuse bowed out. Of course, Pollard was the first African American to play in the Rose Bowl, but the trip was not without challenges. Pollard was refused service by the porters of the Pullman train car that carried his teammates across the country. The hotel the team was staying at in California even refused to give a room to Pollard. It wasn't until an assistant coach threatened to remove the entire Brown team that the hotel acquiesced and let him stay.

And the game itself was a disappointment. The entire team was ill-equipped to play the game—literally. The team arrived in California without "weather" cleats and a rare rainstorm in January turned the Rose Bowl turf into a quagmire. Pollard and the entire Brown squad were ineffective. Even a last-ditch effort to wear shoes multiple sizes too big couldn't save the day for Pollard. His biggest contribution might have been his theatrics as he begged his coach to put him back in. Brown lost to Washington State, 14-0. The game might not have worked out in Pollard's favor, but he was still one of the biggest names in football.

During the summer of 1916 Pollard worked at a resort in Narragansett Pier making a few dollars. While there he met Paul Robeson, who had just completed his freshmen year at Rutgers. Pollard recalled seeing Robeson wearing a black sweater with a big R on it. "What's that stand for?" Pollard asked. The huge New Jersey linemen fired back, "Rutgers." That fall when Rutgers played Brown the two teams played the most "murderous game" in which Pollard ever played. In the end, though, he became very good friends with Robeson.

That fall Pollard helped Brown University continue its winning ways. He worked on his change of direction and his cross-step dodge, which would now be considered a stutter-step, to make him an even better player in 1916. Brown won their first eight games beating the likes of Rutgers, Yale and Harvard, and outscoring their opponents by a score of 254–9! But in their last game of the year, they lost the "national championship" by losing 28–0 to Colgate.

At the end of the year Pollard was honored with many accolades. The *New York Times* named him to the All-Eastern football team, devoting six paragraphs to his spectacular season. Two weeks later the Father of American Football, Walter Camp, named Pollard the first team left halfback on his All-American squad, making Pollard the first African American back to be named to Walter Camp's All-American Team.

After the 1916 season Pollard left Brown. He went to Philadelphia, studied to be a dentist at the University of Pennsylvania, coached football at Lincoln University and served in the Army during World War I, before he was finally recruited to play professional football. He was contacted to play halfback for the Akron Indians by his former Brown teammate, Clair Purdy.

In October 1919, Pollard stepped off a train in Akron on a Sunday morning and caught a taxicab downtown to the city's local cigar store. He had been summoned by its owner, Frank Neid, who was also the fedora-wearing manager of the Akron Indians. Two weeks earlier, the Indians had lost 9–6 to their Ohio League rival, the Massillon Tigers. That defeat set Neid looking to sign the best running back in the country for the upcoming rematch. Akron was a four-time champion of the Ohio League, the semi-pro setup that was the seed of the National Football League. When the Indians offered Pollard $200 for the game against the Tigers, he caught an overnight train to Ohio, arriving just behind this headline in the *Akron Beacon-Journal*: "The Akron Indians ... have landed the kingpin of them all: Pollard, the great All-American halfback from Brown has been signed to play with Akron for the remainder of the season."[3]

After getting to Akron, Pollard made his way to Neid's cigar shop. Neid spotted Pollard and invited him upstairs to his office. The manager was a little disappointed by his new acquisition's runtiness—Pollard was only 5-9, 165 pounds, while Neid had been expecting a six-footer. "Frank Neid the manager said, 'You're not Pollard,'" recalled Pollard. "Then we went out to practice and they had some old kind of plays that I used to hear about back in 1909, 1910 and what not, and it was simple to catch onto them. Fortunately, Neid called the fellows together and said, 'This is Pollard, he's going to play' and that was that. And I happened to get away and play a good game."[4]

Akron lost the grudge match against Massillon, 13–6, but the Tigers' threat to "get Pollard" failed, as he scored the Indians' only touchdown. As the only Black player on his high school team, and later at Brown, Pollard had learned to avoid the violence of opponents who resented his intrusion on a white man's gridiron. A running back's task is evasion—sidestepping and sprinting away from defenders trying to drag him down. Pollard was an early master of that art, with speed, a nimble crossover step, and the ability to cut away from tacklers, slipping out of their trajectory, leaving behind empty air and frustration. But as an African American player, and a prominent one, he'd also been forced to develop an after-the-whistle game, to avoid cheap shots by racist tacklers. If they tried, Pollard had learned to roll over and pull his legs up cleats first, so the defense couldn't wrench his ankles. If they tried, he delivered a kick to the nose, which was usually effective in those leather-helmeted days, when players weren't protected by facemasks.

"When I first came into the league, they didn't want me to play because I was Black," said Pollard in 1972. "But I ignored them and went out and played as well as I could. When they saw how good I was, they began to overlook the fact that I was Black."[5]

Pollard quickly became Akron's headline attraction, drawing fans not only for the novelty of seeing an All-American from an Ivy League school, but a diminutive Black man threading through ponderous defensive lines. Pollard's influence was bigger than Akron's 5–5 overall record. "I turned the whole complexion of the Akron team around," recalled Pollard. "This is 1919 and I started giving them the Brown system. I think the only team later that I found out was using anything near that was Canton. So, we began winning games. [Teammates] didn't say anything and they accepted what I said because the manager told them if they didn't like what I said the hell with them, because he saw that I was developing a good team, that was 1919." The following year saw Akron reach the top of the mountain, this time in an organized league that would change the outlook of professional football for good. Again, Pollard would make history.[6]

In 1920, Akron joined the American Professional Football Association—the precursor to the NFL. Lightning fast and equally quick, Pollard was one of the best players in the inaugural year of the APFA-NFL. Pollard led Akron to the championship with an 8–0–3 overall record. He was brilliant all season on end runs as he scored seven touchdowns—five rushing, one receiving, one via punt return. His best game came late in the season against the Dayton Triangles on November 28 when he scored both TDs in a 14–0 win, keeping Akron in first place.

He was also excellent on defense, helping the Pros outscore their opponents 151–7; they allowed only a single TD all season. Pollard is our 1920 Retro-MVP, the NFL's first Most Valuable Player. "Fritz Pollard, the colored Akron flash, was supreme in the open field with the possible exception of [Paddy] Driscoll. His speed can be sensed by the fact that he was the lightest player in the conference, weighing under 150 pounds. The little halfback was the hero of nearly all of Akron's victorious marches up and down the field," wrote the *Rock Island Argus* naming Pollard First Team All-Pro in 1920.[7]

Pollard was gaining the trust of his teammates who defended him on and off the field. "Very seldom that any opponents ever got a chance to slug me," said Pollard. "This fellow by the name of Charles Copley and this fellow from Tennessee, Rip King, big brutes, they used to say, 'Get away from him, get away from him,' and they stand around me and wouldn't let the guys come in there and jump on me after I was down. I had a way of rolling over and putting my legs up so that nobody could hit them and it was very seldom that they tackled me and tried to wrench my ankles."[8]

On Halloween in 1920, the Pros returned to Canton for a rematch against Jim Thorpe's Bulldogs, who had not been beaten since 1917. Thorpe predicted Pollard wouldn't show up. He boasted crudely. Pollard did show up—again an hour late. "Hello, little Black boy," Thorpe greeted him. "Hello, big Black boy," Pollard said back. Thorpe was dumbfounded by the brashness, but by the end of the game, Pollard had his respect. The Pros won, 10–0, on a field goal and an interception return. Pollard didn't score but executed two "sensational" punt returns.[9]

Pollard's devotion to pro football cost him his head coaching job at Lincoln University. In 1921, he was operating solely in Akron, so Pollard moved his family to Ohio and was named co-head coach of the Pros with Elgie Tobin. He was a player-coach and the first African American head coach in NFL history. In truth, he had been playing that role since he'd joined the Akron team, teaching "the Brown system" to teammates who were still running primitive offensive schemes. Pollard's first move was to sign Paul Robeson, his old rival from Rutgers. A 6-2, 225-pound end, Robeson was also named to Walter Camp's All-America team, making the Pros not only the first NFL team with an African American coach, but the first to start two African American players.

That fall Pollard guided Akron to an 8–3–1 record and a third-place finish in the NFL. He scored seven touchdowns and tied for second in the NFL in scoring with 42 points, trailing Buffalo's Elmer Oliphant's 47. "Small and quick. Once [Pollard], after he had been knocked down repeatedly by players huskier than himself, I asked him how he kept from getting killed. Fritz replied, 'Where do they think I is, I ain't,'" recalled Bob "Nasty" Nash, Akron end, 1920.[10]

Led by Pollard, the 1921 Pros started the season with eight straight shutouts. In the second game, Pollard scored three touchdowns against Cincinnati, even though he didn't play until the second half, joining the game after fans taunted, "Hey, Pollard, you make a good spectator!" In November, though, Robeson and Pollard were injured, and the Pros suffered a three-game losing streak, including a 14–0 Thanksgiving loss to Canton that eliminated them from title contention.

Pollard would leave Akron in 1922, ending up with the Milwaukee Badgers, where he teamed up with Paul Robeson again. The Milwaukee Badgers went 2–4–3 that season. Pollard played in seven games and scored 20 points including three touchdowns. Also, about this time Pollard assembled an all-Black team, "Fritz Pollard and His All-Stars," which played an exhibition game against an all-white team in Chicago. Pollard's team won, 6–0, when he threw a 20-yard touchdown pass to Robeson.

Pollard then became somewhat of a vagabond player, playing with the Hammond Pros (NFL) in 1923 and '25, the Gilberton Cadamounts, an independent professional team located in the coal region of eastern Pennsylvania in 1923 and 1924, and a few games with the Providence Steam Roller in 1925. In 1926, he returned to Akron to play four games for the Pros. After a truncated 1–4–3 season witnessed by dwindling crowds, Akron's NFL franchise folded. That fall would be the last time Pollard played in the NFL.

As the Depression hit the country and the NFL's major league ambitions grew, somehow the NFL had no room for African American players, who had mainly been hired by town teams desperate for a draw. In 1933, the Depression was cutting into the NFL's gate receipts and inciting white resentment against Black people who competed for good jobs. The following year (1934), the NFL would have no African American players.

Over the past eight decades, historians have searched for evidence on how the color line was instituted. Fritz Pollard always blamed George Halas for banning Black people from the NFL. It was a grudge, Pollard suggested, that went all the way back to their high school days in Chicago, when Lane Tech had bested Halas' Crane Tech at baseball and football. Pollard was especially bitter because at the end of the 1920 season, Halas had proposed a game in Chicago between the unbeaten Pros and his 10–1–1 Staleys. The Pros felt they had nothing to prove, but Pollard insisted they play, and the game ended in a tie.

In the end Pollard finished his NFL career with 19 touchdowns (16 rushing, two receiving, one on a muffed punt return). He also is unofficially credited with five touchdown passes. Playing defensive halfback, Pollard was a notch below some of the better halfbacks on defense, but there's no questioning that he was feared as one of the era's greatest breakaway threats.

Fritz Pollard died on May 11, 1986, at the age of 92.

Pollard was not elected to the Pro Football Hall of Fame while he was alive. It was an egregious error by the voters for decades. Up until his death, Pollard felt burned by the fact that he was not a member of the Pro Football Hall of Fame. Finally in 2005, he was placed on the Hall of Fame Seniors Committee ballot. Pollard's time had finally come. "It just seemed like a no-brainer to me," said Don Pierson, a retired *Chicago Tribune* sportswriter who sat on the committee. "Here's the first Black coach, a superstar at the time." Pierson figured Pollard had "slipped through the cracks" of NFL history.[11]

Pollard was inducted along with two-way era quarterback Benny Friedman, and modern-day quarterbacks Dan Marino and Steve Young. "I had a lot of fun playing pro football," said Fritz Pollard in 1976. "I got a chance to play the game when you played all sixty minutes, while today, you have an offensive team and a defensive team. Unless you got seriously hurt, they wouldn't take you out. I liked the era I played in. I'm very thankful that I had a chance to play professional football."[12]

No. 24

Albert "Turk" Edwards
Tackle

Full Name: Albert Glen Edwards
Nicknames: "Turk"; "Rock of Gibraltar"
b: September 28, 1907 (Mold, WA); d: January 12, 1973 (age 65; Seattle, WA)
High School: Clarkston (WA); College: Washington State
Height/Weight: 6–2, 255 pounds
Position: Tackle
Teams/Years: 1932–1940 Boston Braves-Redskins/Washington Redskins
Pro Football Hall of Fame: Class of 1969
Retro-MVPs: No
All-Time Teams: C. Cagle (1937); D. Clark (1942); R. Flaherty (1990); M. Hein (1944, 1968, 1974); D. Hutson (1948); R. Richards (1944); C. Storck (1939)

A notch below the big three at tackle—Cal Hubbard (#9), Pete Henry (#11) and Link Lyman (#14)—is Turk Edwards. Another Hall of Famer, the 6-2, 255-pound Edwards played 86 games over nine years with the Boston/Washington Redskins, helping protect quarterback Sammy Baugh (#3) and opening holes for halfback Cliff Battles (#19) from his left tackle spot.

After a stellar All-American career at Washington State—playing alongside center Mel Hein (#4)—Edwards signed with the Boston Braves in 1932 for $150 a game, turning down offers from the New York Giants and Portsmouth Spartans. "I got a letter from Boston and one from New York, and they both offered me the same amount of money," Edwards recalled. "I wrote each one of them back and I said I play for the team that gave me the most dough." Edwards was worth all the money he got.[1]

On film Edwards consistently showed raw power and intimidation. His game emphasized strength more than speed, and his 255-pound frame usually did the work for him. He was also more agile than his appearance indicated. Nicknamed the "Rock of Gibraltar" because he played with such immovable and impregnable force, the amiable and easygoing Edwards was all business on the gridiron. "When he got mad, which was rarely, he could play the whole side of the line himself," recalled Wayne Millner, Redskins Hall of Fame end and teammate.[2]

Edwards' former college teammate Mel Hein battled his friend for nearly a

Turk Edwards, tackle, Washington Redskins, ca. 1937 (courtesy Washington Commanders).

decade in the NFL. He held Edwards in high esteem. "I consider Turk Edwards the greatest tackle who ever lived—college or pro," commented Hein. "He could handle anyone. I've seen him on defense pick up an opposing lineman and throw him backward, and break up a single-wing sweep before it even got started. He was absolutely awesome."[3]

As a rookie in 1932, Edwards instantly became one of the league's best two-way tackles.

On offense, he was just a building on the line; defenders just couldn't get around him. With him blocking for fellow rookie halfback Cliff Battles, the fledgling Boston Braves had the nucleus of a championship team.

On defense, Edwards used his 255-pound frame to disrupt the line of scrimmage, whether the opposing team was trying to run or pass. "Edwards was a great tackle, he was just a bull of tackle, hard to block. I knew he was going to be hard to block right from the beginning. He was hard to handle, offense and defense. Turk is one of the best," said George Musso, Bears Hall of Fame lineman.[4]

Turk had the toughest assignment for the Redskins when opposing the single-wing offenses they mostly faced. He played left tackle, the strong side by which most running plays were directed, and invariably he would be double-teamed by the tackle and blocking back. "I stood up a little more than they do now," said Turk Edwards in 1973, "but otherwise the techniques haven't changed. And I played both ways. In one 15-game season, I missed only 10 minutes of playing time. Anybody who couldn't play more than they do now, there must be something wrong with them. I'd like to see some of these modern specialists have to play all the time."[5]

Even at his massive size, Edwards rarely left the field. Opponents and sportswriters routinely named Turk one of the best tackles. "[Turk] Edwards was plenty tough and liked it. For a big fellow he had lots of speed and often was down the field as fast as his ends," wrote the *Green Bay Press-Gazette*, naming Edwards First Team All-Pro in 1933.[6]

Edwards would eventually win a championship with the help of one of the game's greatest quarterbacks. Starting in 1937, Edwards had a new role—to protect rookie quarterback Sammy Baugh, which he did well for the next three seasons. Edwards blocked for Baugh as the Redskins won the 1937 NFL championship by defeating the Chicago Bears, 28–21. It was a season of many crazy moments. Coach Flaherty developed a play that had the entire kickoff return team gather together to fake the opposing cover team into who had the ball. "We called it the 'squirrel cage,'" recalled Wayne Millner, Redskins Hall of Fame end. "On kickoff all of us huddled around the receiver after he caught the ball. He'd give it to one of us, or maybe keep it himself, then on a signal we'd take off in all directions, holding our arms as if trying to hide the ball.... Turk kept after us to let him carry it so one day we did, but he was so eager he broke before the rest of us and a tackle caught him. He could have gone all the way if he'd been a little more patient."[7]

The play must've occurred in 1937 because that year is the only year Edwards is listed as returning a kickoff—for 18 yards. Edwards was always considered an intelligent player who knew what he was doing on the field. "Know what's going on around you," said Edwards in 1938. "Don't let an opponent slip up and block or tackle you without your seeing him, for then you don't have a chance." Besides his play on both sides of the line Edwards was also known for blocking punts—including three in a game against the Giants in 1937 to help clinch the division title.[8]

After winning the 1937 NFL title, Edwards was considered the best tackle in the NFL. He was a consensus First Team All-Pro, named by the NFL, UPI, *I.N.S.*, *Collyer's* and the *New York Daily News*. Being named first team became a yearly habit for Edwards. For eight straight years from 1932 to 1939, Edwards was named to at least one First Team All-Pro, just an incredible streak.

How his career would end would be straight out of *Ripley's Believe it or Not*. Edwards' career ended when he suffered a knee injury during the coin toss against the Giants in 1940 with his good friend Mel Hein. Edwards had just shaken hands with Hein right before the coin toss took place. After shaking hands, Edwards turned toward the sidelines and his cleats caught the turf. His knee was so badly wrenched that he never played again. The "Rock of Gibraltar" had finally crumbled.

Selected to the NFL 1930s All-Decade Team (as one of four tackles), Edwards comes in just a notch below the other three great two-way tackles of this era, but he wasn't denied the greatest honor of any NFL player. Edwards was elected to the Pro Football Hall of Fame in 1969. Mel Hein was Edwards' presenter; he spoke at length about his greatest rival and good friend: "We played many games against each other; we were still the best of friends except on that football field. He hated the Giants on the football field, and I hated the Redskins, and to prove it to each other, we used to take pot shots against each other all during the ball game, but after the game, we were friends ... the Giants players never looked forward to playing against Turk Edwards because he would be at his peak. Because it was the [big] game, and they respected him. They felt that Turk was the greatest professional football tackle that we ever had to play against. In all the years that he played he was not only a man that had ability, he had strength. He was a big man for that time. You wouldn't say now if you would compare him with some of the 270, 80, 90-pound football players that he's so big, but at that time, he was the big man. But he had that agility and he had that speed, he had leadership, and he had football brains. He was very smart. But the thing that I remember about Turk Edwards more than anything else was he was a true sportsman, he was a true gentleman. I'll give you Glen 'Turk' Edwards."[9]

Edwards spoke next: Thank you. Mel didn't leave me very much for me to say. I want to say this, it gives me great pleasure to have been selected to join this elite group of men in Pro Football's Hall of Fame. It certainly is the greatest honor that could ever happen to a professional football player, and I accept this honor with great pride and humility. Thank you."[10]

After his playing career was over, Edwards went into coaching. He started out as an assistant with the Redskins, 1941–1945, before becoming the team's head coach for three seasons, compiling an overall record of 16–18–1 from 1946 to 1948. After he retired from coaching, Edwards returned to the Pacific Northwest and operated a sporting goods store.

Turk Edwards passed away on January 12, 1973, at the age of 65.

No. 25

Ox Emerson

Guard

Full Name: Gover Connor Emerson
Nickname: "Ox"
b: December 16, 1907 (Douglas, TX); d: November 26, 1998 (age 90; Austin, TX)
High School: Orange (TX); College: Texas
Height/Weight: 5–11, 203 pounds
Position: Guard
Teams/Years: 1931–1937 Portsmouth Spartans/Detroit Lions; 1938 Brooklyn Dodgers
Pro Football Hall of Fame: No
Retro-MVPs: No
All-Time Teams: P. Clark (1947); M. Gantenbein (1966); R. Grange (1955); B. Nagurski (1939); J. Stydahar (1951, 1952)

Rounding out the top 25 is one of the NFL's best guards during the two-way era, who for decades has been overlooked by the Pro Football Hall of Fame. His name is Gover "Ox" Emerson.

Emerson's nickname did not come from his considerable strength but rather from an impatient quarterback. At Orange (TX) High School, Emerson was still learning the game when he made a mistake in practice. "Emerson, you're dumb as an ox," yelled the quarterback. The nickname stuck. But Ox was no dummy, as his two future college degrees would attest.[1]

Emerson became an all-conference guard at the University of Texas, was elected a captain and helped the Longhorns win a conference championship in 1930. When his eligibility was questioned by a sportswriter in 1931, he left Austin to play in the NFL. "I finally got tired of them trying to straighten it out," Emerson recalled. "The team up at Portsmouth, Ohio, wrote to come up there and play and I went up." Ox signed for $75 a game.[2]

The man nicknamed "Ox" played eight seasons in the NFL with the Portsmouth Spartans-Detroit Lions (1931–1937) and Brooklyn Dodgers (1938). In his rookie year (1931), the former Longhorn quickly became a stalwart on the Portsmouth Spartans line, learning Potsy Clark's single-wing offense. Emerson used all his roughly 200 pounds to dominate his opponent. "There weren't many over 250 pounds in the league then," recalled Emerson in 1987. "But there were a lot that weighed 220 and

230. I was a little punk. Most of the time I weighed 190 pounds or a little less, depending on whether it was the first or end of the season. I was the smallest starting lineman in the league for a number of years."³

Emerson used good strength, speed and quickness to consistently beat opponents. On film the 5–11, 203-pound Emerson always showed excellent technique and savviness at right guard. He could also pull from his guard position on end runs and sweeps in the Lions offense. "I was pretty quick and for the first five yards I was pretty good. The main thing, I guess, was I hated like hell to get beat," said Emerson. In 1935—after naming Ox to First Team All-Pro—the United Press wrote: "Emerson plays guard like an end, big, fast and smart."⁴

On defense, he was a sure tackler and a tough man to block. "[Ox] Emerson, the Detroit guard, is the fastest, 'slicing' forward and the hardest to block, that I ever met in football," said Link Lyman, Bears Hall of Fame tackle.⁵

Ox Emerson, guard, Detroit Lions, ca. 1934 (courtesy Detroit Lions).

During the two-way era, Emerson was one of the most decorated players at his position, earning First Team All-Pro honors from multiple media outlets, including five straight years by the United Press and four straight by *Collyer's Eye*. "Emerson's low charging made him one of the toughest guards to drive out of play, while he was fast enough to pull out and block on the Lions' intricate reverse plays," wrote the United Press on Emerson when naming him first team in 1936. He was named First Team All-Pro five times by the United Press, four times by *Collyer's* and three times by the *Chicago Daily News*.⁶

As well as his many First Team All-Pro honors, Emerson was easily selected as a member of the NFL 1930s All-Decade Team at guard—along with Dan Fortmann (Bears), Buckets Goldenberg (Packers) and Russ Letlow (Packers).

Currently, there are four guards from the two-way era in the Pro Football Hall of Fame: Dan Fortmann, Mike Michalske, Walt Kiesling and George Musso (played some tackle). In the chart below are comparisons of the guards in the Hall of Fame and on the All-Decade teams of the 1920s and 1930s.

Hall of Fame and All-Decade Guards Comparison (1920–1939) First Team All-Pros

Dan Fortmann (HOF, All-Decade) = 6 times
Mike Michalske (HOF, All-Decade) = 5 times
Ox Emerson (All-Decade) = 5 times
Walt Kiesling (HOF, All-Decade) = 2 times
George Musso (HOF) = 2 times (one each at G-T)
Russ Letlow (All-Decade) = 1 time
Hunk Anderson (All-Decade) = 0
Buckets Goldenberg (All-Decade) = 0

(Note: 1930s Buckets Goldenberg [No First Team All-Pros; 120 games, 69 starts; did win three NFL championships]; 1930s Russ Letlow [two Pro Bowls, one All-Pro, two NFL championships])

Looking at his resume, Emerson compares very well to the other Hall of Fame guards of his era and was much better than the other guards on the All-Decade teams.

Emerson was also highly thought of by his opponents during the era he played, especially by the Chicago Bears players from the 1930s—a team that won two championships and lost two during that decade. In 1999, I interviewed two former Bears players who competed against Ox. George Musso, Bears Hall of Fame tackle-guard (1933–1938, 11 games vs. Ox) and Charles "Ookie" Miller, Bears All-Pro center (1932–1938, 15 games vs. Ox):

"He was an ox. He was hard to handle. Ox was just a good guard, hard to block," said George Musso.[7]

"I played against Ox several times. He's fast and elusive. Tried to outsmart you. Did a lot of times. I tried to do it myself. I saw what he was doing and I copied him," said Charles "Ookie" Miller.[8]

In a 1939 interview with the Associated Press, Bronko Nagurski (#6) selected his own All-Time Team. At the guard position, he chose Mike Michalske (#16) and Ox Emerson. In 1955, Red Grange was asked to name an NFL All-Time Team. His chore was to pick 11 players to win one game. At guard, he chose Michalske and Ox Emerson over Bears Dan Fortmann (#12), who is our top-ranked guard. Emerson was clearly an elite player at his position. "Say, there was a guard. Ox Emerson, played for [Detroit]. Well, I tried for a long while to figure out how to handle him, but he always fooled me," said Mel Hein to *Collier's* magazine in 1939. His opponents confirm that Emerson was one of the best guards ever to play in the two-way era.[9]

For seven seasons, Emerson had a huge impact on the success of the Portsmouth Spartans and Detroit Lions—both on offense and defense. Ox was part of a Lions offensive line that helped lead the NFL in rushing twice (1936–1937) and finish second two more times (1934–1935). He blocked for Hall of Fame halfback Dutch

Clark and All-Pros Glenn Presnell, Ernie Caddell and Ace Gutowsky. "Ox wasn't very big for a professional guard; he weighed about 195 pounds. But he was so quick and agile that he made a lot of tackles and was hard to block. So, he was in the opponent's backfield an awful lot. He was very exceptional," said Glenn Presnell in 1999.[10]

In 1936, the Lions set an NFL record for rushing yards in a season with 2,885 yards (in 12 games), a record that stood until 1972 when the undefeated Miami Dolphins broke it (in a 14-game season; 2,960). Both teams were heavy run teams, as the Lions ran 80 percent of the time compared to the Dolphins' 70 percent.

Comparison Chart of 1936 Lions vs. 1972 Dolphins

1936 Lions: 80% Run and 20% Pass (total plays = 737 [591 rush & 146 pass])
1972 Dolphins: 70% Run and 30% Pass (total plays = 872 [613 rush & 259 pass])

"We ran from the single-wing unbalanced to the right and we never shifted," once said Emerson in 1970. "We had a terrific running attack. I was surprised at how strong it looked. The Chicago Bears looked like they were running kindergarten stuff compared to our offense."[11]

Emerson was part of an offensive line that helped the Lions establish an NFL record that still stands today with 426 yards rushing in a single game when the Lions played the Pittsburgh Pirates on November 4, 1934. (The Lions won the game, 40–7.) That same year Emerson was part of a defensive front for the Lions that started the '34 season with an NFL-record seven straight shutouts—giving up only 59 points that season, number one in the league. That is more proof that Emerson excelled on both offense and defense, a true team player.

Emerson played on one of the best teams in the NFL during the 1930s. The Spartans/Lions squads were highly competitive under Potsy Clark. Emerson never had a losing season in eight NFL seasons (1931–1938) and his teams had an overall record of 59–28–9 (winning 67.8 percent of games).

Win-Loss Records of Teams from 1931 to 1938

Bears = 68–21–10 (.764)
Packers = 67–30–3 (.690)
Lions = 59–28–9 (.678) (Dodgers one year in 1938)
Giants = 58–34–7 (.630)
Redskins = 38–34–7 (.527) (only played from 1932 to 1937)

In 1932, his Portsmouth Spartans played the Chicago Bears in the famous "Indoor Game" in Chicago Stadium to determine the league champion. Playing without Dutch Clark, the Spartans lost, 9–0, missing out on being a world champion. Three years later, Emerson got another chance at a title in a season that was probably his signature moment in the NFL.

Best Season: 1935

In 1935, Emerson missed the first five games of the season with a broken vertebrae in his back. The Lions struggled without their top lineman, going just 2-2-1. Ox came back to play the final seven games with the Lions, going 5-1-1 to win the Western Division. "I regard Emerson one of the greatest linemen I have ever seen perform on a football field. Having him out of our first five games hurt us more than anyone will ever know," said Lions coach Potsy Clark in 1935.[12]

At season's end, they played in the NFL championship game against the Eastern champs—New York Giants—who were looking to win back-to-back titles. Emerson helped the Lions pound the Giants to defeat. Behind a fierce running game led by Dutch Clark, the Lions rushed 65 times for 246 yards and four touchdowns, while completing just two passes (on five attempts) for 51 yards. The defense gave up just one touchdown in a convincing 26-7 victory.

In 1938, Emerson followed Potsy Clark to Brooklyn. The team was not quite as talented as the Lions squads, but still went 4-4-3 (third place, Eastern). Ox retired after the season.

After stepping away from the NFL, Emerson worked for Ford Motor Company and served in the Navy for World War II, reaching the rank of lieutenant commander. After the war he and his wife Virginia returned to his home state of Texas where he coached high school football for years—as well as serving as line coach at the University of Texas (1951-1956). On November 26, 1998, in Austin, Texas, Ox Emerson passed away from pneumonia at the age of 90.

Ox Emerson's NFL resume has it all. A resume worthy of being in the Pro Football Hall of Fame:

1. Elite Player: one of the best at his position during his era. Respect from opponents—especially the Chicago Bears.

2. Winner: Won one NFL championship (1935 Detroit Lions) and never had a losing season in eight years in the NFL.

3. Honors: Named First Team All-Pro five times; NFL 1930s All-Decade Team.

4. Stats: Helped Lions to establish single-season rushing record in 1936 (12 games) and to rank first or second in rushing for four consecutive seasons (1934-1937); played great defense.

5. Signature Moment: In 1935 with Lions at 2-2-1 comes back after a broken back to guide the Lions to the NFL championship (Lions went 6-1-1 when he returned).

No. 26

Arnie Herber

Quarterback

Full Name: Arnold Charles Herber
Nicknames: "Arnie"; "Flash"
b: April 2, 1910 (Green Bay, WI); d: October 14, 1969 (age 59; Green Bay, WI)
High School: Green Bay West; College: Wisconsin, Regis (CO)
Height/Weight: 5-11, 203 pounds
Position: Quarterback
Teams/Years: 1930–1940 Green Bay Packers; 1944–1945 New York Giants
Pro Football Hall of Fame: Class of 1966
Retro-MVPs: No
All-Time Teams: G. Corbett (1938); M. Gantenbein (1966); C. Hinkle (1942, 1946); C. Storck (1939)

Coming in behind the big three at quarterback on the list—Baugh (#3), Luckman (#8) and Friedman (#17)—at number 24 is Arnie Herber.

A stocky, powerful passer, the 5-11, 203-pound Herber played 13 NFL seasons with the Packers (1930–1940) and New York Giants (1944–1945). He is mainly remembered for his decade playing in Green Bay, firing long passes for Curly Lambeau.

Because of short fingers and pudgy hands, Herber gripped the ball with his thumb over the laces, helping him throw long passes without a wiggle. "Most passers put their fingers over the lacing, I put the laces right in the palm of my hand. I figure I got a little more distance because that's the heaviest part of the ball," said Arnie Herber. "Nobody ever taught me to do it, when I was a kid I just started throwing it that way. It's the best way to throw a wet ball, too.... Those days there wasn't anybody giving you a fresh towel after every play either. It was harder to grip then—the ball was different shape. You couldn't just throw it, as they do today, you had to guide it with your fingers."[1]

A Green Bay native, Herber briefly played college football at Wisconsin and tiny Regis College in Colorado, but it was his play at Green Bay West High where Packers head coach Curly Lambeau remembered Herber's athletic abilities—especially his passing prowess. In 1930, he offered Herber a contract for about $75 a game. Herber didn't hesitate; he said yes. Herber joined a loaded Packers team that had just won their first NFL title behind the backfield play of Verne Lewellen and Red Dunn. In 1930, Lambeau had retired as a player, leaving a spot for Herber, who tossed three touchdowns over the next two years as a reserve player. By 1932 Dunn had retired and Lewellen was in his last year. It was now time for Herber to take over as signal caller.

Nicknamed "Flash" by the press, Herber helped continue the Packers' aggressive offensive style of football. Mainly throwing out of a tailback spot in Lambeau's Notre Dame box offense, Herber thrived for over a decade in passing downfield.

Arnie Herber, quarterback, Green Bay Packers, ca. 1930–1931 (courtesy Green Bay Packers).

"Herber is the best long passer ever," once said Curly Lambeau. "There never was a long passer like him. He throws them pretty accurately up to 35 yards, but he has no equal when it comes to heaving 'em from 35 to 60 yards. His accuracy is uncanny. He throws perfect strikes and on the dead run, mind you."[2]

In 1932, Herber didn't disappoint, as he led the NFL in attempts (101), completions (37), passing yards (639) and passing touchdowns (9). Although the Packers didn't win a fourth NFL championship in a row, Herber made First Team All-Pro by the NFL and United Press, and second team by *Collyer's* and *Brooklyn Times-Union*.

Herber was a passing machine during his career. He threw 81 career TD passes, including 31 that were 30 yards or more. He held all the NFL career passing marks, until Sammy Baugh supplanted him. He finished his career with 1,175 attempts, 481 completions, and 8,041 passing yards. However, he was not quite the runner as the big three quarterbacks—Baugh, Luckman, Friedman—and only had three career rushing TDs.

Although he was not the all-around athlete that some above him on this list were, Herber was no doubt one of the toughest. Film studies show him to be not the best defensive player during his career, but he was a sure tackler. He also was a very durable player during his career playing in 129 NFL games. "[Arnie] Herber had a sixth sense of when to throw," said Mike Michalske, Packers Hall of Fame guard. "Herber could absorb punishment. He could take more punishment than any two men I know." Herber always knew he would get the rough part of passing the ball so much in Lambeau's offense. "I never threw a pass without getting knocked down … never," recalled Herber.[3]

In 1935, his career really took off when he was teamed with Don Hutson (#2). "Lil Arnie," as Hutson called his battery mate in his Southern drawl, became an instant star as the two connected routinely for scores. From 1935 to 1940 the two connected for 29 scores, including a career-high eight times in 1936. "Herber is the person responsible for Don Hutson's place with the Green Bay Packers. When the going was toughest, he was always at his best. In the clutch he was right on the spot. It is I who owes Arnold Herber the most," said Don Hutson in 1941.[4]

Herber had his best year in 1936. He led the NFL in attempts (173), completions (77), passing yards (1,239) and touchdowns with a career-high 11, as he guided the Packers to a 10–1–1 record and the Eastern Division title. Herber capped off his best year with a sterling performance against the Boston Redskins in the NFL championship game held at the Polo Grounds in New York. In the first quarter he tossed a 48-yard scoring strike to Don Hutson to give the Pack an early 7–0 lead. Then in the third quarter, ahead 7–6, Herber connected with Milt Gantenbein for an eight-yard touchdown pass to help finish off the Redskins in a 21–6 victory. The efficient Herber completed six of 14 passes for 129 yards, two TDs and one INT. "Sure Hutson was good, but it's the passer that counts. Herber never got the credit due him. Why he's the only man in football who can control a 50-yard pass. I'd say Luckman and Baugh are great but when their aerials travel over 35 yards, they lack the precision of those hurled by Herber," said Red Smith, Packers back. "Herber is my type of football player. He can pass without much protection. He learned the hard way, for when he was setting all those Herber-to-Hutson records the passer used to take quite a bit of roughing. Today it's a little different; roughing the passer means a 15-yard penalty."[5]

Herber was named First Team All-Pro by the *Chicago Daily News* and second team by the NFL, *Collyer's* and the *Milwaukee Sentinel*, behind the great Dutch Clark. Herber would finish in second place in the Retro-MVP vote, again behind Clark.

After a rough 1937 season when he suffered an injury, Herber was joined in the backfield with Cecil Isbell as the two men alternated as quarterback. The Packers were back in the title game in 1938, as Herber gave a great effort to try and win another championship. He completed five of 14 passes for 123 yards and one TD. He also rushed three times for 22 yards, but the Packers came up short, losing to the Giants, 23–17. The following year the outcome would be different.

For the third time in four years, Herber started in a championship game in 1939. Once more the Giants stood in their way. This time the Packers steamrolled the Giants, as Herber contributed one scoring pass in an easy 27–0 win. Thus, Herber won his second NFL championship in four seasons.

Herber was a consistent winner at quarterback with the Packers. From 1930–1940 (11 seasons) the Packers went 92–39–5, winning 70 percent of their games with Herber. He led the NFL in attempts, completions and TD passes three times: 1932, 1934 and 1936. He finished in the top five in TD passes nine times.

After sitting out for three seasons, Herber returned to the NFL due to the man-shortage during World War II. He signed to play for the New York Giants and Steve Owen, who thought highly of Herber's talents. "Now about Arnold Herber. Herber was playing when I was playing. He was a great passer," said Owen in 1945. "But what they all forget is this—Herber at 60 will still be a better passer than most of those now around. He is still the greatest long distance, the most accurate long-distance passer in football today, not even barring Sid Luckman, Sammy Baugh, or Bob Waterfield. He is the deadliest of all the touchdown snipers we have."[6]

In 1944, Herber contributed to a Giants team that won the Eastern Division, and he played in his fourth NFL championship game. Facing the Packers that day, Herber had one of his worst games, completing only eight passes and tossing four interceptions in a tough 14–7 loss to his former team. After the 1945 season, he would retire for good at the age of 35.

Herber quickly earned some very high honors, being named to the NFL 1930s All-Decade Team, the Pro Football Hall of Fame in 1966 and the Packers Hall of Fame in 1972. "Thank you. I had a little speech all prepared I was gonna make for just a few words and now after I got here they're so inadequate that I don't dare say anything because the feeling in my heart no one can realize how great it is. Thank you," said Arnie Herber at his Hall of Fame induction speech.[7]

Arnie Herber passed away in Green Bay on October 14, 1969, at the age of 59.

No. 27

George Trafton
Center

Full Name: George Edward Trafton
Nickname: "The Brute"
b: December 6, 1896 (Chicago, IL); d: September 5, 1971 (age 74; Los Angeles, CA)
High School: Oak Park (IL); College: Notre Dame
Height/Weight: 6–2, 230 pounds
Position: Center-Linebacker
Teams/Years: 1920–1921, 1923–1932 Decatur Staleys/Chicago Bears
Pro Football Hall of Fame: Class of 1964
Retro-MVPs: No
All-Time Teams: B. Bell (1940); B. Cahn (1943); J. Conzelman (1941); R. Grange (1934, 1947); G. Halas (1940–1941); D. Slater (1949)

At 6–0 and 230 pounds, big George Trafton was a durable center who played 12 seasons, appearing in 148 games in the NFL—all of them with the Chicago Bears. Nicknamed "The Brute" for his natural brute strength, Trafton was not only a great player in the two-way era but a big personality, too. He was considered to be the toughest player of the two-way era.

Trafton served in the Army during World War I. When the war was over, he attended Notre Dame coached by Knute Rockne, but that didn't last too long. He left Notre Dame to play professional football. In 1920, George Halas signed him to play for his Decatur Staleys, and Trafton quickly became one of the best players in the league.

That first year of the APFA, Trafton was the best center in the league, stabilizing the Staleys offensive and defensive lines. After the season, Bruce Copeland, sports editor of the *Rock Island Argus,* named Trafton to his First Team All-Pro squad—the first documented All-Pro team named by a newspaper. Copeland wrote: "It is conceded in every professional camp this year that Trafton of the Staleys has no superiors, or any opponents who could outlast or out game him, whichever way they chose.... Perfect physical condition was largely responsible for Trafton's super playing. He grew stronger as a game progressed until, at the end, he could have started and finished another contest without weakening one iota."[1]

On the field, Trafton was nobody to mess with. His size helped in any confrontation or potential fistfight. "Trafton was tough," said John Alexander, New York Giants tackle. "Trafton was vocal and open. If Trafton was going to hit you, he'd tell you before he hit you. He didn't make any bones about it."²

No opposing player or team liked to play against "The Brute." Some of the stories that passed down over the years always made Trafton the bad guy. "I tackled a Rock Island halfback named [Fred] Chicken and, after I hit him," recalled Trafton, "he spun against a fence that was very close to the field and broke a leg. After that, the fans really did get on me."³

George Trafton, center, Chicago Bears, ca. 1920 (courtesy NFL Films Research Library).

Halas knew of Trafton's reputation in Rock Island; once when collecting the gate receipts of nearly $7,000 he handed the money to big Trafton. "I knew that if trouble came Trafton would be running for his life. I would only be running for $7,000," said Halas.⁴

Since Trafton had gained an early reputation of being a tough guy—a role he relished—most games became a serious tussle for the Bears. Trafton would do his part to help his team win at any cost. "If a great player was having a good day, we—shall we say—took care of him," said Trafton in 1949. "For instance, there was Cal Hubbard, who was a great lineman playing with the Packers. We worked out a system to eliminate him from contention. He was too damn big and tough to rack up, so we played it subtle like. I'd wind up and whack him one right in the teeth and then hustle over to an official and tell him to keep an eye on Hubbard, that the guy had been slugging the socks off me. On the next play, Cal would figure to get even and as soon as the ball was snapped he'd bust me one. The official would be looking and Hubbard would find himself booted out of the game."⁵

But Trafton was far more than a roughneck on the gridiron. His play shouldn't be overlooked. He was a very skilled lineman during the two-way era and is considered the very first player on offense to center the football with only one hand.

The following year (1922) Trafton stepped away from pro football to coach at Northwestern as the line coach. Trafton missed the game, especially the contact. Red Grange called Trafton the "toughest, meanest, most ornery critter alive." The best center in the NFL in the 1920s, Trafton was also efficient on defense. He was one of the first centers to rove on defense like a linebacker. "That I loved," once said Trafton. "You could really find the action on defense."[6]

A very durable player, Trafton participated in 148 NFL games during his career. In newspaper accounts, Trafton's play improved every year. He was a pioneer on the field, too. "He was the first at being a roving center in the early 1920s. The roving center is now called a middle linebacker," said Ed Healey, Bears Hall of Fame tackle. "George never made a bad snap or pass while playing the center position."[7]

"None of them looked any better than George Trafton at center. The Bears snapper-back was a demon on the defense and he passed perfectly to his backs," wrote the *Green Bay Press-Gazette* in 1924, after naming Trafton First Team All-Pro center.[8]

All while not backing down from a fight, even with a baseball player or a world heavyweight champion. Trafton was known as the "toughest man in pro football," while crosstown Chicago White Sox outfielder Arthur Shires was known as the "toughest man in baseball." The two got together in the boxing ring to prove who was the real toughest man. On December 16, 1929, at the White City Amusement Park, 5,000 fans came to watch "The Brute" fight Shires "The Great." Sportswriters called it the "Match of the Century." Trafton didn't disappoint his fans by knocking down Shires three times in the first round on his way to a five-round decision. "I busted him up pretty good," Trafton recalled. "I also got a couple of thousand bucks, which wasn't peanuts in those days."[9]

The fight got Trafton some national attention with the victory. Associated Press sportswriter Charles Dunkley later called it a legendary bout "which was as vicious and spectacular as it was hilarious." Trafton fought three more bouts in January and February 1930, winning two of those matches by knockout and a third by disqualification. Then on March 26, 1930, Trafton faced future world champion Primo Carnera in Kansas City. Trafton was knocked out by Carnera in the first round of their fight. In the aftermath of the fight, Trafton was suspended indefinitely by the Missouri Boxing Commission for failing to provide more resistance in the 54-second bout.[10]

In 1932, Trafton played his 12th and final season in the NFL. Although he was not the starter at center anymore, "The Brute" helped the Bears tie for first place in the standings with the Portsmouth Spartans. In Trafton's last game as an NFL player, he played in the famous "Indoor Game" in Chicago Stadium against the Spartans. In a fitting end to his rough-and-tough career, Trafton went out a winner against the Spartans, 9–0, on a dirt field indoors. It was his first NFL championship since 1921.

It was an end to an era for one of the NFL's best ever two-way centers. Trafton was 36 years old. "George Trafton played 12 seasons for the Bears, retiring under protest," wrote George Halas in 1967. "Nobody loved football more—or played with greater gusto."[11]

Trafton's toughness would be his ultimate legacy. "The tough one was that George Trafton," recalled Ed Healey, Bears Hall of Fame tackle. "You couldn't get him out of the game if he only had one leg and arm left. We were down south someplace and he cut his leg from his knee to his ankle. I told him he was going to bleed to death. But we couldn't get him out of the game."[12]

Trafton would always miss the game. He loved being on the field for 60 minutes. He never wanted to leave. "We didn't have specialists back in the '20s. You played offense and defense until your tonsils hung out. If a player left the game, he couldn't return until the next quarter. So, the good players didn't leave," said Trafton in 1949. "Imagine, thirty-three players on one squad. Why, when I started with the Bears, we had fifteen. You were hired to play a football game and you played it—all 60 minutes of it, brother. That Halas used to come into the dressing room between halves and say, 'Now boys, this half Trafton will replace Trafton, Hunk Anderson will replace Hunk Anderson, and Healey you better relieve Healey.'"[13]

In 1949, long-time referee Bobbie Cahn retired from the NFL after officiating for over two decades. He named an All-Time Team, selecting Trafton as the best player he ever saw. "Trafton had everything, including a lot of lip for the officials," said Cahn. "He could diagnose a play quicker than any man who ever played football and he knew what to do about it."[14]

After his playing career was over, Trafton went into coaching. He made stops as line coach with the Green Bay Packers in 1944 and then with the Cleveland-Los Angeles Rams from 1945 to 1949, being part of league championships in '44 and '45. Trafton moved from assistant coach to promotions director for the Rams in 1950–1951 before leaving the team. In 1951, he was hired as the head coach of the Winnipeg Blue Bombers (CFL), where he coached for three seasons, going 28–17–1. In 1953, he led the Bombers to the Grey Cup, losing out to the Hamilton Tiger-Cats. After losing the Cup, Trafton retired from coaching.

Trafton was honored by being selected to the NFL 1920s All-Decade Team as the only center on the squad. In 1964, he was elected to the Pro Football Hall of Fame in just the second ever class. The big, rugged Trafton nearly broke down while speaking at his Hall of Fame induction speech. "I have fought the good fight. I have finished my course. I have kept the faith. Today, I am the luckiest man in the world. I have reached the climax of my entire career. The panoramas of God's gifts have unfolded before me, and this is the final reward of my athletic life. I accept this honor with humbleness and pride. Thank God for the thoughtful people who have made this honor possible, who let a small light of happiness into each of our fading lives. Thank you."[15]

George Trafton passed away on September 5, 1971, at the age of 74.

No. 28

Ray Flaherty
End

Full Name: Raymond Paul Flaherty
Nickname: N/A
b: September 1, 1903 (Spokane, WA); d: July 19, 1994 (age 90; Coeur d'Alene, ID)
High School: Gonzaga Prep (WA); College: Washington State, Gonzaga
Height/Weight: 6-0, 190 pounds
Position: End
Teams/Years: 1926-1928 New York Yankees; 1928-1929, 1931-1935 New York Giants
Pro Football Hall of Fame: Class of 1976
Retro-MVPs: No
All-Time Teams: E. Cuneo (1973); R. Grange (1934, 1947); V. Lewellen (1936)

Primarily known for his Hall of Fame coaching career, Ray Flaherty was a standout end in the NFL before that. After playing one year in the rival AFL in 1926, the rangy, 6-0, 190-pound Flaherty played in 88 games over eight seasons in the NFL with the New York Yankees (1927-1928) and New York Giants (1928-1929, 1931-1935).

Born in the Pacific Northwest in 1903, Ray Flaherty spent his youth learning all he could about football in Spokane. He parlayed that into being a three-sport star (basketball and baseball) at Gonzaga University. Flaherty was a member of the Zags football team coached by Gus Dorias that went undefeated in 1924. Flaherty would go on to earn all-conference honors at the end.

After playing his college ball at Gonzaga, Flaherty signed in 1926 with the rival American Football League—the Red Grange League—instead of the NFL by joining the Los Angeles Wildcats. Coached by former University of Washington All-American halfback George "Wildcat" Wilson, the squad was mainly a traveling team based out of Chicago. In a 1976 interview, Flaherty said he made $150 a game with the Wildcats. "You didn't make much money, but in those days $4,000 was like $10,000 now. And all our expenses were paid. Everything!" said Ray Flaherty in 1955.[1]

Flaherty's first year of pro ball was played on a traveling team. After just one year the AFL folded, leaving Flaherty to join the NFL. He signed with Grange's New York Yankees. On November 8, 1927, while playing with the Yankees, Flaherty became the second player in NFL history to catch three touchdowns in a single game in a 26-6 victory over the Bears—two weeks after Duluth end Joe Rooney did it

PRICE 15 CENTS

NEW YORK FOOTBALL GIANTS
vs.
CHICAGO BEARS

RAY FLAHERTY
Popular Giants' End

Sunday, Nov. 6, 1932   **Polo Grounds, New York**

HERE NEXT SUNDAY, NOVEMBER 13th

KEN STRONG AND THE STATEN ISLAND STAPES

Ray Flaherty, end, New York Giants (1932 game program courtesy NFL Films Research Library).

against Pottsville on October 23. In 1928, Flaherty was named First Team All-Pro for the first time by the *Green Bay Press-Gazette*, while the *Chicago Tribune* named him second team.

Flaherty caught a break when in 1929 he joined the New York Giants the same year as Benny Friedman. That season Flaherty caught a career-high eight touchdowns with seven being tossed by Friedman. His 49 points scored was fourth in the NFL. The Giants went 7–0 in games he caught a touchdown pass. The Giants came up short of winning an NFL championship that season, losing out by one game to the Packers. Flaherty, though, had elevated his play as one of the NFL's best ends. That season he was named First Team All-Pro by *Green Bay Press-Gazette*, *Collyer's*, *Chicago Tribune* and coach Leroy Andrews. "Flaherty, once of Gonzaga and an All-Western end during that time, possesses the ability to snag passes so necessary to playing the flank of Friedman's scrimmage line. His defensive play rates with that of [Lavvie] Dilweg, and both are perfect judges of opponents' plays," wrote Wilfrid Smith of the *Chicago Tribune*, naming Flaherty to his First Team All-Pro team.[2]

Catching passes from Benny Friedman was special for Flaherty. "I had a pretty good passer throwing to me, Benny Friedman," recalled Flaherty. "He didn't throw the ball too well long. But he was a very good short passer. So, quite a few of our passes were cross-field patterns or some other patterns of that kind, breaking in or out. I was catching a lot of them over the middle."[3]

After the outstanding 1929 season, Flaherty took a break from pro football, returning to his alma mater, Gonzaga, to coach. But he missed the game too much, returning to the Giants after a one-year absence. In 1931, Curly Lambeau selected his own Lavvie Dilweg and Ray Flaherty at end on his own All-Pro Team. Opponents and teammates could easily see that Flaherty was a relentless competitor. "Winning was everything to me," said Flaherty in 1985. "I was a competitor. I loved to win. I didn't like to lose. It broke my heart every time I lost."[4]

In 1932, at the age of 29, Flaherty maybe had his best year when he led all receivers in receptions (21), receiving yards (350), and touchdowns (five). He finished the year third in the NFL in scoring with 30 points—behind Dutch Clark (55) and Red Grange (42). During that season, he also had the best stretch of his career while playing three games in a week:

> November 20, he scored the game's only touchdown with a 33-yard reception from Jack McBride for a 6–0 upset win over the Green Bay Packers.
> November 24, he scored a touchdown catch in a 13–13 tie with Staten Island.
> November 27, he caught two touchdown passes from McBride to defeat the Brooklyn Dodgers, 13–7.

Flaherty scored four receiving touchdowns in three games to help the Giants go 2–0–1. At the end of the year, George Kirksey of United Press named Flaherty to his First Team All-Pro squad, saying, "Flaherty of the New York Giants catches a football like a baseball, and is almost impossible to cover."[5]

After missing out on winning an NFL championship in his first five seasons, Flaherty got a taste of it over the next three seasons. A very intelligent player, Flaherty was now becoming a coach on the field—as his coaching career would prove—as he spent his last three years with the Giants as player, captain and assistant coach. Starting in 1931, he was paired with fellow Hall of Famer Red Badgro to form one of the NFL's best end duos with the Giants (1931–1935). "Ray Flaherty was another one of our favorites on the team. He was a tremendous competitor. We had two of the toughest players ever at our two ends in those days—Flaherty and Red Badgro—and at the same time they were two of the nicest guys you'd ever meet," said Wellington Mara, Giants Hall of Fame owner.[6]

Flaherty was more than a pass catcher during his career. He was one of the best all-around ends in blocking and playing defense. Maybe not as dominant as the previous ends on the list—Hutson (#2), Chamberlin (#5), or Hewitt (#15)—but he wasn't that far behind. "I think I was a very good blocker for my size," once said Flaherty. "I was blocking against fellas that were usually much larger than I was. Some of them shook me up pretty good sometimes. But I held my own most of the time in blocking. I was always considered to be a very good blocker. They always had me play the strong end, which is the side you run to most of the time. We used to switch our lineman from left to right. I always played the strong end. That's where you put your best blocker."[7]

Flaherty always showed toughness. "I recall one particular incident concerning Flaherty," recalled Wellington Mara. "He hurt his hand in one game, really didn't hurt it badly but the doctor put a big bandage on it. Ray held it like it was broken and in a sling, and was pretending to be in great pain. Everyone was very solicitous toward him. I don't remember who the player was, but it was one of Ray's particular friends and he was helping Ray over to the bench on the sideline. 'Are you all right, Ray?' he asked. 'Yeah, I'm all right,' Flaherty said and then punched his friend in the stomach with his supposedly broken hand."[8]

Flaherty was part of the great Giants squads that won the Eastern Division three straight years (1933–1935). A hardnosed player for 60 minutes, Flaherty was also one of the smartest and aided Steve Owen as an assistant coach. His quick mind helped the Giants win the 1934 NFL championship game. During pregame on the frozen field at the Polo Grounds, Flaherty suggested to coach Steve Owen that they should wear basketball sneakers in the 1934 NFL championship game, which they won 34–13 over the Bears, after playing in "sneakers." "I told Steve [Owen], when Jack Mara told me the field was frozen, I told Steve 'We better get some tennis shoes.' We told our clubhouse man [Abe Cohen] to go down to Manhattan College to gather all the shoes from the basketball team there. I told him to go," recalled Flaherty. "When he came back all of the guys were anxious to put them on. When we finally put them on for the second half some of the Bears looked at them and told [George] Halas, 'Those guys got tennis shoes on over there.' Halas says, 'Step on their toes with the cleats.' We started the second half and we just pushed them all over the field. There was no contest from there on. We beat them 30–13. That's how we won that game. I don't think we'd have won it without the tennis shoes."[9]

In 1935, Flaherty was mainly an assistant coach for the Giants, playing in only two games as the Giants won the Eastern Division for the third year in a row. But they lost the title game to the Detroit Lions.

In his career Flaherty scored 21 total touchdowns, with 20 coming on receptions. When Flaherty caught a TD pass his team was 17-2-1, including a perfect 7-0 in 1929. He led the NFL in touchdown catches three times: 1927, 1929, and 1932. "Well, I played sixty minutes of every game practically," said Flaherty in 1985. "I don't think I'd ever hardly ever came out of the game."[10]

After losing out on the NFL championship in 1935, Flaherty was given a new opportunity to get back on top. George Preston Marshall, owner of the Boston Redskins, was looking for a new coach. He was told that the best man for the job was Ray Flaherty. Giants owner Tim Mara told Marshall that if he hired Flaherty, "You'll never regret it."[11]

After Flaherty coached Boston to the division title in 1936, the team moved to Washington. In that first year in the nation's capital, Flaherty had rookie quarterback Sammy Baugh to help him win the 1937 NFL championship. Coach Flaherty had his prize quarterback throw a few new screen passes that surprised the Chicago Bears in the title game. "They were breaking their necks trying to rack up Baugh," recalled Flaherty about calling the behind-the-line screen pass. "That's what made the screen pass go. It had been nullified downfield, but we put it in behind the line of scrimmage and the Bears didn't know how to stop it."[12]

A few years later in 1940, Flaherty suffered his worst defeat, losing the famous 73–0 game to the Bears. "We just kept throwing the ball and they kept picking it off. You might as well get beat 73–0 as 7–0. If you lose, you lose," recalled Ray Flaherty. But his squad would get its revenge against the Bears in the 1942 championship game, upsetting the unbeaten Bears, 14–6, and giving Flaherty his second title as a head coach. "He knew football, but his biggest asset was in knowing how to handle players," said Jim Barber, Redskins All-Pro tackle. "He knew when to chew a fanny or pat somebody on the back. The players liked him, but he was no patsy." After the big win Flaherty left coaching to join the Navy during World War II.[13]

After serving during the war, Flaherty returned to coaching, this time with the New York Yankees of the AAFC. He won back-to-back division titles in 1946 and 1947 before resigning four games into the 1948 season after a fall out with Yankees owner Dan Topping. He finished his career coaching the AAFC's Chicago Hornets in 1949.

In his 11 years as a head coach in pro football, Flaherty compiled an overall record of 80–37–5, a winning percentage of .684. He won the two NFL championships with the Redskins (1937, 1942) and was honored by the Giants when they retired his number 1 jersey. Then Flaherty earned the highest honor. A quarter century after coaching his last pro football game, Flaherty was elected to the Pro Football Hall of

Fame in 1976 at the age of 72. "I'm very happy," said Flaherty to the *Washington Star*. "It's about the greatest honor you can have in football. I'm a bit surprised that anybody who has been out of football as long as I have, and played and coached so long ago, would still be remembered."[14]

Flaherty continued: "If I were still coaching, I'd still be stressing fundamentals. You've got to block and tackle and play defense. It's a specialist's game now, but it's still a game of fundamentals. That's how you win."[15]

Ray Flaherty passed away on July 19, 1994, at the age of 90.

No. 29

Clyde "Bulldog" Turner
Center

Full Name: Clyde Douglas Turner
Nickname: "Bulldog"
b: November 10, 1919; d: October 30, 1998 (age 79; Gatesville, TX)
High School: Sweetwater (TX); College: Hardin-Simmons (TX)
Height/Weight: 6–1, 237 pounds
Position: Center-Linebacker
Teams/Years: 1940–1952 Chicago Bears
Pro Football Hall of Fame: Class of 1966
Retro-MVPs: No
All-Time Teams: S. Baugh (1949, 1999); P. Driscoll (1956); R. Grange (1946–1947, 1955);
    M. Hein (1944, 1968, 1974); C. Hinkle (1942); D. Hutson (1948); D. Slater (1949)

At number 26 is the man they called Bulldog—a perfect nickname for a two-way player who played center and linebacker and was never called by his real first name. "I'm 50 years old now and it's a little embarrassing to be called Bulldog. But I guess it beats the hell out of Clyde," said Clyde "Bulldog" Turner in 1970.[1]

Growing up in West Texas, Turner picked cotton on his father's farm. Tough labor for a tough boy. Turner picked up football at Sweetwater High School, the same school from which Sammy Baugh graduated a few years earlier. Turner then had an outstanding collegiate career at tiny Hardin-Simmons in Texas.

It was there that Turner got his famous nickname. A high school teammate named A.J. Roy was being recruited to Hardin-Simmons, but only agreed if Turner could come too. The two friends decided to help each other out. "So, we decided that if we got into a scrimmage at Hardin-Simmons and one of us wasn't looking too good, why, here's how we'd handle it," recalled Turner. "If it was A.J. looking bad, I'd say, 'Hey, Tiger! You're not acting as tough as you did back home.' And if it was me looking bad, he'd say, 'Hey, Bulldog! Get in there and hit 'em like you did at home!'" Bulldog, of course, made the team, and his nickname became his permanent moniker.[2]

Despite playing at a tiny college in Texas, Turner's exploits did not go unnoticed by NFL teams, even if he hadn't heard much about the league. "I didn't know there was such a thing as pro football until I was a senior and saw a short subject [MGM]

Clyde "Bulldog" Turner, center, Chicago Bears (1948 book cover courtesy NFL Films Research Library).

on the Green Bay Packers at the movies. Even then I didn't understand what it was all about," said Bulldog Turner.[3]

A Hardin-Simmons fan tipped off Turner's name to Bears scout Frank Korch who passed on his glowing report of Turner to George Halas. Papa Bear drafted him in the first round of the 1940 NFL Draft, number seven overall. For the next decade, Turner would be the anchor of the Monsters of the Midway offensive line that would lead the NFL in rushing five times during his career (1940–1942, 1946, 1951). "He just controlled the middle of the line of scrimmage. Easily the best center to come along for years and years," said Jim Parmer, Eagles back and NFL scout for 35 years.[4]

Very athletic for his size at 6-1, 237 pounds, Bulldog could run just as fast as some NFL backs. He roamed from sideline to sideline as well as anyone during his playing time. As a center, he was a flawless snapper, similar to the Giants' Mel Hein (#4). Tough as nails and with a nickname of "Bulldog," he played that way. He said that he had his nose broken at least a half dozen times and later in his career he began wearing a facemask.

Turner brought his own technique to the center position. "Most guys would get over the ball like an ol' hen over a nest o' eggs, their elbows all bent, and you could knock them back if you hit them up high," recalled Turner. "But I started keepin' my shoulders and head up. And now I noticed that these pros kept their arms straight, which I was the first one to do." Turner continued about playing center: "You have no idea of the pressure on a center.... Centering the ball on a dry field is no problem, but get it on mud, or snow, or just wet grass, and you've got to be careful. And when you're playing in the rain, you got to just baby the ball back to the punter."[5]

On defense from his linebacker position, Turner had a great knack of dropping back into coverage and playing passing angles. He had great timing when leaping in the air for the ball and finished his career with 17 interceptions, including a then–NFL record eight in 1942. In 1947 against the Redskins, Turner showed off his speed and athleticism when he returned a Sammy Baugh interception 96 yards for a touchdown—the longest interception return for a TD in Bears history until 1962. "It shows in the films. I went 96 yards for a touchdown, the last seven with Sammy Baugh on my back," recalled Turner.[6]

Turner always played with an attitude. He set the tone for the 1940s Monsters of the Midway. He would beat his man to a pulp if he could—even if that man was his best friend. "I hate everybody when I walk on a football field," Turner once said. "I wouldn't even speak to my best friend in a game ... not even Sammy Baugh and we graduated from the same high school in Sweetwater, Texas. Yeah, Sammy'd wink at me when he was calling signals for the Redskins, but I'd just glare back and do my best to rack 'em up."[7]

Turner seemed to have no weaknesses on both sides of the ball. "You couldn't possibly block him. He'd center the ball and be the first man downfield under punts.... He made a science of snapping the ball. He never made a bad pass. He knew just how many revolutions he needed to get the ball back with the laces up ... he was the first center quick enough to block the onside guard on sweeps, the first linebacker to cover receivers coming out of the backfield and he'd be with them stride for stride," said Luke Johnsos, Bears All-Pro end.[8]

Turner was a stickler for details, especially on offense. With the Bears he learned the assignments of every position on every play. "What would amaze you most about Bulldog was his ability as an analyst. He knew what would make a play go," recalled Hugh Gallarneau, Bears back. During practice sessions he would drill, not only at center, but all the other positions except quarterback. He was a sponge. He also never wanted to leave the field. "I think players were a little more versatile back then," said Turner in a 1980 interview. "Not that the players today couldn't be. It was just the nature of the game at that time. I liked it that way, too. I enjoyed staying out there the whole game. Back then, you didn't want to sit down. You were afraid you might miss something. Besides, even if we got a little tired, we were all in such good shape, it didn't bother us none."[9]

George Halas loved Bulldog Turner, once saying, "In the 40 years I coached, Turner was the smartest player we had. He knew every assignment for every player, on every play. That's why he was in the right spot at the right time to make the key tackle or interception. When he came into professional football, everyone played both ways. On defense, he was a destructive linebacker, a savage tackler, and a prowling pass defender. On offense, he was a fearsome blocker for our quarterback Sid Luckman and a charm on the draw—a play we used quite well in those days." "Who knows what kind of player he would have been if he ever got to rest during a game," said George Musso, Bears Hall of Fame lineman.[10]

Turner joined a Bears team that was maturing into a team of greatness, led by five future Hall of Famers in quarterback Sid Luckman (#8), guards Dan Fortmann (#12) and George Musso (#33), tackle Joe Stydahar (#34) and back George McAfee. At his first practice Halas yelled out, "Give me a center," in which the tradition would be the returning center, in this case Frank Bausch, would take his spot on the line. Instead, Turner jogged out to take the spot. "I assumed that Chicago had hired me to play center," recalled Turner. "Some people thought I was cocky, but I was just ignorant." Well, Turner did play center and linebacker his rookie year and for the next 12 seasons.[11]

His rookie year (1940) Turner, at the age of 21, was on a Bears team that won the Eastern Division and went on to destroy the Redskins, 73–0, in the championship game. In that game Turner returned an interception 24 yards for a score. "It was my first score in pro ball, in my years at Hardin-Simmons, or my play at Sweetwater High, it was great," recalled Turner. "Any lineman always gets a big buzz from a chance to score, and I got an extra big one because it was in a championship game." His Bears would win two more titles over the next three years (1941, 1943 and four total when you count the 1946 championship win). Turner picked off four passes in the five NFL championship games in which he played.[12]

During his career with the Bears, Turner quickly became one of the leaders, earning the respect of all of his teammates. "When he walked on the field, he was all class. He was motivated. He played both ways and he was a vicious football player," recalled Sid Luckman. "He looked out for all of us. If there was trouble, Bulldog was there. If we were having problems moving the ball he'd be saying,

'Just come right over me.' [Turner] was Dick Butkus on defense and Jim Ringo on offense."[13]

"Bulldog Turner was the best football player and smartest player I ever knew in my whole life. He could do everything," said George Connor, Bears Hall of Fame lineman.[14]

Retro-MVP: 1942 NFL Season

In 1942, Turner had his best season. He led the NFL in interceptions with eight, setting a record for linebackers, and returned one for a touchdown. Turner's all-around play on both offense and defense helped lead the Bears to an undefeated regular season at 11–0. They outscored their opponents 376–84—both tops in the league.

But Turner's high school mentor, Sammy Baugh, and the Redskins got their revenge for the 1940 73–0 blowout by upsetting the Bears, 14–6, denying them an unbeaten season. Turner would finish runner-up in our 1942 Retro-MVP voting behind Don Hutson (#2) of the Packers. "After Nagurski, the most powerful was Bulldog Turner," said Clarke Hinkle, Packers Hall of Fame fullback. "He came along in 1940. He used to rattle my ribs a lot, too. I lit into him to protect myself, as I had to do against Nagurski. Ah, that Bulldog, he weighed 245 and had a twenty-one-inch collar, was a great blocker on offense and on defense was as fine a linebacker as ever played this game. They talk about Dick Butkus, but I'm not sure Butkus could carry Bulldog's shoes."[15]

In 1945, Turner played just two games before joining the Army. He failed to be the consensus First Team All-Pro for the first time in six seasons. He ended up making one First Team All-Pro for nine straight seasons (1940–1948); most of those years he was a consensus First Teamer. His longevity was unique in an era when most players were done with the game after three or four seasons.

His ability to outsmart his opponent never waned during his long career. "Before we played the Bears," recalled Jimmy Conzelman, Cardinals Hall of Fame coach, "I thought of a special formation, so I called a secret practice. I locked all the doors and had the windows covered. Well, came the day of the game, and we sprang that spread. Bulldog Turner of the Bears looked across the line, grinned, and said, 'Oh, here comes that spread again.'"[16]

Turner's play never diminished during his long career with the Bears. "I played right next to Bulldog Turner my rookie year," said Bill George, Bears Hall of Fame linebacker. "That was Bulldog's 13th year and right then he was the best football player I've ever seen. It was great playing next to him because Bulldog liked me immediately. I think it was because I was uglier than he was."[17]

Turner played six seasons during our two-way era (1940–1945) criteria. He made First Team All-Pro four times by Associated Press and *NYDN*; three times by United

Press and *Chicago Herald-American*; twice by I.N.S. and once by *Detroit Free Press*, *Collyer's*, and *Pro Football Illustrated*. He was selected to the NFL 1940s All-Decade Team. Turner was also elected to the Pro Football Hall of Fame in 1966 and the Bears retired his number 66 jersey.

After the 1952 season Turner finally called it quits at the age of 33. "I had been wanting to quit for three or four years. You get where your pride draws against your earning capacity," said Turner. "I was proud that Halas always said I could play anywhere but I never wanted to be anything but a center and a linebacker."[18]

When elected to the Pro Football Hall of Fame in 1966, Turner gave one of the shortest acceptance speeches of all time. After former Bears tackle Ed Healey introduced him, Turner spoke these 17 words: "Thank you, Ed. I want to thank all of you very much for this honor, thank you."[19]

Turner and Mel Hein (#4) were rivals for the league's top center. In 1999, I interviewed former Bears Hall of Fame lineman George Musso, who compared Mel Hein and Bulldog Turner, saying: "Bulldog Turner and Mel Hein were two of the greatest that's ever played pro football. They're great blockers, great centers. They could block on that line. Mel Hein was a little taller than Bulldog. Bulldog was stockier. Both of them were great ballplayers. The name fits him [Turner]. He was a bulldog. He'd get a hold of you, he wouldn't turn you loose. He's like a pit bull."[20]

"I always had the greatest respect for Mel Hein, who already had been All-Pro seven times when I came along, and consider myself fortunate to have duplicated his feat," said Turner in 1965.[21]

After the 1952 season Turner retired and went into coaching, becoming an assistant with the Bears for four years (1953–1956). After a few years out of football, Turner was hired by Harry Wismer in 1962 to be the new head coach of the New York Titans in the then-struggling American Football League (AFL). The Titans went 5–9 that year. After the season, Wismer sold the Titans—who would become the Jets—so Turner stepped away to return to his ranch in Texas.

In 1948, Turner wrote a book titled *Playing the Line*, a small hardback volume published by Ziff-Davis Publishing Company out of Chicago. At the end of the book, he wrote: "A professional football player has to love the game itself, just as the amateur does. Otherwise, he can never make the grade. He has to love the sound of the tackler meeting the tackled. He has to thrill to crashing into an opponent and knocking him to the turf. He has to enjoy the challenge of outmaneuvering the man opposite him. This zest for the game, as a game, is essential if you are to be success in 'Playing the Line.'"[22]

That is a perfect description of Bulldog Turner, two-way football star.

No. 30

Tuffy Leemans
Halfback-Fullback

Full Name: Alphonse Emil Leemans
Nickname: "Tuffy"
b: November 12, 1912 (Superior, WI); d: January 19, 1979 (age 66; Hillsboro Beach, FL)
High School: Superior East (WI); College: Oregon, George Washington
Height/Weight: 6–0, 195 pounds
Position: Halfback (Fullback)
Teams/Years: 1936–1943 New York Giants
Pro Football Hall of Fame: Class of 1978
Retro-MVPs: No
All-Time Teams: J. Stydahar (1952)

Previously on the list we have seen players named "Dutch," "Fats," "Blood," "Ox," and "Bulldog." Now at number 30, we have a "Tuffy." One thing is for sure, the two-way era loved their nicknames.

Alphonse Leemans was raised in northern Wisconsin near the iron mines off Lake Superior. A rugged son of Belgian immigrants, Leemans loved contact sports, especially football. "When I was a kid playing ball in Superior, Wisconsin, I probably had a little more heart than the ordinary kid, and I wasn't afraid to stick my nose in where it was rough. As a matter of fact, that's how I picked up the name Tuffy," recalled Tuffy Leemans. "After I dumped a couple of big boys, why, they started to call me Tuffy and it stuck. My first name really is Alphonse. Naturally you'd want to change that right away, so I kept calling myself Al, but it never took. People would keep calling me Tuffy."[1]

After a brilliant prep career in Wisconsin, Leemans traveled out west to play for "Doc" Spears at the University of Oregon. But a year later the head coach got fired, so Leemans left the west coast for George Washington University. It was at GWU where Leemans made his mark, attracting the attention of pro teams, but one team on the East Coast took the most interest.

After leaving George Washington University, Leemans was a second round draft pick by the New York Giants in the 1936 Draft (number 18 overall). It was said that Leemans was scouted by a 19-year-old Wellington Mara while he saw GWU play Alabama in 1935. "He was exactly what his name implied. And he was the first player

I ever signed for the Giants," recalled Wellington Mara. "If I am remembered for nothing else, I'd like to be remembered for discovering Tuffy Leemans. It's a good thing the Redskins didn't move to Washington until 1937 or we could never have gotten Tuffy." Mara signed Leemans to a rookie contract of $3,500.[2]

The 6–0, 195-pound Leemans played eight seasons (80 games) with the New York Giants. Leemans could do everything really well: run, pass, catch and play defense, as well as return kicks. "I played sixty minutes, so I had to do it all," recalled Leemans in 1978. "Today, if a guy runs like a reindeer, you put him on the outside as a wide receiver. The game is better today, but it's not as much fun. We played football the way it was supposed to be played."[3]

Not the fastest runner, like a Cliff Battles (#19), Leemans had a unique running style. Watching film, it's obvious he had an uncanny ability to wiggle his hips, make a sudden twist or cut back to avoid any big hits. "He was not fast, but his change of pace was uncanny, and he always seemed to be running with a touchdown in prospect.... Leemans is best remembered for his hips. Tacklers would bounce off those hips. He would roll and pivot with a tackler, shake him loose and come up running," wrote Giants head coach Steve Owen in his book, *My Kind of Football*. Owen continued: "Leemans' secret was this: if he was within three yards of a tackler, Tuffy figured he had the man beat and would look for the next one eight to ten yards downfield. The average back concentrates on the nearest threat, and a subsequent one therefore comes as no surprise to him."[4]

Absolutely a workhorse from the start, Leemans led the NFL in rushing as a rookie in 1936 with 830 yards on a league high 206 carries. He earned First Team All-Pro by the NFL and *Collyer's*. His rushing yards was a Giants single-season record until 1951 when Eddie Price ran for 971. He would go on to have 100 or more carries in six straight seasons (1936–1941). "I wasn't very fast, but I started quick and had good leg strength," recalled Leemans. "If you were going to tackle me, it had to be around the shoulders. Greasy Neale, the Eagles coach, told his players they would be fined if they tried to tackle me below the waist."[5]

Leemans made it tough on his opponents trying to slow him down. He became the Giants number one threat on offense. "Tuffy Leemans had it all. He could run, pass and catch and he played truly outstanding defense. He was aggressive, dedicated and gave 100 percent at all times to a game he loved. In my opinion, he ranks among the all-time greats," said Wayne Millner, Redskins Hall of Fame end.[6]

Tuffy was no meek moniker. He played both sides of the ball with equal toughness. He never gave an inch. "When we'd play the Giants and they needed two or three yards, they almost always would call on Tuffy to smash over tackle," recalled Cliff Battles, former Redskins All-Pro back. "But no matter how prepared we were, Tuffy usually would make it. He had great balance and great competitiveness. I never saw a better player than Leemans!"[7]

"Tuffy Leemans of the Giants could play pretty rough. He had legs like posts, when you tackled him you felt like you were tackling a pair of posts," recalled Clarke Hinkle, Packers Hall of Fame fullback.[8]

While on defense Leemans held up on that side of the ball. "He blocked and ran like a bull, tackled like a fool, and caught the ball beautifully. [But] Leemans was probably greater on defense than on offense. He was a bugger on defense, all over the field, always in on the action," recalled Alex Wojciechowicz, former Lions-Eagles Hall of Fame center.[9]

Leemans was a key cog in the Giants lineup during his eight seasons, helping the Giants consistently challenge for the Eastern Division and NFL championship with the likes of fellow All-Pros Mel Hein (#4), Ward Cuff (#32), and Ed Danowski (#41). Over his eight years the Giants won three division titles and the 1938 NFL championship. On a team with a bunch of stars, Leemans was usually the man who took charge. "Mel Hein is considered the number one Giant of all-time," said Wellington Mara, Giants owner. "In a lot of ways, Tuffy was more Mr. Giant than Hein. Mel was quiet and did things by example. Tuffy was an extrovert. He stepped on the field and took charge. He had an aura about him. He'd walk into a room and you knew the leader had just arrived."[10]

Tuffy was the one calling the signals in the huddle. He was a pure leader. "I've seen Tuffy make a run when the blocking was not up to standard. But upon returning to the huddle to call the next signal, the first thing he'd say was: 'Nice blocking, gang, let's hit 'em again.' He always gave his mates credit," wrote Steve Owen in his book *My Kind of Football*.[11]

Playing 60 minutes sometimes didn't come easy for Leemans under Steve Owen. "Steve was a tough coach but fair as hell," recalled Tuffy Leemans. "Yes, he was a fair man. His famous saying to the squad was, 'I only ask one thing of you guys. I want your ass for one hour of playing time every Sunday.' He would tell me, 'Tuffy, keep playing out there till you can't keep going any longer, then put up your hand and I'll get you out of there.' I'd have that hand up in the air so long that I felt like my arm would fall off.... Oh, cripe! It was nothing for Steve Owen to say to us after we'd just lost a game, 'Well, boys, we're going to work a little bit now.' So right there, right after the game was over, we'd practice. One time we went at it for two and half hours. Knocked heads all the way."[12]

In 1939, Leemans earned his other First Team All-Pro honor by rushing for 429 yards and posting career highs with 185 receiving yards and five total touchdowns. He helped the Giants win the Eastern Division, although they lost the NFL championship game, 27–0, to the Packers.

Leemans led the Giants in rushing five times (1936, 1938–1941) but probably was known more for passing later in his career. He excelled as a passer, throwing for 2,318 yards and 25 touchdowns, including a career-high seven in 1942 (sixth best in the NFL). He led the Giants in passing three times, 1941–1943. In the end, Leemans had more passing touchdowns than rushing scores. He finished his career with 3,132 rushing yards and 17 rushing TDs plus three receiving scores (20 total TDs).

Tuffy did have mixed results in four postseason games. He had an excellent performance in the 1938 NFL championship game, rushing 12 times for 43 yards and one TD in the victory against the Packers; the other three games (all losses), he carried 28 times for just 49 yards and zero scores. After he retired Leemans was honored by the Giants, being selected a member of the team's Ring of Honor and having his number 4 jersey retired. He was also selected to the NFL 1930s All-Decade Team. Despite his accolades Leemans seemed to miss out on being elected to the Pro Football Hall of Fame.

"He wasn't really fast, but he had everything else a good runner needed—balance, the ability to pick a hole, things like that. And he was tough. In those days, you weren't really down until they held you down, so he'd always scratch and crawl and fight for a few extra yards," said Jim Lee Howell, Giants end and teammate, 1937–1942.[13]

"Tuffy Leemans was one of the toughest guys in the world to tackle. He just had strong legs and great maneuverability. Not much speed, but he was a good athlete," said Vic Sears, former Eagles All-Pro tackle.[14]

After 35 years since his last NFL game, Leemans did receive the greatest honor of any professional football player—he was elected to the Hall of Fame in 1978, at the age of 65. "I didn't know if I was ever going to make it," Leemans once said. "It was like I had two yards to go, had used up three downs and had only one more chance to make it."[15]

In Canton for the ceremony, Leemans was purely joyful for being elected so late in his life. During his speech Leemans showed his gratitude. "Ladies and gentlemen, 35 years that's what it took me and it is worth every bit of it—I have met the finest people in the world. It has been a long haul and a lot of injuries on the way, but I assure you today after seeing what I have seen, it is worth every bit of those bumps," said Leemans during his Hall of Fame induction speech. To end his speech Leemans said, "I want to say this, that I am probably the proudest guy in the world and I am so happy that today I never before allowed anyone to call me Alphonse, but you all can call me Alphonse today, thank you."[16]

Unfortunately, Leemans didn't get to celebrate being a Hall of Famer very long. Six months after being inducted Leemans died of a heart attack. "I just loved the game," once recalled Tuffy Leemans. "I know a lot of players back then, and myself included, who would have played for nothing."[17]

No. 31

Duke Slater

Tackle

Full Name: Fredrick Wayman Slater
Nickname: "Duke"
b: December 9, 1898 (Normal, IL); d: August 14, 1966 (age 67; Chicago, IL)
High School: Clinton (IA); College: Iowa
Height/Weight: 6–1, 215 pounds
Position: Tackle
Teams/Years: 1922 Milwaukee Badgers; 1922–1926 Rock Island Independents (NFL/AFL); 1926–1931 Chicago Cardinals
Pro Football Hall of Fame: Class of 2020
Retro-MVPs: No
All-Time Teams: E. Cuneo (1973); R. Grange (1947); E. Nevers (1932); P. Robeson (1941)

Duke Slater is one of the true pioneers in the NFL, the first African American tackle in league history. Slater was born on the south side of Chicago as the son of a college-educated minister. He enjoyed playing on the sandlots, craving the physical contact of the sport. He first learned the game with the neighboring boys on the south side of Chicago and once claimed that his favorite part of playing football was tackling.

During this time Slater picked up his royal nickname. "As a boy, I had a dog named Duke, and somehow or other the boys started calling me Duke," explained Slater. After his mother suddenly passed away when Duke was 11 years old, Slater's father moved the family from Chicago to Iowa, taking a job at a church in the town of Clinton. Here, Slater continued to improve his skills on the football field.[1]

The Slater family lived on a shoestring budget, so Duke found it hard to afford football equipment while growing up. He rarely had the money for cleats, shoulder pads and helmet. "We were too poor to buy both headgear and shoes. My father said I could take my choice," recalled Duke. "Shoes were more essential than a helmet. Since I couldn't quite see playing barefoot, I went without headgear. I never could get used to wearing one after that." Playing for Clinton High School, Slater made a name for himself as a rugged lineman, someone who not only had the talent to play with brawn but with his brains.[2]

Those talents allowed him to play at the University of Iowa. He became a two-time All-American at tackle, and the *Chicago Defender* called him "the man mountain of football." While playing with the Hawkeyes, Slater was one of the strongest, fastest tackles in the country. He learned to control his temper and was well regarded for his skills. Knute Rockne, the great Notre Dame coach, once said that there was "no better tackle ever trod a western gridiron ... this fellow Slater just about beat my team single-handed in the only contest we lost."³

In 1922, Slater decided to sign with the NFL's Rock Island Independents. Slater mentioned he was paid $1,500 for that first season. Jimmy Conzelman, the Rock Island player-coach, went to sign Slater. "We drove over to Iowa City and found the 'Duke' out on a corner lot throwing the ball around for the pleasure and delight of a gang of neighborhood worshipers. He shuffled over to our car with his size 13 shoes and after a bit of bargaining, signed a contract. For the next 10 years he was regarded as one of the top tackles in the league."⁴

Duke Slater, tackle, Chicago Cardinals, ca. 1921 (courtesy Iowa University Athletics).

Slater was excited to play pro football. "I'm quick at picking up signals," Duke told the *Rock Island Argus*. "I'll be in great shape, too." His rookie year Slater played against the mighty Chicago Bears twice and held his own. Bears great guard Hunk Anderson once called Slater "a rough piece of furniture." Slater proved he belonged against the NFL's defending champions.⁵

Slater goes down in history as the NFL's first Black lineman and one of the dozen or so early Black players in the NFL's first decade, joining such names as Fritz Pollard (#23), Paul Robeson and Inky Williams. Filling out at 6–1, 215 pounds, Slater was hard to block on defense, making many tackles at or behind the line of scrimmage, while on offense he was one of the hardest to get around. "Nobody opened holes like Duke Slater," said Vince McCarthy, former Rock Island back and teammate. "He was 215 pounds but with arms as big as my legs. The team loved him." One of his better skills that was consistently noted in game recaps was Slater's ability to run down on punts, making many tackles.⁶

From 1922 to 1925, Slater played four seasons under four head coaches—Jimmy Conzelman, Herb Sies, John Armstrong, Rube Ursella—with the team going a combined 16–10–9. Despite the turnover at coaches, Slater played at a high level each season. Twice he was named First Team All-Pro by *Collyer's Eye*, in 1923 and 1925. "Duke was a helluva body blocker and you couldn't play him outside nor inside because he was big and quick and could easily sideswipe you out of the play with his body block," recalled Hunk Anderson.[7]

Opposing players and coaches took notice of Slater for his talent, not the color of his skin. "Slater was a whiz-bang in Sunday's game," Franklin Fausch, player-coach for the Evansville Crimson-Giants (NFL) said after a 1922 game. "He hammered tirelessly against the Evansville forward wall. At the end of the game he seemed fresh as when he went in. At the kickoff Slater booted the ball over the fence with seemingly little effort."[8]

After Rock Island completed their schedule at the end of the 1922 season, Slater joined the Milwaukee Badgers and teamed up with fellow Black pioneer players Fritz Pollard and Paul Robeson. Duke quickly earned Robeson's respect: "Milwaukee was playing Racine and it was an annual 'blood' game. Our club got Slater to play for us—Rock Island had finished its season. He played next to me and I don't think I made a tackle all afternoon. Didn't have to. Whenever I felt like loafing, I'd say, 'You take care of 'em, Duke.' Jeez, he was a whole side of a line by himself."[9]

Despite being one of the only Black players in the league at times, Slater became recognized as one of the best linemen in the NFL. Then his team left the league. In 1926, the Independents joined the American Football League (AFL) founded by Red Grange and his agent, C.C. Pyle. It was in the AFL that Slater went up against Grange for the first time. The Galloping Ghost came away impressed. "They can bring all the tackles in the country," Grange said in an interview with the *Philadelphia Inquirer*. "But this fellow Slater is the best of 'em all. Slater is a marvel, and is so strong and powerful that he seems one half of the line aside when he charges. I've played against Slater, and I know what I'm talking about."[10]

Although Slater played well in 1926, the Independents ran out of money and folded before the season was completed. Instead of packing up his equipment for good, Slater joined the Chicago Cardinals to finish out the season. Wilfrid Smith of the *Chicago Tribune* selected an All-Pro team that combined AFL and NFL players and named Slater first team, writing, "Slater, who started the season with Rock Island and finished with the Chicago Cardinals, is one of the best tackles who ever donned a suit. His phenomenal strength and quickness of charge make it almost impossible for his opponents to put him out of the play directed at his side of the line."[11]

In 1927, Slater joined the Cardinals full time, becoming the lead blocker for All-Pro fullback Ernie Nevers (#18). Duke quickly became one of Nevers' best friends, on and off the field. In 1928, Slater graduated from Iowa with his law degree and the following year, while still playing in the NFL, he passed the Illinois bar exam. The law would be Slater's life work. But first he had to finish his football career. In 1929, he took part in a game renowned in NFL history.

Slater blocked for Nevers when Ernie scored his six rushing TDs (his 40-point game) in 1929 vs. the Bears, accounting for an NFL record of 40 points in one game, including four XPs. It's a record that still stands today. "Duke Slater, the veteran colored tackle, seemed the dominant figure in that forward wall which had the Bear front wobbly. It was Slater who opened the holes for Nevers when a touchdown was in the making," wrote the *Chicago Herald-Examiner* the day after the game. "I can't say enough about Duke Slater as a football player and as a gentleman," said George Halas. "In the old Cardinals-Bears games, I learned it was absolutely useless to run against [Duke] Slater's side of the Cardinal line. They talked about Fordham's famous seven Blocks of Granite in the mid–1930s and what a line that was. Well, Slater was a One Man Line a decade before that. Seven Blocks of Granite? He was the Rock of Gibraltar."[12]

Two weeks after the Nevers six-touchdown game, Slater found himself in the end zone for the first time ever. On December 8 he scored his only NFL touchdown on an interception return in a 26–0 Cardinals victory over the Orange Tornadoes. Slater was named again First Team All-Pro by the *Chicago Tribune* while the *Green Bay Press-Gazette* selected him to the second team for the fifth time in his career.

A dominate tackle during his 10-year career in the NFL who played 90 games for Milwaukee, Rock Island and the Chicago Cardinals, Slater retired after the 1931 season at the age of 33. "I hung up my suit in 1931 when I realized that football is a young man's game," said Slater. His play that year was just as good as when he played his rookie year. "Slater makes the most of his position: is powerful, has huge hands, is very seldom caught, and hasn't slowed a bit in the six years I have played opposite to him," wrote Lavvie Dilweg in the *Green Bay Press-Gazette* in naming Slater to his 1931 All-Opponent Team.[13]

In 1932, Ernie Nevers was asked by the *Los Angeles Times* to give his five greatest players he knew in pro football. Nevers listed Red Grange, Mike Michalske, Bronko Nagurski, Walt Keisling and Duke Slater.[14]

In 1934, the Associated Press wrote: "The immense Duke Slater [was] one of the greatest tackles who ever developed. Duke was the idol not only of those who knew and respected his ability, but who had a weakness as well for sportsmanship, good nature, and manliness, regardless of race or color. He never lost his temper, never lost the grin that continually split his huge face, and never more than an arm's length, either, from the man with the ball."[15]

When the NFL's unwritten ban on Black players occurred, Slater wasn't quite done with football. He played for Fritz Pollard's Chicago Blackhawks with Sol Butler, Ink Williams and Joe Lillard. Then he went on to coach a few all-Black pro football teams, including the Brown Bombers (1937) and Chicago Panthers (1940).

Besides sports, Slater continued to make waves in his profession on his way to the top. Slater was voted to the Cook County (IL) Municipal Court as a sitting judge in 1948—thus becoming just the second African American elected as a judge in the city of Chicago. He would eventually become the first to ascend to Chicago's Supreme Court in 1960. While Slater sat on the judicial bench, pro football was gaining a Hall of Fame, built in 1963 in Canton, Ohio. After the Pro Football Hall of Fame opened, Slater's name was prominently on the list of top candidates. However, Slater never heard his name called for election, and he passed away from stomach cancer in 1966 at the age of 67.

One of Slater's teammates with the Chicago Cardinals, Herb Blumer, a former All-Pro guard, talked about his former roommate:

> It's been such a long time ago, but I've never forgotten Duke Slater and the effect he had both on his teammates and the players on the other teams. I think he might have been one of the only Negro players in the league at the time, but I've never gotten over the way he gained everyone's respect … especially players from the southern colleges.
>
> I was his roommate while we were on trips for two reasons, I guess. First, because I had a high regard for him as a person, and, second, because in my own way, I wanted to take the harshness off some of the insults he had to endure because he was a Negro living in those times. He was a decent man, a real gentleman. There were times when we'd sit alone and we'd discuss his feelings about segregation. Of course, he was bitter about it but he always held those under control.[16]

In the early years of the Pro Football Hall of Fame voting, Slater's name was listed with the other greats of the game. Twice, he was a Hall of Fame Finalist, in 1970 and 1971. Then his name disappeared. It seemed Slater's achievements and career were forgotten. Nearly 50 years later he was finally elected to the Pro Football Hall of Fame in 2020 as part of the Hall's Centennial Class. It was about time. At least now, football fans know the name of Duke Slater as one of the greatest NFL players of all time. Football had been good to Slater. "Football is a rugged, demanding sport, and it teaches you to put every effort forth. The finest thing about playing is that you retain a lot of the give and take the rest of your life," said Slater.[17]

No. 32

Ward Cuff
Halfback-Wingback

Full Name: Ward Lloyd Cuff
Nickname: N/A
b: August 13, 1912 (Redwood Falls, MN); d: December 24, 2002 (age 90; Vallejo, CA)
High School: Redwood Valley (MN); College: Oregon, Marquette
Height/Weight: 6-1, 192 pounds
Position: Halfback-Wingback
Teams/Years: 1937–1945 New York Giants; 1946 Chicago Cardinals; 1947 Green Bay Packers
Pro Football Hall of Fame: No
Retro-MVPs: No
All-Time Teams: M. Hein (1944); T. Leemans (1945)

    Another overlooked Hall of Fame candidate—joining Verne Lewellen (#7) and Ox Emerson (#25)—who could do almost everything on the gridiron from his wingback position was Ward Cuff.
    The 6-1, 192-pound Cuff played 11 years (110 games) for three teams, including the Cardinals and Packers, but played nearly his entire career with the New York Giants. After graduating from Marquette, Cuff was drafted in the fourth round of the 1937 NFL Draft (34th overall) by the New York Giants. Cuff was personally scouted by Giants head coach Steve Owen. Although Marquette was led by their All-American halfback Ray Buivid—who finished third in the Heisman ahead of Sammy Baugh—and brothers Art and Al Guepe, Owen's eyes became fixated on Marquette's blocking back. He was the man doing all the dirty work, making all the tackles and lead blocking for the star backs. Owen knew he wanted Cuff.
    At that first training camp coach Owen made it a priority to use Cuff in any way possible. At Marquette Cuff never kicked, but Owen saw something in his prized recruit. Every day for three weeks Owen drilled Cuff for a half-hour in the art of place kicking. He liked what he saw. Owen recalled that first training camp in an article he wrote for *Collier's* magazine in 1942: "Cuff had tremendous leg drive and an excellent sense of balance. I was not too certain about the third necessary qualification but that was speedily discovered when we scrimmaged. Mr. Cuff has nothing but ice water in his veins. Nothing rattles him. He looked like a perfect prospect."[1]
    Cuff was a very durable player that would play through any aliment. "Ward

was outstanding as a runner, a receiver, and a defensive halfback. Above all, he was an Iron Man who could play with so many injuries that he often seemed to be taped from head to toe before he put on his uniform," wrote Steve Owen in his book *My Kind of Football*. On offense, Owen had developed a new offensive system he called the A-formation. He had the perfect center, Mel Hein, to snap the ball; he had plenty of halfbacks and quarterbacks like Tuffy Leemans, Ed Danowski and Hank Soar; what he was missing was the wingback—the man who would go in motion at times to be a decoy, be a ball carrier every so often, run pass routes, but mainly be used as a lead blocker. Cuff was the man for the job. "Our motto was to keep knocking men down until the whistle blew ending the play," said Cuff to the *Milwaukee News* in 1938. What Owen didn't know was that Cuff, almost from the start, was his best receiver, blocker and defensive back.[2]

Ward Cuff, halfback, New York Giants, ca. 1936 (courtesy Marquette University Athletics).

In his second season, Cuff helped the Giants win the Eastern Division. He led the team in scoring with 45 points, while helping the defense only surrender a league-low 79 points—including only 10 points in their final five games. In the NFL championship game, they faced off against the Green Bay Packers at the Polo Grounds. In the first quarter Cuff booted a 14-yard field goal to give the Giants an early 3–0 lead. Then the Packers and Giants started to trade touchdowns as New York took a 16–14 lead into halftime.

Early in the third quarter the Pack took the lead for the first time, 17–16. Then Ed Danowski hit Hank Soar with a 23-yard scoring strike to give the Giants the lead back at 23–17. In the fourth quarter the Packers had the ball four times but came close to scoring only one time. In the red zone, Packers quarterback Arnie Herber connected with Wayland Becker, but Cuff nailed Becker and forced a fumble that was recovered by the Giants' Kayo Lunday who returned the ball to their own 22-yard line. The Packers never got closer. Cuff was a world champion. Although he was just doing his job, Cuff's name made plenty of newspaper headlines as the "hero of game."

Cuff's overall numbers don't blow you away. He finished his career with 3,410 yards from scrimmage (1,851 rushing, 1,559 receiving) and averaged a robust 5.4 yards per carry. While playing with New York Cuff was never the top dog in the Giants rushing game, mostly overshadowed by Hall of Fame teammate Tuffy Leemans, but twice he led the NFL in rushing average per carry, in 1943 (80 carries) with a 6.5 average and in 1944 with a 5.6 average (tied with the Eagles' Steve Van Buren). His 80 rushing attempts in 1943 was a career high.

Ward Cuff's passion for the game always came out in the way he played on the field, going a hundred miles an hour to help his team win. He didn't care if he carried the ball or made the block. On film, Cuff was always around the ball and consistently made plays—on both offense and defense. He showed excellent ball skills and was very durable, playing in over 100 games. Rarely did he get to carry the football, but he might've been the most important piece in the backfield. Another strength was as a skilled receiver for Tuffy Leemans (#30) and Ed Danowski (#41). From 1937 to 1943 he caught 78 passes for 1,170 yards—averaged a gaudy 16.7 yards per catch—and 10 touchdowns.

Watching game footage of Cuff on the defensive side of the ball, he consistently showed great range and timing as a defensive halfback with 13 career INTs for 263 return yards. He always seemed to be around the ball, breaking up many passes and never being out of position. In the championship season of 1938, he had a 96-yard INT return for a touchdown against the Redskins (won game 36–0) to help clinch the Eastern Division title and set a Giants team record that lasted 20 years when Erich Barnes broke it in 1961 (102 yards). In 1941, he led the NFL in interception return yards with 152. In a 1985 NFL Films interview, Washington Hall of Fame coach Ray Flaherty remembers the 1938 Cuff interception: "We took the ball down to the Giants one-yard line. It was first down and a yard to go for a touchdown. I was just sitting there relaxing, waiting for them to go across the goal line. Frank Filchock lined up in the tailback position and threw a pass into the right side of our offense against the best, probably the best defensive back in the league, Ward Cuff. He picked it off and went 96 yards for a touchdown."[3] During his career Cuff made three Pro Bowls (1938–1939, 1941) and was named First Team All-Pro three times in 1941 and 1943–1944. He was named Honorable Mention by the NFL four times (1937–1939, 1941).

After all his success on offense and defense, Cuff was even better on special teams. He was the premiere kicker of his time—among the likes of Ken Strong, Ralph Kercheval, and Jack Manders. He converted 43 FGs and was an impressive 155 of 162 on extra points, a clip of 96 percent. He led the NFL in FGs made four times, 1938–1939, 1943, and 1947—at the age of 35—and finished in the top 5 of field goals made eight times. He also was in the top 10 in scoring eight times and helped the Giants win four divisional titles and the 1938 NFL championship—where he kicked two XPs and one FG against the Packers, a 23–17 victory.

Cuff still ranks second all-time with most seasons leading league in field goals made behind Lou Groza's five times. In 1938, Cuff explained his kicking process: "There's no trick to it. The mechanics of the thing are simple, and the only thing I take credit for are the hours I devote to practice. Practice is essential; it develops the right timing. First and foremost, the kicker must keep his eye on the ball. That's why so many kickers miss. Rushing linemen distract them, and involuntarily they take their eyes off the ball. That's fatal. I start off with my right foot, take one step with the left and let go."[4]

In 1946, at the age of 34, Cuff was traded by the Giants to the Chicago Cardinals, so he could be closer to his family's Milwaukee home. That season he finished third in the NFL in scoring with 55 points, behind the Packers' Ted Fritsch with 100 points and the Rams' Bob Waterfield with 61 points. Cuff played his final season in the NFL with the Green Bay Packers in 1947. When he retired, Cuff finished with 411 career points, 305 with the Giants.

In 2000, I interviewed Hank Soar, one of Cuff's teammates with the Giants. He praised Cuff for his all-around play. "Ward could punt a ball. He would kick off, too, his ball would always be right there at the goal line. He was a strong kicker. Ward was a great defensive player. He could run. He could just play football, and he was a great defensive man. He'd intercept passes like nobody in football could do."[5]

Because he was never the focal point of the offense, Cuff's overall stats come up short with other Hall of Fame backs from the two-way era, especially his contemporaries like George McAfee, Bill Dudley, Tony Canadeo or his teammate Tuffy Leemans. But nobody might've been more important for their team's success than Ward Cuff for the Giants. Offense, defense and special teams—the premiere kicker of his era—Cuff was simply an outstanding two-way player. Footage shows us that too. Once speaking in 1943, Steve Owen told the *New York Times*, "If I had to choose up sides, Ward would be the first man I pick. He does everything and does it remarkably well."[6]

Giants Jersey Number 14 Retired

Despite his lack of recognition, Ward Cuff was honored with one of the greatest achievements any player can have when the Giants retired his number 14 jersey in 1946—the year he was traded to the Cardinals. That fall Cuff returned to his old stomping grounds wearing a different uniform but a familiar jersey number. On October 20, 1946, Cuff jogged out in front of over 50,000 fans at the Polo Grounds wearing his Cardinals number 14 jersey. The fans gave him an ovation.

In the game program that day, Giants vice president Wellington Mara wrote a one-page tribute to Ward Cuff, praising the former Giants hero. He wrote:

> In his nine years with the club, Ward Cuff was truly a "Giant Among Giants." From the very first he was a regular. He scored more points for the Giants than anyone has ever scored for them. He paved the way for many more with his unselfish blocking. When an important game hung in the balance for want of a field goal or point after touchdown he never failed. He was always the best pass defender and tackler on the team that excelled in defense....
>
> The Giants miss Cuff. They miss his running and blocking and tackling but most of all they miss him "in the clutch." For when the chips were down, he was always there to say "I'll make it, let me try," when a first down was needed or a field goal would mean the ball game.
>
> This year, when family ties and business interests were such that Cuff couldn't come east,

arrangements were made to permit him to play near his Milwaukee home. That explains his presence with the Cardinals today. No one can ever take his place on the Giants nor will anyone ever wear his No. 14 jersey. That number has been retired for all time.[7]

That day Cuff played his heart out trying to beat his former team. He accounted for 12 points on a touchdown run, one field goal and three extra points. But it wasn't enough as the Giants pulled out a tough 28–24 victory.

Cuff's jersey wasn't retired quite yet. In 1961 when the Giants traded for Y.A Tittle they brought out jersey number 14 for him. But since 1965 no New York Giants player has worn the number 14.

After doing some high school coaching and working for Boeing, Ward Cuff passed away on December 24, 2002, at the age of 90. "We were contemporaries," Giants owner Wellington Mara said to the Associated Press. "He came to camp in 1937 as a rookie, and we roomed together from then on in camp and on the road. I have a lot of fond memories of him. He was a terrific competitor."[8]

Not too many players get their jersey retired. It's a special honor, for a special player. A player that should be in the Pro Football Hall of Fame.

No. 33

George Musso
Guard-Tackle

Full Name: George Francis Musso
Nickname: "Moose"
b: April 8, 1910 (Collinsville, IL); d: September 5, 2000 (age 90; Edwardsville, IL)
High School: Collinsville (IL); College: Millikin
Height/Weight: 6–2, 262 pounds
Position: Guard-Tackle
Teams/Years: 1933–1944 Chicago Bears
Pro Football Hall of Fame: Class of 1982
Retro-MVPs: No
All-Time Teams: B. Bell (1940); R. Richards (1944)

At number 33 is George Musso, the 6–2, 262-pound mammoth lineman who played for the Chicago Bears' Monsters of the Midway.

Musso was born in Collinsville, Illinois, the son of a coal miner. The younger Musso grew up with a passion for sports, not the dusty mines of southern Illinois. He wanted to go to school and play football. Some of Musso's school friends had to persuade his father to allow him to go to high school and then on to Millikin College as an alternative to working in the mines. Eventually, Musso's father said yes.

Musso used his size and unique athletic abilities to make a name for himself at Millikin, lettering in four sports: football, baseball, basketball and track & field. While at tiny Millikin, Musso crossed paths with a future Hollywood star who would go on to become president of the United States.

In 1929, Musso was a lineman for Millikin playing against Eureka College. Millikin won easily 45–6, but across from him that day was a skinny 165-pound guard named Ronald Reagan.

"He played left guard and I was right tackle. Of course, we played right in front of one another," recalled George Musso. "He weighed about 165 pounds, I was weighing about 235, 240 at that time. He was supposed to be handling me, of course, he couldn't do it. To begin with, because I was just too much weight for him, I pushed him back. In fact, we beat them 45–6 or something like that. He was quick. He was a good ballplayer, but he was no comparison with the size. I could push him whatever way I wanted to push him. But he was a good ballplayer, that's all I can tell you about that."[1]

George Musso, guard-tackle, Chicago Bears, ca. 1932 (courtesy Millikin University Athletics).

After graduating from Millikin, Musso got the itch to play pro football. Musso received two offers, one from the New York Giants and one from the Chicago Bears. Bears owner George Halas became aware of Musso from the recommendation of George Corbett who had played with Musso at Millikin before joining the Bears for his rookie year in 1932. "George Corbett, a teammate of mine at Millikin, had already joined the Bears and Chicago was closer to home. In those days you played because it was fun, not because of money," recalled Musso.[2]

Halas gave the small-school star a chance to play pro ball. "He sent a money order for $5 [for expenses]," Musso recalled. "The round-trip train ticket on the Wabash [RR] was $3. That left $2 for me to really do the town. I came. Mr. Halas offered me $90 a game. I accepted."[3]

Musso struggled in his first training camp with the Bears. Halas was unhappy with his investment. He suggested that Musso move down a notch and play for a farm team in Cincinnati to get his confidence up. Musso wanted nothing of that, telling Halas that Curly Lambeau of the Packers was interested in signing him. Not wanting to lose a potential good player to the hated Packers, Halas countered. He would keep Musso on for half his salary and if he didn't make the team, he would trade him to Green Bay. Musso agreed.

The rookie still felt down about his play with the Bears until Red Grange, the Galloping Ghost, gave Musso some confidence. "We talked for a while," Musso recalled. "He told me I could make the club if I just played up to my capability. It was a shot in the arm. The next Sunday at Brooklyn I played about a half, gaining confidence as I went along. That was the last time I ever heard about being traded."[4]

Musso joined a Bears team that had just won the NFL championship—winning the famous "Indoor Game." He earned a spot on a squad that featured All-Pros Bronko Nagurski, Red Grange, Bill Hewitt, Luke Johnsos, Joe Kopcha and Ookie Miller. They were looking to repeat.

Musso quickly picked up the nuances of the pro game, combining his size with speed and quickness, gliding his 260-pound body around with ease. He quickly earned the nickname "Moose." His rookie year Musso helped the Bears win the 1933 NFL championship game, 23–21, over the New York Giants. Musso was named First Team All-Pro by the *Brooklyn Eagle* and second team by the NFL.

In the 1934 College All-Star Game Musso played against another future United States president, facing off against former Michigan All-American center Gerald Ford. He is the only Pro Football Hall of Famer to face off against two presidents. "I played against another fella that became president. Ford." recalled Musso. "He was a center on the All-Star team. Of course, we played a five-man front and I played right in front of him. He was pretty rugged. He was pretty tough. Trying to move him out of there. But he was a good ballplayer."[5]

Musso quickly became one of the Bears' leaders, both on and off the field. He became someone that the team, and in particular, Coach Halas could trust. "George was one of the finest guards ever in professional football. He was tough, mobile, agile and intimidating, with an indomitable competitive spirit," said George Halas.[6]

But Halas saw more than a great player, he saw the perfect Bears player. "He was a great leader and from his third season on he was our captain," continued Halas. "He could get along with anybody." Halas thought so much of Musso that the man they called "Moose" was one of the few players he allowed to give the pregame talk. "George Musso was a man that would 'play down' his individual performance [to the press]. He was 100 percent a team player," said Clyde "Bulldog" Turner, Bears Hall of Fame center and teammate.[7]

After playing his first four seasons with the Bears at tackle, Musso moved to guard in 1937 and stayed there until his retirement after the 1944 season. Musso's versatility of being knocked inside to guard proved why he was one of the best linemen during his era. He was very durable, appearing in 128 games over 12 seasons while helping the Bears to four NFL championships in 1933, 1940–1941 and 1943.

Playing both ways thrilled Musso. He never wanted to leave the field. "Back in my days we played offense, defense, kicking team, receiving team you name it," said Musso. "Most of the fellas played 60 minutes, the whole game. The only time they'd replace me because of an injury or something. We were worn out by the time that the game was over. A lot of us just walk into the shower room, uniform and all. Just walk in and get under the cold shower to cool off."[8]

Playing on a team with an array of All-Pros and future Hall of Famers, it was hard to stand out. But the "Moose," did his best. Watching game film shows that Musso was a slightly better player on defense than offense. "Excellent on defense against running plays directly at him," said Bruiser Kinard, Hall of Fame tackle. "George was the outstanding lineman of his time. His size and speed made him a difficult target, particularity on defense," said Ray Flaherty, Redskins Hall of Fame coach.[9]

Musso gained a reputation of roughing it up. Early in his career he didn't wear a helmet. Watching footage of Bears games in the 1930s and early '40s, you can see the big 262-pounder making tackles and blocking without a helmet. "We played without headgear until they put a rule in that you had to play with them," recalled George Musso.[10]

He sometimes played with a cast on his arm and getting into scuffles, especially against the Packers, was commonplace. Once Packers All-Pro guard Russ Letlow was fined $75 for fighting with Musso. "[George] always had a broken arm and he battered me with his cast," once recalled Russ Letlow. "We were rolling around in the dirt while the play was 40 yards downfield ... [with a wry smile] I took the fine to Lambeau and he paid for it."[11]

"That man right in front of that center is me. When he's getting that ball between his legs with one hand, but as soon as that ball moves, you're in there under his chin," recalled Musso. "Of course, back in our days, you could go ahead and slap their head. It didn't make any difference if you hit them in the head, you could slap the hell out of them. Our line coach Hunk Anderson used to tell us, 'You hit a man's head and knock him to the left, he's going to fall to the left. If you knock him to the right, he's going to fall that way.'"[12]

Part of one of the NFL's greatest dynasties, Musso's teams went 104–26–6 and won six division titles and four NFL championships during his tenure. Musso became one of the rare players during the two-way era to be named First Team All-Pro at two different positions—guard and tackle. He played in three Pro Bowls and was named to the NFL 75th Anniversary Two-Way Team (1994).

In 1962, Musso suffered a near-fatal auto accident where he had 54 separate bone breaks. This didn't stop Musso, who after his playing career was over was elected Madison County treasurer and sheriff, serving in office for over three decades.

Once the Pro Football Hall of Fame opened in 1963, Musso's name was bypassed by voters. His accomplishments seemed to get lost over time. Finally, in 1982, Musso's name came up as a finalist for the Hall of Fame. During the process several former opponents gave their endorsement for "Moose" to be selected. Alex Wojciechowicz, Bruiser Kinard, Clarke Hinkle and Art Rooney wrote endorsement letters affirming that Musso was definitely a Hall of Famer. "He was as tough as they make them. A big hulk but a very aggressive player," wrote Alex Wojciechowicz, former Hall of Fame center.[13]

"[Musso] was big and tough. Anchored the Bears five-man line with authority. Had good speed for a big man. He was hard to fool," wrote Hinkle.[14]

Bears teammates Dan Fortmann, Bulldog Turner, George McAfee and Sid Luckman also wrote letters. Thirty-eight years after his last NFL game Musso was finally elected to the Pro Football Hall of Fame. He was 71 years old. "After being away from the game 38 years I thought people had forgotten about me," said Musso. "This is the greatest moment of my life. Making the Hall of Fame is something that I've always dreamed about."[15]

George Musso passed away on September 5, 2000, at the age of 90.

No. 34

Joe Stydahar
Tackle

Full Name: Joseph Lee Stydahar
Nickname: "Jumbo Joe"
b: March 17, 1912 (Kaylor, PA); d: March 23, 1977 (age 65; Beckley, WV)
High School: Shinnston (WV); College: Pittsburgh, West Virginia
Height/Weight: 6-4, 233 pounds
Position: Tackle
Teams/Years: 1936–1942, 1945–1946 Chicago Bears
Pro Football Hall of Fame: Class of 1967
Retro-MVPs: No
All-Time Teams: S. Baugh (1949, 1957, 1999); R. Grange (1947); C. Hinkle (1942);
   C. Lambeau (1955); T. Leemans (1953); D. Slater (1949)

Just like the father of his future Bears teammate, George Musso (#33), Stydahar's dad worked in the coal mines in West Virginia. Stydahar grew up quickly in a family with 10 siblings. He blossomed physically, too, eventually standing 6-4 and weighing 233 pounds. In high school in West Virginia, Stydahar was named all-state as a fullback and as a tackle. He also was all-state and captain of the basketball team. His football skills attracted attention with some of the nearby colleges. Joe chose to go to Pittsburgh, but after a few weeks he became homesick, so he decided to return home and attend West Virginia University, located 35 miles from his home in Shinnston.

At West Virginia, Stydahar was sensational. In his first two seasons in Morgantown, Stydahar was coached by future Hall of Fame coach, Earle "Greasy" Neale. He was a three-year starter at tackle who earned every honor you could achieve: All-Eastern, Little All-American and national All-American. After his senior year, he played in the East-West Shrine Game and the College All-Star Game in Chicago—a city that would be his NFL home.

The first NFL Draft was held right after Stydahar finished his senior season. George Halas selected him in the first round, number six overall, in the 1936 NFL Draft. "That was the turning point of my life," said Stydahar in 1952. "Halas has been like a second father to me. I didn't know anything about football until I had a chance to play football for him." "Jumbo Joe" was a mainstay for the Monsters of the Midway. He was a starter for nine years (84 games)—although he missed two years due to World War II (1943–1944).[1]

Stydahar was a member of three NFL championship squads with the Bears, 1940–1941 and 1946, protecting Sid Luckman and paving rushing lanes for Hall of Fame backs George MacAfee and Bronko Nagurski with a bulldozing style throwing around his 233-pound frame. On the Monsters of the Midway line, Stydahar would be paired next to fellow '36 NFL Draft pick, guard Dan Fortmann (#12), who saw the benefits of playing next to "Jumbo Joe." "It helped me tremendously to play next to Joe for so many years. A true partnership built up. We got to know exactly what to expect from one another," said Dan Fortmann, teammate and Hall of Fame guard.[2]

Joe Stydahar, tackle, Chicago Bears, ca. 1940 (courtesy NFL Films Research Library).

Film study shows that Stydahar was better on defense than offense. He was a hard-hitter and ferocious tackler on the Bears front line. "When you charge, you have to keep your head up. Sure, you lose a lot of teeth that way, but you make a lot of tackles," said Stydahar. On offense, he was a consistent blocker from his tackle position and helped anchor a line that included two Hall of Famers next to him in Fortmann and center Bulldog Turner (#29).[3]

Stydahar was always a student of the game who had a future as a coach, learning from Halas. Not only did he learn the Xs and Os of the pro game, but he also learned to not back down from any battle on the football field. When the Bears battled their biggest rivals, the Green Bay Packers, it was always a slugfest. "I remember the time big Joe Stydahar promised to meet me and punch me full of holes after a Bears game in Green Bay. I accepted the invitation and looked him up at the hotel," recalled Pete Tinsley, Packers Pro Bowl guard. "Joe greeted me by asking 'Imagine a little squirt like you trying to tangle with me?' Next thing I knew, he was saying 'Let's have a beer.' We did. That's the way it usually is."[4]

Stydahar left the Bears to fight in World War II, joining the Navy, where he became a lieutenant. While serving he didn't play any football. "I just don't have the heart to play against those kids," said Stydahar. "They're just too damned small."[5]

He came back to the Bears in 1945 at the age of 33. Stydahar told Halas to pay him what he thought he was worth. Unflinchingly, Halas filled in a contract for $8,000. "That was twice as much as I'd ever been paid before," recalled Stydahar.⁶

In 1946, he helped the Bears win another NFL championship. Then he retired at the age of 34 and went into coaching. He was hired by the Los Angeles Rams to be their line coach in 1947, working mainly with head coach Clark Shaughnessy. In 1950, he replaced Shaughnessy as head coach. In his first season as the head man he led the Rams to the NFL Western Division championship with a 9–3 record. The Rams had the top offense in the NFL, averaging a record 38.8 points per game. In the 1950 NFL championship game, the Rams lost, 30–28, to the Cleveland Browns on a last second Lou Groza field goal. The following year, Stydahar led the Rams back to the NFL championship game in a rematch with the Browns. This time the Rams came out on top with a long late touchdown pass from Norm Van Brocklin to Tom Fears for the 24–17 win.

The winning ways didn't last long for Stydahar. One game into the 1952 season, he found he could no longer work with assistant coach—and former Bears teammate—Hamp Pool and owner Dan Reeves. He resigned. He was quickly hired by the Chicago Cardinals as their head coach. But after two terrible seasons, going 3–20–1, Stydahar was fired. A few years later, he returned to football coaching the defensive line for the Chicago Bears (1963–1965) under his mentor George Halas. He helped the Bears win the 1963 NFL championship 14–10 over the New York Giants, stopping Y.A. Tittle and the Giants' number one scoring offense that averaged 32 points per game.

Stydahar was elected to the Pro Football Hall of Fame in 1967 and was selected to the NFL 1930s All-Decade Team, as well.

Stydahar passed away from a heart attack in 1977 at the age of 65. "Joe is something special for me," said George Halas, when hearing of Stydahar's death. "Football fans know him as the first lineman drafted in the first round in 1936 and as a true All-Pro, as a great player, as one of the Bears' all-time greats, and a Hall of Famer. But more important to any of these football accomplishments, Joe Stydahar was a man of outstanding character and loyalty. We had a warm personal relationship all these years."⁷

"You look back, and you count the years, so many of them," said Stydahar. "So many good times, so many memories, so many friends. And you wonder maybe if you had another swing at it would you do anything different. And you think not."⁸

No. 35

George Christensen
Tackle

Full Name: George Washington Christensen
Nickname: "Big Chris"
b: December 13, 1909 (Pendleton, OR); d: July 1, 1968 (age 58; Detroit, MI)
High School: Pendleton (OR); College: Oregon
Height/Weight: 6-2, 238 pounds
Position: Tackle
Teams/Years: 1931–1938 Portsmouth Spartans/Detroit Lions
Pro Football Hall of Fame: No
Retro-MVPs: No
All-Time Teams: P. Clark (1947): B. Hewitt (1937); D. Hutson (1948); J. Stydahar (1952)

Nicknamed "Big Chris," the rather large, 6-2, 238-pound George Christensen appeared in 95 games over eight seasons with the Portsmouth Spartans/Detroit Lions franchise. His name and accomplishments have been overlooked, especially by the voters of the Pro Football Hall of Fame. He is the seventh tackle on the list. The previous six are all enshrined in the Hall of Fame. Christensen has a resume equal to some of the other Hall of Fame tackles.

The Pacific Northwest was very good to young George Christensen, growing up among the woods in northeast Oregon. After playing football at Pendleton High School, Christensen ventured some 300 miles west to Eugene and the University of Oregon. Already standing over six feet tall and weighing nearly 200 pounds, Christensen became an immediate starter at tackle with the Ducks. One summer Christensen worked as a placer miner—panning for gold—when he returned to Oregon weighing over 230 pounds.

In his senior year at Oregon in the fall of 1930, Christensen was coached by Clarence "Doc" Spears, who had just coached Bronko Nagurski at the University of Minnesota. Christensen learned even more about the tackle position from Spears, who had played pro football with Jim Thorpe and the Canton Bulldogs. He prepared Christensen for the next step.

After being named All-Pacific Coast at tackle while playing at Oregon, Christensen was an instant starter as a rookie for the Portsmouth Spartans in 1931. Playing under Potsy Clark, Christensen was an intelligent tackle learning both sides of the line. He worked well with fellow linemates, guard Ox Emerson (#25), center Clare Randolph, and ends Bill McKalip and Harry Ebding, to give the Spartans a lethal ground game. Blocking for the best player in the league, Dutch Clark (#1), the Spartans jumped to the top of the standings. After the season, the *Green Bay Press-Gazette* named Christensen First Team All-Pro at tackle with Cal Hubbard of the Packers. They wrote: "This was Christensen's first season in post-graduate ball, but he showed plenty of class. In several games he blocked punts that turned the tide in favor of Portsmouth."[1]

A big, fast, athletic tackle, Christensen would sometimes pull on end runs for halfbacks Clark, Glenn Presnell and Ernie Caddel in Potsy's single-wing offense.

George Christensen, tackle, Detroit Lions, ca. 1935–1936 (courtesy Detroit Lions).

"George Christensen was the biggest man on the team at 238 pounds and we used to consider him a freak. But I'll tell you, he was one of the fastest men we had," recalled Jim Steen, Lions teammate, 1935–1936, in 1974. "George Christensen played tackle for us, he was around 240 pounds and could run," recalled Dutch Clark. "He was fast for a big man. He played in the single-wing and he played right tackle. He would lead all the weak-side offensive plays." Christensen was a key cog in the ground-oriented Spartans offense.[2]

In 1931, the Spartans finished in second place behind the champion Packers, then challenged for the NFL title in 1932, before losing the NFL's first play-off game, 9–0, to the Chicago Bears in the famous "Indoor Game." Christensen hoped this wouldn't be his final shot at an NFL title.

So highly respected on the Lions team that he was voted team captain, Christensen also served as "unofficial" line coach under coach Clark. "He was a real nice guy and an outstanding tackle," recalled Glenn Presnell, Spartans/Lions All-Pro halfback, 1931–1936. "He was pretty big for a tackle, for a player back in those days. He weighed about 240, 245 pounds, which was large. It wouldn't be large today, but it was large back in those days. He was a very strong tackle and a very good defensive player."[3]

"Good tackles were numerous with Christensen of Portsmouth the best of the lot. This husky Spartan was a demon on the attack, while on the defense he raised havoc with every club Potsy Clark's hirelings bumped into this past season," wrote George W. Calhoun of the *Green Bay Press-Gazette* in 1933 after naming Christensen First Team All-Pro.[4]

Christensen continued his dominant play over the next two years as the Spartans moved from tiny Portsmouth to the Motor City in 1934 to become the Detroit Lions. That season Christensen was a consensus All-Pro, being named first team by the NFL, *Boston Post*, *Brooklyn Times-Union* and *Collyer's*. The following year he became a champion.

The big tackle was a key contributor to the Lions' run to the 1935 NFL championship. That Lions squad was pretty loaded with the likes of halfback Dutch Clark (#1), guard Ox Emerson (#25), halfback Glenn Presnell (#44), fullback Ace Gutowsky, and of course Christensen. "We had pretty good material," said Potsy Clark in 1947. "In Chris [Christensen] we had just about the best tackle I ever saw and I never knew a better guard than Ol' Ox Emerson. We had Dutch Clark, still number one in my book in the backfield."[5]

After winning the Western Division with a 7–3–2 record, Christensen helped the Lions rush for over 240 yards and four touchdowns in a convincing 26–7 win over the New York Giants in the NFL championship game that season. Now a champion, Christensen gained a reputation of being a tough player against whom to face off.

Playing nearly 60 minutes a game, even late in his career, Big Chris always played at a high level that would get the attention of all his opponents. Former Bears Pro Bowl end Edgar "Eggs" Manske remembers his battles with "Big Chris": "First time we met, I hit him and 'boom,' nothing happened. I couldn't move him. Next play, I shot out a quarter-count fast and tattooed Christensen right under the chin. He didn't say a word. The next play, he knocked my head underneath my shoulder blades. I said to him, 'Let's just forget it.'"[6]

In 1936, Christensen was on a Lions line with All-Pro guard Emerson, All-Pro tackle Jack Johnson and center Clare Randolph that established an NFL record for rushing yards in a single-season with 2,885 yards in 12 games—a record that stood until 1972 when the Miami Dolphins broke it in a 14-game season.

Christensen played that whole season with a broken hand, although he didn't know it. An encounter with big Cal Hubbard (#9) might've caused it. On November 1 in New York the Lions faced off against the Giants. After a back-and-forth hard-fought tussle, the Giants survived with a 14–7 win. The 253-pound Hubbard became agitated with the play of Lions fullback Ace Gutowsky, frustrated that old Ace was gaining too many yards late in the game. According to Gutowsky, Hubbard muttered that he would "get" Gutowsky after the game. When the game ended Ace walked up to Hubbard and said, "Here I am."[7]

Hubbard started to swing, but Christensen stepped in and beat him to the "punch," with a left to the mouth. Right after the punch connected, Dutch Clark,

Giants coach Steve Owen and several other leaped in to stop the fracas and escorted the players—with the aid of the police—to their separate dressing rooms. "We're all one big happy family," said Potsy Clark to the *Detroit Free Press*, "and if Big Chris did steal a fight from Gutowsky, we'll preserve peace by making Chris give Ace one of his before the season is over. Our motto is, 'Justice for Everybody!'" Big Chris always stuck up for his teammates; it's what made him a great leader on and off the field for the Lions.[8]

After the 1936 season, Christensen stepped away from pro football. He had had enough of the physical pounding, giving his body time to heal. But being away from football didn't last long. In the fall of 1937 Dutch Clark had taken over as player-coach for the Lions when Potsy took the head coaching job with the Brooklyn Dodgers. Old Dutch convinced Big Chris to return to the Lions to play tackle. How could Christensen say no? He returned to help Dutch's boys compete again for an NFL championship. Over the next two seasons, the Lions finished in second place in the Western Division. Christensen came up short of a championship both years. After the 1938 season he finally retired for good at the age of 29.

One of the biggest honors of Christensen's career was being voted as one of the tackles on the NFL 1930s All-Decade Team—joining Hall of Famers Turk Edwards and Joe Stydahar and All-Pros Frank Cope and Bill Lee. Christensen was one of the best tackles to play in the two-way era, slightly behind the previous tackles listed: Hubbard (#9), Henry (#11), Lyman (#14), Edwards (#24), Slater (#31), and Stydahar (#34). All of the tackles above him are Hall of Famers. Big Chris deserves to be right there with them. "On our club was a tackle who I think should be in the Hall of Fame. His name is George Christensen and he was as good a tackle as I ever saw on a pro team. Most of the men who played with him or against him would say the same thing," said Dutch Clark, Lions teammate and Hall of Fame back.[9]

After he retired, Big Chris went into business with Lions teammate Frank Christensen (no relation) in operating a highly successful diamond bit company. Christensen passed away from a heart attack on July 1, 1968, at the age of 58.

Despite his playing resume that includes five consecutive years as a first or second team All-Pro, a spot on the NFL 1930s All-Decades team, opponents' testimonials, and winning one NFL championship, George Christensen still hasn't been elected to the Pro Football Hall of Fame. Hopefully that will change soon.

No. 36

LaVern "Lavvie" Dilweg
End

Full Name: LaVern Ralph Dilweg
Nickname: "Lavvie"
b: January 11, 1903 (Milwaukee, WI); d: January 2, 1968 (age 64; St. Petersburg, FL)
High School: Milwaukee Washington (WI); College: Marquette
Height/Weight: 6-3, 200 pounds
Position: End
Teams/Years: 1926 Milwaukee Badgers; 1927–1934 Green Bay Packers
Pro Football Hall of Fame: No
Retro-MVPs: No
All-Time Teams: J. Conzelman (1941); A. Herber (1946); C. Hubbard (1937, 1947, 1966);
    C. Lambeau (1946, 1948); V. Lewellen (1946); J. McNally (1963); B. Nagurski (1939)

One of the more overlooked players of the two-way era is Lavvie Dilweg, one of the best ends of the era. On our list he is the fifth end to appear; the previous four—Don Hutson (#2), Guy Chamberlin (#5), Bill Hewitt (#15), Ray Flaherty (#28)—are in the Hall of Fame. Dilweg somehow is not.

LaVern Dilweg was born in Milwaukee in 1903 and earned the nickname of "Lavvie" as he quickly fell in love with football, although his biggest supporter at home didn't like the sport. Dilweg's mother was against him playing—she didn't want him to get hurt—so he kept his gridiron participation from her until he went to college. At Marquette he couldn't keep his name out of the local newspapers, so that's when she found out he was participating. Instead of punishing her son, she became his biggest fan, attending many games when her son played at home.

Under the guidance of College Football Hall of Fame coach Frank Murray, Marquette only lost four times in four years (28-4-1) with Dilweg as a starting end. After his 1925 senior year, Dilweg played in the prestigious East-West Shrine game, attracting national attention for his play. The following fall, Dilweg would sign to play pro football with the local Milwaukee Badgers—who had been a member of the NFL since 1922.

Very big for his era, the 6-3, 200-pound Dilweg was a very polished player for his position. He helped the Badgers compete against the NFL's best, but the Badgers didn't have the talent to compete in the NFL that fall, finishing with a disappointing record of 2–7. After the season the Badgers folded, leaving Dilweg without a team.

Dilweg still had a desire to play pro ball and signed with the Green Bay Packers for 1927. His career was about to take off both on and off the field. The same year he joined the Packers, Dilweg earned his law degree from Marquette. He would practice football with the Packers in the morning and practice law in the afternoon. "Everybody was very understanding. If I needed a continuance because of a road trip or something, I'd generally get it. Most of the men in my day did nothing in the afternoons but I was able to use law as a living, with football as a helper," said Dilweg in 1965.[1]

Lavvie Dilweg, end, Green Bay Packers, ca. 1929–1930 (courtesy Green Bay Packers).

The tall, athletic Dilweg ended up playing eight seasons with the Green Bay Packers and appeared in 107 total NFL games as a very complete player from his end position. Like most great players from this era, he never wanted to leave the field. "You know, they talk about platoon systems now, well, Curly Lambeau had one long before anybody else did," recalled Dilweg. "He hit on the idea of keeping players fresh even when he couldn't substitute. Like with [Don] Hutson. He was an end on offense, of course, but Curly got a fellow named Larry Craig from South Carolina as the blocking back. Then when the club was on defense, Craig would move up and play end and Hutson would go into the backfield. That's the kind of innovator Curly was."[2]

Not quite the scorer as some other ends of this era, Dilweg finished with 12 career touchdown catches. He flourished as a blocker in the run game. But Dilweg was praised more for his defense than his offensive skills. "I have always rated Dilweg as the greatest end who ever brought me down," recalled Red Grange in 1937. "I always enjoyed defense," said Dilweg. "Nowadays, of course, the game is full of specialists, and they're wonderful at their jobs. But for me, if I had not been permitted to play both offense and defense, I'm sure I wouldn't have enjoyed it as much as I did."[3]

Unofficially, Dilweg has been credited with 27 career interceptions on defense, mostly with the Packers. And to complete his skills, Dilweg, similar to the previous ends on this list, played very well on special teams, especially covering punts. Only Chamberlin and Hewitt were his equal in covering punts.

Dilweg was a key member of three NFL championship teams with Green Bay from 1929 to 1931. His best game came in 1929 when he had two TD catches in a 12–0 victory over the Cardinals on November 17 to keep Green Bay undefeated during their first championship season. In 1931, Dilweg caught a career-high four touchdown passes—and was named First Team All-Pro by the NFL, United Press, and *Milwaukee Journal*.

Over his career, Dilweg scored 14 total touchdowns (12 receiving, two interception returns)—in those games the Packers went 12–1. Dilweg was an accomplished player of the two-way era on those Packers teams, even though he wasn't quite as dominant as teammate Verne Lewellen, but he was definitely a key cog in the Packers winning those three consecutive championships.

After the 1934 season, Dilweg retired at the age of 31. "I had a couple of more years left, I think, but I could feel myself slowing down," recalled Dilweg. "Bruises that had healed in a week were taking 10 days. And they didn't want to pay me what I thought I ought to get, so I thought I would just get out of it." His accomplishments have been forgotten. "Dilweg faded out of the picture just about the time the seven-man line went out of fashion, but without question was the greatest end the seven-man line type of defense ever developed," said Curly Lambeau, Packers Hall of Fame coach.[4]

Dilweg was named to the NFL 1920s All-Decade Team. Only two of the 18 players selected to the '20s squad are not in the Pro Football Hall of Fame—Dilweg and guard Hunk Anderson. In 1970, he was elected to the Packers Hall of Fame.

In 2020, Dilweg was named as one of the 20 finalists for the Pro Football Hall of Fame Centennial Class. However, he was not selected as one of the 10 enshrinees. Two years later, in 2022, Dilweg was selected as one of 24 Senior Hall of Fame Semi-Finalists. Again, he did not make the cut. Hopefully, that won't be his last chance to make the Hall, where he deserves to be.

No. 37

Joe Kopcha
Guard

Full Name: Joseph Edward Kopcha
Nickname: "Doc"
b: December 23, 1905 (Whiting, IN); d: July 29, 1986 (age 80; Hobart, IN)
High School: Whiting (IN); College: Tennessee-Chattanooga
Height/Weight: 6–0, 221 pounds
Position: Guard
Teams/Years: 1929, 1932–1935 Chicago Bears; 1936 Detroit Lions
Pro Football Hall of Fame: No
Retro-MVPs: No
All-Time Teams: D. Clark (1942); B. Hewitt (1937, 1940); J. McNally (1937)

The fifth and last guard on the list is Dr. Joe Kopcha.

Just like another Chicago Bears lineman, guard Dan Fortmann (#12), Joe Kopcha went on to become a doctor. But first he made a name for himself as one of the NFL's best two-way guards, also like Fortmann.

Kopcha first played organized football on his high school team at Whiting (IN) High that only had 14 players. There he played some fullback and on the line. Through his relationship with his high school coach, Kopcha was introduced to Wilfrid Smith, the sportswriter of the *Chicago Tribune*, who got him to go to the University of Chattanooga (now University of Tennessee at Chattanooga) to play college football. Kopcha took advantage of the opportunity to not just play football but to get an education. Kopcha participated in multiple sports, including basketball, baseball and swimming. On the gridiron, Kopcha played tackle, befitting his 6–0, 220-pound physique. The future doctor was all-conference three times and graduated with honors. At the time, he wasn't quite finished with football.

Once again Wilfrid Smith came to Kopcha with another opportunity. "Wilfrid Smith approached me again, he said, 'Joe, I'll introduce you to Mr. Halas and see if he has a place for you to play [pro] football," recalled Joe Kopcha. "At that time, I applied to the University of Chicago Medical School. They said I should take another six months for my classes for biology and chemistry. I figured well, why should I waste a half a year, I'll just go ahead and see Halas and play football and make enough money, then I can go to medical school on my own without any scholarship affair."[1]

Kopcha continues: "I signed for $90 [a game]. I'll always remember that one. Because when I returned [in 1932], I thought I'd ask for a raise. When I went to Halas to ask for a raise, I had my tongue in my cheek and I kind of swallowed a few times. 'I was wondering, Mr. Halas, do you think $5 a game more, could I get $5 more a game?' He says, 'Joe, you're worth every bit of it.'"[2]

Although Kopcha had played tackle at Chattanooga, Halas had a different position for his newest recruit. "Well, there were six great, big tackles in front of me," recalled Kopcha. "And all of these fellas, were all bigger than I was. I said to myself, 'Gee, maybe I don't have a chance.' So, Halas said, 'Can you play guard?' and I said, 'Yes, sir.' So, as a result of that I became a running guard for five years."[3]

Halas taught Kopcha the ins and outs of playing guard—

Joe Kopcha, guard, Chicago Bears, ca. 1930 (courtesy University of Tennessee–Chattanooga Athletics).

mostly out of the T-formation. "Well, the tackle charges forward, charges straight ahead. Halas, the way the thing is set up, the two guards pull out. The left guard and the right guard pull out to the right or they pull out to the left, and they act as defense. They act as running protection for the backs. So, we have to keep ahead of the running backs in order to give them the interference that they need," recalled Kopcha.[4]

Kopcha quickly learned the guard position and contributed to a Bears team that struggled to a 4–9–2 record. The small-school product got an ear full of trash talk from opposing NFL players while playing on both sides of the ball. "Pro players would try to kid me about Chattanooga. An opposing player in the line would start with, 'Chattanooga, where's that?'" said Kopcha in 1963. "About the time the ball would snap and I would whack that guy extra hard—bingo!—and I would hear no more about Chattanooga. No one ever made me ashamed of going to fine University of Chattanooga."[5]

After playing in 1929, Kopcha took the next two years off to attend medical school at the University of Alabama. Missing football, Kopcha got an idea to get back into playing pro ball. He wanted to get back to the Bears. "If I could be transferred to the University of Chicago Rush Medical School, I could then contact Mr. Halas," said Kopcha. "So, I contacted Mr. Halas and I told him what I had in mind. I then made arrangements with the Dean [Alabama] who made arrangements with the Dean of Chicago Rush Medical School to come back to Chicago. I told Halas 'I am not asking for any favors. I will guarantee you one thing, that when I finish my second year of medical school down at Tuscaloosa, I will be ready to be in shape when we meet in camp in September.'"[6]

Rejoining the Bears in 1932, Kopcha quickly became one of the NFL's best linemen on a Bears team that reloaded with talent since he left with the likes of Red Grange, Bronko Nagurski, Carl Brumbaugh, Bill Hewitt and Luke Johnsos. Starting that season, Kopcha was a perennial All-Pro next to the Lions' Ox Emerson (#25) as one of the two best guards in the NFL in the middle 1930s. He appeared in 72 games over six years with the Bears and Lions and was a starting guard on the Bears back-to-back championship teams of 1932–1933.

Old Papa Bear always looked out for his boys, including Kopcha. "If a teacher [medical] ever got on my back for missing a class due to football, I would tell Halas who in turn would mention it to the dean of the school. And the problem would cease," recalled Kopcha.[7]

Although Kopcha had to work hard at balancing football and his studies, his play on the field never suffered. Hall of Fame tackle Cal Hubbard picked Joe Kopcha as one of the two toughest men he ever played against, along with Link Lyman. "Joe Kopcha…. I remember him, he was some tough guy," said Hubbard in a 1976 interview.[8]

The Bears won back-to-back NFL championships with Kopcha at guard, playing in two of the more famous games in league history, the "Indoor Game" (1932) and the first NFL championship game. Winning back-to-back titles put Kopcha in rare company. "Football for football's sake isn't quite worthwhile. I like to win," said Kopcha in 1935 to the *Chicago Tribune*.[9]

Kopcha helped block for the Bears outstanding backfield of Grange, Brumbaugh and Nagurski. He helped the Bears finish first in the NFL in rushing twice (1934–1935) and second twice (1932–1933). In 1934, he was part of a line that helped Bears rookie halfback Beattie Feathers become the NFL's first 1,000-yard rusher with 1,004 yards, but Joe missed the 1934 NFL championship game, the famous "Sneakers Game," due to a broken arm. "Joe Kopcha was the Bears' best forward. He could do everything well at a guard's position and still have something in reserve to help out his teammates," wrote the *Green Bay Press-Gazette*, naming Kopcha First Team All-Pro in 1934.[10]

Throughout his NFL career Kopcha protected his body and hands, using his intelligence to play against tough opponents during this era. He always knew how to take care of his body. "We used to try and go sixty minutes, as it was considered less than manly to ask to come out," recalled Kopcha. "To conserve on energy, if the play went the other way, we would just lean on an opponent."[11]

After five seasons, Kopcha thought about retiring from pro football. "The money I have received from professional football has enabled me to continue my study and help take care of my parents. Without the assistance of coach Halas, who has raised my salary every year I have been with the club, I could not have done my part at home and continued in medicine. The contacts I make as a member of a recognized professional team will be invaluable to me in the future. It will be tough to give it up, but linemen are not like old man river. They can't just go on rollin' along," said Kopcha in 1935.[12]

Instead of retiring, Kopcha switched teams. Again he consulted with George Halas about his future plans. At this time Kopcha's top priority was finishing medical school. He had just been assigned an internship that would be in Detroit. Kopcha talked to Halas about his future. "I said to myself, 'Well, if I could carry on with my internship and live in the intern quarters [in Detroit] and play with the Detroit Lions, I wouldn't miss out as far as my [medical] training was concerned,'" recalled Kopcha. "So, I asked Halas if he would have any objections if I played for the Detroit Lions. He says, 'No, I'd be more than happy as long as you can continue on with your [medical] training.'" Halas traded Kopcha to the Lions, where he would play for Potsy Clark.[13]

That fall with the Lions, Kopcha made Honorable Mention All-League. Then he finally retired. Kopcha received his medical degree from Rush Medical School (1934), interned at Detroit's Harper Hospital (1935–1937) and did his post-graduate work in obstetrics and gynecology at Western Reserve University (Ohio) Hospitals from 1937 to 1940. Kopcha eventually achieved his goal of becoming an obstetrician, opening his own office in Gary, Indiana. Over the next few decades, Kopcha delivered thousands of babies in Gary and Hobart. "Dr. Joe Kopcha, he was a good guard and a doctor," recalled George Musso, Bears Hall of Fame lineman and teammate. "I asked him, 'How can you be a baby doctor with those big hands?' He said, 'Well, I am.'"[14]

Kopcha passed away on July 29, 1986, at the age of 80.

Kopcha's career was cut short because of his desire to become a doctor. His three straight First Team All-Pros (1933–1935) and two NFL championships put him in a discussion for the Pro Football Hall of Fame. He wasn't named to the NFL's 1930s All-Decade Team which hurts him. He's a notch below all-decade guards Dan Fortmann (#12) and Ox Emerson (#25) but was a better player than the Packers guards Russ Letlow and Buckets Goldenberg who are on the team. If Kopcha had a little longer career, maybe his name would have made the squad or the Hall of Fame.

"Back in those days we played both ways," recalled Kopcha speaking at the Pro Football Hall of Fame in 1979. "Today it's a highly specialized type of football. You have a passer, a kicker, a halfback, a fullback, everyone has a specialty. If you want to compare the players then with the players today—the players today are better prepared, better nourished. But I don't think the players of today could play 60 minutes of football—if I didn't play 60 minutes, I would think something was wrong, that I wasn't on the first team."[15]

No. 38

Cecil Isbell

Quarterback

Full Name: Cecil Frank Isbell
Nickname: "Cece"
b: July 11, 1915 (Houston, TX); d: June 23, 1985 (age 69; Hammond, IN)
High School: Sam Houston (TX); College: Purdue
Height/Weight: 6–1, 190 pounds
Position: Quarterback
Teams/Years: 1938–1942 Green Bay Packers
Pro Football Hall of Fame: No
Retro-MVPs: No
All-Time Teams: P. Clark (1947); C. Hinkle (1942); C. Lambeau (1946, 1948); V. Lewellen (1946); J. McNally (1963)

Cecil Isbell comes in at number 40, below the big five quarterbacks of the two-way era: Sammy Baugh (#3), Sid Luckman (#8), Paddy Driscoll (#10), Benny Friedman (#17) and Arnie Herber (#26). Playing only five seasons and just 54 games has always kept Isbell from being a Hall of Famer, but his skills, passing prowess and accomplishments are right there with any passer during this era.

The son of a Houston barber, Isbell quickly took to the sport of football, like most Texas boys. Isbell would leave the Lone Star State to head north to play his college ball at Purdue. Cecil had three brothers who would also play college football. Cody followed Cecil to Purdue while Dub played at Rice and Larry at Baylor before playing five years in the CFL.

Isbell would play mainly as a halfback in the single-wing at Purdue, becoming more known for his running skills than his passing. While at Purdue, Isbell suffered an injury that would affect him his entire career. In his first Big Ten game against Northwestern, Isbell suffered a dislocated left shoulder. Twice the trainer had to come onto the field to pop it back in. "After that, they decided I should have a chain on my left arm, so I couldn't raise it too high. I wore the chain at Purdue and with the Packers," recalled Isbell. Isbell played the rest of his career with a chain attached from his body under his pads.[1]

Isbell was chosen in the first round of the 1938 NFL Draft by the Green Bay Packers, seventh overall. Before joining the Packers Isbell was the starting halfback for the College All-Stars against the Washington Redskins, the defending NFL champs. Isbell was the best player on the field that night, leading the All-Stars to a surprising 28–16 win over Sammy Baugh's Redskins.

Isbell was named the game's Most Valuable Player.

The tall, athletic Isbell (6–1, 190) played just five seasons in the NFL, all with the Green Bay Packers. His short tenure was one of excellence as he thrived in Lambeau's passing offense from the tailback position. "Isbell was a master at any range. He could throw soft passes, bullet passes, or long passes," said Curly Lambeau.[2]

Eventually Isbell replaced Arnie Herber as starting tailback in Lambeau's backfield. Isbell was just such a player.

Cecil Isbell, quarterback, Green Bay Packers, ca. 1941–1942 (courtesy Green Bay Packers).

Compared to some of his contemporaries, Isbell was known as a better pure passer than Sid Luckman and a better runner than Sammy Baugh. Athletically he was on par with the big two quarterbacks from his time. "We felt we could move with the pass anywhere on the field, and we could," said Isbell. "When I was with the Packers, I called the plays. The quarterback was the blocking back, so the tailback gave the signals. Lambeau would call a play once in a while, but mostly he was too excited. If Hutson or Hinkle got tired, they would tell me to call someone else's number."[3]

He was a strong passer who made all the throws and took over the passing offense from Herber. On film, one of best throws was the out route, and he had great timing with Don Hutson. "I worked with another great passer at Green Bay, Cecil Isbell, he would be in the Hall of Fame today if he hadn't quit playing football so early. If he stayed in the NFL, his name would be all over the record books and they would talk of him in the same terms they do of Luckman and Baugh," said Don Hutson.[4]

Hutson continued: "Isbell really got the ball out in front of you all the time.... His ability to lead his receiver was remarkable. All you had to do was take the ball over your shoulder and scram." Isbell loved the way Lambeau and the Packers put the ball in the air out of the Notre Dame box. "I had the honor of throwing to the greatest receiver: Don Hutson," recalled Isbell in 1978. "In those days we were known as a passing team and I was throwing maybe 18 times a game at the most. Now they throw 35 times. We played a single-wing. I played left half in the old Notre Dame box. If Lambeau had put in the T-formation maybe I'd still be playing."[5]

Isbell's 1938 rookie year was a success, with him passing for 659 yards, fifth in NFL, and eight touchdowns which was second in the NFL behind nine thrown by teammate Bob Monnett. He also averaged an NFL-high 5.2 yards per rush with two touchdowns. He was named Second Team All-Pro by the NFL, UPI, *New York Daily News*, I.N.S. and the Pro Football Writers. Even George Halas was impressed by the rookie after Isbell played the Bears for the first time, telling the *Green Bay Press-Gazette*, "Cecil Isbell is going to make one of the greatest backs in professional football.... I hate to think what might happen in Chicago when the Packers come down there."[6]

That same year, Isbell helped the Packers win the Western Division before losing to the New York Giants in the NFL championship game. But the following year, Isbell and the Packers got their revenge, as the Packers won the 1939 NFL championship, 27–0, over the Giants. Isbell threw just two passes, completing both with one being a touchdown to Joe Laws in the third quarter to give the Packers a 17–0 lead, pretty much sealing the win. To show how the Packers valued Isbell, in 1939 he was paid $7,100 for the season. The great Don Hutson, in his fifth NFL season, was paid $5,075 for the season.

In just two seasons, Isbell had won an NFL championship. Over the next three years, he would elevate his game to even bigger heights. The most underrated aspect of Isbell's game was his ability to run with the ball. In Lambeau's offense at this time Isbell was used as a running weapon just as much as a passer. He led the Packers in rushing for two seasons, 1938–1939, gaining more yards than fullback Clarke Hinkle. He rushed for 10 career TDs—eclipsing Baugh (nine), Luckman (four) and Herber (three)—and over 1,500 yards.

But passing was where he made his mark during this era. He had a great two-year stretch, playing better than Baugh and Luckman. In 1941, Isbell led the NFL in attempts, completions, passing yards with 1,479—breaking Baugh's NFL record—and touchdowns with 15. Lambeau thought his prized signal caller could get better. "I am looking forward to Isbell's best year," said Lambeau to the *Green Bay Press-Gazette*. "Great as he was last season, I still do not believe that he has reached his peak in performance." The Packers coach would help Isbell reach that higher level.[7]

Isbell had a better year in 1942 when he led the league in completions (146), passing yards (2,021) and touchdowns (24)—all new NFL single-season records—helping All-Pro receiver Don Hutson win the NFL Joe Carr MVP award. That season he was the first NFL quarterback to throw for 2,000 yards in a single season.

Isbell also set an NFL record for most consecutive games with a touchdown pass with 24, breaking the old mark of 20 set by Benny Friedman in 1929. Johnny Unitas would eventually break the mark in 1958, before going on to throw a TD pass in 47 straight games through 1960. Isbell's streak was a Packers record until Brett Favre broke it in 2003.

Isbell had an incredible two-game stretch that November. In back-to-back games, he tossed eight touchdown passes. He threw five in just 10 completions against the Chicago Cardinals on November 1 in a 55–24 win. His 331 passing yards that day broke the single-game passing record of 316 that was set by Davey O'Brien in 1940. (A year later Sammy Baugh broke Isbell's mark by passing for 376 against Brooklyn.) The following week, he threw for three scores in a 30–12 win over the Cleveland Rams on November 8. Five of the eight touchdowns went to Don Hutson. Both years the Packers fell short of winning the Western Division, losing out to the Bears. After the 1942 season, Isbell retired.

One of the more impressive stats of Isbell's 54-game career is that he threw more touchdowns (61) than interceptions (52), very uncommon for this era. Over his tenure, he was a key contributor to his team winning. When Isbell threw a touchdown pass the Packers went 33-7-1 (61 career TDs). On defense, Isbell also performed well. "Of course, I also played defense then," recalled Isbell in 1967. "I figured that, in my five seasons, I played the equivalent of 10 years by present standards."[8]

Isbell made four Pro Bowls, 1938–1939 and 1941–1942, in five seasons. He was so highly thought of that he was selected to the NFL 1930s All-Decade Team along with Dutch Clark (#1) and Arnie Herber (#26), despite playing just 54 games overall and just two years in the '30s, 1938–39. He is the only All-Decade quarterback who is eligible but NOT in the Pro Football Hall of Fame. "If ever there was a man who deserved to be in the Hall of Fame, it is Cec Isbell," once said Sid Luckman in 1967. He was elected to the Packers Hall of Fame in 1972.[9]

After retiring from the NFL, Isbell accepted a job as an assistant coach at his alma mater, Purdue, for one-third of his $10,000 salary. "I hadn't been up in Green Bay long when I saw Lambeau go around the locker room and tell players like Arnie Herber and [Milt] Gantenbein and [Hank] Bruder that they were all done with the Packers. I sat there and watched, then I vowed it would never happen to me. I'd quit before they came around to tell me." Isbell was just 27 years old. If Isbell had played just two or three more seasons, he would be a lock for the Hall of Fame. But playing just 54 games has kept him out.[10]

Isbell coached at Purdue for three seasons (1944–1946), compiling an overall record of 14-14-1. In 1947, he moved to Baltimore to become the first coach of the Colts in the AAFC. With the Colts he helped develop Y.A. Tittle into a promising quarterback. He finished his coaching career as an assistant with the Chicago Cardinals (1950–1951) under Curly Lambeau and at LSU (1952–1953) before going into business. Although he was out of football, the love of the game never left Isbell. "Oh, sure, that's in your blood," Isbell said in 1967. "I haven't tried getting back into it, I'll say that, but it stays in your blood forever."[11]

Isbell passed away from liver and kidney problems on June 23, 1985, at the age of 69.

In 2020, Isbell was one of the 20 finalists for the Pro Football Hall of Fame Centennial Class. His first time as an HOF finalist, he was not selected. "Played a couple of years with Cecil. In my book he ranks along the side of Sid Luckman and Sammy

Baugh. He had a nice soft pass, he was a pinpoint passer, he could pass to a spot. He was a beautiful passer," recalled Clarke Hinkle, Packers Hall of Fame fullback.[12]

Two years later in 2022, Isbell was again named a finalist for the Pro Football Hall of Fame as one of 24 Senior nominees. Once again, he was not selected. Despite the setback, Isbell's name still has a chance to make it to Canton.

No. 39

Jack McBride

Fullback

Full Name: John F. McBride
Nickname: "Jack"
b: November 30, 1901 (Conshohocken, PA); d: October 11, 1966 (age 64; Conshohocken, PA)
High School: Conshohocken, Bellefonte Academy; College: Syracuse
Height/Weight: 5-11, 185 pounds
Position: Fullback
Teams/Years: 1925–1928, 1932–1934 New York Giants; 1929 Providence Steam Roller; 1930–1932 Brooklyn Dodgers
Pro Football Hall of Fame: No
Retro-MVPs: 1927
All-Time Teams: None

A notch below the "Big Four" fullbacks on our list (Nagurski, Hinkle, Nevers, Strong) is Jack McBride. Very underrated, McBride played in the shadow of Ernie Nevers and then Bronko Nagurski at the fullback position during his playing career. The 5-11, 185-pound McBride did everything well—he could run, block, tackle. He was a better passer than Nagurski but not quite as good as Nevers with the arm.

From eastern Pennsylvania, McBride was born in 1901 the son of a steel-mill worker. He picked up the game while playing in high school in Conshohocken. He stayed on the East Coast to attend college, as he made his way to Syracuse. Coached by Chick Meehan, McBride became a star in the Orangeman backfield, leading them to eight-win seasons in 1923 (8-1) and 1924 (8-2-1). In his senior year, McBride made a national name for himself when he kicked three field goals to single-handedly defeat Columbia, 9–6. That fall, McBride finished second in the country in scoring with 92 points—behind Heinie Benkert of Rutgers with 100. Soon Benkert and McBride would be teammates in the NFL.

The 5-11, 185-pound McBride signed with the newly formed New York Giants, founded by New York bookie Tim Mara in 1925. That fall Mara also signed Penn State halfback Hinkey Haines, Vanderbilt end Lynn Bomar, and Rutgers halfback Heinie Benkert. They would help establish pro football in the Big Apple. "McBride, the former Syracuse star, was a line crusher, extraordinary yet speedy enough on his feet to make splendid interference for the other backs. McBride was there plenty

PRICE **15** CENTS

N. Y. FOOTBALL GIANTS
vs.
ERNIE NEVERS ESKIMOS

JACK McBRIDE
Giants Battering Ram

Sunday
November 6, 1927

Polo Grounds
New York

Jack McBride, fullback, New York Giants (1927 program cover courtesy NFL Films Research Library).

when it came to backing up the line," wrote the *Green Bay Press-Gazette* in 1925, naming McBride First Team All-Pro.[1]

McBride's tough running style made him an effective runner. He had such supreme confidence in his running ability that he didn't even worry about blockers. His classic cry, as one sports reporter described, as he received the pass from center, was, "Interference, follow me!" Former Giants tackle and teammate Steve Owen once said in 1954 that McBride was "a tremendous fullback, a fellow who could do anything and do it brilliantly."[2]

McBride would play 10 seasons (106 games) with three teams—Providence and Brooklyn, but primarily the New York Giants (seven years). He scored 26 total touchdowns, all rushing, as his teams went 18-2-2 when he scored. He also kicked, making five field goals and 62 extra points for 233 career points during his career.

One of McBride's biggest strengths was as a passer, throwing 31 career touchdowns. His teams went 21-2 in those games. In a 1925 Giants program, McBride's right-hand throwing style is described as "an unusual power to forward pass the pigskin with the control of a baseball catcher throwing to second base. No matter how many opponents loom up in his path, McBride manages to get away his passes either just over the line of scrimmage or far down field."[3]

Another skill that McBride showcased often was his ability to return punts, a rare skill for a fullback during the two-way era. McBride did it better than almost anybody. "Oh, how some of those little men could field those punts on the dead run and get good yardage," once said John Alexander, Milwaukee Badgers and New York Giants tackle. "Fritz Pollard was tremendous. So was Paddy Driscoll, but the best I ever saw was Jack McBride of the New York Giants. He had a real knack for it. You see, the best ones would time the catch so that they could field the punt on the dead run. I mean running at top speed, catch the ball, and be gone past the men that were coming downfield to cover the punt before they knew what went by. McBride was the best at this. I liked it when he was on my team, which wasn't often enough, and dreaded it when I had to play against him."[4]

McBride's best year came in 1927. That season McBride finished the year with six touchdown runs and seven TD passes, while leading the NFL in scoring with 57 points. He also helped a defense that only allowed 20 points and had 10 shutouts in 13 games. All of this led the Giants to an 11-1-1 record and an NFL championship. He earned First Team All-Pro honors from the *Chicago Tribune* and second team by the *Green Bay Press-Gazette* and coach Leroy Andrews. McBride was the Retro-MVP of the NFL that season.

In 1930, McBride left the Giants and joined the Brooklyn Dodgers. That season he helped Brooklyn to a 7-4-1 record by scoring eight TDs; the Dodgers were 6-0 when he scored. On November 30, McBride's fourth quarter TD and extra point conversion helped upset the Giants, 7-6, and kept the Giants out of first place. He finished the season with 56 points scored, tops in the NFL. McBride returned to the Giants in 1932 and 1933.

In 1934, McBride left the NFL to become player-coach for the minor league Paterson (N.J.) Panthers. At age 33, McBride could still plow for a first down or throw for a score. So much so that late in the football season when the Giants starting quarterback, Harry Newman, was lost for the final few games McBride was asked to join the team. But McBride wouldn't give up on his team in New Jersey. He played on Thanksgiving for the Giants against the Brooklyn Dodgers and threw a touchdown pass to Dale Burnett to help the Giants to an easy 27–0 win. Three days later he was in the starting lineup for his Panthers against the Shenandoah Presidents. Playing quarterback, McBride helped the Panthers to a 13–13 tie.

Despite playing in only one regular season game for the Giants during the 1934 season, McBride dressed for the 1934 NFL championship game against the Chicago Bears. In the famous "Sneakers Game," McBride came off the bench to help in the 30–13 upset victory. He had two carries for 10 yards, spelling starter Ed Danowski. This was McBride's second NFL championship title. McBride continued to coach a few non–NFL teams with the Paterson Panthers and the New York Yankees of the second American Football League (AFL).

McBride passed away on October 11, 1966, at the age of 64.

Not quite the equal of Nagurski, Hinkle, Nevers or Strong, McBride still has a very good resume. His 1927 Retro-MVP helps his case as he was the best player in the NFL that season while leading the Giants to the NFL championship.

No. 40

Red Dunn
Quarterback

Full Name: Joseph Aloysius Dunn
Nickname: "Red"
b: June 21, 1901 (Milwaukee, WI); d: January 15, 1957 (age 55; Milwaukee, WI)
High School: Marquette Academy (WI); College: Marquette
Height/Weight: 5-11, 177 pounds
Position: Quarterback
Teams/Years: 1924 Milwaukee Badgers; 1925–1926 Chicago Cardinals; 1927–1931 Green Bay Packers
Pro Football Hall of Fame: No
Retro-MVPs: No
All-Time Teams: A. Herber (1946); C. Lambeau (1946, 1948); V. Lewellen (1946)

At number 43 is the third player on our list nicknamed "Red." Of course, if you have reddish hair, you automatically get that moniker. Red Dunn was sometimes asked about his real first name. "It's Joseph," once said Dunn. "But no one ever used it but my mother."[1]

Dunn is the seventh member of the Green Bay Packers first dynasty squad that won three consecutive NFL championships, 1929–1931, on our list, joining Verne Lewellen (#7), Cal Hubbard (#9), Mike Michalske (#16), Johnny "Blood" McNally (#21), Arnie Herber (#26), and Lavvie Dilweg (#36). Dunn was the little spark plug that revived Curly Lambeau's team. Just like Dilweg and Lewellen, he is not in the Pro Football Hall of Fame.

Born in Milwaukee, Dunn went on to play his college ball at local Marquette University under John Ryan (1920–1921) and Frank Murray (1922–1923). Under Murray, Dunn led the Golden Avalanche to unbeaten records of 8-0-1 in 1922 and 8-0 in 1923. He was named to the third team on Walter Camp's All-American Team and was a basketball letter winner, too. The freckle-faced, skinny Dunn, who maxed out at 5-11, 177 pounds, never backed down from a fight. In 1924, Dunn signed with the local Milwaukee Badgers. One local paper reported that Dunn was to get $200 per game, a very substantiable amount. He would be worth every penny as Dunn was the Badgers' best player. He led the team in scoring with 47 points as the Badgers went 5-8 (12th place in NFL).

The talented Dunn left the Badgers to join the Chicago Cardinals, led by All-Pro quarterback Paddy Driscoll. Dunn would make an immediate impact with the 1925 Chicago Cardinals championship team. That season with the Cardinals, Dunn threw nine touchdown passes to help the Cards to a first-place finish in the standings. This was Dunn's first taste of being a champion.

After playing his first three seasons with Milwaukee and the Chicago Cardinals, Dunn joined the Green Bay Packers in 1927. "We got him from the Cardinals. Paid $250 for him but that was a lot of money in those days," said Curly Lambeau in 1957.[2]

The quarterback they called "Red" was the main engine that helped the Packers win three straight NFL championships, 1929–1931. Lambeau encouraged Dunn to take charge of the huddle. On a squad that featured six members already on our list, Dunn, with Verne Lewellen (#7), was the main engine that made the team run. "Red was responsible for our three straight championships," said Lavvie Dilweg, Packers teammate. "It was his leadership that paved the way. We had confidence in every play he called."[3]

The 5–11, 177-pound Dunn could do everything within Lambeau's offense while with the Packers. Usually, the quarterback in the Notre Dame box was a blocker, but with Dunn's running and passing skills Lambeau encouraged his new signal caller to use the forward pass as often as he wanted. During his NFL career Dunn was overshadowed only by Benny Friedman in the passing game during his time, the era before Baugh and Luckman. "He was a great ball handler; a fine passer and he had a good head. When Red got you on the 10-yard line you never had to worry about

Red Dunn, quarterback, Green Bay Packers, ca. 1929–1930 (courtesy Green Bay Packers).

scoring; he always took us in," recalled Lambeau. "He gave us our first championship and he was the best quarterback in the league his last three years. He played under the center—like the winged-T now. We went to the single-wing after Red left."[4]

Along with Lewellen, Dunn became a quiet leader on the Packers who would dominate the NFL for three years. "He was a very good passer and very good signal caller. He had charge of the team on the field and was a leader," said Mike Michalske, Packers Hall of Fame guard.[5]

He had his best year in 1930 with the Packers, throwing a career-high 11 TD passes in a championship year, including tossing three to defeat Frankford on Thanksgiving (November 27). He followed that up with eight TD passes in the 1931 championship season.

Dunn was just a notch below Friedman during his era but can make a strong case to be a Hall of Famer. "Red Dunn could throw the ball as well as anybody at the time. Benny Friedman was considered the best pro passer then, because he had the big college reputation, but every time we played the Giants, Red outplayed Benny as far as I'm concerned," said Johnny "Blood" McNally, Packers Hall of Fame back.[6]

Dunn unofficially accounted for 48 career TD passes and twice tossed three scores in a single game. He ran for five touchdowns and even caught one in 1927 against Duluth. Dunn was also an excellent kicker, converting 75 XPs and 13 FGs, while scoring 150 career points.

On defense, Dunn was an ideal "safety" man. He was a sure tackler that nobody would get by and a consistent ball hawk. Unofficially, Dunn was credited with returning more punts than any other Packers player during his five years with the team, showing another example of his great athletic abilities put to use by Lambeau.

In his five years as a Packer, the team went 47–11–6, a .781 winning percentage. Dunn played his final NFL game against the Chicago Bears at Wrigley Field. Despite losing the game, 7–6, Dunn and the Packers won their third straight NFL championship that season. He retired after the 1931 season. He finished his career playing eight NFL seasons—total of 92 games. Instead of returning to the Packers in 1932, Dunn became an assistant football coach at his alma mater, Marquette, and stayed there until 1940. He then went on to run a very successful insurance business in Milwaukee.

Since his retirement, Dunn has often been overlooked. His accomplishments and NFL resume are definitely Hall of Fame worthy. Dunn played most of his career competing for honors and prestige against fellow quarterback Benny Friedman (#17). From 1927 to 1931, Friedman and Dunn played five seasons against each other. Friedman's overall record was 48–17–4, Dunn's 47–11–6. Dunn won three NFL championships, Friedman none. Dunn had 31 TD passes to Friedman's whopping 56. The Packers were the better overall team, but those Giants teams from 1929 to 1931 were loaded, too. Dunn held the winning advantage over Friedman, going 5–1. Friedman was always the choice for First Team All-Pro, 1927–1930, while Dunn was named second team in 1930 and 1931. Except for the passing touchdowns and First Team All-Pros, Dunn's resume seems very close to Friedman's.

In 1946, the *Green Bay Press-Gazette* had several former players pick their All-Time Packers team. Jug Earpe, Arnie Herber, Verne Lewellen and Charlie Mathys all chose Dunn for their quarterback spot. That same year Curly Lambeau also selected Dunn for his All-Time Packers team.[7]

Red was elected to the Packers Hall of Fame in 1976.

Dunn passed away unexpectedly from a heart attack on January 15, 1957, at the age of 55.

No. 41

Ed Danowski

Quarterback

Full Name: Edward Frank Danowski
Nickname: "Big Ed"
b: September 30, 1911 (Jamesport, NY); d: February 1, 1997 (age 85; East Patchogue, NY)
High School: Riverhead (NY); College: Fordham
Height/Weight: 6-1, 198 pounds
Position: Quarterback
Teams/Years: 1934–1939, 1941 New York Giants
Pro Football Hall of Fame: No
Retro-MVPs: No
All-Time Teams: None

Probably the most underrated quarterback on the list is former New York Giants signal caller, Ed Danowski. Just like Red Dunn (#40), he probably should be on the short list of potential Hall of Fame quarterbacks from the two-way era.

Growing up on Long Island, Danowski was a son of Polish immigrants. His father operated the family farm, mainly selling cauliflower and potatoes. Danowski was part of a rather large family, being one of 15 children. He was a three-sport star at Riverhead High School where the local paper called him "one of the crack players on the Riverhead High School eleven for several years," before going on to play his college ball at Fordham. He was coached by Frank Cavanaugh for his first three years, then by Jim Crowley, one of the famous Four Horseman of Notre Dame, in his senior year (1933). That season Danowski was named team captain while leading the Rams to a 6-2 record, earning Honorable Mention All-American honors by the United Press.

Ed was a college teammate of guard John Dell Isola who would also play with Danowski with the New York Giants after the Fordham star was signed by them. One report said that he received $200 a game. Playing for head coach Steve Owen, Danowski quickly learned you had to have a good sense of humor. "I remember the first time I suited up with the Giants," recalled Danowski in 1966. "I was one of 15 children from Jamesport, a little town way out on Long Island. I guess all my relatives were on hand in the Polo Grounds. They were shouting, 'Danowski, Danowski!' Coach Owen called me, 'Hey, Danowski!' 'Who will I go in for, Coach?' I asked.

Ed Danowski, quarterback, New York Giants, ca. 1934 (courtesy NFL Films Research Library).

'Don't go in for anybody,' Coach said. 'Go up in the stands, they're calling for you.'"[1]

  Danowski did eventually see the field. Coach Owen would make sure he was always there. Danowski quickly adapted to the pro game, knowing the difference between college and the pros. "Most of the pro backs are quite versatile," said Danowski in 1935. "For example, we all can pass quite well. And if you can't block by the time you get into the pros, you're no use to the team. It's taken for granted that you can run. College teams rarely, if ever, have the men able to kick, pass and run."[2]

Maybe not quite as gifted a passer as Sammy Baugh, Arnie Herber or Cecil Isbell during his time, the 6-1, 198-pound Danowski made up for it with great leadership and passing accuracy. "Ed Danowski was a great player. But he didn't think he was a good player. He was timid. I loved playing with him. He could throw the football, it was like picking it off a table, right in your hands. Hit you right there. He could punt and he could run with the ball," recalled Hank Soar, Giants Pro Bowl back. Danowski had small hands but could throw the pigskin with great accuracy. "I used to throw the short passes very well," recalled Danowski.[3]

"Ed was easy to catch. He had a soft touch," recalled Jim Lee Howell, New York Giants end. "Ed didn't rifle the ball, but it came to you smoothly and within your grasp."[4]

Danowski gave a stacked Giants team a much-needed boost in 1934 when their starting quarterback Harry Newman suffered a serious back injury. At the end of his rookie season Danowski helped the Giants win the Eastern Division. Then he played his best game of the year in the championship comeback against the Bears in the famous "Sneakers Game." "We weren't prepared for weather that cold," recalled Danowski. "You've got to remember the game was played on December ninth, which was late for us … [but] I always looked forward to the Bears games." Against the Bears, Danowski had an interception on defense, then during the fourth quarter rally, he threw one touchdown and rushed for another in the 30-13 victory. He finished the game with 59 rushing yards on 20 carries.[5]

The following year (1935), Danowski had his best statistical year, leading the NFL in attempts (113), completions (57), yards (794), and touchdowns (10), while guiding the Giants to another Eastern Division title. He was named consensus First Team All-Pro at the "halfback" position.

One of the most accurate passers during the two-way era, Danowski would go on to play 71 games over seven NFL seasons, all with the Giants. He completed 48.5 percent of his passes, compared to Herber at 40.9; Parker at 46.7; Isbell at 50.2, Luckman at 51.8; and Baugh at 56.5. Danowski led the NFL in passing completion percentage twice (1934-1935). "Ed Danowski was one of the finest passers the Giants ever had, and one of the most accurate in football history. Danowski never paid any attention to a rusher. He never took his eyes off his receivers. He threw many a pass which he never saw completed, when rifled the ball he was hit and went down," wrote Steve Owen in his book, *My Kind of Football*.[6]

Danowski would throw 37 career touchdown passes and rush for four scores. His leadership and accuracy always came up big in big games. In four postseason games he completed over 50 percent of his passes and threw four TDs, with the Giants going 2-2. Ed was a big-time performer in two NFL championship games.

Besides his great performance in the Sneakers Game, Danowski played great in the 1938 NFL title game against the Packers, where he went seven of 11 for 74 yards and tossed two TDs, including the go-ahead score in the third quarter to defeat Green Bay, 23–17. He also threw a touchdown pass in the 1935 NFL championship game against the Lions, although they lost 26–7.

In the 1935 championship game, Danowski set a record that still stands today. Not known for his punting prowess, he actually only had 31 punts in his career, but against the Lions Danowski booted one 76 yards, setting an NFL postseason record of longest punt that has since been tied by Mike Horan of the Denver Broncos against the Buffalo Bills in 1991.

"Big Ed," as he was sometimes called, became one of the more popular players in the NFL, so much so that he was able to get an endorsement from Wheaties. In the advertisement cartoon, the headline read, "Bullet Ball" Danowski, with the Giants quarterback in passing form. "I had one commercial, for Wheaties," recalled Danowski. "I got a box of Wheaties. That was my pay."[7]

After the championship game loss in 1935, Danowski continued his good play under Steve Owen. During the 1930s, he threw for 3,688 yards; in that decade, only Herber threw for more with 6,464 yards. During the 1938 championship season, Danowski once again proved he was one of the best quarterbacks in the NFL. He led the league in completions (70) and completion percentage (54.3) and was third in passing yards—with a career-high 848—and passing touchdowns with seven. After the season, he was named a consensus First Team All-Pro—his second first team honor—and played in the Pro Bowl.

In 1940, Danowski played for the American Association's Jersey City Giants, who were owned by Tim Mara, coached by Bill Owen and whose backfield coach was Ken Strong. Danowski, at the age of 29, was the starting halfback. He was one of the best players in the league. He led Jersey City to a 6-3-1 league record. He was second in passing touchdowns (7), attempts (101) and passing yards (732), and first in completions (63) and completion percentage (62.4). In the playoffs, Jersey City beat Newark (7–6) and the Wilmington Clippers, 17–7, to win the championship. Danowski was named First Team All-League by the coaches.

The following year he re-joined the Giants, age 30, where he played in just six games. He retired after the 1941 season. Danowski joined the Navy for World War II in 1942, reaching the post of lieutenant commander, and served until 1946. Once he returned from the war, Danowski was hired as head coach at his alma mater, Fordham. He lasted nine seasons, 1946–1954, compiling a record of 29-44-3. He hired a former Fordham Ram to be one of his assistants—Vince Lombardi, who lasted two seasons, 1947–1948.

His best year as the head man came in 1950 when he guided the Rams to an 8–1 record. After Fordham dropped its football program, Danowski became a physical education teacher and football coach in the East Meadow (N.Y.) school district until his retirement in 1977, a job that he relished. He never returned to coaching at the college ranks. "Not for me," said Danowski in 1967. "I played and coached college football, played professionally and enjoyed it all. But working with these young boys in high school as I do now gives me more satisfaction than I've ever had from any other phase of the game."[8]

In 1958, Stanley Woodward, editor of the *Dell Pro Football Annual*, selected an All-Time Team of pro football players. For the quarterback position he selected six names—Sammy Baugh, Otto Graham, Arnie Herber, Sid Luckman, Bob Waterfield and, yes, Ed Danowski—over the likes of Benny Friedman, Red Dunn, Ace Parker, and Cecil Isbell. But since then, his name has been overlooked. His career is on par with some of the other quarterbacks of the two-way era, mainly Cecil Isbell (#38), Ace Parker (#42) and Jimmy Conzelman. But like Red Dunn (#40), he's never been a Hall of Fame finalist.

Ed Danowski passed away from complications of Alzheimer's disease on February 1, 1997, at the age of 85.

No. 42

Ace Parker

Quarterback

Full Name: Clarence McKay Parker
Nickname: "Ace"
b: May 17, 1912 (Portsmouth, VA); d: November 6, 2013 (age 101; Portsmouth, VA)
High School: Woodrow Wilson (VA); College: Duke
Height/Weight: 5–10, 178 pounds
Position: Quarterback
Teams/Years: 1937–1941 Brooklyn Dodgers; 1945 Boston Yanks; 1946 New York Yankees (AAFC)
Pro Football Hall of Fame: Class of 1972
Retro-MVPs: 1940 (Joe F. Carr MVP Trophy)
All-Time Teams: S. Baugh (1999); P. Clark (1947); C. Hinkle (1942)

One of the best all-around athletes to play the quarterback position during the two-way era is our tenth and final signal caller—Ace Parker.

Parker was born in Portsmouth, Virginia, where his father worked for the railroads as a master mechanic and foreman in the shops in nearby Norfolk. Hard work and toughness were passed down to his son. Parker learned the game of football in his hometown. "I was about fourteen when I first took up the game of football, played sandlot ball over in a city park in Portsmouth. It was a big thing in the city back then. Every Saturday we'd have pickup games with kids from all over the city. Sometimes we'd have as many as seven or eight teams show up," recalled Ace Parker.[1]

Parker became obsessed with sports, especially football, even if it meant getting an earful from his parents when he returned home from the sandlots. "It was all street clothes. No one had any uniforms. We all used to catch hell always. We'd go home with our clothes all tore off. Things like that. No, there was no uniforms. No gear at all. It was just plain clothes," recalled Parker.[2]

After a stellar career at Woodrow Wilson High School, Parker was encouraged by his parents to attend Duke University. There he would play for Wallace Wade, one of the best coaches in the country. The triple-threat athlete used his small frame, 5–10, 178 pounds, to the best of his abilities, becoming an All-American. Reportedly, it was here that a local sportswriter wrote, "Parker was Duke's ace in the hole," giving the future Hall of Famer his famous nickname. Parker also lettered in baseball, the sport he thought would be his future.

No. 42—Ace Parker

Ace Parker, quarterback, Brooklyn Dodgers, ca. 1936 (courtesy Duke University Athletics).

Parker was selected in the second round of the 1937 NFL Draft by the Brooklyn Dodgers, number 13 overall—just a few spots below TCU quarterback Sammy Baugh (number six overall) who went to the Washington Redskins. Parker and Baugh shared a mutual respect for each other their entire careers.

The smallish Parker could go toe-to-toe with some of the bigger players during the two-way era. "There was no in and out. When you went in, you went in to play unless you got killed. There wasn't no such thing as being hurt. You had to play," recalled Parker.[3]

Although Parker was considered a great pro football prospect, he thought his professional career would be played on a diamond, not a gridiron. Parker played Major League Baseball for two seasons with the Philadelphia A's (1937–1938). "I thought I was a better baseball player. But I wasn't good enough to stay up there," recalled Parker. Ace got off to a fantastic start with the A's, hitting a home run in his first Major League at-bat against the Boston Red Sox at Fenway Park. But it would go all downhill after that. Parker struggled hitting Major League pitching. He batted just .179 in 228 at-bats with the A's. "I thought of myself as a baseball player first at that time and I told them I wasn't really that interested in playing pro football," said

Parker. "But as the season wore on I kind of got to know that my chances of being a good baseball player were marginal. So around August I started to think more and more about football. And the football Dodgers contacted me again. It was Don Topping and Shipwreck Kelly, the owners, who came to see me. Potsy Clark also talked to me about this time."[4]

Late in the summer of 1937, Parker got permission from the A's to leave the team to play for the football Dodgers. Parker claimed he joined the Dodgers for $2,500. Parker adjusted to playing in the NFL, but he also adjusted to living in New York City. "It was hard for me to get used to. I was a little country boy. Everything would move so fast," recalled Parker.[5]

Very versatile, Ace could run, pass and play defense with the best of them and was tough as nails on the field. Watching game film shows that Parker was very instinctive in the passing game—like contemporary Sammy Baugh—and could impact the game with his creativity. "I'll tell you the best I ever saw: Ace Parker. He could punt, he could pass, he could run, he could play defense. I mean, he could do it all," said Sammy Baugh.[6]

Throwing passes seemed natural to Baugh, but not so much with Parker. Throwing a plum-shaped ball was a challenge for Parker. "You had to almost grip it on the end," said Parker. "It was kind of fat. Everybody was having the same trouble. Seemed liked everybody had trouble except Sammy Baugh. He and I went in the [NFL] same year. He was the best I've ever seen."[7]

Parker played his first three seasons with the Dodgers under Potsy Clark, former Lions head man, playing in the single-wing. Parker would play the role of Dutch Clark in Potsy's offense. He would run, pass and punt. "I ran with the ball a lot. I wasn't exceptionally fast, but I was quick," recalled Parker. Ace's running style became his trademark. He was not a hard runner, since he only weighed 178 pounds, but he was a master of faking; most opponents found it hard to know which direction he was going. On film he made good use of his blocking and interference as well as anybody who played quarterback during this era. "Parker could throw the ball. He could kick. He could call signals. He could do all those things," said Hank Soar, Giants Pro Bowl back.[8]

In 1938, Parker had a breakout season. He led the NFL in passing attempts (148) and passing yards (865)—beating out Baugh and Cecil Isbell of the Packers—while finishing second in completions behind Ed Danowski of the Giants. "There is no greater thrill than blocking for a fellow like Ace," said Frank "Bruiser" Kinard, Dodgers Hall of Fame tackle. He was named First Team All-Pro over Baugh, Isbell and Danowski by the NFL, United Press, I.N.S., Pro Football Writers, *New York Daily News* and *New York Daily Mirror*.[9]

In 1939, Parker threw for a career-high 977 yards but only went 4–6–1. Potsy Clark left the Dodgers after the season. "Playing football in those days wasn't nearly as formal as it is today," recalled Parker. "We practiced in the morning and had our team meetings at the end of the morning and that was it. We had the afternoons off and most of us just took it easy, lay around, none of us had other jobs during the season. Everybody had off-season jobs, you had to in those days because you couldn't really get by on what you got paid for playing football. My job was better than most, playing baseball, at least in 1937 and 1938. I also managed in the minor leagues for four years, too. I played and managed at Portsmouth in the Piedmont League up until I'd have to leave and go play football."[10]

In the summer of 1940, Parker was playing minor league baseball with the Syracuse Chiefs of the International League. Batting near .400 at the time, Parker suffered a broken fibula and a dislocated ankle during a collision at the plate. Despite missing the rest of the baseball season, Parker came back to play for the football Dodgers. He used a padded steel brace that covered his left leg from his knee to his ankle. He would play his best football.

That fall, Potsy Clark left the Dodgers to be replaced by Jock Sutherland, the great University of Pittsburgh coach. "Jock Sutherland replaced Potsy Clark in 1940. He was quite a coach, changed the whole football team around when he took over," recalled Parker. "Up until then Potsy would let you do fundamentally what you'd learned to do in college. Now when Sutherland came in you had to adapt and do everything his way, which brought us all together and that's when we started to produce and win. He was a perfectionist, a helluva coach."[11]

Retro-MVP: 1940 NFL Season

Despite the bad leg Parker had his best year in 1940 when he won the NFL's Joe F. Carr MVP Award. He was second in the NFL in passing touchdowns with 10 (Baugh had 12); third in punting; first in extra points made (19) and was tied for first in interceptions on defense with six—he led the NFL in interception return yards (146) while guiding Brooklyn to an 8–3 record, one game back of the Eastern Division champion Redskins. Parker was named First Team All-Pro by the NFL, I.N.S., *Collyer's* and *New York Daily News*.

Parker played his best as a pro for two years under Jock Sutherland in 1940–1941. "Greatest competitor I have ever seen," said Jock Sutherland in 1940. It was during these couple of seasons that Parker cemented his legacy as a great quarterback.[12]

"You can kick Ace Parker in the head and you can break both his ankles but you can never hurt his heart," said Wellington Mara, Giants Hall of Fame owner. Parker finally took it to Mara's squad in 1940. From 1930 to 1939 the football Dodgers had played 20 games against their crosstown rivals. They had a record of 1-16-3 with their only win in 1930. Parker had had enough. On December 1 at the Polo Grounds, Parker put on a show for the Polo Grounds crowd of 54,993. The Giants were a 6-3-1 team celebrating "Mel Hein Day" that day. Parker spoiled that by throwing two touchdown passes in a 14-6 upset win. The following year, the Dodgers swept the Giants. "For instance, Red Grange was a marvelous runner but not a passer, kicker or field general. You've asked for the best all-around man and so I give you Ace Parker!" said Mel Hein, Giants Hall of Fame center, in 1949. "Tell me what he couldn't do with a football. He could pass as well as Sammy Baugh or Otto Graham or Frankie Albert. He could punt with anybody who played. He was smart calling signals. He was a wonder running the ball and deadly on defense. What more do you want?"[13]

Parker proved that he was one of the toughest and best players in the NFL. "I never thought I would ever be this kind of player. In the first place, I was really too small to start with. I thought to be a great player, the difference was I was tough. Had a lot of determination. That was what carried me, was the desire to play. Once I got started in football I forgot baseball and just went head-first into football," said Parker.[14]

In 1942, Parker joined the Navy to fight in World War II, losing three of his prime football playing years. "I didn't play any football while I was in the service, but I did get to play some baseball," said Parker.[15]

In 1945, Parker returned to the NFL, joining the Boston Yanks (at the age of 33), then finished his career playing one season in the AAFC for the New York Yankees. He retired following the 1946 season. "I was 34 years old. Wallace Wade offered me a coaching job at Duke and I accepted," said Parker.[16]

Parker finished his career with 30 passing touchdowns, while scoring 13 rushing, three receiving, two on interception returns and one on a punt return, and kicked 25 extra points. Although Parker had retired from pro football, he did continue to play and manage baseball in the minor leagues. He played his last game at the age of 40 with the Durham Bulls of the Carolina League. He also coached at Duke as an assistant football coach and head baseball coach.

It was not until 26 years after his last game that he was selected to the Pro Football Hall of Fame in 1972. When Parker received the phone call from the Hall of Fame, he was shocked. "I just got the greatest thrill of my life," said Parker after the call. "Of all the honors I've had in football this is the greatest." During his Hall of Fame speech Parker said: "I really didn't know I was that good. If I had I probably should have asked for more money.... I never expected to be selected for this, but since I have been selected, I'm sure glad it happened when I'm still around."[17]

Parker passed away of natural causes on November 6, 2013, at the age of 101. "Just love of the game, that's all I can say. And a determination to win," said Parker about his passion for football.[18]

No. 43

Charley Brock
Center

Full Name: Charles Jacob Brock
Nicknames: "Pea Head"; "The Thief"
b: March 15, 1916 (Columbus, NE); d: May 25, 1987 (age 71; Green Bay, WI)
High School: Kramer (NE); College: Nebraska
Height/Weight: 6–2, 207 pounds
Position: Center-Linebacker
Teams/Years: 1939–1947 Green Bay Packers
Pro Football Hall of Fame: No
Retro-MVPs: No
All-Time Teams: C. Hinkle (1946); C. Lambeau (1946, 1948); V. Lewellen (1946); J. McNally (1963)

    The fourth and final center on the list is Charley Brock.
    During the two-way era Brock is usually thought of as a notch below the previous three centers on our list, Mel Hein (#4), George Trafton (#27), and Bulldog Turner (#29). But he's worthy of their company as Pro Football Hall of Fame centers. He's also the 11th full-time Packers player to make the list.
    A Nebraska native, Brock grew up as a son of a railroad worker who was a veteran of the Spanish-American War. While his father worked hard for over 40 years as a bridge and building foreman for the Union Pacific Railroad, Brock became tough on the farm playing roughhouse with his six brothers. All the Brock boys knew how to be competitive in whatever they did.
    At Kramer High School, the Brock brothers all made a name for themselves. During their time at Kramer, the brothers earned more than 60 athletic letters with six of the seven playing college football. Mike (Midland Lutheran College), Tom (Notre Dame), Bill (Creighton), Fred (Creighton/Purdue), Johnny (Kansas), and Bob, who didn't play in college because he lost a lung from dust pneumonia, all participated in the game they loved. As for Charley, he stayed close to home by attending the University of Nebraska.
    It would be nothing but hard work during his time in Lincoln as Brock went to work running an elevator at night and washing dishes during the day. In between, he went to classes and practice. Playing for the Cornhuskers, Brock would be taught

Charley Brock, center, Green Bay Packers, ca. 1941–1942 (courtesy Green Bay Packers).

the intricacies of center and line play by one of the greatest linemen of all time. Link Lyman (#14) was the Cornhuskers line coach at this time who taught Brock how to play the center position. The Hall of Fame tackle was more than impressed by Brock. "I've played with and against many fine centers in my time," once said Lyman in 1937, "and when it all narrows down, he tops them all. A great competitor, he never has been licked."[1]

During the summers, Brock continued to work hard by digging ditches and cellars. His body was also growing. He now stood at 6–2 and weighed 207 pounds. His play at center was noticed when he was named to several All-American teams. His leadership shone through from the start. He was captain and All-American at Nebraska his senior year, was captain of the West team in the East-West Shrine game played January 1, 1939, and was captain of the College All-Stars in the 1939 game against the New York Giants. He knew he was one of the best football players in the country. He also knew that several other Nebraska stars had some success in the NFL with the likes of Link Lyman, Verne Lewellen, Guy Chamberlin and Glenn Presnell, all earning First Team All-Pro honors. He was ready for the challenge.

Brock was drafted by the Green Bay Packers in the third round of the 1939 NFL Draft (24th overall). Curly Lambeau visited Brock in Nebraska to offer him a contract. "He could sell you on the idea that you were going to be great," said Brock about his future coach. Although Lambeau was a good salesman, Brock was going to get as much as he could. At breakfast, Lambeau offered Brock $2,500 for his first year with the Packers. "I can't play for [that]," Brock insisted. Lambeau then offered $2,800 and if the Packers were to win the championship, he would get another $1,000. Brock quickly said yes.[2]

Lambeau liked what he saw of the young Cornhusker, both on offense and defense, as Brock became an integral part of a team that had just played for an NFL championship in 1938. Brock was built perfectly as a center-linebacker for the two-way era. "You could tell Charley was going to be a player," recalled Herman Schneidman, Packers back, 1935–1939. "Curly liked to draft players from Minnesota, Notre Dame, Wisconsin, Nebraska, the big colleges in the Midwest. Charley earned the respect of coaches and his teammates with his play."[3]

Brock arrived at his first camp in Green Bay nervous. Although he had been an All-American, he still had to make the team. "You had to earn your job or you wouldn't stick around," recalled Brock. "You never knew whether you were going to get fired from one week to the next. I've seen him [Lambeau] fire guys on the road after a bad game. They'd have to get home on their own." But Brock didn't have to worry about his spot on the team. He was there to stay. He let his play do all the talking.[4]

Brock would go on to play nine seasons (92 games) in the NFL, all with the Packers. Despite not starting, Brock learned the center and linebacker positions during his first few years with the Packers. Red Smith, Packers line coach under Lambeau, took Brock under his wing, pushing the promising lineman to reach his potential. "I was a small country boy out of Nebraska when I came to the Packers in 1939," recalled Brock in 1974. "Red Smith called me over the first day of practice and said, 'What's your name, kid?' After I told him, he said, 'Run to the other end of the field and back.' After I had done it, he said, 'I don't know, kid, but I think maybe we can make a football player out of you.' The second year when I came back, Red was calling me 'boy.' 'Just keep doing what I tell you, boy,' he said, 'and you might make it.' The next year when I came back, he said, 'You're doing fine. I think you might make it.' Then I finally had arrived as a pro football player."[5]

Brock gained a reputation of being a hard-nosed player around the ball, so much so that he received a rather unique nickname. "His teammates call him 'Pea Head.' That's because his head is small for the rest of his body. We have a stock saying on our team: 'If you want to know where the ball is, look for Charley,'" said Lambeau. Brock was around the ball often.[6]

The Packers were around the top of the standings throughout Brock's career in Green Bay. He was a member of two NFL championship teams with the Packers, 1939 and 1944. In the 1939 NFL championship game against the New York Giants, Brock had two interceptions on defense, in a game where the Packers had six total interceptions.

Brock played center most of his career in Lambeau's Notre Dame box offense that required him to repeatedly deliver sure, short snaps to any of the four backs. "As a center, he never made a bad pass [snap]," recalled Clarke Hinkle, Packers Hall of Fame fullback. Film study shows Brock with excellent power, great movement, and the ability to make all the blocks. His snaps were always clean, even if he didn't get his face out of the way after he passed the ball through his legs. "You took a lot of beatings," said Brock. "I had my nose broke five or six times."[7]

Brock always showed outstanding athletic ability in space, especially while playing on defense. He was excellent in pass coverage, having a knack for interceptions with 20 career picks with four career touchdowns—with three on interception returns. "Brock is the best center in professional football, I include Bulldog Turner. I have a great deal of respect for Bulldog Turner. He is fast, too, but does not maneuver with the skill of Brock, who has the coordination of a halfback," said Curly Lambeau in 1945.[8]

Lambeau knew he had a special player in Brock, especially with his knack to be around the ball, so much so that he taught Brock how to rip the ball away without the runner getting away. The technique paid off in a big way in 1942. In a game against the Chicago Cardinals (October 4), the Packers were trailing 13–10 in the fourth quarter. Curly Lambeau turned to Brock to get the ball back. That's what the ball hawk did. Stealing the ball away from Cardinals back Bob Morrow and sprinting 20 yards for the game winning score, Brock kept the Packers in the championship hunt. "[Cardinals fullback Morrow] was running quite high and all I could see was the football in his arms," recalled Brock. "I stole it and ran for a touchdown. When the whistle blew the officials were surprised because I was standing in the end zone. Some of them thought the ball was still at the line of scrimmage. It worked pretty well. It got to be kind of a knack. That's why I was called 'the Thief.'"[9]

Despite his great overall play on both sides of the ball, Brock's strongest trait, maybe, was his leadership. He served as permanent captain of the Packers his final three seasons. As a team leader Brock studied the game hard, becoming a true student of the game. He knew what every player was supposed to do. If a player wasn't performing up to his standards, Brock would order him to the bench. "That made them mad, and they'd play a little better. Other guys, you'd chew out and they'd fall apart," recalled Brock.[10]

An appendectomy in the middle of the 1943 season cost Brock four games, but he returned to play in the regular season finale at Philadelphia, a 38–28 victory over the Steagles, showing his toughness and his desire to not let his teammates down. When the 1944 Packers team went on to win the NFL championship, Brock always said that was his favorite season of playing in Green Bay. "I don't think we had the personnel that year, but we had a bunch of boys who wanted to play football and we won the championship with probably less talent than we had in other years," recalled Brock. In 1945, Brock led the NFL in interception return yardage with 122 and returns for touchdowns with two—both returns coming in wins. After the 1947 season, Brock called it quits at the age of 31. After retiring, Brock spent several years coaching with Omaha University and one year (1949) as an assistant with the Packers under Lambeau.[11]

Brock was selected as a member of the NFL 1940s All-Decade Team but has not been a finalist for the Pro Football Hall of Fame. His resume is right with the other three listed two-way centers in the Hall (Hein, Trafton, Turner) and is probably better than a few centers already in.

Brock stayed in Green Bay when he retired, working as an insurance agent in town, as well as becoming president of the Packer Alumni Association and regularly attending Packer games. He was elected to the Packers Hall of Fame in 1973.

Reflecting back, Brock always cherished his time playing in Green Bay. "We didn't lose many ball games. We didn't want to lose because of the people," recalled Brock. "Everybody in town knew you. When you walked down the street, they wanted to know what happened. They backed us whether we won or lost, but I hated to lose. I didn't want to let these people down. That was it more than anything else. If you lost, they were nice on Monday, but you knew you had let them down. But it was great to say that you played on a championship team, the best pro team in the country."[12]

Charley Brock passed away on May 25, 1987, from natural causes at the age of 71.

No. 44

Glenn Presnell
Halfback

Full Name: Glenn Emery Presnell
Nickname: "Press"
b. July 28, 1905 (Gilead, NE); d. September 13, 2004 (age 99; Ironton, OH)
High School: DeWitt (NE); College: Nebraska
Height/Weight: 5–10, 195 pounds
Position: Halfback
Teams/Years: 1928–1930 Ironton Tanks (non–NFL); 1931–1936 Portsmouth Spartans/ Detroit Lions
Pro Football Hall of Fame: No
Retro-MVPs: No
All-Time Teams: J. Carr (1934)

After playing three years with the semi-pro Ironton (OH) Tanks, Glenn Presnell played six NFL seasons (74 games) with the Portsmouth Spartans/Detroit Lions. Presnell was severely underrated during his playing career. Two things have kept him out of the Hall of Fame discussion. His first three years were played outside of the NFL, although with a good Tanks team that defeated NFL teams during this era, and the fact that he played behind the number one player on our list—the great Dutch Clark.

Presnell was born in the heartland of the country in 1905, surrounded by cornfields. "I was born in Nebraska and when I was about ten years old my family moved to Kansas. My father was a foreman on the railroad and got transferred a lot," recalled Glenn Presnell. "We lived in Kansas for about five years then he was transferred to Colorado and back to Dewitt, Nebraska." Growing up in Nebraska, Presnell suffered an early tragedy at the age of 16 when his father passed away. The youngster they called "Press" quickly took to the football field to take out his grief. "In 1922, I was a sophomore in high school in DeWitt, Nebraska, which was a pretty small town, and that's when I played my first game of football. I was a running back," recalled Glenn Presnell.[1]

The local high school was not a hotbed for coaching as Presnell found out. "We didn't have a coach, our coach was a local dentist in town who had played football at Creighton University," recalled Presnell. After the death of his father, Presnell quickly grew up. He went to school, played football and worked at a dairy farm a mile out of town to earn money. "A fella owned a dairy farm and wanted me to milk the cows every morning and evening, and go to high school. Which I did. I did that for a couple of years," recalled Presnell.[2]

Encouraged by a few of his teammates on the high school team, Presnell made his way 40 miles to the University of Nebraska. "When I arrived in Lincoln in 1924, I thought, 'Wow, now this is the big, big place.' We had about 100 kids in our whole high school, so you could say I was impressed by Lincoln's size. I was just a real country boy who had worked hard growing up," recalled Presnell.[3]

Glenn Presnell, halfback, Detroit Lions, ca. 1935 (courtesy Detroit Lions).

If Presnell was impressed by the campus, his coaches and teammates were impressed by Presnell's skills on the gridiron. Compact at 5–10, 195 pounds, Presnell made Nebraska one of the best teams in the country. During his time as a Cornhusker, Presnell faced off against the likes of Red Grange of Illinois and Ken Strong of New York University. Presnell held his own against the best All-Americans in the country.

In his senior year, Presnell led the nation in rushing and was named First Team All-American. Despite playing at a high level, the small-town boy from DeWitt didn't know much about professional football. "Just what I'd read. I didn't know anything about it. It wasn't as publicized as it is today," recalled Presnell in 1999. Even though he didn't know much about pro football, the teams knew about the All-American from Nebraska. Several NFL teams wrote to Press to see if he was interested in playing pro ball. "I had several offers to play professional football. The New York Giants offered me a contract, the Kansas City Cowboys and Providence Steam Roller also contacted me," recalled Presnell. "But it was Nick McMahon, the manager of the Ironton Tanks, who contacted me to consider playing for the Tanks. They offered me the same kind of contract as the NFL teams per game, but they also offered me a job teaching school in the school system there. That appealed to me because I figured if I couldn't play pro ball or if I got hurt, I'd have the teaching job to drop back on. So, I decided to take the offer from the Ironton Tanks."[4]

Presnell played halfback for the Tanks while teaching science at the high school. Coached by future Hall of Fame coach Greasy Neale, Presnell became a star with the Tanks. "He was an exceptional coach. He was an innovator," said Presnell. The small-town Tanks squad was definitely unique with most of the Tanks players being teachers. "They had flood lights on top of the [Ironton] stadium and we had to practice at night. Most of the players taught in the county, so they had to practice their teams after school," said Presnell.[5]

The Tanks were one of the best semi-pro football teams in the country, despite not being a part of the NFL. In 1930, the Tanks played and defeated many good teams including the New York Giants. Later that year Presnell had his greatest moment as a pro. "A couple of weeks later we played the Bears. We outscored them 28–14," recalled Presnell. "I had a pretty good day against the Bears. I ran 88 yards on one touchdown. I remember that very clearly because I had sprained my ankle the week before and had my ankle taped. They taped it up real tight. I broke loose off-tackle and went 88 yards for a TD. We beat the Bears, which was considered quite an accomplishment in those days."[6]

In a midst of the Depression, the Tanks folded after the 1930 season. Presnell had played three years of pro ball and was ready to move on. But he then received an enticing offer. "I had taken a high school job across the river at Russell, Kentucky. But Portsmouth made me a real good offer to play with them," said Presnell in 1999. "The contract was worth, I think, $2,800 a season. That wouldn't be one game today, but that was quite a bit of money back in those days. So, I decided to go ahead and play with them."[7]

In 1931, Presnell was the backup halfback who would sometimes get paired in the backfield with the great Dutch Clark. The Spartans were coached by Potsy Clark, who made an immediate impression on Presnell. "I joined the Spartans right at the same time they hired Potsy Clark as their head coach," recalled Glenn Presnell. "We called Potsy 'the Little General' because he was a strict disciplinarian. He worked us real hard. He was a stickler for conditioning. I think we were always in better shape than most of the teams we played. Potsy wouldn't stand for any horseplay. He just wouldn't take any lip from anybody. He would teach just straight-up football. He was an exceptional coach. We didn't travel by train much in those days; it was mainly by Greyhound bus. Some of our road trips east would be pretty long and we wouldn't have a chance to work out, so Potsy told us to pack a pair of shoes and a sweatshirt on the bus with us. We'd be going along sometime in the middle of the afternoon and he'd see this open field, so he'd have the driver stop the bus. We'd put on our shoes and sweatshirts and practice in this open field. We'd get back on the bus after the workout smelling like a bunch of goats. Those were great days."[8]

Only a player who played during the Depression would think that practicing on the side of the road and smelling like goats would be a great time. The 1931–1932

Spartans were a championship caliber team, going 17–5–4. Dutch Clark was the star of the show, but Presnell made his presence felt every time he played. "My greatest years were with Portsmouth when they just joined the NFL," said Presnell. "If I had played in Chicago or New York at the time, I would have got a lot of publicity. But in a small town such as Portsmouth not many people knew much about me."[9]

Presnell might've been in the shadows of Dutch Clark and overlooked, but his play never suffered. At the end of the 1932 season, Presnell got his chance to be the top dog. The Spartans had tied the Chicago Bears for first place, and that set up the famous "Indoor Game" to decide the NFL championship. With Dutch Clark not playing because of his coaching duties at Colorado College, Presnell stepped in, and he never forgot playing in the famous "Indoor Game" at Chicago Stadium. "It was an unusual environment to play a football game, and the footing was very treacherous. My favorite play was an off-tackle dive. Once, we were down near the goal line and I was going off right tackle. As I planted my foot, it skidded out from under me and I went down. There was a big hole, and I would've easily scored to give us the lead," recalled Presnell. Unfortunately, the Spartans couldn't score, losing 9–0 to the Bears.[10]

An excellent all-around player, Presnell excelled in many areas; he was a productive runner, above average passer, solid defender, and one of the best kickers in the NFL during his time. Although never the focus of the Lions offense—that was Dutch Clark—Presnell was highly thought of by opponents. "Presnell was a good player. He was hard to bring down when he had the ball. You had to get him down around the shoe tops. You couldn't hardly bring him down," recalled George Musso, former Bears Hall of Fame lineman. While on defense Presnell was a solid tackler and cover man. "Potsy had more confidence in me," said Presnell. "We'd get the lead and Potsy would always turn to me and say, 'Get in there Glenn and hold 'em.'" "Glenn Presnell was a brilliant football player. Outstanding on offense and defense," said Ralph Kercheval, Dodgers back, 1934–1940.[11]

To show how great Presnell could be, when Dutch Clark decided not to play in 1933, Presnell became the focus of Potsy Clark's offense. He had a career year, leading the NFL in rushing TDs (six) and scoring with 64 points. "The following year I assumed Dutch Clark's role when Dutch decided not to come back to the Spartans. I had a real good season. I led the league in scoring and made All-Pro. I also played eight straight games for 60 minutes. I would've played some more except I hurt my shoulder against the Giants. That was the way it was in those days. You didn't have a lot of substitutions. You just stayed in there and played," recalled Presnell.[12]

He was named First Team All-Pro by the NFL, United Press, *Brooklyn Eagle*, *Collyer's* and the *Green Bay Press-Gazette*. After the season, George Musso, tackle for the Chicago Bears, told the *Decatur Herald*, "Glenn Presnell, the old Nebraska star of the Portsmouth Spartans, was the hardest man to stop in the entire pro circuit."[13]

Presnell was ready to move on from the Spartans after the 1933 season. The Spartans were sold to G.A. Richards who moved the team to Detroit and renamed them the Lions. The new owner convinced Dutch Clark to return to pro football. Then he talked to Presnell. "I took a coaching position at the University of West Virginia. In the meantime, the Spartans, who had folded because of financial difficulties, were sold to Mr. Richards in Detroit. He was going to move the team to Detroit and since I made All-Pro and led the league in scoring, he couldn't understand why I wanted to retire from football. So, he called me up and made me an offer I couldn't refuse," recalled Presnell.[14]

In 1934—with Dutch Clark back on the team—Presnell finished third in the league in scoring (63 points) and rushing TDs (seven). He had the best moment of his career that season when he booted an NFL-record 54-yard field goal to help defeat the Packers, 3–0. That record lasted until 1953 when Colts kicker Bert Rechichar kicked a 56-yard field goal. "We figured a field goal attempt would be just as good as a punt. Besides, our offense wasn't making much ground against those big Packers. There really wasn't anything to it; I just booted the ball and it sailed over the crossbar," said Presnell in 1936.[15]

Throughout his career kicking was a strength for Presnell. "It's a lot like golf," once said Presnell in 1936. "You've got to keep your eye on the ball and when you kick the ball make your leg follow through just like a golf club. The moment your toe meets the ball relax all over." Every year Presnell worked hard on his kicking since it didn't come naturally to him like Dutch Clark. "You know, I never even knew I could kick better than the average player until I turned pro. Coach Clark used to have us kick 25 field goals every morning during practice and I guess I just had a flair for it, because I soon became the team's regular kicker," said Presnell in 1936.[16]

In 1935, Presnell would come in to spell Clark at halfback and proved his worth again, helping the Lions win the 1935 NFL championship over the New York Giants that year. Just like Clark, Press was part of a rushing offense that in 1936 set an NFL record for rushing yards in a season with 2,885 yards (in 12 games), a record that stood until 1972 when the Miami Dolphins broke it (in a 14-game season), and part of a Lions rushing offense that helped lead the NFL in rushing once (1936) and finished second twice more (1934–35).

Presnell finished his career with 1,593 rushing yards (3.9 average) and scored 218 points—including converting 15 FGs and 41 XPs. He also finished his career with 22 total touchdowns—including 18 rushing—that was more than such Hall of Fame backs from the two-way era as Fritz Pollard, Joe Guyon and Tuffy Leemans. He also tossed 17 career passing touchdowns.

After the 1936 season, Presnell stepped away from pro football at the age of 31. Coaching would be his passion for the next three decades. Presnell made coaching stops at Kansas (1937), his alma mater Nebraska (1938–1942, 1946), and North Carolina Pre-Flight (1944). In 1947, he accepted a job as an assistant at Eastern Kentucky. He would work his way up from assistant (1947–1953) to head coach (1954–1963), to finally athletic director (1963–1971). His 25 years at EKU would earn Presnell a spot in the school's athletic Hall of Fame in 2014. During his 10 seasons as the head coach at EKU, Presnell compiled an overall record of 42–49–3, with one Ohio Valley Conference title in 1954 (8–1–1).

After his coaching career was over, Presnell retired to a home back in Ironton, Ohio. Over the years he reflected on his time in the NFL. "I suppose playing in Detroit and winning the national league championship was the most standout thing that happened to me," said Presnell in 2002. "It was quite a thrill, I know that."[17]

Over the past few decades, Presnell's name and accomplishments have gotten lost. He's a notch below the names of Verne Lewellen (#7) and Ward Cuff (#32) for the Hall of Fame, as far as halfbacks-wingbacks, goes but he's not too far behind. He should be considered. "I don't know why Glenn Presnell has never made it to the Pro Football Hall of Fame. I've written letter after letter," said Clarke Hinkle, Packers Hall of Fame fullback, in 1984. "I think he should be in there as well as some of the ones already there. He played 60 minutes of football. He very seldom got hurt. He was a triple threat and he won a lot of ball games for Portsmouth and later the Detroit Lions. And I think he belongs in there."[18]

During the early 1980s when the Hall of Fame selection committee looked seriously at some of the two-way era players—electing Red Badgro (1981) and George Musso (1982)—several endorsement letters came in for their support of Presnell. Letters from Clarke Hinkle, Wellington Mara, and George McAfee were received by the Hall. Benny Friedman also wrote one for Presnell: "Gentleman: It is with a great deal of pleasure that I recommend Glenn Presnell to you as one of the great backs of my time. He was not only a great ball carrier, but also a hell of a man on defense. True to the players of his day, he was rugged, he did not get hurt in the days of sixty-minute football. I played against him when he was with the Portsmouth Spartans and had a high regard for him. He was a great competitor and a fine person. I believe he is one of the standouts of our time and well deserving to be in the Hall of Fame. Sincerely, Benny Friedman."[19]

But Presnell has never been named a finalist. "Several people have brought my name up for the Hall of Fame, but I'm not in there. I'd like to be in, but for some reason I've slipped through the cracks. I have as good statistics as some of the people that are in there now. But I don't resent it at all. They do a good job with the Hall of Fame selections," said Glenn Presnell in 1999. He never lost any sleep over not being in.[20]

Glenn Presnell passed away of natural causes on September 13, 2004, at the age of 99.

"It was a challenge to me to see whether I could make it in pro football or not," recalled Presnell in 1999. "I enjoyed my nine seasons of pro ball very much and made a good living while doing it. I'd just like to be remembered as a good football player. That's all."[21]

No. 45

Roy "Father" Lumpkin
Blocking Back

Full Name: Roy L. Lumpkin
Nicknames: "Father"; "Pop"
b: January 27, 1907 (Jefferson, TX); d: April 17, 1974 (age 67; Dallas, TX)
High School: Oak Cliff (Dallas, TX); College: Georgia Tech
Height/Weight: 6–2, 210 pounds
Position: Blocking Back-Fullback
Teams/Years: 1930–1934 Portsmouth Spartans/Detroit Lions; 1935–1937 Brooklyn Dodgers
Pro Football Hall of Fame: No
Retro-MVPs: No
All-Time Teams: C. Hinkle (1942); J. McNally (1944)

Rounding out the list of the greatest two-way players of all-time is the man with two nicknames. Roy Lumpkin, nicknamed "Father" or "Pop," was an absolute beast when it came to knocking opponents down—whether on offense or defense. Playing with reckless abandon, Lumpkin played eight seasons (93 games) with the Portsmouth Spartans/Detroit Lions and Brooklyn Dodgers. One of the premiere blocking backs of his era, Lumpkin could block, hit and tackle with the best of them. His lack of "scoring" stats keeps him lower on the list.

Lumpkin grew up near Dallas, the son of a laundry businessman where he learned the essence of hard work from his father. The younger Lumpkin not only could put in a hard day's work, but he also liked to mix it up with the neighborhood boys in all kinds of sports. Football quickly became his favorite.

After a stellar high school career at Dallas Oak Cliff, Lumpkin made his way to Georgia Tech. The native Texan filled out at 6–2, 210 pounds. Even as a freshman nobody wanted to mess with Lumpkin. One Atlanta sportswriter wrote that Lumpkin was only called by one name at Tech, that the other players "know his name. They call him 'Father,' not that he is old enough to be called 'Father' but because of his fatherly manner at the game [of] football. His last name is Lumpkin, in other words his title on the Tech Flats is 'Father' Lumpkin. He is a freshman fullback."[1]

Because of Lumpkin's size, the freshmen coach wanted to move him to tackle. The outspoken Lumpkin had a different idea. "[Coach,] I'm your fullback. What's more, I'm the only one among this group that's going to play fullback on this team."

And that's what Lumpkin did, he played fullback. In 1928, Lumpkin was the starting fullback on a Yellow Jackets national championship team that went 9-0 and earned a berth in the Rose Bowl. Played on January 1, 1929, Georgia Tech faced California in a game that would feature one of the greatest plays—or follies—in college football history: Roy Riegels wrong-way run.[2]

Midway through the second quarter, California center Roy Riegels picked up a fumble by Tech's Stumpy Thomason. Just 30 yards away from the Yellow Jackets' end zone, Riegels was somehow turned around and ran 65 yards in the wrong direction. Teammate and quarterback Benny Lom chased Riegels, screaming at him to stop. Known for his speed, Lom finally caught up with Riegels at California's three-yard line and tried to turn him around, but he was immediately hit by a wave of Tech players and tackled back at the one-yard line. The Bears chose to punt rather than risk a play so close to their own end zone, but Tech's Vance Maree blocked Lom's punt for a safety, giving Georgia Tech a 2-0 lead. Riegels was so distraught that he had to be talked into returning to the game for the second half. Tech held on to win by a final score of 8-7 to finish undefeated (10-0).

Roy "Father" Lumpkin, blocking back, Detroit Lions, ca. 1934 (courtesy Detroit Lions).

Lumpkin only played two years at Georgia Tech before missing classes cost him a chance to keep playing. Instead of making amends for his missed schoolwork, Lumpkin decided to play pro football. He got an offer to join the Portsmouth Spartans, a semi-pro team in southern Ohio. He was all set to play before returning to Georgia, thinking he might return to college. Fans in Portsmouth were heartbroken. A local newspaper wrote a poem about their disappointment.

> Oh Lumpkin, Father Lumpkin
> To whom the Spartans pray,
> We had you for a moment,
> Oh, why could you not stay?
> You lifted up our spirit,
> Made Peerless grid fans gay,
> But now that you have left us
> We'll paint the Floodwall grey.[3]

In the end, Lumpkin decided to leave school. Since the Spartans were not in the NFL, Lumpkin could play despite the fact that his class hadn't graduated. He helped the Spartans to an impressive 12–2–1 record, with their only two losses coming to the Ironton Tanks and the NFL's Green Bay Packers.

Lumpkin could tell he was playing with the big boys in pro ball. "The professionals have to take a chance because up there all the players are experienced and smart. You can't outfox 'em. You have to outgamble 'em if you expect to win," said Lumpkin in a 1937 interview with the *Atlanta Constitution*. "Open football is the answer, of course. A lot of college coaches would like to call it crazy football. But every coach in the east goes out of his way to attend the professional games, because he knows he is going to see something and learn something, too. Why, we toss all sort of passes behind our own goal lines."[4]

Roy Witt, a former Tennessee back who played with Lumpkin on the 1929 Spartans, was once asked how he gained so many yards that season. "Father Lumpkin was blocking for me," said Witt. "I just got behind him and he sucked me along."[5]

The following year (1930) the Spartans took a big step up in competition by joining the NFL. That season Lumpkin added a new weapon to his game by becoming more involved as a passer, throwing for three touchdowns. Lumpkin started to make a name for himself against the best players. Bull Behman, Frankford Yellow Jacket All-Pro player-coach, said about Lumpkin, "Don't forget this 'Father' Lumpkin, he's a pretty tough cuckoo to stop."[6]

During this time, in the middle of the Depression, Lumpkin turned to boxing and wrestling to earn some extra income. He was in perfect physical condition. But boxing wasn't too kind, as Lumpkin was knocked out several times, leading him to give up the sport, putting all his focus into wrestling. "This rassling racket put me in shape for football," said Lumpkin to the *Portsmouth Times* in 1931. He quickly became a very successful wrestler who became very much in demand.[7]

In 1931, the Spartans hired Potsy Clark as head coach. He changed the environment in Portsmouth, creating a closer team and a winning team. Lumpkin was committed to playing his best on the gridiron. He would take pride in his craft, not listening to some critics who said he didn't take the game seriously. "When the whistle blows, you forgot all the that," once said Lumpkin. "You don't have the feeling that you got to break your neck for the city, or the club. You remember that the guy you have to block, or that man you are trying to tackle, or that safety man you are trying to elude is just as good a ballplayer as you are and you do not want to be outclassed by him. It is a matter more of personal pride with you."[8]

Lumpkin's all-out effort made him a fan favorite with the Spartans fans. They would go nuts when the P.A. announcer would blast the song "Rambling Wreck from Georgia Tech" over the loudspeaker when he was introduced or when he made a tackle.

Lumpkin had a carefree attitude on and off the field that endeared him to his teammates and opponents. Lumpkin was truly one of the greatest characters during the two-way era. "A character, an absolute character, Father Lumpkin. He was just always full of jokes and fun. I don't think he had a serious thought from the time I was around him. Everybody loved him though and was tougher than a cobb," said Ralph Kercheval, Dodgers halfback, 1934–1940.[9]

In 1931, Lumpkin signed a contract with the Spartans for $3,500. Old "Pop" tried to save every dollar. "The Spartans would, they told me, supply a helmet and a jersey for each player, but our pants, shoulder pads, and shoes had to be provided by us. So did the whites—our tee shirts, socks and such," recalled Dutch Clark. "This prompted Father Lumpkin to think of a way to save money. Instead of buying socks, he would plaster his feet and ankles with tape, which was free. He would keep the tape on for a couple of days. Then when it got really dirty, he would tear it off and start on a new set of tape socks."[10]

Lumpkin built a great repartee when blocking for backfield mate Dutch Clark, even if it meant not knowing quite where he would go on certain runs. "Father Lumpkin did a great job of blocking," once said Potsy Clark, Spartans head coach. "Lumpkin was always complaining that he didn't know how to block for Clark. 'I block one way and Dutch goes the other.' My stock answer was, 'Keep on blocking 'em one way or the other and Dutch will be back.' He was that type of player."[11]

Another one of his on-the-field trademarks—besides his nicknames and carefree attitude—was that Lumpkin usually played without a helmet. "Lumpkin always said the helmet made him dizzy," recalled Glenn Presnell. This didn't keep him out of the lineup; he was a very durable player, starting 85 of his 93 career games. He found ways of protecting himself. "I never go down, but I cover up or keep moving." said Lumpkin in 1936. "That's the best defense. Now and then you get a pretty hard blow. But if you learn how to move and cover up you don't get hurt."[12]

But his colorful persona shouldn't overshadow that Lumpkin was a great two-way player. Presnell, Spartans/Lions All-Pro back and teammate said, "Lumpkin was an exceptional blocker. He played blocking back in our offense. He was a real good blocker and a very fine defensive fullback, too. He was a real tough guy, a really hard-nosed player.... He was one of the toughest human beings I ever saw. I remember seeing him wrestle during the off-season. He was just a very athletic individual. He was a great blocker, and he would say if he didn't take out two men on each play, then he wasn't doing his job. He meant putting them on the ground, not just bump them and go ahead."[13]

In 1932, the Spartans tied the Bears for first place in the standings, setting up the famous "Indoor Game." Of course, Dutch Clark missed the game because of his coaching duties at Colorado College. Still, Lumpkin had total confidence in his team. "We can beat the Bears, anytime, anywhere, even without Dutch Clark," proclaimed Lumpkin. But in the end the Bears were the better team, defeating the Spartans 9–0. But Lumpkin never backed down from his boast.[14]

Lumpkin could play with the best of them during this era. In 1942, Clarke Hinkle placed Lumpkin on his All-Time team, saying that he had "many a jolt dished out to this particular line bucker." He would be listed in lineups as halfback or fullback, but his main job was to be a lead blocker in Potsy Clark's single-wing offense. Lumpkin took his job as blocking back very seriously. He had no thoughts of glory and scoring the winning touchdown. Once a reporter asked what position he played, and Lumpkin responded by saying, "Third guard."[15]

When the Spartans ran out of money after the 1933 season, Lumpkin followed the franchise to Detroit, playing one year with the Lions. On September 23, the Lions played their first game in Detroit against the New York Giants at the University of Detroit Stadium. Dutch Clark hit a field goal in the second quarter, but the game was still 3–0 going into fourth quarter. The Giants tried to mount one final attack. The Giants threw a pass down field, but Lumpkin dropped back into coverage to intercept the ball and raced 45 yards down the right sideline for a score. It was the first touchdown scored in Lions history and clinched a 9–0 victory. A little over a month later, Lumpkin scored his final NFL touchdown on a short run of six yards in a 38–0 convincing win over the woeful Cincinnati Reds.

Lumpkin was a part of that 1934 Lions defense that started the season with seven straight shutouts. On defense, he excelled at disrupting the run game while being effective when dropping back into coverage. Old "Pop" was just a pure football player.

After the 1934 season, Lumpkin and the Lions didn't see eye-to-eye about his commitment to football. The team wanted Lumpkin to give up wrestling. Lumpkin didn't want to; he was making good money during the Depression. In the end the Lions got rid of Lumpkin. "The Lions had to trade him away because he took up pro wrestling on the side. The Lions said it gave football a bad name," said Sam Knox, Lions guard, 1934–1936.[16]

In 1935, Lumpkin was sent to the Brooklyn Dodgers. Newspaper reports claimed he was "sold," but no amount was ever reported. After playing two seasons with the Dodgers, Lumpkin was reunited in 1937 with Potsy Clark who became the Dodgers' new coach. Old Pop didn't last long with his old coach. He only played in five games for the Dodgers that fall before being released. Potsy offered Lumpkin a chance to stay as an assistant coach, but Lumpkin wasn't interested. "Playing the game is the only part of football that interests me," said Lumpkin to the *Brooklyn Daily Eagle*. "I'm through. I have been offered a good business post and I'm going to take it." He retired from the NFL after the season.[17]

Lumpkin's stats don't match his overall play and worth to the two NFL teams he played on. He scored just five career rushing TDs, all from short distances (six, one, two, one, six yards) and had just two receiving touchdowns. He did throw six career passes (from 1932 on) and that was mostly with Brooklyn later in his career. In 1937, Lumpkin named the two greatest ends he ever went up against. He named Bill Hewitt (#15) number one and Don Hutson (#2) number two.[18]

In 1939, at the age of 32, Lumpkin became the player-coach of the Louisville Tanks (AFL), who finished with a 2–9 record. Lumpkin then retired from football. However, he continued to wrestle for several more years before he quit that sport, too.

Lumpkin passed away in his hometown of Dallas on March 31, 1974, at the age of 67.

Lumpkin always appreciated the effort he gave while playing pro football, especially coming from Texas. "I knew there is considerable criticism of professional football in the south," Lumpkin said in 1930. "But it really is a fine game. Our league was organized as efficiently as the major leagues in baseball, and none but old college players participated. And it was real football. We all knew the game thoroughly and played with more speed, flash and skill than I had ever seen before."[19]

The Best of the Rest
Nos. 46–100

No. 46—Red Badgro, End (Hall of Famer), 1927–1928 New York Yankees, 1930–1935 New York Giants, 1936 Brooklyn Dodgers

No. 47—Ed Healey, Tackle (Hall of Famer), 1920–1922 Rock Island Independents, 1922–1927 Chicago Bears

No. 48—Jimmy Conzelman, Quarterback (Hall of Famer), 1920 Staleys, 1921–1922 Rock Island Independents, 1922–1924 Milwaukee Badgers, 1925–1926 Detroit Panthers, 1927–1930 Providence Steam Roller

No. 49—George Halas, End (Hall of Famer), 1920–1929 Chicago Bears

No. 50—Byron "Whizzer" White, Halfback, 1938 Pittsburgh Pirates, 1940–1941 Detroit Lions

No. 51—George McAfee, Halfback (Hall of Famer), 1940–1941, 1945–1950 Chicago Bears

No. 52—Alex Wojciechowicz, Center-Linebacker (Hall of Famer), 1938–1946 Detroit Lions, 1946–1950 Philadelphia Eagles

No. 53—Jim Benton, End, 1938–1940, 1944–1947 Cleveland/Los Angeles Rams, 1943 Chicago Bears

No. 54—Joe Guyon, Halfback (Hall of Famer), 1919–1920 Canton Bulldogs, 1921 Cleveland Indians, 1922–1923 Oorang Indians, 1924 Rock Island Independents, 1924–1925 Kansas City Cowboys, 1927 New York Giants

No. 55—Ace Gutowsky, Fullback, 1932–1938 Portsmouth Spartans/Detroit Lions, 1939 Brooklyn Dodgers

No. 56—Beattie Feathers, Halfback, 1934–1937 Chicago Bears, 1938–1939 Brooklyn Dodgers, 1940 Green Bay Packers

No. 57—George "Wildcat" Wilson, Halfback, 1927–1929 Providence Steam Roller

No. 58—Frank "Bruiser" Kinard, Tackle (Hall of Famer), 1938–1944 Brooklyn Dodgers/Tigers, 1946–1947 New York Yankees (AAFC)

No. 59—Luke Johnsos, End, 1929–1936 Chicago Bears

No. 60—Riley Matheson, Guard, 1939–1942, 1944–1947 Cleveland/Los Angeles Rams, 1943 Detroit Lions, 1948 San Francisco 49ers (AAFC)

No. 61—Doc Elliott, Fullback, 1922–1923 Canton Bulldogs, 1924–1925, 1931 Cleveland Bulldogs/Indians

The Best of the Rest: No. 46–100

No. 62—Hank Gillo, Fullback, 1920–1921 Hammond Pros, 1922–1924, 1926 Racine Legion/Tornadoes, 1925 Milwaukee Badgers

No. 63—Wayne Millner, End (Hall of Famer), 1936–1941, 1945 Boston/Washington Redskins

No. 64—Swede Youngstrom, Guard, 1920–1925 Buffalo All-Americans, 1921 Canton Bulldogs, 1925 Cleveland Bulldogs, 1926–1927 Frankford Yellow Jackets

No. 65—Jim McMillen, Guard, 1924–1928 Chicago Bears

No. 66—Al Nesser, Guard, 1910–1917 Columbus Panhandles, 1917–1926 Akron Pros/Indians, 1925 Cleveland Bulldogs, 1926–1928 New York Giants, 1931 Cleveland Indians

No. 67—Bill Osmanski, Fullback, 1939–1943, 1946–1947 Chicago Bears

No. 68—Gaynell Tinsley, End, 1937–1938, 1940 Chicago Cardinals

No. 69—Bill Karr, End, 1933–1938 Chicago Bears

No. 70—Jack Manders, Halfback, 1933–1940 Chicago Bears

No. 71—Buckets Goldenberg, Guard, 1933–1945 Green Bay Packers

No. 72—Joey Sternaman, Quarterback, 1922–1925, 1927–1930, 1926 Chicago Bulls (AFL), 1923 Duluth Kelleys

No. 73—Curly Oden, Quarterback, 1925–1928, 1930–1931 Providence Steam Roller, 1932 Boston Braves

No. 74—Walt Kiesling, Guard (Hall of Famer), 1926–1927 Duluth Eskimos, 1928 Pottsville Maroons, 1929–1933 Chicago Cardinals, 1934 Chicago Bears, 1935–1936 Green Bay Packers, 1937–1938 Pittsburgh Steelers

No. 75—Hinkey Haines, Halfback, 1925–1928 New York Giants, 1929, 1931 Staten Island Stapletons

No. 76—Keith Molesworth, Halfback, 1931–1937 Chicago Bears

No. 77—Curly Lambeau, Quarterback, 1919–1929 Green Bay Packers

No. 78—Jim Poole, End, 1937–1941, 1945–1946 New York Giants, 1945 Chicago Cardinals

No. 79—Tony Latone, Fullback, 1925–1928 Pottsville Maroons, 1929 Boston Bulldogs, 1930 Providence Steam Roller

No. 80—Harry Robb, Halfback, 1921–1923, 1925–1926 Canton Bulldogs

No. 81—Doug Wycoff, Halfback, 1927, 1931 New York Giants, 1929–1930, 1932 Staten Island Stapletons, 1934 Boston Redskins

No. 82—Dutch Sternaman, Halfback, 1920–1927 Chicago Bears

No. 83—Len Grant, Tackle, 1930–1937 New York Giants

No. 84—Ernie Caddell, Halfback-Wingback, 1933–1938 Portsmouth Spartans/Detroit Lions

No. 85—Henry "Two-Bits" Homan, Halfback, 1925–1930 Frankford Yellow Jackets

No. 86—Tommy Hughitt, Quarterback, 1920–1924 Buffalo All-Americans/Bisons

No. 87—Tillie Voss, End, 1921 Buffalo All-Americans, 1921 Detroit Tigers, 1922 Akron Pros, 1922 Rock Island Independents, 1923 Toledo Maroons, 1924 Green Bay Packers, 1925 Detroit Panthers, 1926 New York Giants, 1927–1928 Chicago Bears, 1929 Buffalo Bisons, 1929 Dayton Triangles

No. 88—Joe Carter, End, 1933–1940 Philadelphia Eagles, 1942 Green Bay Packers, 1943 Brooklyn Dodgers, 1945 Chicago Cardinals

No. 89—Steve Owen, Tackle (Hall of Famer), 1924–1925 Kansas City Blues/Cowboys, 1925 Cleveland Bulldogs, 1926–1933 New York Giants

No. 90—Kink Richards, Halfback, 1933–1939 New York Giants

No. 91—Ralph Kercheval, Halfback, 1934–1940 Brooklyn Dodgers

No. 92—Hap Moran, Halfback, 1926–1927 Frankford Yellow Jackets, 1927 Chicago Cardinals, 1928 Pottsville Maroons, 1928–1933 New York Giants

No. 93—Duke Osborn, Guard, 1921–1923 Canton Bulldogs, 1924 Cleveland Bulldogs, 1925–1928 Pottsville Maroons

No. 94—Russ Letlow, Guard, 1936–1942, 1946 Green Bay Packers

No. 95—Frank Bausch, Center, 1934–1936 Boston Redskins, 1937–1940 Chicago Bears, 1941 Philadelphia Eagles

No. 96—Hunk Anderson, Guard, 1922–1925 Chicago Bears, 1923 Cleveland Indians

No. 97—Larry Craig, Blocking Back, 1939–1949 Green Bay Packers

No. 98—Harry Newman, Quarterback, 1933–1935 New York Giants

No. 99—Dale Burnett, End, 1930–1939 New York Giants

No. 100—Jim Thorpe, Halfback (Hall of Famer), 1915–1917, 1919–1920, 1926 Canton Bulldogs, 1921 Cleveland Indians, 1922–1923 Oorang Indians, 1924 Rock Island Independents, 1925 New York Giants, 1928 Chicago Cardinals

Final Analysis

After researching and ranking the players from the two-way era of the NFL's first 25 years, 1920–1945, Portsmouth Spartans/Detroit Lions halfback Dutch Clark is number one. He beats out the very greatest of the era: Don Hutson, Sammy Baugh and Mel Hein.

There are some unique numbers when you look at the final analysis of the greatest NFL players of the two-way era. Among the players on the list are a few non–Hall of Famers, with Packers halfback Verne Lewellen the highest on the list at number seven. These players should be looked at in-depth by the Hall of Fame selection Seniors committee. Several players have been overlooked for far too long. Two-way players such as Verne Lewellen, Ox Emerson, Ward Cuff, George Christensen, Lavvie Dilweg, Joe Kopcha and Cecil Isbell are no-brainers for enshrinement in Canton, Ohio, while Jack McBride, Red Dunn, Ed Danowski, Charley Brock, Glenn Presnell, and Father Lumpkin have resumes worthy of discussion.

The players from the two-way era have a unique bond together, more than the other 75 years of NFL history, when players became more specialized and took the game to new heights. But nobody can deny the special talent that played both offense and defense from 1920 to 1945. There are some players who could've played in any era. "There could never be a better fullback than Bronko Nagurski, or a better center than Mel Hein," said Bulldog Turner in 1962. "We only had 10 teams in the league then and there were 330 pro football players. If those players were in competition today, they could all make the grade with a pro team—and don't you ever think otherwise."[1]

"Well, all the running backs do today is run with the ball," recalled Clarke Hinkle, Packers Hall of Fame fullback, in 1983. "When I was playing fullback, I had to block for the passer. I had to lead the ball carrier. I had to do the kicking. I did the kickoffs. I was pretty busy on the football field. You take the running backs today; all they do is run with the ball. You can't compare the two eras of the game. Ours was a combat sport. We played sixty minutes."[2]

Hinkle continues: "I'm very proud of our era. We had to have every ability available in order to go both ways. I've had people ask me if I would have been qualified to make a modern team. Of course I would and so would an awful lot of my contemporaries. I still have yet to see a better passer than Sammy Baugh or a better pass catcher than Don Hutson. We had great players in my day, too."[3]

Dutch Clark, Don Hutson, Sammy Baugh, Mel Hein, Bronko Nagurski, Verne Lewellen, Cal Hubbard, Paddy Driscoll, and the list goes on and on, could've played in any era. Dutch Clark, the number one player on our list, once said, "These days I'm just a fan. I don't miss a game and I think the game has never been better. But I have to say that some of the men from my time could play in any era. Nagurski, Hinkle, Strong, Battles, and later Baugh and Luckman. And some of the lineman like Hein and Turk Edwards. And of course, George Christensen, who belongs in the Hall of Fame if anyone does." Great players know great players, and great players could play anywhere, anytime.[4]

Going through the testimonials and interviews, one can see that the majority of the players who played in the two-way era loved being on the gridiron for 60 minutes. They routinely said they wouldn't like the modern game because they would sit for half of it. It was a different era. It was a different game. A game played by 60-minute men who played for the love of it.

Appendix I:
The Author's All-Time Two-Way Teams

Position	*First Team	*Second Team
End	Don Hutson, Green Bay Packers	Bill Hewitt, Chicago Bears
End	Guy Chamberlin, Canton Bulldogs	Ray Flaherty, New York Giants
Tackle	Cal Hubbard, New York Giants, Green Bay Packers	Link Lyman, Canton Bulldogs, Chicago Bears
Tackle	Pete "Fats" Henry, Canton Bulldogs	Turk Edwards, Washington Redskins
Guard	Dan Fortmann, Chicago Bears	Ox Emerson, Portsmouth/Detroit Lions
Guard	Mike Michalske, Green Bay Packers	George Musso, Chicago Bears
Center	Mel Hein, New York Giants	George Trafton, Chicago Bears
Quarterback—Single-Wing	Sammy Baugh, Washington Redskins	Benny Friedman, Cleveland Bulldogs, New York Giants
Quarterback—T	Sid Luckman, Chicago Bears	Paddy Driscoll, Chicago Cardinals, Chicago Bears
Halfback	Dutch Clark, Portsmouth/Detroit Lions	Verne Lewellen, Green Bay Packers
Halfback-Wingback	Johnny "Blood" McNally, Green Bay Packers	Ward Cuff, New York Giants
Fullback	Bronko Nagurski, Chicago Bears	Clarke Hinkle, Green Bay Packers
Punter	Verne Lewellen, Green Bay Packers	Sammy Baugh, Washington Redskins
Kicker	Ward Cuff, New York Giants	Jack Manders, Chicago Bears
Drop-Kicker	Dutch Clark, Portsmouth/Detroit Lions	Paddy Driscoll, Chicago Cardinals, Chicago Bears
Defensive Specialist	Red Grange, Chicago Bears	Al Nesser, Akron Pros/Indians, New York Giants

Position	*First Team	*Second Team
Player-Coach	Guy Chamberlin, Canton Bulldogs, Frankford Yellow Jackets	**(Tie) George Halas, Chicago Bears; Curly Lambeau, Green Bay Packers

*Player listed with team he played the longest or had the most impact on.

**(Tie)

Appendix II: Historical Sources of NFL All-Pro and All-Time Teams, 1920–1945

NFL All-Pro Teams, 1920–1945

Below are the sources that named an NFL All-Pro team during the period from 1920 to 1945. Most of them selected a First and Second Team, while a few selected players making a Third Team and Honorable Mention. Throughout this two-way era, several coaches and players also selected an All-Pro squad, and those teams are included here too. If a specific sportswriter selected the team, his name is included.

Newspapers/Coaches/Players

Rock Island Argus (1920)
Buffalo Evening News (1921)
Buffalo Courier (1921)
Guy Chamberlin (1922–1923)
George Halas (1922)
Collyer's Eye Magazine (Red Grange; 1923–1926, 1929–1941)
Green Bay Press-Gazette (George W. Calhoun/Art Bystrom; 1923–1935)
Canton Daily News (1923)
Ohio State Journal (1925)
Pottsville Journal (Walter Farquhar; 1925)
Joe F. Carr (*Liberty* magazine; 1925–26)
Chicago Tribune (Wilfrid Smith; 1926–1929)
Roy Andrew (1927, 1929)
Milwaukee Sentinel (1930, 1936)
Ernie Nevers (1930)
Red Grange (1930)
Lavvie Dilweg (1931)
NFL Official Team (1931–1942)
United Press (1931–1941, 1943–1944)
Curly Lambeau (1931)

New York Post (1931)
Chicago Daily News (1933–1936)
Brooklyn Daily Eagle (1932–1933)
Brooklyn Times Union (Lou Niss; 1932–1934)
Harry Newman (1933)
Potsy Clark (1934)
Boston Post (1934–1935)
New York Journal (1935)
Ray Flaherty (1936, 1938)
International News Service (1937–1940, 1942, 1944)
New York Daily News (1937–1948)
Professional Football Writers Association (1938–1939)
Chicago Herald-American (1939–1941, 1943)
Associated Press (1940–1944)
Pro Football Illustrated (1943–1944)
New York Journal-American (1943)
Detroit Free-Press (1944)

NFL All-Time Teams Selected by Those Who Were There

I researched newspapers, publications, books, magazines and much more to find every NFL All-Time team selected by the men who played, coached, owned, officiated or wrote about the NFL from 1920 to 1945. Most of these teams included a full 11-man squad, while some other teams included their top five opponents or greatest players they ever saw. Over the years some individuals would repeat or give another All-Time team; those are included here too.

Throughout my research I tried to find at least one All-Time team from every Hall of Famer of the two-way era. At the start of the 2023 NFL season there were 55 total players/coaches/executives from the two-way era (1920–1945) inducted into the Hall of Fame—including 46 players. Some Hall of Famers never selected a team, or it was never printed.

Here is the list of NFL All-Time teams, including the year it was given and the source it came from.

Pro Football Hall of Fame Players

Red Badgro: None
Cliff Battles: None
Sammy Baugh: 1949, 1957, 1999 (*Los Angeles Times*, December 9, 1949; *Dayton Daily News*, May 10, 1957; *Knoxville News-Sentinel*, January 24, 1999)
Tony Canadeo: None
Guy Chamberlin: None

Dutch Clark: 1942 (*Sporting News*, December 31, 1942)
Jimmy Conzelman: 1941 (*Nebraska State Journal*, August 5, 1941)
Paddy Driscoll: 1956 (*Miami Herald*, April 5, 1956)
Turk Edwards: None
Ray Flaherty: 1990 (*Spokesman-Review,* January 28, 1990)
Dan Fortmann: None
Benny Friedman: None
Red Grange: 1934, 1946–1947, 1955 (*San Francisco Examiner*, January 17, 1934; *Cedar Rapids Gazette,* December 1, 1947; *Nashville Banner*, January 12, 1955)
Joe Guyon: None
George Halas: 1939, 1940–1941 (*Minneapolis Star-Tribune*, May 7, 1939; *New York Daily News*, December 8, 1940; *Dayton Herald*, December 20, 1941)
Ed Healey: None
Mel Hein: 1944, 1968, 1974 (*New York Times,* December 17, 1944; *Quad-City Times*, March 12, 1968; *Spokesman-Review,* June 19, 1974)
Pete Henry: None
Arnie Herber: 1946 (Packers All-Time Team, *Green Bay Press-Gazette*, November 7, 1946)
Bill Hewitt: 1937, 1940 (*Dayton Daily News,* January 21, 1937; *Piqua Daily Call*, January 9, 1940)
Clarke Hinkle: 1940, 1942, 1946, 1986 (*Appleton Post-Crescent,* March 29, 1940; *Clarke Hinkle Scrapbook*, 1942; Packers All-Time Team, *Green Bay Press-Gazette*, November 7, 1946; *Green Bay Press-Gazette*, September 7, 1986)
Cal Hubbard: 1937, 1947, 1966 (*Oshkosh Northwestern*, April 26, 1937; *Honolulu Star-Bulletin*, December 6, 1947; *Pittsburgh Press*, December 12, 1966)
Don Hutson: 1948, 1986 (*Green Bay Press-Gazette*, November 24, 1948; *Green Bay Press-Gazette*, September 7, 1986)
Walt Kiesling: 1936, 1942 (*Pittsburgh Sun-Telegraph*, February 9, 1936; *Sporting News*, December 31, 1942)
Bruiser Kinard: None
Curly Lambeau: 1946, 1948, 1955 (*Green Bay Press-Gazette*, November 5, 1946; *Salt Lake Telegram,* December 13, 1948; *Los Angeles Times,* January 27, 1955)
Tuffy Leemans: 1945, 1947, 1953 (*Chicago Tribune*, December 6, 1945; *Fort Worth Star-Telegram*, December 12, 1947; *Nashville Banner*, January 10, 1953)
Sid Luckman: None
Link Lyman: None
George McAfee: None
Johnny "Blood" McNally: 1937, 1944, 1963, 1971 (*Green Bay Press-Gazette*, July 24, 1937; *Marshfield News-Herald*, August 4, 1944; *Minneapolis Star-Tribune*, October 11, 1963; *Wisconsin State Journal*, June 4, 1971)
Mike Michalske: 1982 (*Green Bay Press-Gazette*, July 24, 1982)
Wayne Millner: None

George Musso: 1964 (*Woodstock Daily Sentinel*, December 3, 1964)
Bronko Nagurski: 1939, 1944 (*Reading Times*, November 11, 1939; *Wisconsin State Journal*, August 7, 1944)
Ernie Nevers: 1932 (*Los Angeles Times,* January 26, 1932)
Steve Owen: 1942, 1952, 1955 (*Baltimore Sun*, December 10, 1942; *My Kind of Football* biography, 1952; *Nashville Banner*, January 12, 1955)
Ace Parker: None
Fritz Pollard: None
Duke Slater: 1949, 1957 (*Davenport Times,* September 29, 1949; *Mason City Globe-Gazette*, March 27, 1957)
Ken Strong: None
Joe Stydahar: 1951, 1952 (*Los Angeles Times*, November 23, 1951; *The All-Sports News*, January 16, 1952)
Jim Thorpe: 1951 (*Fort Worth Star-Telegram,* February 6, 1951)
George Trafton: None
Bulldog Turner: None
Alex Wojciechowicz: None

Pro Football Hall of Fame Owners/Executives

Bert Bell: 1940 (*Decatur Daily Review*, November 15, 1940)
Charlie Bidwill: None
Joe F. Carr: 1934 (*Green Bay Press-Gazette*, September 19, 1934)
Tim Mara: None
Wellington Mara: None
George Preston Marshall: None
Greasy Neale: None
Hugh "Shorty" Ray: None
Art Rooney: None

Non-Hall of Fame Players/Coaches/Officials/Executives

Charley Brock: player, 1986 (*Green Bay Press-Gazette*, September 7, 1986)
Chris Cagle: player, 1937 (*Reading Times*, October 20, 1937)
Bobbie Cahn: game official, 1943 (*Chicago Tribune,* June 11, 1943)
Potsy Clark: coach, 1940, 1947 (*Fort Worth Star-Telegram*, November 20, 1940; *Madison Capital Times*, August 30, 1947)
George Corbett: player, 1938 (*Decatur Daily Review,* December 11, 1938)
Ernie Cuneo, player, 1973 (*Paterson News*, August 20, 1973)
Gus Dorias: coach, 1952, 1954 (*Pittsburgh Sun-Telegraph,* November 23, 1952; *Wisconsin State Journal*, January 13, 1954)
Milt Gantenbein: player, 1946, 1966 (Packers All-Time Team, *Green Bay Press-Gazette,* November 7, 1946; *La Crosse Tribune,* December 18, 1966)

Verne Lewellen: player, 1936, 1946 (Top Six Greatest Players, July 30, 1936; Packers All-Time Team, *Green Bay Press-Gazette*, November 7, 1946)
Roy "Pop" Lumpkin: player, 1937 (*Atlanta Constitution,* January 12, 1937)
Jim McMillian: player, 1939 (*Nashville Banner,* February 9, 1939)
Ray Richards: player, 1944 (*Los Angeles Times,* May 29, 1944)
Paul Robeson: player, 1941 (*Wilmington Morning News,* December 9, 1941)
Carl Storck: coach-executive, 1939 (*Green Bay Press-Gazette,* November 3, 1939)
Dan Tehan: game official, 1963 (*Chattanooga Daily Times,* May 26, 1963)

Media/Publications Pro Football All-Time Teams

1942 Sporting News (December 31, 1942; team selected by NFL coaches Curly Lambeau, Steve Owen, Walt Kiesling, Dutch Clark, Mel Hein, Bull Karcis, Mike Getto; and *Sporting News* writer Joe King)
1947 Pro Football Illustrated Annual (editors selected 51 "Famous Players" in NFL history)
1952 Official NFL Football Encyclopedia (selected three teams; Roger Treat, editor)
1957 Pro Football (Peterson Publications Football Annual; team selected by Maxwell Stiles of *Los Angeles Mirror-News*)
1958 Dell Pro Football Annual (selected a 43-man All-Time team; Stanley Woodward, editor)
Pro Football's 100 Greatest Players: Rating the Stars of Past and Present (by George Allen, 1982)

Pro Football Hall of Fame/National Football League

Pro Football Hall of Fame: All-Decade Teams (1920s, 1930s, 1940s)
NFL 50th Anniversary Team (1969)
NFL 75th Anniversary Team (1994)
NFL 75th Anniversary Two-Way Team (1994)
NFL 100th Anniversary Team (2019)

Chapter Notes

Introduction

1. Paul Gallico, *The Golden People* (New York: Doubleday, 1965), 27.
2. David Neft, Richard Cohen, and Rick Korch, *The Football Encyclopedia* (New York: St. Martin's Press, 1994), 19.
3. Gallico, *The Golden People*, 27–28.
4. Neft, *The Football Encyclopedia*, 19.
5. Ibid., 19–20.
6. Ray Flaherty, 1985 NFL Films interview.
7. *Austin American*, July 7, 1944.
8. Dan Daly and Bob O'Donnell, *The Pro Football Chronicle* (New York: Macmillan, 1990), 16.
9. Richard Whittingham, *What a Game They Played* (New York: Harper & Row, 1984), 135.
10. *Lima News*, December 29, 1959.
11. Milton Richman, *Pro! Official Magazine of the NFL* XI, no. 4 (September 7, 1980); "Sammy Baugh: I'll Never Forget ... Bronx Cheers," 10E.
12. *Miami News*, December 17, 1983.
13. *Sun Sentinel*, January 31, 1978.
14. Charles Johnson, *The Green Bay Packers: Pro Football's Pioneer Team* (New York: Thomas Nelson & Sons, 1961), 54.
15. Cliff Christl email, September 1, 2022.
16. *Waterloo Daily Courier*, January 25, 1955.
17. Ray Flaherty, 1985 NFL Films interview.
18. Sid Luckman, 1994 NFL Films interview.
19. *Houston Chronicle*, July 26, 1998.
20. Murray Oldermann, *The Running Backs* (Englewood Cliffs, NJ: Prentice-Hall, 1969), 83.
21. Ibid.
22. Potsy Clark, *Football: A Book for Players and Football Fans* (Chicago: Rand McNally, 1935), 8.
23. *1939 Official Guide of the National Football League* (New York: American Sports Publishing, 1939), 101.
24. *Toledo Blade*, July 20, 1975.
25. Clark, *Football: A Book for Players and Football Fans*, 10.
26. Bill Morgan, Pro Football Hall of Fame file, clipping, undated.
27. Clark, *Football: A Book for Players and Football Fans*, 12.
28. Ibid.
29. Ibid.
30. *1939 Official Guide of the National Football League*, 104.
31. *Rocklin Placer Herald*, January 28, 1998.
32. *Chicago Tribune*, October 31, 1998.

No. 1. Dutch Clark

1. *Detroit News*, November 27, 1934.
2. Myron Cope, *The Game That Was* (New York: World, 1970), 85.
3. Ibid., 90.
4. Chris Willis, *Dutch Clark: The Life of an NFL Legend and the Birth of the Detroit Lions* (Lanham, MD: Scarecrow Press, 2012), 23.
5. *Denver Post*, March 14, 1965.
6. Willis, *Dutch Clark: The Life of an NFL Legend and the Birth of the Detroit Lions*, 130.
7. *Detroit Free Press*, January 30, 1963.
8. Dutch Clark, audio interview, 1969.
9. Dutch Clark quote, Cleveland Rams at Detroit Lions game program, September 29, 1940, 4.
10. Glenn Presnell, author interview, February 21, 1999.
11. Ray Flaherty, 1985 NFL Films interview. Ralph Kercheval, author interview, July 12, 2001.
12. *Billings* (MT) *Gazette*, April 27, 1937.
13. *Knoxville Journal*, November 30, 1932.
14. Cope, *The Game That Was*, 90.
15. Dutch Clark, 1962 Detroit TV interview.
16. *Detroit Free Press*, November 27, 1934.
17. Willis, *Dutch Clark: The Life of an NFL Legend and the Birth of the Detroit Lions*, x.
18. Joe Kopcha, 1979 Pro Football Hall of Fame interview.
19. George Musso, author interview, April 6, 1999.
20. *Detroit News*, November 27, 1934.
21. George Halas quote, Chicago Bears at Detroit Lions game program, November 25, 1937.
22. Jack McDonald, "I'll Never Forget ... First Pro Football Hall of Fame Selection Meeting," *Pro! Official Magazine of the NFL*, vol. 1, p. 15A.
23. 1963 Pro Football Hall of Fame transcript.
24. Bob Curran, *Pro Football's Rag Days* (New York: Bonanza Books, 1969), 121; *Pueblo Chieftain*, August 6, 1978.
25. *Portsmouth Times*, January 12, 1940.
26. *Pueblo Chieftain*, November 23, 2019.
27. Curran, *Pro Football's Rag Days*, 96.

No. 2. Don Hutson

1. *St. Louis Post-Dispatch*, September 6, 1940.
2. Richard Whittingham, *What a Game They Played* (New York: Harper & Row, 1984), 120; *Green Bay Press-Gazette*, February 11, 1942.
3. *Rutland* (VT) *Daily Herald*, September 23, 1969.
4. Whittingham, *What a Game They Played*, 124.
5. Arthur Daley, *Pro Football's Hall of Fame* (New York: Tempo Books, 1963), 156.
6. *Chicago Tribune*, November 5, 1962.
7. Daley, *Pro Football's Hall of Fame*, 154.
8. *Indianapolis Star*, December 27, 1987; Whittingham, *What a Game They Played*, 121.
9. Clarke Hinkle, 1983 NFL Films interview.
10. *San Bernardino County-Sun*, October 24, 1975.
11. Charles Johnson, *The Green Bay Packers: Pro Football's Pioneer Team* (New York: Thomas Nelson & Sons, 1961), 81–82.
12. Ibid.
13. Don Hutson, 1983 NFL Films interview.
14. Ibid.
15. Ace Parker, 2000 NFL Films interview.
16. Ray Flaherty, 1985 NFL Films interview.
17. *Cushing Daily Citizen*, January 15, 1940.
18. Johnson, *The Green Bay Packers: Pro Football's Pioneer Team*, 71.
19. *Boston Globe*, December 11, 1943.
20. Mel Hein, 1983 NFL Films interview.
21. George McAfee, interview conducted by Cliff Christl, July 15, 1996.
22. *Green Bay Press-Gazette*, July 3, 1994.
23. Dan Fortmann, Pro Football Hall of Fame file, undated clipping.
24. *Manitowoc Herald-Times*, October 22, 1999.
25. *Appleton Post-Crescent*, June 27, 1997.
26. *Des Moines Register*, December 16, 1945.

No. 3. Sammy Baugh

1. Whittingham, *What a Game They Played*, 171.
2. Ibid.
3. Ibid.
4. *USA Today*, December 18, 2008.
5. Joe Holley, *Slingin' Sam: The Life and Times of the Greatest Quarterback Ever to Play the Game* (Austin: University of Texas Press, 2012), 29.
6. Ibid.
7. Ibid.
8. Ibid.
9. Ibid.
10. Sammy Baugh, 1994 NFL Films interview.
11. *Spokesman-Review*, January 30, 1983.
12. *Washington Star*, January 27, 1976.
13. Holley, *Slingin' Sam: The Life and Times of the Greatest Quarterback Ever to Play the Game*, 127.
14. *Mansfield* (OH) *News-Journal*, January 7, 1938.
15. Ibid.; *Sport Life*, December 1951, 15.
16. Sammy Baugh, 1994 NFL Films interview.
17. *Salinas Morning Post*, December 14, 1937; Ace Parker, 2000 NFL Films interview.
18. Ralph Kercheval, 2001 NFL Films interview.
19. Steve Owen, *My Kind of Football*, edited by Joe King (New York: David McKay, 1952), 189.
20. *Nashville Banner*, January 10, 1953.
21. *Los Angeles Times*, January 30, 1963.
22. Sammy Baugh, 1994 NFL Films interview.
23. Bob Addie, "What Makes Sammy Baugh?" *Sportsfolio*, December 1947, 16; *Fort Worth Star-Telegram*, December 24, 1952.
24. Sammy Baugh, 1994 NFL Films interview.
25. Holley, *Slingin' Sam: The Life and Times of the Greatest Quarterback Ever to Play the Game*, 246–247.
26. Sammy Baugh, 1994 NFL Films interview.
27. Addie, "What Makes Sammy Baugh?" *Sportsfolio*, 9.
28. Ibid.
29. Tom Barnidge, *The Sporting News: Football Hall of Fame Fact Book* (St. Louis: The Sporting News, 1983), 8.
30. George Sullivan, *Pro Football's All-Time Greats: The Immortals in Pro Football's Hall of Fame* (New York: G.P. Putnam's Sons, 1968), 21.
31. Whittingham, *What a Game They Played*, 179.
32. Frank Dennis, "Rifle-Arm Sammy," *Collier's*, September 11, 1948, 24.

No. 4. Mel Hein

1. Whittingham, *What a Game They Played*, 54.
2. Mel Hein, 1978 NFL Films interview.
3. Ibid.
4. Ward Cuff, Pro Football Hall of Fame file, clipping, 1941.
5. Whittingham, *What a Game They Played*, 56–57.
6. *Sporting News*, November 26, 1942.
7. Whittingham, *What a Game They Played*, 59.
8. Bob Curran, *Pro Football's Rag Days* (New York: Bonanza Books, 1969), 119.
9. Quentin Reynolds, "Block and Tackle," *Collier's*, November 4, 1939, 30.
10. Ibid.
11. *New York Daily News*, November 17, 1946.
12. Bronko Nagurski, 1983 NFL Films interview.
13. Clarke Hinkle, 1983 NFL Films interview.
14. Michael Eisen, *Gameday! NFL Program*, Washington Redskins at New York Giants, September 19, 1994, "Giant of the Decade: 1930's Mel Hein (1931–1945)," 11.
15. *Passaic Herald-News*, October 21, 1978.
16. Whittingham, *What a Game They Played*, 62.
17. Ibid.
18. *New York Daily News*, May 5, 1974; *Time*, March 21, 1969.
19. Daley, *Pro Football's Hall of Fame*, 137.

20. Don Hutson, 1983 NFL Films interview.
21. Owen, *My Kind of Football*, 190.
22. Eisen, "Giant of the Decade: 1930's Mel Hein," 12.
23. *New York Daily News*, May 5, 1974.
24. Curran, *Pro Football's Rag Days*, 122.
25. Cope, *The Game That Was*, 178.
26. *Harrisburg Telegraph*, December 6, 1945.
27. Mel Hein, Pro Football Hall of Fame file, undated clipping.
28. Curran, *Pro Football's Rag Days*, 123.
29. *New York Times*, February 2, 1992.
30. *Spokane Spokesman-Review*, June 18, 1974.
31. *Ibid.*

No. 5. Guy Chamberlin

1. *Omaha World-Herald*, December 1, 1912.
2. *Lincoln Star*, December 12, 1943.
3. Paddy Driscoll, 1964–1965 Pro Football Hall of Fame audio interview.
4. Guy Chamberlin, 1965 Pro Football Hall of Fame audio interview; *Saturday Evening Post*, November 23, 1957.
5. *Canton Repository*, April 15, 1965.
6. *Lincoln Journal-Star*, August 21, 1951.
7. Link Lyman, 1964–1965, Pro Football Hall of Fame audio interview.
8. *Philadelphia Daily News*, August 29, 1991.
9. Owen, *My Kind of Football*, 47.
10. Guy Chamberlin, Pro Football Hall of Fame file, *Philadelphia Evening Public Ledger*, clipping, 1926.

No. 6. Bronko Nagurski

1. *Kenosha Evening News*, February 18, 1937.
2. *Huntingdon Daily News*, December 29, 1978.
3. Bronko Nagurski Oral History interview, Voyageurs National Park, August 17, 1976; *St. Paul Pioneer-Press*, January 21, 1979.
4. Bronko Nagurski Oral History interview, Voyageurs National Park, August 17, 1976.
5. *Ibid.*
6. Murray Olderman, *The Running Backs* (Englewood Cliffs, NJ: Prentice-Hall, 1969), 155.
7. *Chicago Sun-Times*, July 3, 1973.
8. *Boston Globe*, October 8, 1957.
9. *Fort Lauderdale News*, December 28, 1965.
10. Ray Flaherty, 1985 NFL Films interview.
11. *Miami Herald*, October 5, 1973.
12. *Houston Chronicle*, July 26, 1998.
13. Whittingham, *What a Game They Played*, 61.
14. Bronko Nagurski, Pro Football Hall of Fame file, interview quotes, undated.
15. *Ibid.*
16. Red Grange, audio interview, Wheaton College Special Collections, Red Grange Papers, July 26, 1978.
17. *Minneapolis Star*, December 10, 1933.
18. Glenn Presnell, author interview, February 21, 1999.
19. *Duncannon Record*, March 25, 1971.

No. 7. Verne Lewellen

1. Verne Lewellen, Pro Football Hall of Fame file, clipping, *Omaha World-Herald*, 1965.
2. Lewellen punting stats from Richard M. Cohen and David Neft, *Pro Football: The Early Years (An Encyclopedic History, 1895–1959)* (Ridgefield, CT: Sports Products, 1978).
3. *Green Bay Press-Gazette*, December 22, 1948.
4. *Green Bay Press-Gazette*, April 16, 1980.
5. *New York Daily News*, November 20, 1943.
6. *New York Daily News*, November 25, 1929.
7. *Appleton Post-Crescent* (wire report), November 27, 1929.
8. *Brooklyn Daily Eagle*, November 25, 1929.
9. Pete Rozelle letter to Verne Lewellen, February 9, 1967, Verne Lewellen family collection.
10. Charlie Mathys, original interview by Cliff Christl, Packers historian.
11. *Ibid.*
12. *Appleton Post-Crescent*, February 3, 1963.

No. 8. Sid Luckman

1. Timothy J. Gilfoyle, "Stars of Chicago: Interviews with Etta Barnett and Sid Luckman," *Chicago History*, Fall 1999, 62.
2. Whittingham, *What a Game They Played*, 196.
3. Ed Fitzgerald, "Sid Luckman—Hail and Farewell," *Sport*, December 1949, 17, 92.
4. Sid Luckman, *Luckman at Quarterback* (Chicago: Ziff-Davis, 1949), 1.
5. Robert Cannon, "Sid Luckman and the Destruction of Washington," *Sports Collector's Digest*, March 10, 1995, 142.
6. *Ibid.*
7. Whittingham, *What a Game They Played*, 197.
8. *Montpelier* (VT) *Evening Argus*, November 22, 1938.
9. *Chicago Tribune*, July 6, 1998; Whittingham, *What a Game They Played*, 197.
10. Murray Olderman, *The Pro Quarterbacks* (Englewood Cliffs, NJ: Prentice-Hall, 1966), 145.
11. *Chicago Tribune*, July 11, 1995.
12. *Chicago Tribune*, January 30, 1994.
13. Whittingham, *What a Game They Played*, 198.
14. Ray Robinson, "Luckman, T-Formation Pioneer," *Sport*, December 1965, 35.
15. Curran, *Pro Football's Rag Days*, 156.
16. *Chicago Tribune*, July 6, 1998.
17. Curran, *Pro Football's Rag Days*, 163.
18. Cannon, "Sid Luckman and the Destruction of Washington," *Sports Collector's Digest*, March 10, 1995, 144.
19. Whittingham, *What a Game They Played*, 204.
20. Curran, *Pro Football's Rag Days*, 167; Gilfoyle, "Stars of Chicago: Interviews with Etta Barnett and Sid Luckman," *Chicago History*, Fall 1999, 66.

21. *Oakland Tribune*, October 17, 1984.
22. Ibid.
23. Steve Bisheff, "Yesterday's Heroes: Clyde 'Bulldog' Turner," *Pro: Official Program of the National Football League* XI, no. 12 (1980), 10E; Hamp Pool, 2000 NFL Films interview.
24. Whittingham, *What a Game They Played*, 202.
25. Fitzgerald, "Sid Luckman—Hail and Farewell," *Sport*, 79.
26. Cannon, "Sid Luckman and the Destruction of Washington," *Sports Collectors Digest*, 145.
27. Whittingham, *What a Game They Played*, 203.
28. Gilfoyle, "Stars of Chicago: Interviews with Etta Barnett and Sid Luckman," *Chicago History*, Fall 1999, 69.

No. 9. Cal Hubbard

1. Daley, *Pro Football's Hall of Fame*, 104.
2. Murray Olderman, *The Defenders* (Englewood Cliffs, NJ: Prentice-Hall, 1973), 148.
3. Ibid.
4. *Knoxville News-Sentinel*, July 28, 1954; Gary Ronberg, "Pigskins and Horsehides," *Pro! Official Program of the National Football League* 7, no. 10 (1976), p. 17C.
5. *Nashville Banner*, January 5, 1950; *Shreveport Times*, December 1, 1926.
6. Clarke Hinkle Scrapbook, Pro Football Hall of Fame file, clipping, Gordon Mackay sports column, circa 1932.
7. *Atlanta Constitution*, December 5, 1962.
8. *Shreveport Times*, November 18, 1964.
9. Olderman, *The Defenders*, 150.
10. *Central New Jersey Home News*, December 24, 1976.
11. *Milwaukee Journal*, October 21, 1965.
12. Olderman, *The Defenders*, 150.
13. *Central New Jersey Home News*, December 24, 1976.
14. *Green Bay Press-Gazette*, December 8, 1932.
15. Whittingham, *What a Game They Played*, 62; Red Grange, with George Dunscomb, "The College Game Is Easier," *Saturday Evening Post*, November 5, 1932, 14.
16. Whittingham, *What a Game They Played*, 113.
17. *Sports Illustrated*, September 5, 1994, 65.
18. *Green Bay Press-Gazette*, October 30, 1977.
19. *Chicago Tribune*, October 17, 1977.
20. *Central New Jersey Home News*, December 24, 1976.
21. *New York Times*, October 18, 1977; *Central New Jersey Home News*, December 24, 1976.
22. Daley, *Pro Football's Hall of Fame*, 112; *Green Bay Press-Gazette*, October 30, 1977.
23. Cal Hubbard, Pro Football Hall of Fame file, wire to Cal Hubbard, February 3, 1976.
24. *New York Times*, October 18, 1977.

No. 10. Paddy Driscoll

1. Paddy Driscoll, Pro Football Hall of Fame file, clipping, by Leo Fischer, 1947.
2. *Chicago Tribune*, June 29, 1968.
3. *Chicago American*, June 29, 1968.
4. *Chicago American*, August 26, 1965.
5. Whittingham, *What a Game They Played*, 23.
6. *Chicago Tribune*, December 8, 1956.
7. *Green Bay Press-Gazette*, September 10, 1926.
8. George S. Halas, with Arthur Veysey and Gwen Morgan, *Halas: An Autobiography* (New York: McGraw Hill, 1979), 124.
9. *Chicago Tribune*, December 19, 1926.
10. *Allentown Morning Call*, June 24, 1929; Halas, *Halas: An Autobiography*, 126–127.
11. *Chicago Tribune*, June 2, 1963.
12. 1965 Pro Football Hall of Fame transcript.

No. 11. Pete "Fats" Henry

1. *Canton Daily News*, October 8, 1919.
2. *New York Times*, September 9, 1962.
3. *Canton Repository*, September 18, 1920.
4. *Madison Capital Times*, February 13, 1952.
5. *Pittsburgh Post-Gazette*, September 10, 1963.
6. Chris Willis, "The Perfect Tackle: The Career of Hall of Famer Pete Henry," *Coffin Corner* 27, no. 5 (2005), 5.
7. Ibid.
8. Ibid.
9. Ralph Hickok, *Vagabond Halfback: The Saga of Johnny Blood McNally* (Self-published, 2017), 92.
10. Olderman, *The Defenders*, 151.
11. Sullivan, *Pro Football's All-Time Greats*, 54.
12. *The Red and Black*, October 23, 1953.
13. *New York Times*, September 9, 1962.
14. 1963 Pro Football Hall of Fame transcript.
15. *Mansfield News-Journal*, November 10, 1954.
16. *Mansfield News-Journal*, July 13, 1958.

No. 12. Dan Fortmann

1. *Billings Gazette*, November 24, 1984.
2. *Rochester Democrat and Chronicle*, October 29, 1942.
3. George Musso, author interview, 1999.
4. *Madison Capital Times*, November 2, 1962.
5. *Chicago Tribune*, September 16, 1965.
6. *Detroit Free Press*, September 2, 1993.
7. Dan Fortmann, Pro Football Hall of Fame file, *Pro! Official Magazine of the NFL*, 1973 program, clipping.
8. Ibid.; *Pittsburgh Press*, December 22, 1946.
9. *New York Daily News*, December 15, 1940.
10. *Pro Football Digest*, September-October 1970, 62.
11. *Honolulu Advertiser*, March 12, 1975.
12. *Daily Press*, November 25, 1942.
13. *Pittsburgh Press*, December 22, 1946.
14. *Detroit Free-Press*, December 2, 1943.

15. Cope, *The Game That Was*, 185.
16. Dan Fortmann, Pro Football Hall of Fame file, undated clipping.

No. 13. Clarke Hinkle

1. Whittingham, *What a Game They Played*, 92.
2. Robert C. Barnett, "Playing for the Pack in the 30's: Interview with Clarke Hinkle," *The Coffin Corner* 4, no. 5 (1982), 1.
3. Ibid.
4. Whittingham, *What a Game They Played*, 94.
5. Sullivan, *Pro Football's All-Time Greats*, 111.
6. Clarke Hinkle, Pro Football Hall of Fame file, undated clipping.
7. Cope, *The Game That Was*, 104.
8. Clarke Hinkle, 1983 NFL Films interview.
9. *Nashville Banner*, February 3, 1939.
10. Sullivan, *Pro Football's All-Time Greats*, 111; *Pro! Official NFL Program*, November 21, 1971, p. 4C.
11. Olderman, *The Running Backs*, 165.
12. *Pro! Official NFL Program*, November 21, 1971, p. 5C.
13. Ray Flaherty, 1985 NFL Films interview.
14. Sullivan, *Pro Football's All-Time Greats*, 112.
15. Cope, *The Game That Was*, 104.
16. Ibid.
17. *Green Bay Press-Gazette*, February 28, 1964.
18. Clarke Hinkle, 1983 NFL Films interview.
19. *Pro! Official NFL Program*, November 21, 1971, p. 5C.
20. *Tyler Courier-Times*, January 9, 1990.
21. *Green Bay Press-Gazette*, September 7, 1986.
22. *Chicago Tribune*, November 2, 1962.

No. 14. Roy "Link" Lyman

1. Chris Willis, *Old Leather: An Oral History of Early Pro Football in Ohio, 1920–1935* (Lanham, MD: Scarecrow Press, 2005), 58.
2. Owen, *My Kind of Football*, 46–47.
3. *Detroit Free-Press*, August 15, 1976.
4. *Nebraska State Journal*, January 20, 1937.
5. *Spokesman-Review*, October 26, 1941.
6. Link Lyman, Pro Football Hall of Fame file, clipping, undated.
7. *Lincoln Journal-Star*, September 8, 1964.
8. *Rutland Daily Herald*, February 11, 1979.
9. *Nebraska State Journal*, January 20, 1937.
10. *Nebraska State Journal*, December 26, 1936.
11. *Green Bay Press-Gazette*, December 16, 1934.
12. *Washington Evening Star*, February 2, 1935.
13. Link Lyman, Pro Football Hall of Fame file, obituary, 1972.
14. *Lincoln Journal-Star*, September 8, 1964.

No. 15. Bill Hewitt

1. Whittingham, *What a Game They Played*, 61.
2. *Chicago Tribune*, November 20, 1940.
3. *Chicago Tribune*, December 2, 1933.
4. *Chicago Tribune*, December 9, 1933.
5. Ibid.
6. *Chicago Tribune*, December 6, 1933.
7. *New York Daily News*, February 5, 1971.
8. *Los Angeles Times*, January 22, 1937.
9. *Chicago Tribune*, January 15, 1947; *Los Angeles Times*, January 29, 1935.
10. *Montana Standard*, December 17, 1933.
11. *Jackson Clarion-Ledger*, February 11, 1971.
12. *Chicago Tribune*, December 9, 1933.
13. *Madison Capital Times*, January 20, 1956.
14. Matthew Algeo, *Last Team Standing: How the Steelers and the Eagles—The Steagles—Saved Pro Football During World War II* (Cambridge: Da Capo Press, 2006), 56.
15. 1971 Pro Football Hall of Fame transcript.
16. NFL Network All-Time Team TV show, 2019 broadcast, NFL Network.
17. *Saturday Evening Post*, October 21, 1944, 93.

No. 16. Mike Michalske

1. *Saturday Evening Post*, October 21, 1944, 93.
2. *Austin American*, February 10, 1955.
3. *Green Bay Press-Gazette*, December 3, 1929.
4. *Green Bay Press-Gazette*, October 26, 1983.
5. *Milwaukee Journal*, November 18, 1965.
6. *Green Bay Press-Gazette*, October 26, 1983.
7. *Milwaukee Journal*, November 18, 1965.
8. *Green Bay Press-Gazette*, January 6, 1950.
9. Herm Schneidman, archival interview by Cliff Christl, May 13, 2000.
10. *Milwaukee Journal*, November 18, 1965.
11. *Green Bay Press-Gazette*, September 2, 1979.
12. *Green Bay Press-Gazette*, August 8, 1993.

No. 17. Benny Friedman

1. Benny Friedman, *The Passing Game* (New York: Steinfeld, 1931), 13.
2. Murray Greenberg, *Passing Game: Benny Friedman and the Transformation of Football* (New York: Public Affairs, 2008), 9.
3. *New York Daily News*, February 4, 1967; Barry Gottehrer, *The Giants of New York* (New York: Putnam, 1963), 65.
4. Curran, *Pro Football's Rag Days*, 6; Benny Friedman, Pro Football Hall of Fame file, clipping, Blackie Sherrod column, March 11, 1966.
5. Dave Klein, *The New York Giants, Yesterday, Today and Tomorrow* (Chicago: Henry Regnery, 1973), 41.
6. Whittingham, *What a Game They Played*, 135.
7. Curran, *Pro Football's Rag Days*, 68.
8. *New York Times*, October 27, 1961.
9. *Chicago Tribune*, August 4, 2005.
10. Olderman, *The Pro Quarterbacks*, 14.
11. Curran, *Pro Football's Rag Days*, 109.
12. *Escanaba Daily Press*, August 27, 1938.

No. 18. Ernie Nevers

1. Jim Scott, *Ernie Nevers: Football Hero* (Minneapolis: T.S. Denison, 1969), 11.
2. Chuck Frederick, *Leatherheads of the North: The True Story of Ernie Nevers & the Duluth Eskimos* (Duluth: X-Communication, 2007), 54.
3. Ibid.
4. Scott, *Ernie Nevers: Football Hero*, 47.
5. Frederick, *Leatherheads of the North*, 51.
6. *Sporting News*, May 22, 1976.
7. Scott, *Ernie Nevers: Football Hero*, 77.
8. Ibid.
9. Frederick, *Leatherheads of the North*, 54.
10. Ibid.
11. Johnny "Blood" McNally, NFL Films interview, 1983; John Alexander, 1983 NFL Films interview.
12. Scott, *Ernie Nevers: Football Hero*, 91.
13. *Dayton Daily News*, February 20, 1977.
14. *Chicago Tribune*, November 29, 1929.
15. *Clinton Herald*, December 31, 1956.
16. Ray Flaherty, 1985 NFL Films interview.
17. Friedman, *Passing Game*, 166.
18. Scott, *Ernie Nevers: Football Hero*, 137.
19. Ibid.

No. 19. Cliff Battles

1. Cope, *The Game That Was*, 114.
2. Ibid.
3. Ibid.
4. Curran, *Pro Football's Rag Days*, 121.
5. *Nashville Banner*, January 10, 1953.
6. *Pittsburgh Sun-Telegraph*, December 30, 1933.
7. *Richmond News Leader*, January 16, 1953; *New York Daily News*, November 17, 1946.
8. Curran, *Pro Football's Rag Days*, 134.
9. Ibid.
10. Olderman, *The Running Backs*, 177.
11. Curran, *Pro Football's Rag Days*, 133.
12. *St. Joseph News-Press*, December 29, 1979; Olderman, *The Running Backs*, 173.
13. *Richmond Times Dispatch*, December 29, 1940.
14. Olderman, *The Running Backs*, 171; *Boston Globe*, October 8, 1957.
15. *Knoxville Journal*, October 2, 1958.

No. 20. Ken Strong

1. *Baltimore Sun*, September 6, 1939; *Hartford Courant*, December 16, 1999.
2. Curran, *Pro Football's Rag Days*, 103.
3. Ibid., 104.
4. *Richmond Times-Dispatch*, July 20, 1943.
5. Mel Hein, 1983 NFL Films interview.
6. Curran, *Pro Football's Rag Days*, 106.
7. Ibid.
8. Mel Hein, 1978 NFL Films interview.

9. Pittsburgh Steelers at New York Giants game program, November 24, 1946, 5.
10. *Long Beach Independent*, December 17, 1967.
11. Whittingham, *What a Game They Played*, 139.

No. 21. Johnny "Blood" McNally

1. Whittingham, *What a Game They Played*, 30.
2. Denis J. Gullickson, *Vagabond Halfback: The Life and Times of Johnny Blood McNally* (Madison: Trails Books, 2006), 26.
3. Ibid.
4. Ibid.
5. Ibid.
6. Ibid.
7. Ibid.
8. Ibid.
9. Ibid.
10. Ray Flaherty, 1985 NFL Films interview.
11. *Minneapolis Tribune*, December 22, 1931.
12. Gullickson, *Vagabond Halfback: The Life and Times of Johnny Blood McNally*, 126.

No. 22. Red Grange

1. Red Grange, as told to Ira Morton, *The Red Grange Story: The Autobiography of the Galloping Ghost* (New York: G.P. Putnam's Sons, 1953), 6.
2. Ibid.
3. *Chicago American*, November 12, 1925.
4. *Boston Globe*, October 8, 1957.
5. *Woodstock* (IL) *Daily Sentinel*, December 3, 1964; *Muncie Star-Press*, October 9, 1938.
6. Ray Flaherty, 1985 NFL Films interview.
7. George Musso, author interview, 1999.
8. Clarke Hinkle Scrapbook, Pro Football Hall of Fame, clipping, 1932–1933.
9. John M. Carroll, *Red Grange and the Rise of Modern Football* (Urbana: University of Illinois Press, 1999), 175.
10. Ibid.
11. *Wisconsin State Journal*, July 30, 1936; *Wisconsin State Journal*, August 7, 1944.

No. 23. Fritz Pollard

1. Fritz Pollard, 1976 NFL Films interview.
2. Ibid.
3. *Akron Beacon-Journal*, October 25, 1919.
4. Fritz Pollard, 1970 Brown University Archives interview, conducted by John Barry.
5. *Akron Beacon-Journal*, January 2, 1972.
6. Fritz Pollard, 1970 Brown University Archives interview, conducted by John Barry.
7. *Rock Island Argus*, December 2, 1920.
8. Fritz Pollard, 1970 Brown University Archives interview, conducted by John Barry.
9. Fritz Pollard, 1976 NFL Films interview.
10. *Akron Beacon-Journal*, December 21, 1975.

11. *Green Bay Press-Gazette*, February 9, 2005.
12. Fritz Pollard, 1976 NFL Films interview.

No. 24. Albert "Turk" Edwards

1. *Longview Daily News*, January 15, 1972.
2. *Washington Star*, September 29, 1969.
3. Turk Edwards, Pro Football Hall of Fame file, clipping, undated.
4. George Musso, author interview, 1999.
5. Olderman, *The Defenders*, 153.
6. *Green Bay Press-Gazette*, December 22, 1931.
7. *Washington Star*, September 29, 1969.
8. *Scottsbluff Daily Star-Herald*, October 12, 1938.
9. Pro Football Hall of Fame 1969 transcript.
10. *Ibid.*

No. 25. Ox Emerson

1. *Austin American-Statesman*, November 28, 1998.
2. *Austin American-Statesman*, July 13, 1969.
3. *Austin American-Statesman*, July 10, 1987.
4. *Green Bay Press-Gazette*, December 12, 1935; *Austin American-Statesman*, July 10, 1987.
5. *Pittsburgh Press*, November 28, 1934.
6. *Austin American*, December 18, 1936.
7. George Musso, author interview, 1999.
8. Charles "Ookie" Miller, author interview, 1999.
9. *Nashville Banner*, January 12, 1955; Reynolds, *Collier's*, November 4, 1939.
10. Glenn Presnell, author interview, 1999.
11. *Austin American*, August 18, 1970.
12. *Windsor Star*, October 26, 1935.

No. 26. Arnie Herber

1. *Green Bay Press-Gazette*, October 1, 1965.
2. *Arizona Republic*, February 9, 1939.
3. *Green Bay Press-Gazette*, September 12, 1982; "Arnie Herber: The Greatest Long Passer," *1966 Green Bay Packers Yearbook*, 43.
4. *Green Bay Press-Gazette*, November 17, 1941.
5. *Spokesman-Review*, September 24, 1944.
6. *Harrisburg Telegraph*, December 8, 1945.
7. 1966 Pro Football Hall of Fame transcript.

No. 27. George Trafton

1. *Rock Island Argus*, December 2, 1920.
2. John Alexander, 1983 NFL Films interview.
3. Sullivan, *Pro Football's All-Time Greats*, 122.
4. *Ibid.*
5. *Los Angeles Daily News*, June 24, 1949.
6. *Indianapolis Star*, September 10, 1971.
7. *Benicia Herald*, June 11, 1991.
8. *Green Bay Press-Gazette*, December 19, 1924.
9. *Alton Evening Telegraph*, September 24, 1971.
10. *Cincinnati Enquirer*, July 7, 1944.
11. *Ft. Lauderdale News*, January 24, 1967.
12. *Chicago Sun-Times*, August 2, 1973.
13. Sullivan, *Pro Football's All-Time Greats*, 124.
14. *Chicago Tribune*, June 11, 1943.
15. 1964 Pro Football Hall of Fame speech transcript.

No. 28. Ray Flaherty

1. *Spokane Chronicle*, September 16, 1955.
2. *Chicago Tribune*, December 22, 1929.
3. Ray Flaherty, 1985 NFL Films interview.
4. *Ibid.*
5. *Green Bay Press-Gazette*, December 6, 1932.
6. Wellington Mara, 1999 NFL Films interview.
7. Ray Flaherty, 1985 NFL Films interview.
8. Whittingham, *What a Game They Played*, 138.
9. Ray Flaherty, 1985 NFL Films interview.
10. *Ibid.*
11. Ray Flaherty, Pro Football Hall of Fame file, clipping, no date.
12. Don Smith, "Ray Flaherty," *The Coffin Corner* 6 (1984).
13. *Washington Star*, January 27, 1976; *Longview Daily News*, July 20, 1994.
14. *Washington Star*, January 27, 1976.
15. *Ibid.*

No. 29. Clyde "Bulldog" Turner

1. Steve Weller, "Bulldog Turner: Carmel Candy on a Penny a Say," *Pro Quarterback*, June 1970, 68.
2. Cope, *The Game That Was*, 195–96.
3. Steve Weller, "Bulldog Turner: Carmel Candy on a Penny a Say," *Pro Quarterback*, June 1970, 66.
4. *Chicago Tribune*, October 31, 1998.
5. Cope, *The Game That Was*, 201; *Chicago Tribune*, October 31, 1998.
6. *New York Times*, November 2, 1998.
7. *Gatesville Messenger and Star-Forum*, July 30, 1965.
8. Steve Weller, "Bulldog Turner: Carmel Candy on a Penny a Say," *Pro Quarterback*, June 1970, 64.
9. *Ibid.*; Steve Bisheff, "Yesterday's Heroes: Clyde 'Bulldog' Turner," *Pro XI*, no. 12 (1980), 10E.
10. *Paris* (TX) *News*, September 19, 1975; *Chicago Tribune*, October 31, 1998.
11. Olderman, *The Defenders*, 165.
12. *The Brand*, December 14, 1940.
13. Steve Weller, "Bulldog Turner: Carmel Candy on a Penny a Say," *Pro Quarterback*, June 1970, 65.
14. Michael Barr, *Remembering Bulldog Turner: Unsung Monster of the Midway* (Lubbock: Texas Tech University Press, 2013), xiv.
15. Whittingham, *What a Game They Played*, 100.
16. *Billings Gazette*, October 20, 1948.
17. Olderman, *The Defenders*, 163.
18. Steve Weller, "Bulldog Turner: Carmel Candy on a Penny a Say," *Pro Quarterback*, June 1970, 67.

19. 1966 Pro Football Hall of Fame speech transcript.
20. George Musso, author interview, 1999.
21. *Gatesville Messenger and Star-Forum*, July 30, 1965.
22. Bulldog Turner, *Playing the Line* (Chicago: Ziff-Davis, 1948), 111.

No. 30. Tuffy Leemans

1. Cope, *The Game That Was*, 153–54.
2. Olderman, *The Running Backs*, 196; Don Smith, "Tuffy Leemans: A Real Tuffy," *Coffin Corner* 7, no. 1 (1985).
3. Alphonse (Tuffy) Leemans, *Pro! Official Magazine of the National Football League* 9, no. 1, p. 9C.
4. Owen, *My Kind of Football*, 222–23.
5. Alphonse (Tuffy) Leemans, *Pro! Official Magazine of the National Football League* 9, no. 1, p. 9C.
6. *Salisbury Daily Times*, April 23, 1978.
7. *Ibid.*
8. Whittingham, *What a Game They Played*, 99.
9. *Asbury Park Press*, January 24, 1979.
10. Alphonse (Tuffy) Leemans, *Pro! Official Magazine of the National Football League* 9, no. 1, 9C.
11. Owen, *My Kind of Football*, 205.
12. Cope, *The Game That Was*, 153.
13. *Hackensack Record*, October 20, 1978.
14. Vic Sears, 1999 NFL Films interview.
15. Don Smith, "Tuffy Leemans: A Real Tuffy," *Coffin Corner* 7, no. 1 (1985).
16. 1978 Pro Football Hall of Fame transcript.
17. Don Smith, "Tuffy Leemans: A Real Tuffy," *Coffin Corner* 7, no. 1 (1985).

No. 31. Duke Slater

1. *Waterloo Courier*, August 16, 1966.
2. *Des Moines Register*, August 16, 1966.
3. *Green Bay Press-Gazette*, December 6, 1921.
4. *St. Louis Post-Dispatch*, September 15, 1940.
5. *Rock Island Argus*, September 11, 1922; *Mt. Pleasant News*, March 28, 1953.
6. *Rock Island Argus*, March 4, 1990.
7. Heartley W. Anderson, with Emil Klosinski, *Notre Dame, Chicago Bears and "Hunk"* (Orlando: Daniels, 1976), 32.
8. *Evansville Press*, October 19, 1922.
9. *Des Moines Register*, December 10, 1944.
10. *Philadelphia Inquirer*, October 20, 1926.
11. *Chicago Tribune*, December 19, 1926.
12. *Chicago Herald-Examiner*, November 28, 1929; *Chicago Tribune*, August 20, 1966.
13. *Green Bay Press-Gazette*, December 12, 1931.
14. *Los Angeles Times*, January 26, 1932.
15. *Syracuse Herald*, October 24, 1934.
16. *Iowa City Press-Citizen*, August 25, 1966.
17. *Mount Pleasant News*, March 5, 1953.

No. 32. Ward Cuff

1. Steve Owen, with Art Daley, "Keeping the Foot in Football," *Collier's*, October 31, 1942, 23.
2. Owen, *My Kind of Football*, 70; *Milwaukee News*, December 19, 1938.
3. Ray Flaherty, 1985 NFL Films interview.
4. Ward Cuff, Pro Football Hall of Fame file, clipping, dated 1938.
5. Hank Soar, author interview, July 12, 2000.
6. Ward Cuff, Pro Football Hall of Fame file, *New York Times* clipping, 1943.
7. Chicago Cardinals at New York Giants game program, October 20, 1946, 24.
8. *Newsday*, December 28, 2002.

No. 33. George Musso

1. George Musso, author interview, April 6, 1999.
2. *Edwardsville Intelligencer*, January 29, 1982.
3. *Chicago Sun-Times*, September 6, 2000.
4. George Musso, author interview, April 6, 1999.
5. *Ibid.*
6. *Pro! Official Magazine of the National Football League* XIII no. 1 (1982), p. 8B.
7. George Musso, Pro Football Hall of Fame file, endorsement sheet.
8. George Musso, author interview, April 6, 1999.
9. George Musso, Pro Football Hall of Fame file, endorsement letters.
10. George Musso, author interview, April 6, 1999.
11. *San Luis Obispo County Telegram*, April 29, 1980.
12. George Musso, author interview, April 6, 1999.
13. George Musso, Pro Football Hall of Fame file, endorsement letters.
14. *Ibid.*
15. *Edwardsville News*, January 29, 1982.

No. 34. Joe Stydahar

1. *The All-Sports News*, January 16, 1952.
2. *Billings (MT) Gazette*, November 24, 1984.
3. Tom Barnidge, *The Sporting News: Football Hall of Fame Fact Book* (St. Louis: The Sporting News, 1983), 99.
4. *Madison Capital Times*, November 2, 1962.
5. Sullivan, *Pro Football's All-Time Greats*, 219.
6. *Ibid.*
7. *Chicago Sun-Times*, March 25, 1977.
8. *Buffalo Evening News*, April 20, 1967.

No. 35. George Christensen

1. *Green Bay Press-Gazette*, December 19, 1931.
2. Dutch Clark, 1962 Detroit TV interview.

3. Glenn Presnell, author interview, February 21, 1999.
4. *Green Bay Press-Gazette*, December 28, 1933.
5. *Capital Times*, August 30, 1947.
6. *Escondido Times-Advocate*, January 30, 1989.
7. *Detroit Free-Press*, November 2, 1936.
8. *Detroit Free Press*, November 12, 1936.
9. Dutch Clark, 1962 Detroit TV interview.

No. 36. LaVern "Lavvie" Dilweg

1. *Milwaukee Journal*, October 7, 1965.
2. *Ibid.*
3. *Ibid.*; *Chicago Tribune*, August 21, 1937.
4. *Milwaukee Journal*, October 7, 1965.

No. 37. Joe Kopcha

1. Joe Kopcha, 1979 Pro Football Hall of Fame interview.
2. *Ibid.*
3. *Ibid.*
4. *Ibid.*
5. *Chattanooga Times*, September 17, 1963.
6. Joe Kopcha, 1979 Pro Football Hall of Fame interview.
7. Stanley Grosshandler, "Dr. Joe: The Last Renaissance Man," *Coffin Corner* 8 (1986).
8. *Detroit Free-Press*, August 15, 1976.
9. *Chicago Tribune*, December 5, 1935.
10. *Green Bay Press-Gazette*, December 16, 1934.
11. Stanley Grosshandler, "Dr. Joe: The Last Renaissance Man," *Coffin Corner* 8 (1986).
12. *Chicago Tribune*, December 5, 1935.
13. Joe Kopcha, 1979 Pro Football Hall of Fame interview.
14. George Musso, author interview, April 6, 1999.
15. Joe Kopcha, Pro Football Hall of Fame file, clipping, April 3, 1979.

No. 38. Cecil Isbell

1. Ed Gruver, "Cecil Isbell," *Coffin Corner* XIX, no. 2.
2. *Ibid.*
3. Cecil Isbell, Pro Football Hall of Fame file, *Milwaukee Journal* clipping, undated.
4. Whittingham, *What a Game They Played*, 127.
5. *Green Bay Press-Gazette*, May 21, 1978.
6. *Green Bay Press-Gazette*, September 19, 1938.
7. *Green Bay Press-Gazette*, July 20, 1942.
8. *Green Bay Press-Gazette*, May 10, 1967.
9. *Fond Du Lac Commonwealth Reporter*, May 25, 1967.
10. *Muncie Evening Press*, June 24, 1985.
11. *Green Bay Press-Gazette*, May 10, 1967.
12. Clarke Hinkle, 1983 NFL Films interview.

No. 39. Jack McBride

1. *Green Bay Press-Gazette*, December 18, 1925.
2. *Syracuse Post-Standard*, November 5, 1965; *Syracuse Post-Standard*, February 27, 1954.
3. Chicago Bears at New York Giants game program, December 6, 1925.
4. Jim Campbell, "John Alexander: Pro Football Pioneer," *Coffin Corner* 16, no. 2.

No. 40. Red Dunn

1. *Green Bay Press-Gazette*, December 3, 1936.
2. *Green Bay Press-Gazette*, January 15, 1967.
3. *Green Bay Press-Gazette*, December 15, 1942.
4. *Green Bay Press-Gazette*, January 15, 1957.
5. *Green Bay Press-Gazette*, January 25, 1976.
6. Hickok, *Vagabond Halfback: The Saga of Johnny Blood McNally*, 96.
7. *Green Bay Press-Gazette*, November 7, 1946.

No. 41. Ed Danowski

1. *Asbury Park Press*, March 6, 1966.
2. *Hackensack Record*, November 2, 1935.
3. *Asbury Park Press*, March 6, 1966.
4. *Passaic Herald-News*, October 21, 1978.
5. *Newsday*, February 3, 1997; *Newsday*, January 6, 1986.
6. Owen, *My Kind of Football*, 89.
7. *Newsday*, January 6, 1986.
8. *Mamaroneck Daily Times*, April 3, 1964; Rochester Democrat-Chronicle, March 5, 1967.

No. 42. Ace Parker

1. Whittingham, *What a Game They Played*, 145.
2. Ace Parker, 2000 NFL Films interview.
3. *Ibid.*
4. *Ibid.*; Whittingham, *What a Game They Played*, 146.
5. Ace Parker, 2000 NFL Films interview.
6. *Boston Globe*, November 10, 2013.
7. Ace Parker, 2000 NFL Films interview.
8. *Ibid.*; Hank Soar, author interview, 2000.
9. Bruiser Kinard quote, 1941 Brooklyn Dodgers program, clipping.
10. Whittingham, *What a Game They Played*, 150.
11. *Ibid.*
12. *St. Louis Post-Dispatch*, November 7, 1976.
13. *Raleigh News and Observer*, May 28, 1972; *Scranton Tribune*, November 11, 1949.
14. Ace Parker, 2000 NFL Films interview.
15. Whittingham, *What a Game They Played*, 151.
16. *Virginian-Pilot*, February 9, 1972.
17. 1972 Pro Football Hall of Fame transcript.
18. Ace Parker, 2000 NFL Films interview.

No. 43. Charley Brock

1. *Fremont Tribune*, December 11, 1937.
2. *Wisconsin Rapids Daily Tribune*, November 15, 1986.
3. *Milwaukee Journal-Sentinel*, June 9, 2010.
4. *Wisconsin Rapids Daily Tribune*, November 15, 1986.
5. *Green Bay Press-Gazette*, January 23, 1974.
6. *Chicago Tribune*, July 18, 1945.
7. *Wisconsin Rapids Daily Tribune*, November 15, 1986.
8. *Chicago Tribune*, July 18, 1945.
9. *Green Bay Press-Gazette*, September 12, 1958; *Wisconsin Rapids Daily Tribune*, November 15, 1986.
10. *Wisconsin Rapids Daily Tribune*, November 22, 1986.
11. Evans Kirkby, "Packers of the Past: Brock a Leader, as Collegian, as All-Star, as Packer," *Milwaukee Journal*, no date, 19.
12. *Wisconsin Rapids Daily Tribune*, November 15, 1986.

No. 44. Glenn Presnell

1. Glenn Presnell, author interview, February 21, 1999.
2. Ibid.
3. Ibid.
4. Ibid.
5. *Mansfield (OH) News-Journal*, July 23, 2002.
6. Glenn Presnell, author interview, February 21, 1999.
7. Ibid.
8. Ibid.
9. *Ironton Tribune*, July 20, 1980.
10. Glenn Presnell, author interview, February 21, 1999.
11. George Musso, author interview, April 6, 1999; *Ashland Daily Independent*, September 15, 2004; Ralph Kercheval, author interview, July 12, 2001.
12. Glenn Presnell, author interview, February 21, 1999.
13. *Decatur Herald*, February 25, 1934.
14. Glenn Presnell, author interview, February 21, 1999.
15. *Los Angeles Times*, January 16, 1936.
16. Ibid.
17. *Portsmouth Daily Times*, August 5, 2002.
18. Clarke Hinkle quote, *Pro Football: Once a Small Town Sport*, PBS documentary, 1984.
19. Glenn Presnell, Pro Football Hall of Fame file, Benny Friedman letter, April 27, 1981.
20. Glenn Presnell, author interview, February 21, 1999.
21. Ibid.

No. 45. Roy "Father" Lumpkin

1. *Waco News-Tribune*, December 12, 1927.
2. *Charlotte Observer*, January 26, 1944.
3. *Ironton Times*, July 7, 1929.
4. *Atlanta Constitution*, January 12, 1937.
5. *Knoxville News-Sentinel*, March 27, 1973.
6. *Green Bay Press-Gazette*, October 29, 1930.
7. *Portsmouth Times*, June 21, 1931.
8. *Louisville Courier-Journal*, September 17, 1939.
9. Ralph Kercheval, author interview, July 12, 2001.
10. Curran, *Pro Football's Rag Days*, 91.
11. *Des Moines Register*, December 14, 1950.
12. *Atlanta Constitution*, July 28, 1936.
13. Glenn Presnell, author interview, February 21, 1999.
14. Robert C. Barnett, *The Spartans and the Tanks* (North Huntingdon, PA: Pro Football Researchers Association, 1983), 26.
15. Clarke Hinkle Scrapbook, Pro Football Hall of Fame file, 1942 clipping; *Atlanta Constitution*, January 12, 1937.
16. *Cincinnati Post*, October 24, 1973.
17. *Brooklyn Daily Eagle*, October 26, 1937.
18. *Atlanta Constitution*, January 12, 1937.
19. *Chattanooga Daily Times*, March 19, 1930.

Final Analysis

1. *Sheboygan Press*, November 7, 1962; *Alamogordo Daily News*, April 21, 1968.
2. Clarke Hinkle, 1983 NFL Films interview.
3. *Butte Montana Standard*, December 9, 1971.
4. Curran, *Pro Football's Rag Days*, 96.

Bibliography

Primary Sources

Author Interviews

Kercheval, Ralph. July 12, 2001.
McCaskey, Virginia. June 8, 1999.
Miller, Charles. April 2, 1999.
Musso, George. April 6, 1999.
Newman, Harry. April 1, 1999.
Presnell, Glenn. February 21, 1999; July 2, 2000.
Soar, Hank. July 12, 2000.
Steverson, Norris. July 5, 2002.

Archival Interviews

Badgro, Red. NFL Films, 1997.
Bowser, Arda. NFL Films, 1994.
Canadeo, Tony. NFL Films, 2000.
Chamberlin, Guy. Pro Football Hall of Fame, 1965.
Clark, Dutch. Colorado College Oral History Project, Tutt Library, Special Collections, Colorado College, 1977.
Clark, Dutch. Detroit TV Station, 1962.
Grange, Red. Audio interview, Wheaton College Special Collections, Red Grange Papers, July 26, 1978.
Grange, Red. NFL Films, 1976; 1978.
Halas, George. NFL Films, 1976; 1981.
Hein, Mel. NFL Films, 1983.
Hein, Mel. Pro Football Hall of Fame, 1978.
Hinkle, Clarke. NFL Films, 1983.
Hinkle, Clarke. *Packers: Grandstand Franchise* documentary, 1983.
Hutson, Don. NFL Films, 1983; 1993.
Kopcha, Joe. Pro Football Hall of Fame, 1979.
Luckman, Sid. NFL Films, 1994.
Lyman, Link. Audio interviews, Pro Football Hall of Fame, 1964; 1965.
Mara, Wellington. NFL Films, 1999.
McNally, Johnny. NFL Films, 1976; 1983.
Nagurski, Bronko. NFL Films, 1976; 1983.
Nagurski, Bronko. Voyageurs National Park Oral History Interview, August 17, 1976.
Parker, Ace. NFL Films, 2000.
Pollard, Fritz. Brown University Oral History Interview, 1970.
Pollard, Fritz. NFL Films, 1976.
Pool, Hamp. NFL Films, 2000.
Rooney, Art. PBS-TV, 1984.
Sears, Vic. NFL Films, 1999.

Secondary Sources

Books

Anderson, Heartley W., with Emil Klosinski. *Notre Dame, Chicago Bears and "Hunk."* Orlando: Daniels, 1976.
Barr, Michael. *Remembering Bulldog Turner: Unsung Monster of the Midway.* Lubbock: Texas Tech University Press, 2013.
Carroll, Bob, Michael Gershman, David Neft, and John Thorn, eds. *Total Football II: The Official Encyclopedia of the National Football League.* New York: HarperCollins, 1999.
Carroll, John. *Fritz Pollard: Pioneer in Racial Advancement.* Urbana: University of Illinois Press, 1992.
Clark, Potsy. *Football by Potsy Clark: A Book for Players and Football Fans.* Chicago: Rand McNally, 1935.
Cohen, Richard M., and David Neft. *Pro Football: The Early Years (An Encyclopedic History, 1895–1959).* Ridgefield, CT: Sports Products, 1978.
Cope, Myron. *The Game That Was.* New York: World, 1970.
Curran, Bob. *Pro Football's Rag Days.* New York: Bonanza Books, 1969.
Daley, Arthur. *Pro Football's Hall of Fame.* New York: Tempo Books, 1963.
Frederick, Chuck. *Leatherheads of the North: The True Story of Ernie Nevers & the Duluth Eskimos.* Duluth: X-Communication, 2007.
Friedman, Benny. *The Passing Game.* New York: Steinfeld, 1931.
Gill, Bob, and Tod Maher. *The Pro Football Encyclopedia.* New York: Macmillan, 1997.
Grange, Red, as told to Ira Morton. *The Red Grange Story: An Autobiography.* Urbana: University of Illinois Press, 1993.
Greenberg, Murray. *Passing Game: Benny Friedman and the Transformation of Football.* New York: Public Affairs, 2008.
Gullickson, Denis J. *Vagabond Halfback: The Life and Times of Johnny Blood McNally.* Madison: Trails Books, 2006.
Halas, George S., with Arthur Veysey and Gwen Morgan. *Halas: An Autobiography.* New York: McGraw-Hill, 1979.
Hickok, Ralph. *Vagabond Halfback: The Saga of Johnny Blood McNally.* Self-Published, 2017.

Holley, Joe. *Slingin' Sam: The Life and Times of the Greatest Quarterback Ever to Play the Game*. Austin: University of Texas Press, 2012.

Hubbard, Mary Bell. *Strike 3! And You're Out: The Cal Hubbard Story*. Marceline, MO: Walsworth Press, 1976.

Luckman, Sid. *Luckman at Quarterback*. Chicago: Ziff-Davis, 1949.

Olderman, Murray. *The Defenders*. Englewood Cliffs, NJ: Prentice-Hall, 1973.

———. *The Pro Quarterbacks*. Englewood Cliffs, NJ: Prentice-Hall, 1966.

———. *The Running Backs*. Englewood Cliffs, NJ: Prentice-Hall, 1969.

Owen, Steve. *My Kind of Football*. Edited by Joe king. New York: David McKay, 1952.

Peterson, Robert W. *Pigskin: The Early Years of Pro Football*. New York: Oxford University Press, 1997.

Rozendaal, Neal. *Duke Slater: Pioneering Black NFL Player and Judge*. Jefferson, NC: McFarland, 2012.

Scott, Jim. *Ernie Nevers: Football Hero*. Minneapolis: T.S. Denison, 1969.

Sullivan, George. *Pro Football's All-Time Greats: The Immortals in Pro Football's Hall of Fame*. New York: G.P. Putnam's Sons, 1968.

Turner, Bulldog. *Playing the Line*. Chicago: Ziff-Davis, 1948.

Whittingham, Richard. *What a Game They Played*. New York: Harper & Row, 1984.

Willis, Chris. *Dutch Clark: The Life of an NFL Legend and the Birth of the Detroit Lions*. Lanham, MD: Scarecrow Press, 2012.

Willis, Chris. *Old Leather: An Oral History of Early Pro Football in Ohio, 1920–1935*. Lanham, MD: Scarecrow Press, 2005.

Willis, Chris. *Red Grange: The Life and Legacy of the NFL's First Superstar*. Lanham, MD: Rowman & Littlefield, 2019.

Zimmerman, David. *Curly Lambeau: The Man Behind the Mystique*. Hales Corner, WI: Eagle Books, 2003.

Index

*Numbers in **bold italics** indicate pages with illustrations*

Akron Pros 5, 70, 168–169, 171–174
Albert, Frankie 260
Alexander, John 142, 189, 245
Allen, George 289
American Football League (AFL) 8, 101, 141–142, 165, 192, 210
Anderson, Hunk 21, 112–113, 191, 209, 221, 232, 280
Andrews, Leroy 136, 153, 194, 245
Armstrong, John 210
Artoe, Lee 112

Badgro, Red 64, 150, 154, 195, 271, 278
Barber, Jim 196
Baseball Hall of Fame 97
Battles, Cliff 10, 12, 56, 63, 75, 81, 117, 119, 147–151, 166, 175–176, 205, 282
Baugh, Sammy 1, 12–15, 22, 29, 41–42, 52–59, 65, 67, 76, 81, 90, 100. 112, 138, 147, 150, 175, 177, 184–187, 196, 198, 200, 202, 213, 238–242, 248, 253, 255, 257–258, 281–283, 286
Bausch, Frank 201, 280
Becker, Wayland 214
Behman, Bull 8, 274
Belichick, Bill 42–43, 129
Bell, Bert 129, 156, 288
Benkert, Heinie 243
Benton, Jim 15, 90, 278
Bergman, Dutch 75
Berry, Charlie 2, 7, 101
Bezdek, Hugo 131
Blaine, Dan 153–154
Blumer, Herb 212
Bomer, Lynn 243
Boston Braves-Redskins 10, 12, 50, 117, 147–149, 175–178, 186
Boynton, Benny 6
Brock, Charley 261–265, 281, 288
Brooklyn Dodgers 9, 11, 13, 46, 135, 138, 179, 183, 194, 229, 241–246, 257–259, 272, 276
Brown, Jim 75, 78
Bruder, Hank 241
Brumbaugh, Carl 235
Bryant, Paul 45

Buffalo All-Americans 5, 70, 106
Buffalo Bisons 6
Buivid, Ray 213
Burnett, Dale 246, 280
Butkus, Dick 76, 96, 202
Butler, Sol 211

Caddell, Ernie 37, 40, 182, 227, 279
Cagle, Chris 288
Cahn, Bobbie 191, 288
Calhoun, G.W. 124, 228, 285
Camp, Walter 99, 104–105, 171, 173, 247
Canadeo, Tony 15, 50, 216
Canton, Ohio 2, 19, 41, 105, 173, 207, 212, 281
Canton Bulldogs 5–6, 18, 22, 27, 68–72, 99, 103, 105–108, 120–123, 161, 172, 226
Carnera, Primo 190
Carr, Joe 3, 5, *12*, 13–15, 19, 46, 50, 58, 64, 70, 90, 113, 123, 240, 259, 285, 288
Carroll, Bird 106
Carter, Joe 280
Chamberlin, Guy 5–6, 23, 68–72, 80, 105–106, 120, 122–123, 129, 195, 230, 232, 263, 283–285
Chicago Bears 6, 8–15, 19–20, 25, 56, 58, 63, 73–78, 85–91, 95, 106–107, 110–114, 117, 120, 122–129, 133, 141, 143–144, 155, 163–167, 177, 182, 188–191, 196, 209, 211, 218–225, 227, 233–235, 249, 268–269
Chicago Cardinals 5–7, 9–10, 46, 68, 72, 99–102, 107, 139, 143–144, 161, 209–213, 216–217, 225, 232, 241, 248, 264
Chicago Stadium (1932 Indoor Game) 19, 38, 77, 127, 167, 182, 190, 220, 227, 235, 269, 276
Christensen, Frank 229
Christensen, George 36, 123, 226–229, 281–282
Christl, Cliff 25
Clark, Dutch 1, *10*, 11, *12*, 29, 34–44, 52, 56, 67, 77, 79, 81–82, 84, 90, 95, 100, 119, 147, 149, 167,

182–183, 186, 194, 227–229, 241, 258, 266, 268–270, 275–276, 282–283, 287, 289
Clark, Potsy 23, 26, 30–31, 34, 36–37, 39, 63, 125, 179, 182–183, 226, 228–229, 258–259, 268, 274–276, 286, 288
Cleveland Bulldogs 6, 8, 22, 68, 71–72, 122–123, 135–136, 143–144
Cleveland Rams 13, 15, 41, 59, 191, 241
Cocozza, Mary 129
Cohen, Abe 195
Columbus Panhandles-Tigers 19, 100
Comp, Irv 15, 113
Comstock, Rudy 107, 122
Connor, George 202
Conzelman, Jimmy 5–6, 23, 44, 62, 70, 81, 99, 102, 113, 145, 202, 209–210, 255, 278, 287
Cope, Frank 229
Copeland, Bruce 188
Copley, Charles 173
Corbett, George 219, 288
Craig, Larry 50, 231, 280
Csonka, Larry 76
Cubs Park 99
Cuff, Ward 13–15, *26*, 206, 213–217, 271, 281, 283
Cuneo, Ernie 288
Cutler, Jay 90

Danowski, Ed 11–13, 206, 214–215, 246, 251–255, 258, 281
Davis, Al 66–67
Dayton Triangles 5, 107, 122, 143–144, 172
Decatur-Chicago Staleys 5, 69–70, 99, 105, 188
Dell Isola, John 251
Detroit Lions 11–12, 15, 36–42, 50, 58, 156, 180–183, 196, 226–229, 236, 254, 266–268, 270–271
Detroit Panthers 6, 70
Detroit Wolverines 9, 135–136
Deutsch, Sam 71, 107, 122
Dilweg, Lavvie 72, 95–96, 132, 194, 211, 230–232, 247–248, 281, 285

303

Index

Dinsmore, Bob 8
Dorias, Gus 192, 288
Driscoll, Paddy 5-6, 7, 8, 10, 12, 41, 70, 81, 98-102, 107, 119, 172, 238, 245, 282-283, 287
Dudley, Bill 2, 14, 56, 81, 216
Duluth Eskimos 139, 141-144, 160, 192, 244, 249
Dungy, Tony 42
Dunn, Red 6, 80, 82, 95-96, 132, 185, 247-251, 255, 281

Earp, Jug 84, 131, 250
Ebding, Harry 227
Eckersall, Walter 98
Edwards, Cap 105
Edwards, Turk 57-58, 61, 123, 175-178, 229, 282-283
Elliott, Doc 22, 71, 106, 278
Emerson, Ox 11, 179-183, 213, 227-228, 235-236, 281, 283
Evans, Lon 96, 134
Evansville Crimson-Giants 210

Farkas, Andy 13
Fausch, Frankie 210
Favre, Brett 240
Feathers, Beattie 11, 76-77, 235, 278
Filchock, Frankie 215
Flaherty, Ray 21, 23, 27, 30, 37, 48, 55-56, 62, 76, 118, 144, 149, 161, 166, 192-197, 215, 221, 230, 283, 286-287
Folwell, Bob 104
Ford, Gerald 220
Forte, Aldo 112
Fortmann, Dan 1, 13-14, 50, 57, 110-114, 117, 131, 134, 180-181, 201, 222, 224, 233, 236, 283
Francis, Sam 129
Frankford Yellow Jackets 6, 8-9, 68, 71-72, 94, 120, 123, 249, 274
Friedman, Benny 8-9, **20**, 56, 75, 81-82, 86-87, 123, 133, 135-138, 143-144, 151, 154, 165, 184, 186, 194, 238, 240, 248-249, 255, 271, 283
Fritsch, Ted 216
Fritz Pollard All-Stars, 173, 211

Gallarneau, Hugh 201
Gantenbein, Milt 186, 241, 288
George, Bill 202
Getto, Mike 289
Gifford, Frank 156
Gilberton Cadamonts 174
Gill, Frank 279
Goldenberg, Buckets 112, 117, 119, 134, 180-181, 236, 279
Gordon, Lou 56
Gould, Alan 36, 43
Graham, Otto 255, 260
Grange, Garland 143
Grange, Red 8-10, 17, 29, 40-41, 75-77, 79, 81-82, 94-96, 100-101, 107-108, 123-124, 127, 129, 131, 137, 141, 147, 149-151,

153-154, 163-167, 181, 190, 192, 194, 210-211, 220, 231, 235, 259, 267, 283, 285, 287
Grant, Lou 279
Great Lakes Naval Station 99, 101
Green Bay Packers 6, 9-15, 38, 40, 44-51, 65, 79-84, 92-96, 115-119, 131-134, 142, 149, 158, 161-162, 182, 184-187, 194, 199, 206, 213-215, 219, 224, 231-232, 238-242, 247-250, 263-265, 274
Groza, Lou 215, 225
Gutowsky, Ace 12, 37, 182, 228, 278
Guyon, Joe 82, 270, 278

Haines, Hinkey 243, 279
Halas, George 21, 23, 25, 39, 41-42, 47, 56, 64, 69-70, 72, 75, 87-88, 97, 99-102, 105-106, 110, 113, 127-128, 130, 136, 165, 167, 174, 188, 191, 195, 199, 201, 219-220, 223-225, 233-236, 240, 278, 284-285, 287
Hall, Parker 13
Hamer, Tex 6
Hammond Clabbys-Pros 99, 174
Haugsrud, Ole 139-143, 160
Hay, Ralph 107
Healey, Ed 21, 30, 102, 190-191, 203, 278
Hein, Mel 1, 3, 11-14, 32, 41-42, 49, 57, 60-67, 76, 95, 125, 129, 134, 149, 154-157, 175-178, 181, 200, 203, 206, 259, 261, 265, 281-283, 287, 289
Henry, Pete 6, 27, 71, 103-109, 122-123, 161, 175, 229, 283
Herber, Arnie 10-12, 47, 81, 117, 149, 184-187, 238, 240-241, 247, 250, 253, 255, 287
Herigstad, Ollie 35
Hewitt, Bill 1, 77, 122-123, 125-130, 195, 220, 230, 232, 235, 277, 283, 287
Hinkle, Clarke 12-13, 29, 42, 47, 63, 78, 81, 115-119, 133, 139, 145-146, 149, 189, 202, 206, 221-222, 239-240, 242-243, 264, 271, 276, 281-283, 287
Hoffman, Bill 72
Homan, Henry 8, 279
Horween, Arnie 100
Houston Oilers 59
Howell, Jim Lee 64, 150, 207, 253
Hubbard, Cal 1, 8-9, 37, 41-42, 46, 76, 81, 84, **92-98**, 107-108, 116, 121, 123-124, 132-133, 143, 157, 166, 175, 189, 227-229, 235, 247, 282-283, 287
Hughitt, Tommy 105, 138, 279
Hutson, Don 1, 13-15, 22, **26**, 40, 42, **44-52**, 65, 67, 81-82, 90, 100, 111-112, 117-119, 129, 134, 149, 161-162, 186, 195, 202, 230-231, 239-241, 277, 281-283, 287

Ironton (OH) Tanks 266-268, 274

Isbell, Cecil 13-14, 47-48, 117-118, 137, 186, 238-242, 253, 255, 258, 281

Johnson, Jack 228
Johnsos, Luke 88, 127-128, 200, 220, 235, 278
Jones, Ben 107, 123

Kansas City Cowboys 267
Karcis, Bull 289
Karr, Bill 77, 128, 279
Kavanaugh, Ken 89
Kelly, Shipwreck 11, 46, 258
Kercheval, Ralph 37, 48, 56, 215, 269, 275, 280
Kiesling, Walt 180, 211, 279, 287, 289
Kinard, Bruiser 129, 221, 258, 278
King, Joe 289
King, Rip 173
Kirksey, George 128, 194
Knox, Sam 276
Kopcha, Joe 39, 127, 220, 233-237, 281
Korch, Frank 199
Kotel, Eddie 132
Kramer, Jerry 114
Kreuz, Al 8

Lambeau, Curly 6, 23, 25, 44, 46-47, 63, 70, 72, 79-80, 82, 95-96, 116, 118, 132-134, 161-162, 166, 184-186, 194, 219, 231-232, 239-241, 247-248, 250, 263-265, 279, 284-285, 287, 289
Latone, Tony 7, 161, 279
Laws, Joe 240
Lee, Bill 229
Leemans, Tuffy 12, 23, 57, 81, 128, 149, 204-207, 214-216, 270, 287
Letlow, Russ 134, 180-181, 221, 236, 280
Lewellen, Verne 3, 9-10, 12, 25, 29, 79-84, 96, 100, 132, 147, 162, 167, 185, 213, 232, 247-250, 263, 271, 281-283, 288
Lillard, Joe 211
Little, Lou 86-87, 105, 109, 151
Lombardi, Vince 83, 129, 254
Los Angeles Rams 114, 225
Los Angeles Wildcats (AFL) 192
Louisville Tanks 277
Luckman, Sid 14-15, 29, 58, 81, 85-91, 100, 111-112, 184, 186-187, 201, 222, 224, 238-241, 248, 253, 255, 282-283
Lumpkin, Father 38, 272-277, 281, 288
Lunday, Kayo 214
Lyman, Link 6, 71. 105-107, 120-124, 175, 180, 229, 235, 262-263, 283

Madden, John 42
Mahrt, Al 5
Malone, Charley 58
Manders, Jack 12, 215, 279, 283

Index

Manske, Eggs 87, 228
Mara, Tim 19, 136, 138, 153–154, 196, 243, 254
Mara, Wellington 21, 65, 116, 127, 137–138, 157, 195, 204–206, 216–217, 259, 271
March, Harry 94
Marino, Dan 174
Marshall, George Preston 19, 55, 148, 151, 196
Massillon Tigers 104, 171
Matheson, Riley 278
Mathys, Charlie 84, 250
Mays, Willie 47–48
McAfee, George 14, 49, 81, 112, 119, 201, 216, 222, 224, 271, 278
McBride, Jack 6, 8–9, 94, 154–155, 194, 243–246, 281
McCarthy, Vince 209
McKalip, Bill 227
McMahon, Nick 267
McMillen, Jim 279, 289
McMillin, Bo 93–94
McNally, Johnny 10, 81–82, 84, 95–96, 107, 132–134, 142, 144, 156–162, 247, 249, 283, 287
Mercer, Ken 9
Meyer, Dutch 54
Miami Dolphins 182, 228, 270
Michalske, Mike 42, 80, 95–96, 123, 131–134, 180–181, 186, 211, 247, 249, 283, 287
Miller, Charles 181, 220
Millner, Wayne 56–57, 175, 177, 205, 279
Milwaukee Badgers 94, 100, 158, 160, 168, 173, 210, 230–231, 245, 247–248
Molenda, Bo 82
Molesworth, Keith 279
Monnett, Bob 240
Moran, Hap 280
Morgan, Bill 31
Muller, Brick 140
Musick, Jim 148
Musso, George 40, 42, 111, 166, 176, 180–181, 201, 203, 218–223, 236, 269, 271, 283, 288

Naguarski, Bronko 10–11, 29, 39, 41, 63, 73–78, 81, 115–117, 119, 127, 129, 139, 145–146, 167, 181, 202, 211, 220, 224, 226, 235, 243, 281–283, 288
Nash, Bob 173
National Football League (NFL) 2, 17–23, 32, 34, 36–42, 44, 46–47, 49–52, 54–56, 58–60, 62, 64–72, 75–79, 81–83, 85, 87–91, 94, 96–97, 99–102, 106–107, 109, 111–114, 117–119, 121–124, 127–129, 131–139, 141–145, 148–158, 160–163, 165–168, 172–174, 176–188, 190–192, 194–196, 200–203, 205–216, 220–225, 227–232, 234–236, 238–241, 243, 245–249, 253–254, 257– 260, 263–271, 274, 276–277, 281, 285–286, 289
Neale, Greasy 129, 205, 223, 268
Neid, Frank 171
Nesser, Al 5, 8, 94, 279, 283
Nevers, Ernie 8–10, 29, 41, 56, 78, 81, 132, 134, 139–146, 154, 160–161, 167, 210–211, 243, 285, 288
New York Giants 6, 8–9, 11–15, 57, 62–66, 77, 82, 86, 89–90, 92, 94, 102–103, 107, 116, 123, 128, 135–138, 148, 152–157, 162, 167, 175, 177, 182–184, 187, 189, 192–196, 204–207, 213–217, 219–220, 228, 240, 243–246, 251–254, 263–264, 267–268, 270, 276
New York Titans (AFL) 59
New York Yankees (AFL-NFL) 8, 79, 131, 163, 165, 192
New York Yanks 152
Newman, Harry 11, 56, 77, 96, 123, 126, 149, 155, 246, 253, 280, 286
Newsome, Ozzie 42

O'Brien, Chris 101
O'Brien, Davey 241
Oden, Curly 9, 279
Oliphant, Elmer 5, 173
Oorang Indians 122
Orange Tornadoes 211
Osborn, Duke 71, 106, 280
Osmanski, Bill 49, 279
Owen, Steve 21, 23, 48, 55, 57, 62–63, 65–66, 72, 94, 97, 121, 124, 127, 134, 137, 154, 167, 187, 195, 205–206, 213–214, 216, 229, 245, 251–254, 280, 288–289

Parker, Ace 13, **28**, 48, 56, 81, 253, 255–260
Parmer, Jim 200
Paschal, Bill 15
Paterson (NJ) Panthers 246
Payton, Walter 150
Philadelphia Eagles 15, 125, 128–129, 162, 205, 264–265
Philadelphia Quakers 8, 165
Pierson, Don 174
Pittsburgh Pirates-Steelers 14, 92, 97, 158, 162, 182
Plansky, Tony 9
Pollard, Fritz 5, 21, 29, 81, 168–174, 209–210
Polo Grounds 48, 82, 86, 137, 155, 186, 195, 214, 216, 259
Pool, Hamp 89, 225
Poole, Jim 279
Portsmouth Spartans 10–11, 19, 36–38, 62, 77–78, 127, 148, 155, 167, 175, 179, 181–182, 226–228, 266, 268–269, 272–276, 281
Pottsville Maroons 7, 101, 103, 107, 143, 158, 167, 181, 194
Powers, Francis 124
Presnell, Glenn 10–11, 37, 78, 155, 182, 227–228, 263, 266–271, 275, 281

Pro Football Hall of Fame 19, 41, 72, 78–80, 83–84, 91, 97, 102, 108, 124, 129, 134, 138, 144, 157, 162, 167, 174, 178–183, 187, 191, 196–197, 203, 207, 212, 221–222, 225–226, 229–230, 232, 236, 241–242, 247, 249–251, 260, 265–266, 271, 282
Pro Football Journal 1
Providence Steam Roller 9, 62, 94, 168, 174, 245, 267
Purdy, Clair 171
Pyle, C.C. 101, 141, 210

Randolph, Clare 227–228
Ray, Baby 117
Reagan, Ronald 218
Rechichar, Bert 270
Reeves, Dan 225
Rice, Grantland 152
Rice, Jerry 51
Richards, George A. 38, 269–270
Richards, Kink 280
Richards, Ray 289
Riegals, Roy 273
Ringo, Jim 202
Robb, Harry 106–108, 279
Roberts, Gene 148
Robeson, Paul 2, 21, 170–171, 173, 209–210, 289
Rock Island Independents 189, 209–211
Rooney, Art 162, 221
Rooney, Joe 192
Rozelle, Pete 67, 83
Ruth, Babe 17, 141

St. Louis Browns 141
Sauer, George 118
Sayers, Gale 167
Schneidman, Herm 133, 263
Sears, Vic 207
Senn, Bill 8
Shaughnessy, Clark 88, 225
Shires, Arthur 190
Shula, Don 42
Sinkwich, Frankie 15, 50
Sisk, Johnny 49, 118
Slater, Duke **22**, 144, 208–212, 229, 288
Smith, Red 186, 263
Smith, Riley 151
Smith, Wilfrid 210, 233
Smyth, Lou 122
Sneakers Game (1934 NFL Championship) 64, 77, 123, 128, 155–156, 195–196, 246, 253
Soar, Hank 214, 216, 253, 258
Sonnenberg, Gus 94
Spears, Doc 74–75, 100, 204, 226
Stacy, Red 32
Staten Island Stepletons 37–38, 152–154, 193–194
Steen, Jim 227
Stein, Russ 109
Sternaman, Dutch 5–6, 70, 75, 279
Sternaman, Joey 6, 279

Index

Storck, Carl 289
Strong, Ken 11, 77, 81, 118, 138, 152–157, 215, 243, 254, 267, 282
Stydahar, Joe 110, 112, 201, 223–225, 229, 288
Sutherland, Jock 259

Taylor, Lawrence 125, 142
Tehan, Dan 289
Thorpe, Jim 3, 19, 41, 69, 81–82, 99–100, 105, 107–108, 140–141, 152, 173, 226, 280, 288
Tinsley, Pete 111, 134, 224, 279
Tittle, Y.A. 217, 225, 241
Tobin, Elgie 173
Todd, Dick 13
Trafton, George 21, 70, 95, 127, 165, 188–191, 261, 265, 283
Treat, Roger 289

Tryon, Eddie 8, 131
Turner, Bulldog 14, 23, 32, 89, 112, 118, 198–203, 220, 222, 224, 261, 264–265, 281
Turney, John 1

Unitas, Johnny 90, 240
Ursella, Rube 210

Van Buren, Steve 2, 215
Voss, Tille 279

Warner, Pop 140–141, 143
Washington Redskins 12–15, 77, 89, 112, 147–151, 182, 196, 200–202, 205, 215, 239
Waterfield, Bob 15, 59, 100, 187, 216, 255
White, Byron 278

Williams, Inky 209, 211
Wilson, George 9, 192, 278
Wilson, Mule 94
Wismer, Harry 203
Witt, Roy 274
Wojciechowicz, Alex 66, 113, 206, 221, 278
Wolf, Ron 42, 51
Woodard, Stanley 255, 289
Wray, Lud 105, 148
Wrigley Field 143, 249
Wycoff, Doug 94, 279

Yost, Fielding 136
Young, Steve 59, 174
Youngstrom, Swede 5, 105, 279

Zuppke, Bob 165

www.ingramcontent.com/pod-product-compliance
Lightning Source LLC
Chambersburg PA
CBHW060336010526
44117CB00017B/2844